SECOND

EDITION

# Counseling
# Today's Families

SECOND

EDITION

# Counseling
# Today's Families

**HERBERT GOLDENBERG**
*California State University, Los Angeles*

**IRENE GOLDENBERG**
*University of California, Los Angeles*

Brooks/Cole Publishing Company
Pacific Grove, California

**I(T)P**™ The trademark ITP is used under license.

**C** A CLAIREMONT BOOK

**Brooks/Cole Publishing Company**
A Division of Wadsworth, Inc.

Printed in the United States of America

10   9   8   7   6   5   4   3   2   1

**Library of Congress Cataloging-in-Publication Data**

Goldenberg, Herbert.
    Counseling today's families / Herbert Goldenberg and Irene
Goldenberg. —2nd ed.
        p.    cm.
    Includes bibliographical references and index.
    ISBN 0-534-20526-7
    1. Family social work—United States.  2. Problem families-
-Counseling of—United States.  3. Family—United States-
-Psychological aspects.  4. Behavioral assessment.  I. Goldenberg, Irene.  II. Title.
HV699.G65  1993
362.82'86'0973—dc20
                                                                            93-29235
                                                                            CIP

Sponsoring Editor: *Claire Verduin*
Editorial Associate: *Gay C. Bond*
Production Editor: *Marjorie Z. Sanders*
Manuscript Editor: *Bernard Gilbert*
Permissions Editor: *Elaine Jones*
Interior and Cover Design: *Laurie Albrecht*
Cover Illustration: *Laurie Albrecht*
Art Coordinator and Interior Illustration: *Lisa Torri*
Typesetting: *Bookends Typesetting*
Printing and Binding: *Malloy Lithographing, Inc.*

Credits continue on p. 329.

*To our parents—in the shadow of their absence, we stand;
and to all parents—struggling to create light as well as shade.*

# CONTENTS

# PREFACE

We wrote the first edition of this text because we recognized that profound changes were taking place in the everyday living experiences of a significant portion of our population and that no counseling text had as yet addressed these issues. Single-parent–led families, stepfamilies, cohabiting heterosexual adults, gay and lesbian couples, and couples in dual-career marriages were appearing in our offices in greater number than ever before, and census data supported our observations that the traditional intact family was no longer the expected norm. The "changing American family" was indeed a phenomenon that was beginning to have a portentous impact on all aspects of our society.

What is notable about this revision is that the changing American family has become part of a shared cultural experience. It is a rare and sheltered person who has no experience of the fracturing and restructuring of contemporary families. Moreover, today's greater openness allows us to discuss lifestyle choices that in the past were hidden or closeted from public view.

With such increased awareness has come new interest in the problems of today's client families and new discoveries about how best to intervene in troubled or dysfunctional situations. We have tried to report on the accompanying advances in both knowledge and intervention procedures in this new edition, taking care to elaborate on what we know about how counselors can best help flawed relationships in each of the lifestyles considered here.

As our country experiences greater awareness of ethnic minority life, and as new waves of immigrants come here seeking a better life, it behooves the counselor to learn how best to help in what is for many—counselors and families alike—uncharted waters. Thus, in this edition we have added a long chapter in which we consider multicultural issues, especially in regard to counseling African-American, Hispanic-American, and Asian/Pacific-American families.

As in the first edition, a major goal is the preparation of counselors to deal most effectively with the families they are likely to encounter today. We remain convinced that counselors need an appreciation of how a family functions as a social system, along with how dysfunction may come about, how to tap into family strengths, and how to utilize community resources where available. Although we continue to believe that each family presents the counselor with a unique configuration and a new and distinctive set of transactional patterns, we nevertheless feel he or she will be better prepared if aware of common sets of problems within each family type. To that end, we offer a problem checklist in each chapter, to help focus attention on common patterns a counselor might encounter.

We believe we are presenting a representative sample of what counselors might expect in their daily work. To aid in their understanding and compassion, we have included numerous case studies from our files to reflect the real human beings we have counseled, as they struggled to cope with relationship issues within their families.

Second editions give authors another chance to get it right and, to the extent that we have succeeded, we have been aided in that effort by a number of academic and counseling colleagues who deserve mention: Edwin S. Cox, California Family Study Center; Lawrence Ganong, University of Missouri; Sonja Matison, Eastern Washington University; Ronnie Priest, Memphis State University; and Donald G. Unger, University of Delaware.

As always, our many friends at Brooks/Cole deserve our heartfelt thanks for turning a manuscript into a book. Their faith in our ability to carry it off makes the task so much easier and the work environment so much more conducive to producing this finished product.

*Herbert Goldenberg*

*Irene Goldenberg*

P A R T

O N E

# Understanding Today's Families

# Counseling Today's Changing Families

We live today in a complex and increasingly varied society. The family, no less than other institutions, is undergoing rapid and dramatic changes in form, composition, and structure. Nontraditional families (led by **single parents,**[1] for example) are becoming more commonplace and the traditional **nuclear family** (in which the male as sole breadwinner and the female as full-time homemaker, wife, and mother remain together in an intact marriage till death do them part) less and less the American norm. Skyrocketing divorce rates (which doubled between 1965 and 1985), the surge of women into the work force, the need to have two or more incomes in order to make ends meet, marriage postponement, the greater prevalence of stepfamilies, children living in poverty, single people living alone or with a partner of the same or opposite sex, childless families, mothers with out-of-wedlock children—these are just some of the contemporary realities in what Skolnick (1991) calls an "age of uncertainty" for the American family.

The marked increase in new ethnic minorities in recent years also has added greatly to the diversity of value systems, language, family structure, and relationships in our society. The current rapid change in demographics, as we move from a predominantly European and Caucasian base to one with a broader mix of African-American, Asian, and Hispanic peoples, will inevitably influence social mores and likely lead to conflicting value systems. In regard to possible value

---

[1]Terms printed in **boldface** are defined in the Glossary at the back of the book.

clashes, Ho (1987) contends that, while mainstream society is future-oriented, worshipping of youth, and willing to sacrifice for a "better" tomorrow, ethnic groups may reminisce about the past and take pleasure from experiences in the present. Collective behavior may hold higher priority than individual autonomy, again unlike white middle-class American ideals. Competitiveness and upward mobility, highly valued in the middle-class American lifestyle, may in some minority subgroups hold considerably less appeal, and society's traditional emphasis on the nuclear family may in some cases become less crucial than reliance on the extended family.

Not surprisingly then, counselors today are being confronted with new sets and combinations of clients, presenting new sets of attitudes, lifestyles, and relationship problems. Customary diagnostic categories designed for individual clients do not adequately describe a family in which transactional patterns have broken down or a family that is stuck in a period of rapid societal change, unable to adapt old patterns while finding it difficult to discover adaptive new techniques. Today's counselor must be prepared to think in terms of couples, entire families, or combinations thereof, as well as clients who come individually to seek help for relationship woes or the discomfort accompanying the search for new life paths. As Barth (1988) observes, for example, when faced with varying types of couples seeking help to decide whether they should remain together or separate, today's counselor is often hard pressed to decide if marriage counseling, divorce counseling, family counseling, or individual counseling is called for.

Moreover, today's counselor is likely to confront client misfortunes that arise from circumstances that were once rare, such as helping a same-gender couple work out adoption plans. Or, to take another current example, the counselor may be called upon to help a client growing up in a home with successive "fathers," or one where **custody** was shared between divorced parents with the children moving from household to household every three or four days. Or conceivably the problems arise from an alternative[2] family life pattern in which two unmarried heterosexual adults share an intimate living arrangement but struggle over differences in their sense of commitment to the future of their relationship. Or perhaps conflict exists between children from two or more parents joined together in a **stepfamily** situation, forced to develop sibling relationships not necessarily of their choosing. Today's counselor is more likely than at any time in the past to be called upon to help two-career couples work out new role structures in order to balance career and personal or family demands.

---

[2]It might be useful at this point to note the distinction Cazenave (1980) draws between *alternative* and *alternate* lifestyles. He considers the former to be ideologically based, representing a choice made by those who have the resources to do so: they choose to move beyond traditional patterns to a lifestyle more consistent with their values (for example, living together without being married). Cazenave reserves the latter term for involuntary arrangements, often the result of structural constraints (for example, poverty-level African-American women living as single parents because of the absence of eligible African-American men, welfare-system stipulations, or the unavailability of funds for abortions).

Counselors need to alert themselves to the general problems (and strengths) inherent in each of today's many family structures, in addition to grasping the interplay in each specific situation. They need to become more sensitized to the ethnic and social class backgrounds of clients—especially if different from their own—in order to understand and appreciate differing values and relationship emphases, to say nothing of the opportunity that this provides for self-examination of stereotypes and prejudices. The same holds true for client lifestyles (for example, homosexuality or cohabitation) about which they may hold negative prejudgments. Beyond that, they need to become familiar with current counseling strategies for dealing with these new developments in family life.

In this book, we describe six basic contemporary family structures: single-parent–led families, remarried families, cohabiting heterosexual couples, gay male and lesbian female couples, dual-career families, and ethnically diverse families. For each family configuration, we develop a format for assessing its situation and counseling needs, and offer suggestions (along with excerpts from sessions) for delivering effective therapeutic intervention.

## TODAY'S FAMILIES: SOME DEMOGRAPHIC NOTES

American life has changed drastically in the past two decades, and that change is reflected in the workplace, in male-female relationships, and, inevitably, in the family. Whether they are working or going to school, young people today are leaving home earlier than ever before and living on their own longer. Young women, in particular, increasingly plan extended periods of employment and expect to have fewer children than their counterparts even a decade ago. More readily than ever before, they accept the idea that, as young mothers, they can and should work (Morrison, 1986).

Women now account for approximately half of the total work force, in sharp contrast with times as recent as the early 1960s, when they accounted for perhaps one-third of those employed outside the home. The influx of younger generations of women is likely to continue; Morrison (1991) estimates that women will constitute 63% of new entrants to the workforce in the decade ahead. Within the professions, the number of women employed equals the number of men (although most women are still clustered in the less-prestigious and lower-salaried professions of teaching and nursing), according to a recent survey (ABC News, 1986). Today, 18% of all lawyers are women, up 14% in 14 years; 17% of American physicians are women, compared to 10% in 1972; and one out of four of today's MBAs is female.

Clearly, these statistics reveal significant changes in our attitudes and expectations, and profoundly affect the number and kind of decisions faced by today's woman of marriageable age. She is more likely than ever before to have obtained a higher level of education, and her options are more varied than ever before. She must decide if and when to marry; what kind of work to devote herself to; whether to have children and when to do so; the economic feasibility of being a divorced woman, should a marriage be unsuccessful; whether to remarry; and so on. Her far greater sexual freedom than her counterpart of two decades ago, expanded career options, and increased economic power have together helped alter man-woman relationships in ways that the mothers of today's women would likely find incomprehensible. With new choices have come increased uncertainty and, in many cases, role confusion, as today's young women (as well as the men with whom they interact) grapple with changing ideals and evolving notions of personal and interpersonal fulfillment.

Nowhere is the social upheaval of the last two decades more apparent than in family patterns and relationships. As demographer Morrison (1986) points out:

> Fewer and fewer American families conform to traditional stereotypes. They are more diverse and less stable now than ever before. More children are born to unmarried mothers, and more childhood years are spent in fatherless families. Couples marry later and are quicker to divorce. Fully 54% of wives with preschool-age children are now in the work force (only 30% were in 1970). (p. 2)

Figure 1.1 dramatically illustrates some of the changes in types of American households that have occurred over the last three decades. Note especially the jump in numbers of childless married couples, single men and women living alone, and female-headed households over the thirty-year period. Between 1960 and 1975 alone, according to Gullotta, Adams, and Alexander (1986), 8 million more married couples were counted; however, 7.1 million were couples without children at home, primarily young childless families. In addition, substantial increases were found in female-headed families. (This phenomenon, along with its implications for today's counselors, is discussed more fully in Chapter Four.)

From a contemporary perspective, it no longer makes sense to refer to what is "typical" when speaking of American family life. More accurately, we need to consider varying types of families—with diverse organizational patterns, styles of living, and living arrangements. America's idealized and nostalgic portrait of the nuclear family—the carefree family with a suburban residence, sole-provider father and homemaker mother, both parents dedicated to childrearing, remaining together as an intact family for life, children obtaining an education in a neighborhood school, trips to church together on Sunday, plenty of money, supportive grandparents—is the stuff of television make-believe and not reality for the vast majority of the population today (if, indeed, such a picture-postcard family ever existed).

Consider the following facts and forecasts (Gullotta, Adams, & Alexander, 1986; Morrison, 1991; Emery, 1988; Price & McKerney, 1988):

Half the marriages made this year in the United States will probably end in divorce.

Divorce rates are likely to be higher when a marriage is preceded by a premarital pregnancy or out-of-wedlock birth.

Age of the spouses at the time of first marriage is highly related to the divorce rate (those under 20 are two to three times more likely to divorce than those who marry in their 20s).

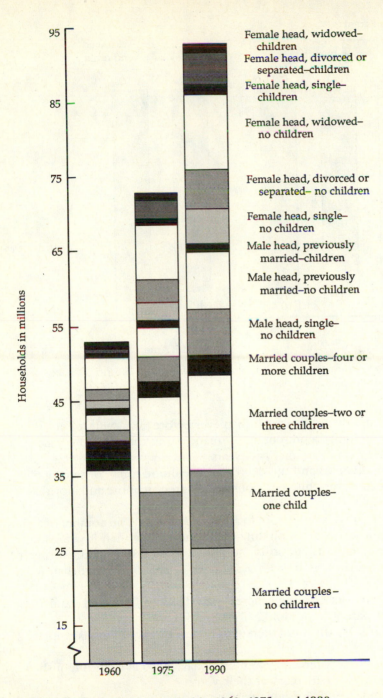

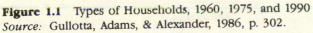

**Figure 1.1**  Types of Households, 1960, 1975, and 1990
*Source:* Gullotta, Adams, & Alexander, 1986, p. 302.

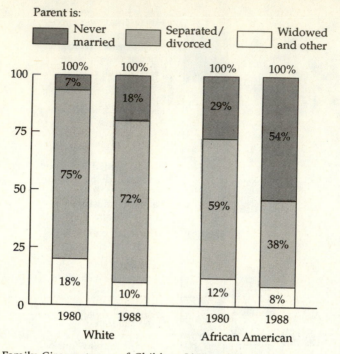

**Figure 1.2**  Family Circumstance of Children Living with One Parent, by Race.
*Source:* Morrison, 1991, p. 6.

Married couples are divorcing earlier than ever before (38% within four years
  of marriage), probably representing for many a breakdown in the marriage
  and separation within the first two years.

Because of early divorces and the decreased likelihood today of staying married "for the sake of the children," younger children are more and more likely
  to be affected.

One out of four children is now born to an unwed mother. The number of teenage unwed mothers is at an all-time high (and higher than in almost any
  other industrial nation), but so is the number of unwed mature women,
  economically self-sufficient, with a stronger desire for a child than for a
  husband.

Today's teenage mother is opting increasingly to keep her child, launching
  another single-parent household.

More than two of every three children under 6 has a mother who is employed
  outside the home.

Fewer than three of every ten adolescents will have lived in a continuously intact family through all 18 years of their youth.

Single-parent families, 90% of which are headed by women, now represent
  more than one out of five families with children. More than half of all black
  children are born into one-parent households (see Figure 1.2).

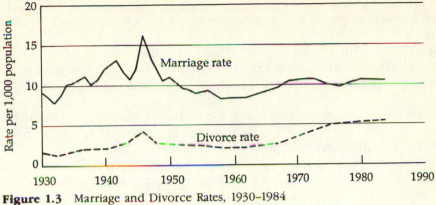

**Figure 1.3**  Marriage and Divorce Rates, 1930–1984
*Source:* National Center for Health Statistics, 1985, p. 4.

Divorce is likely to be followed by remarriage (five out of six divorced men and three out of four divorced women remarry).

None of the family forms we will be describing in detail in the remainder of this book will be entirely atypical or unfamiliar to the reader. What is new is the sharp increase in the proportion of such alternative (as well as alternate) lifestyles today, as well as their partial acceptance by society.

We recognize that there are readers who may be disdainful or rejecting of certain patterns (for example, working mothers) and readers who may have strong religious, moral, or political objections to others (gay couples, young heterosexual couples living together outside of marriage). Before undertaking any clinical work with such families, the counselor should explore his or her feelings regarding a particular lifestyle and, if there is a problem, be honest and straightforward with the clients, perhaps referring them to a more suitable counselor if necessary. It has been our clinical experience that all these lifestyles face certain serious problems, but also have certain internal strengths. In this book we have addressed our attention to the understanding and resolution of these issues rather than to making any judgment or endorsement of a lifestyle.

# CHANGING TIMES: MARRIAGE, DIVORCE, REMARRIAGE

## PATTERNS OF MARRIAGE AND DIVORCE

A central determinant of the sweeping changes in contemporary American family life is the high rate of marital dissolution. While the marriage rate has remained stable in recent years, and the rate of divorce has in fact dropped slightly (National Center for Health Statistics, 1985), it is nevertheless true that the marriages of approximately 50% of today's couples will eventually terminate in divorce. Figure 1.3 illustrates both marriage and divorce trends over the last half century in the United States.

The reasons for marrying are, of course, varied and complex and, not surprisingly, what went wrong in any specific marriage is correspondingly difficult to pinpoint.

Acknowledging the myriad of factors that may influence a couple's decision to separate and perhaps eventually divorce, Bornstein and Bornstein (1986) offer a three-part classification of possible reasons: social, personal, and relationship issues.

Socially, these authors contend, changes in marital and family relations are but a reflection of the current period of rapid change in our society, in which values, beliefs, and customs are continuously being challenged. The complexity and impersonalization of society at large contributes to a further sense of isolation and distrust. Alternative lifestyles (**open marriage**, **nonmarital cohabitation**, **gay couples**, sexually active singles, remarriage), increasingly common and socially acceptable in an increasing number of circles, offer a wider range of relationship choices than ever before. Such an expansion of lifestyle options means that an individual may choose to leave a traditional marriage not simply because it is terribly dissatisfying, but perhaps because other options, not formerly available, appear to be more attractive. The increasing "respectability" (or at least social acceptability) of divorce, as well as the ease with which it may be obtained, may help facilitate the decision to end the marriage.

As Levinger (1979) contends, adopting a social-exchange perspective, three factors determine whether people remain in a marriage: (1) the extent of their *attraction* to the relationship (desire for companionship, esteem for spouse, sexual pleasure, and so on); (2) the *barriers* they perceive to obtaining a divorce (loyalty, feelings of obligation, external pressures from family and friends, needs of dependent children, economic considerations, religious proscriptions, community stigma); and (3) comparisons they make between what they have in their current marriage and the *alternatives* they sense are available outside (the freedom of being single, interest in pursuing another relationship, the possibility of replacing a spouse with someone with whom a relationship of higher quality is likely, and so on). In the event that their marriage has eroded to the point where the first two factors are perceived as weak arguments for remaining in the light of possible alternative attractions, then the likely consequence is the breakup of the marriage.

Price and McKerney (1988) note that, in their effort to make sense of the pending decision, couples who divorce are far more apt to cite specific complaints than to allude to the analytic pros and cons just described. Increasingly, according to their research, the reasons given by middle-class divorcing couples involve personal incompatibilities and personal-growth issues, suggesting that they look to marriage and family as sources of interpersonal nurturance and individual gratification.[3] This is in sharp contrast with a trail-blazing study of

[3]There are important social-class differences here that have been reported and should be noted. Women with more education and higher socioeconomic status are apt to cite internal gender-role conflict, poor communication with their husbands, and emotional incompatibility as sources of marital dissatisfaction. Women with less education and lower socioeconomic status tend to complain of physical and psychological abuse, drinking, financial instability, and the frequency with which their husbands go out with male friends (Kitson & Sussman, 1982).

divorce by Goode (1956), in which he found that nonsupport and excessive authoritarianism were the most common reasons given by women for divorcing their husbands.

Bornstein and Bornstein (1986) also identify a number of personal factors that contribute to marital unhappiness. Unrealistic expectations (for example, that one's spouse will always try to please, never be angry, always be open and honest) based on romantic dreams and false hopes—inevitably unfulfilled—may lead to disappointment and ultimately to despair. Happiness may seem elusive to some partners, who may then withdraw from the relationship and perhaps seek satisfactions in work-related activities or extramarital affairs.

Inevitably, too, people change as they mature, and a couple (particularly if they married at an early age) may discover a growing divergence in interests and values to the point of "irreconcilable differences." Some partners may find that their parents provided poor role models for a successful marriage; others may find themselves too uncomfortable trying to sustain an intimate relationship; still others may become stressed to the point of dysfunction when called upon to care for a newborn child. Serious psychological problems in one or both partners may become exacerbated in the process of living as husband and wife.

Disillusionment with the relationship, a feeling that one's emotional and physical needs remain unmet, and a sense of growing in different directions may build over time, until a precipitating event—the "last straw"—or an accumulation of unfulfilled expectations provides the momentum behind the decision to divorce (Milne, 1988).

Beyond personal factors, interpersonal issues are at the core of most marital breakups:

ineffective communication patterns;
sexual incompatibilities;
anxiety over making and/or maintaining a long-term commitment;
fewer shared activities;
reduced exchange of affection;
infidelity;
lack of sensitivity or indifference to a partner's feelings or wishes;
conflicts over power and control;
underdeveloped problem-solving skills;
conflicts over money, independence, in-laws, or children;
physical abuse;
an inability to respond positively to changing role demands such as those brought about by the birth of a first child or the return to paid work by one partner.

Typically, several of these episodes, transactions, or transition-point experiences, repeated without resolution over a period of time, escalate the growing marital dissatisfaction of one or both partners. In effect, once a partner concludes that the costs of staying together outweigh the benefits, then the marriage is in jeopardy.

## SUCCESSFUL MARRIAGE

While alternative family arrangements and options have penetrated deeply into mainstream American life, marriage continues to be the cultural ideal; there is no other lifestyle that is, even by a sizable minority, viewed as preferable to marriage in the long run (Buunk & van Driel, 1989). The central characteristic of any marital relationship is its interdependence—sexual, economic, emotional, communicational—built and maintained through the partners' continuing attraction and commitment to one another and their efforts, as a couple, to achieve certain goal-directed behavior (Levinger & Huston, 1990).

What makes certain marriages happy and others unsatisfying and conflict-prone? Rice and Rice (1986b) suggest that a healthy marriage is able, flexibly and even synergistically, to adapt to the individual growth of each partner, while a dysfunctional one often is strained by the developmental changes that inevitably occur in each partner. As individuals grow apart, they often make resented accommodations to one another and deny themselves the opportunity for self-growth in an effort to cling to the marriage. Ultimately such compromises become too personally costly, work against the relationship, and stifle the growth of the marriage.

By way of contrast, Beavers (1988) contends that, in healthy couples, the partners by and large respect each other's perceptions; they negotiate, and occasionally fight, without necessarily struggling for a one-up position. They tend to believe in the trustworthiness of their spouse, accepting occasional conflict as inevitable but without fearing abandonment as the result. They tolerate sporadic outbursts of unpleasant or angry feelings from spouse and children without using such experiences to "prove" the others have evil intent.

Their accommodation to one another allows for more equal overt power, without hostile competition and continuous rivalry. Whether their quarrels are loud or quiet, open or covert, intense or emotionally subdued, distancing or embroiling, rationally presented or passionately expressed, they tend to end up, when the smoke lifts, with a clear sense of boundaries (knowing where one person ends and the other begins, recognizing the difference between one person's feelings and wishes and the other's), making productive resolution of the conflict possible. Healthy couples operate mainly in the present, according to Beavers, aware of the past without being its prisoner or being driven repeatedly to behave as in their childhood. The individuals in healthy couples respect each other's opinions and choices (that is, without viewing a difference as an expression of the other's willfulness, selfishness, stubbornness, or ignorance). All of these attributes outlined by Beavers help couples negotiate solutions to problems or opportunities that meet the needs of both partners.

## THE PROCESS OF DIVORCE

Separation and divorce are procedures that occur over time and in stages; the entire process usually involves a great deal of stress, ambivalence, indecision, self-doubt, and uncertainty, even when both partners agree to the action. Although they cannot be fully aware of what lies in store for them, in most cases they are about to undergo a painful, disruptive process from which, more likely than not, it may take much time to recover. Kressel (1985) goes so far as to characterize the process of divorce negotiation as "one of the more demanding tasks that rational beings are expected to perform" (p. 4).

In most cases, one person initiates the process, although the other may be feeling the same urge but be less able or less willing, financially or emotionally, to act; in far fewer cases, the noninitiating person is taken by surprise, although probably because he or she did not want to know and thus denied what was taking place prior to the initiating act. It is the exceptional couple who mutually and simultaneously reach the decision to divorce (Milne, 1988).

However the decision is reached, or by whom, the counselor seeing the couple at any point in the marriage/separation/divorce continuum must be attuned to the blow to self-esteem that separation and divorce inevitably bring. To have invested time, effort, personal resources, and youthfulness, all for naught, is to experience a personal feeling of failure and the sense that perhaps one does not possess the necessary traits to ever achieve or maintain a satisfying marriage. Moreover, marriage bestows a sense of identity, maturity, acceptance, and respectability in most segments of society. For many people, then, despite a veneer of sophistication, to have failed at marriage is to have failed as an adult. Yet, divorce also has a positive potential—offering a new beginning as much as an ending—important for the counselor to impart to the divorcing pair.

Divorce, even a relatively amicable one, rarely occurs abruptly. More likely, couples undergo a series of events together before both partners can let go and begin to lead separate lives. A useful framework for conceptualizing the divorce process has been offered by Paul Bohannan (1970; 1984), who views the entire circumstance as usually requiring six overlapping stages before such disengagement can be accomplished. While these stages do not necessarily occur in an invariant sequence, nor do all persons involved feel the same anguish at each phase, Kaslow (1988) argues that each stage must be experienced and its stumbling blocks removed before a sense of well-being can be achieved by both mates.

First comes the **emotional divorce,** which may or may not involve physical separation; during this stage, often at the instigation of one partner, they both finally recognize that the marriage is deteriorating. This period may be brief or prolonged but, whatever its length, the couple must deal with the decline of the relationship. If one person gives voice to dissatisfaction or disillusionment before the other, the latter may become alarmed, even agitated, and try to cajole or seduce the initiator back into the marriage. Promises to change, declarations of good intentions, desperate pleas, threats of suicide, even a willingness to begin counseling (if previously resisted) may be offered as inducements to stay. Another common scenario is for both marital partners to use this opportunity to hurl criticisms and invectives, each defending his or her own behavior and denouncing the actions, past or present, of the other.

Kessler (1975) has further divided this stage into three phases—disillusionment, erosion, and detachment—during which each partner focuses on the other's weaknesses and deficiencies, blaming the other for the marital unhappiness. Destructive verbal and nonverbal exchanges, avoidance, lack of attention, withdrawal, and perhaps self-pity characterize behavior at this point, as one or both mates prepare to cope with the future, sometimes by seeking solace through outside sexual contacts or affairs (Woody, 1983).

Kaslow (1988) believes that couples who enter conjoint marital counseling at this point—resolving frustrations, ventilating and understanding their suppressed anger, perhaps working on improving the relationship now that it is in jeopardy—are more likely to work out their marital conflict than by one or both entering individual counseling or psychotherapy. Table 1.1 (pp. 16–17) offers a useful description of what a counselor might expect in the form of feelings or actions of divorcing couples at each of Bohannan's (1970) stages of the divorce process.

Returning to Bohannan's stages, next comes the **legal divorce**, during which one partner contacts an attorney, serves legal notice on the other, and begins the judicial process. Until a decade ago, it was necessary in most states to justify the action by alleging some grounds—adultery, mental cruelty—but today almost all states allow partners to terminate the marriage without a presumption of fault by either party. While still adversarial, "no-fault" legislation can be interpreted as an encouraging move toward normalizing divorce in our society (Ahrons & Rodgers, 1987).

Increasingly, as Rice and Rice (1986a) note, divorce has come to be seen as a predictable phenomenon and life-cycle stage, particularly for a segment of society that places great value on individual fulfillment and independence. Today, in Bohannan's view (1984), divorce is as much a societal institution as marriage.

The **economic divorce** follows as decisions are made by the divorcing pair regarding the redistribution of assets, property, child-support payments, possible alimony payments, and so forth, usually with the help of attorneys and sometimes in conjunction with mental health workers. **Divorce mediation** (Coogler, 1978; Folberg & Milne, 1988; Kressel, 1985), an alternative to traditional legal intervention, is a relatively recent innovative attempt to facilitate the negotiation of these emotion-arousing issues by taking into account the affective as well as the legal dimensions of the marital dissolution. As we discuss later in this chapter, divorce mediation is a nonadversarial approach in which professionals (mental health workers, lawyers, or both working together) help a couple arrive at an acceptable and mutually beneficial settlement based on their own agreed-upon choices. By helping the couple reach their own decisions with the aid of a neutral party, divorce mediation is likely to diminish or remove altogether the emotional intensity and blaming behavior commonly associated with adversarial actions.

During Bohannan's fourth stage, that of **coparental divorce**, child-custody and visitation rights are hammered out. While custody has traditionally been awarded to the mother, on the assumption that a young child's interests are best served by his or her mother, that tradition is being increasingly challenged today. More and more fathers are awarded sole custody now, and shared custody or joint custody, in which both parents retain legal custody, is more the norm. One parent may retain **physical custody**; they may take turns caring for the child; or each parent may be granted custody of one or more children. Ahrons and Rodgers (1987) argue that, while marriages may be ended, families (especially with children) continue, even if the parents reside in separate households. These authors prefer the term **binuclear families** to *single-parent* or *broken* families, in order to emphasize that the two households form one family system. (We'll return to these issues in Chapter Four.)

The former partners must next redefine their separate places in the community as single individuals, and must also reestablish relations with family and friends; this all occurs during the stage of **community divorce**. In many cases, as Weiss (1975) observes, decisions to separate (and especially to divorce) may have been postponed for lengthy periods because of reluctance to face friends and family and make the divorce public. Now, relations with others must be reestablished and new lifestyles attempted. Young divorced persons may find it necessary for a variety of reasons (help with child care, finances, feelings of isolation and despair) to move back with their parents, perhaps triggering old parent-child conflicts.

The final stage, for many the most trying, calls for **psychic divorce**, as each former mate must accept the fact of permanent separation, redefine himself or herself as a single and unattached person, and begin the often painful process of seeking and being open to new relationships.

The entire event is a process with roots in the past, before divorce is contemplated, and carries with it effects that extend into the future. As Ahrons and Rodgers (1987), as well as Kaslow and Schwartz (1987), point out, every family member— children as well as adults—will be profoundly affected; as family reorganization results, each person must redefine himself or herself as part of a divorced family and must learn new ways of coping with society at large, as well as with other family members. Feelings of abandonment, betrayal, loneliness, anxiety, rage, inadequacy, disillusionment, continued attachment to the person who has left, desperation at feeling unloved (and thus unlovable), mourning—all are likely to appear in some form (Kessler, 1975). Depression, hostility, and bitterness may continue for many divorced persons, who may persist in struggling with an ex-spouse and/or develop dysfunctional parent-child relationships. Others may rush prematurely into new attachments in an effort to reassure themselves of their worth and attractiveness or to cope with feelings of inadequacy or fear of being alone.

Men are consistently more likely to remarry than are women, for several reasons: they are more apt to marry someone not previously married, and they tend to marry younger women and thus have a larger pool of potential partners than do divorced women (Glick, 1984a). As a group, divorced women, typically with physical custody of their young children, have far less chance of remarriage. Census data as analyzed by Glick, a distinguished demographer, indicate that, among women in their 30s who have divorced, the likelihood of remarriage also declines with increasing levels of education. While divorced women with no college education are likely to remarry rather quickly, other things being equal, those with more education are not, perhaps choosing to enter marriage more deliberately or deciding to remain unmarried. (These data suggest that, generally speaking, the more economically independent a divorced woman feels, the more choices she

**Table 1.1  Common Client Feelings, Actions, Therapeutic Interventions, and Mediation Strategies at Six Stages of the Divorce Process**

| Divorce Stage | Station[a] | Stage | Feelings | Actions and Tasks | Therapeutic Interventions | Mediation |
|---|---|---|---|---|---|---|
| *Predivorce* A time of deliberation and despair | I. Emotional divorce | A | Disillusionment Dissatisfaction Alienation Anxiety Disbelief | Avoiding the issue Sulking and/or crying Confronting partner Quarreling | Marital Therapy (one couple) Couples group therapy | |
| | | B | Despair Dread Anguish Ambivalence Shock Emptiness Anger Chaos Inadequacy Low self-esteem Loss | Denial Withdrawal (physical and emotional) Pretending all is okay Attempting to win back affection Asking friends, family, clergy for advice | Marital therapy (one couple) Divorce therapy Couples group therapy | |
| | II. Legal divorce | C | Depression Detachment Anger Hopelessness Self-pity Helplessness | Bargaining Screaming Threatening Attempting suicide Consulting an attorney or mediator | Family therapy Individual adult therapy Child therapy | Set the stage for mediation Ascertain parties' understanding of the process and its appropriateness for them |
| *During Divorce* A time of legal involvement | III. Economic divorce | D | Confusion Fury Sadness Loneliness Relief Vindictiveness | Separating physically Filing for legal divorce Considering economic arrangements Considering custody arrangements | Children of divorce group therapy Child therapy Adult therapy | Define the rules of mediation Identify the issues & separate therapeutic issues from mediation issues |

| Stage | | Feelings | Tasks | Therapeutic Interventions | Mediation |
|---|---|---|---|---|---|
| IV. Coparental divorce and the problems of custody | E | Concern for children<br>Ambivalence<br>Numbness<br>Uncertainty | Grieving and mourning<br>Telling relatives and friends<br>Reentering the work world (unemployed woman)<br>Feeling empowered to make choices | Same as above plus network family therapy | Negotiate & process the issues & choices<br>Reach agreement<br>Analyze & formalize agreement |
| V. Community divorce | F | Indecisiveness<br>Optimism<br>Resignation<br>Excitement<br>Curiosity<br>Regret<br>Sadness | Finalizing divorce<br>Begin reaching out to new friends<br>Undertaking new activities<br>Stabilizing new lifestyle and daily routine for children<br>Exploring new interests and possibly taking new job | Adults<br>Individual therapy<br>Singles group therapy<br>Children<br>Child play therapy<br>Children's group therapy | |
| VI. Psychic divorce<br><br>*Postdivorce*<br>A time of exploration and reequilibration | G | Acceptance<br>Self-confidence<br>Energetic<br>Self-worth<br>Wholeness<br>Exhilaration<br>Independence<br>Autonomy | Resynthesis of identity<br>Completing psychic divorce<br>Seeking new love object and making a commitment to some permanency<br>Becoming comfortable with new lifestyle and friends<br>Helping children accept finality of parents' divorce and their continuing relationship with both parents | Parent-child therapy<br>Family therapy<br>Group therapies<br>Children's activity group therapy | Return to mediation when changed circumstances require a renegotiation of the agreement |

*Source:* Kaslow, 1988, pp. 88–89.
[a]These stations are taken from the work of Bohannan (1970).

has and the less attractive remarriage may appear to her.) In either case, divorced mothers increasingly are heading single-parent households. Widowed and divorced women with custody of their children were about equally numerous in 1960; but by 1983, divorced mothers outnumbered widowed mothers by five to one (Glick, 1984b). Divorce, separation, and the leap in premarital births have doubled the proportion of single-parent–led families in the last 20 years.

## CHANGING FAMILIES, CHANGING RELATIONSHIPS

Baby boomers—those persons born between 1946 and 1964, the most fertile period in U.S. history—are now in their prime childbearing years, and thus might be expected, themselves, to be producing a bumper crop of children. The facts, however, are otherwise. Whatever the reasons—delayed marriages, career priorities, decisions to remain single, the high cost of childrearing, fear of bringing children into an unstable world, more reliable contraceptive methods, the reluctance to have children in a risky marriage, or simply the desire to enjoy freedom unencumbered by too many family responsibilities; clearly, different factors are important for different couples—the percentage of couples without children today is at the highest point in 50 years.

Consider the options available 50 years ago in order to better understand the dramatic changes in traditional life-cycle events. Then, for the most part, people lived with parents until married; most married by 21; they began to have children almost immediately, as a rule; childbearing typically was over by age 31; marriages remained intact until the death of one of the spouses; widowhood followed by the mid-60s; and, since remarriage at that point was uncommon, men and women both lived out their remaining ten years or so alone. Now, after living with parents, they may live alone, live with a roommate of the same sex, cohabit with an adult of the opposite sex, perhaps marry, have children (in or out of wedlock), get divorced, live alone again or with a lover of the same or opposite sex, remarry, become stepparents, perhaps become widowed or divorced a second time, marry for the third time, and so forth.

Today's Americans are experiencing transition points in their lives unknown to previous generations. People no longer marry in order to start a family; more single American women are having babies than ever before (18% of all Caucasian women, 63% among black women), and many married women are choosing to remain childless or delay childbearing until their late 30s (Morrison, 1991). Childlessness has become a more socially acceptable option for married women, who no longer have to be embarrassed or become defensive or otherwise justify such a choice, their parents' disapproval notwithstanding.

We are once again experiencing important changes in American family life, as we have done repeatedly over the last two centuries. As the historian Hareven (1982) notes, contemporary lifestyles (cohabiting heterosexual couples, homosexual partners, **dual-career marriages**, single-parent–led households, and so on) are not necessarily new inventions, but rather have become more visible as society becomes more tolerant of change and alternative living arrangements. She argues that we are now witnessing not a fragmentation of traditional family patterns, but an emerging acceptance of pluralism in family lifestyles.

The face of the American family has been altered remarkably over the past several decades, during which profound social and demographic changes have taken place. Thriving marriages, successful childrearing, the ability to build and maintain a mature and intimate relationship with another, commitment—these have never been easy to come by, and are probably more difficult than ever today. Conger (1981, p. 1483) calls particular attention to the increased strains on couples, as well as increased challenges:

> Changing sex roles; the rapid increase in women's participation in the work force; the pressure of two-job families; generational differences in values and outlook; continued geographic mobility; relative isolation of the nuclear family; continued age segregation; extremely rapid social, economic, and technological changes and the uncertainty about the future that they create; the economic penalties of parenthood in today's world compared to earlier generations—all of these realities have added to the stresses of marriage and parenthood, as well as to their challenges and exciting opportunities.

## A FAMILY COUNSELING SAMPLER

Family counselors today can expect to deal with at least some of the following situations: married couples attempting in one final way, through joint counseling sessions, to hold a deteriorating relationship together; divorcing couples (see the following section); single parents, usually women, experiencing the emotional and financial hardship of raising children alone (Chapter Four); stepfamilies desperate to work out an arrangement so that they might live together in some degree of harmony despite major differences in background, experiences, and values (Chapter Five); young people in a nonmarital-cohabitation living arrangement, knowing they need to make some decisions about their future but panicked over what a long-term commitment to another person means giving up (Chapter Six); homosexual couples experiencing the agony of breaking up a long-term love relationship (Chapter Seven); ethnic and racially diverse families trying to cope with an unfamiliar or hostile environment (Chapter Eight); and overloaded dual-career couples attempting to juggle career and family while seeking to achieve equity in their relationship (Chapter Nine).

Consider the following brief descriptions from a typical caseload of today's counselor:

❋   ❋   ❋   ❋   ❋

Mr. and Mrs. Brown, married six months, after having each been in marriages ending in divorce, referred themselves for counseling. [Self-referral is actually fairly common with stepfamilies, since one or both parents have had earlier unhappy experiences in marriage and want to avoid a repetition of that trauma.] Both were computer scientists who met as graduate students at a midwestern university. Since both were married at the time, and both were expressing considerable despair about their deteriorating marriages, they found solace in one another, and soon were having a sexual affair. Immediately after graduation, Mr. Brown divorced his wife, left his two preteenage children with their mother, and departed for a job on the West Coast. His wife-to-be shortly thereafter left her husband, took their 6-year-old daughter, and by prearrangement joined Mr. Brown. Within one year, they were married, both employed in rewarding jobs, and living happily with her young daughter in a large urban community. Mr. Brown talked by telephone with his own children on occasion, but saw them rarely, only when he had business in the town where they lived.

Unfortunately, the Browns' honeymoon period was short-lived. For one thing, each of them had been married to people of the same ethnic and social class background as themselves before, and they now experienced some rift as a result of her Baptist and his Jewish background. (Her effort during their first Christmas to maintain a family custom by reading aloud from the New Testament did not go over well with him!) Even more disrupting was the sudden appearance of his daughter, now 13, who had been struggling with her mother and decided to come out, unannounced, to live with her father. Within a short period, during which Mrs. Brown was determined to make her stepdaughter feel at home, conflict erupted in the household. Mrs. Brown was especially upset at what she viewed as her husband's overindulgent and overly permissive childrearing actions, which she believed led to undisciplined and uncontrolled behavior. In addition, she disliked her stepdaughter's intrusiveness—using her perfume, wearing some of her clothes, behaving as though she had proprietary rights over her father. Mr. Brown, caught in the middle, felt concerned about his wife's increasing unhappiness, but also believed he needed to indulge his daughter or she would feel neglected and rejected. One major worry and source of guilt feelings was that his daughter might begin to believe he favored his stepdaughter over his own child. Finally, when conflict in the household had reached an unacceptable level, the Browns contacted a family counselor, who suggested over the telephone that the parents and both children come together for family sessions.

❊   ❊   ❊   ❊   ❊

Andrea and John could not make up their minds about living together, although they had been having an ongoing (and tempestuous) love affair for five years. Both single, in their late 20s, and both employed as salespeople at the same department store where they met, each claimed to be having too much fun to settle down with one person. More likely, however, each had pervasive fears of an intimate relationship, as well as some sense that each would have problems sustaining such closeness over any length of time. Despite these misgivings, and after a long series of on-again, off-again decisions, they determined that they would try living together and decide once and for all whether they should marry or split up permanently. John gave up his apartment and, doubts aside, moved in with Andrea.

It seemed within a month that their worst fears were confirmed. Andrea felt her territory, which she had carefully and lovingly decorated with objects very personal and meaningful to her, was being invaded. John felt very critical of Andrea's way of doing things—cooking, stacking dishes after they were washed, caring for her car, spending money. Accustomed to straight, direct talk—he had been raised in a large family where get-togethers often became free-for-alls—he could not understand Andrea's long silences and quiet weeping. She, on the other hand, an only child raised by a doting mother (who herself had little if any relationship with an increasingly ostracized father), could not understand why John had so many complaints about her if, as he claimed, he loved her so much. After living together two months, both were depressed and confused and, at the suggestion of a fellow employee, sought professional help.

❀   ❀   ❀   ❀   ❀

Glenn and Carl had been lovers more than two years, and had moved into Glenn's house together about a year and a half before their conflicts led them to seek counseling as a couple. Glenn was a Ph.D. historian, graduate of a prestigious university, and himself a university professor, while Carl had had a sporadic education, worked as a bookstore clerk, and was currently taking evening classes at a community college. Glenn had been in individual psychotherapy with a gay psychologist even before living with Carl, and had continued to go after they were together. It was that psychologist who first suggested to Glenn that he was in the midst of a highly intense and disturbing relationship that required the help of a counselor who worked with couples, something that psychologist was not trained to do.

When both partners decided to live together, they believed the relationship would be more or less permanent. Each of them had had experiences with various men—Glenn in relatively long-term relationships, Carl in brief affairs, usually of the pickup, one-night variety. Each was sexually sophisticated about the gay life; each knew how to please the other. In Glenn's case, he had moved from being the more passive, more dependent member in the past to his current situation with Carl of being more active and dominant. Carl had always enjoyed adopting a passive role with other men and continued to do so with Glenn.

Several long-standing issues and certain immediate ones had led to their current crisis. Among the former was Glenn's critical and meticulous behavior; for example, constantly carping about a dirty spot on the sofa or the fact that Carl did not empty ashtrays after each use. Carl's reaction was typically to become increasingly defiant and sloppy. There were additional struggles over status differences, Glenn never failing to remind Carl of the latter's low-level work and the fact that he, Glenn, had lived before with higher-status individuals such as "a physician, a novelist, and a hospital administrator." Perhaps the most acute problem, however, was Carl's return to "cruising" gay bars and being promiscuous, despite (or perhaps because of) Glenn's terror of contacting AIDS.

❀   ❀   ❀   ❀   ❀

Mrs. Taylor, 42, called a male counselor in near-panic, indicating she wanted help for Lois, her 15-year-old daughter, an only child. Mrs. Taylor revealed that she had been in individual counseling with a social worker for three years, since shortly after her husband died, but mainly appeared to be receiving support to resume her life; the matter of dealing with Lois, increasingly a problem, had been a secondary issue until recently. Now, however, the pressures of being a single parent of an adolescent girl were mounting. The school had called several times to report that Lois was not attending class and, when she was present, seemed to be uninterested and uninvolved. What appeared to trigger the call to the counselor, however, was a rare confrontation between mother and daughter in which Lois blurted out that she had visited a clinic to get birth control pills and was having a sexual relationship with Tom, 20, a sometime student at a local junior college. Mrs. Taylor wanted a male counselor in particular, because she felt most of her family problems could be traced to the loss of her husband and her subsequent efforts "to be both mother and father to Lois."

As is often the case with adolescents, especially when seeing a counselor because of a parent's prodding, an individual session with Lois proved of limited value. Although the counselor and Lois hit it off well enough, Lois was guarded and sulky; she was willing to answer questions and seemed to do so honestly, but she volunteered little information and gave most of her responses in as brief a form as possible. She did acknowledge her sexual activity, insisting it was her business alone and that her mother—and now the counselor—were intruding into her life. She was willing to continue the sessions to pacify her mother but, frankly, she felt the problem was her mother's and not hers. The counselor did persuade her to return for a joint session with her mother the following week.

In person, Mrs. Taylor gave the impression of a passive-dependent, uncertain, frightened, and depressed woman. Not knowing how to deal with Lois, and especially her budding sexuality, she had adopted a laissez-faire attitude, abdicating any responsibility for providing guidance for her daughter. She herself barely managed to hold onto a part-time job as a bank teller, and essentially led a fairly solitary and joyless life. Her living standard, now far below what her husband had provided as a self-employed accountant, left her with few options for travel or other social activities she had known in the past. At some level—although she refused to deal with the issue at first—she felt competitive with her young daughter and resentful of the romance in the latter's life.

❀   ❀   ❀   ❀   ❀

Joel, born and raised in a small town and relatively innocent about the outside world, did not stray far from home until he was 18 and went off to college in a nearby state. Lindsay, by contrast, had been brought up in the college town, and was sophisticated, brainy, and beautiful. What this "college queen" ever saw in Joel never ceased to amaze him, since she had a choice of dozens of more attractive men, or so it seemed to him. In any case, choose him she did, and in their last year of school they were married.

Joel completed his premed training, Lindsay continued working on her elementary teaching credential, and their dual-career relationship seemed to flourish. All through his medical school, internship, and residency years, Joel worked hard, continuing to be the high achiever he had been since his earliest school years. Lindsay got a job as a teacher, discovered it was rewarding but demanding and, although she saw herself as a career person, seemed to welcome Joel's urging that she stop working and have a baby. Within two years, they had another child, Joel was busy establishing his practice in internal medicine, and Lindsay, like many another woman in a dual-career marriage, was trying to decide whether to return to work part-time or on a substitute-teacher basis while their preschool children still needed her attention. Intent on resuming her career, with aspirations toward becoming a school psychologist, Lindsay nevertheless was torn between the needs of her children and the requirements of a demanding profession. She was unable to find satisfactory child care for her two children and, rather than return to teaching and take evening classes to obtain an advanced degree and school psychologist credential, Lindsay decided to interrupt her career somewhat longer until the children were more self-sufficient or more fully grown. Increasingly, however, Lindsay began experiencing periods of depression and feelings of worthlessness. Bored and dissatisfied at home, she tried a variety of part-time jobs: secretary in a large office, assistant to a book publisher, private tutor. None challenged her intellectually. She felt despondent over not living up to her career potential and resentful that Joel was gaining recognition and her career aspirations were stalled. Typically, when morose, she would return home, have dinner with the family (Joel had picked up the children from the day-care center near his office and prepared dinner), spend a brief period with the children, and go to bed. Weekends were similar: Joel playing the role of mother and father, taking the children shopping for clothes, to the movies, or to kiddyland activities, preparing dinner, and getting them to bed.

During this time, Lindsay stayed in bed most of the day, slept on and off, and hardly seemed to notice the comings and goings of people around her. More and more, the children turned to Joel as a single parent; more and more, they shared his unexpressed contempt and rage at Lindsay's behavior. After some initial fruitless attempts to get Lindsay to seek professional help, little changed in this family pattern for two years. By then, however, Joel was receiving enough satisfaction from his martyrdom that he no longer allowed Lindsay to share in raising the children, even at those times when she expressed a desire to do so. Curiously, despite Joel's self-righteousness and Lindsay's escapist behavior, their sex life seemed to continue and give pleasure to both of them. Whether such physical intimacy represented the exchange of true affection or simply the seeking of comfort and reassurance by two needy, dependent people was never considered. However, even this tentative effort to reach out to one another ultimately dwindled and, as a last resort before filing for divorce, they contacted a family counselor.

❋    ❋    ❋    ❋    ❋

Rao and Sanjay Singh were sister and brother who came from India to the United States with their parents when they were still of a preschool age. Their parents had brought them with the hope that the children's future would be brighter than theirs, since neither of the parents had had much education or opportunity in their native land. The parents worked very hard, seven days a week, in a clothing store they owned, just managing to make a living, and expected the children to help out once they were old enough to do so. Both children were taught to be compliant, to respect their parents' wishes, and to only engage in social activities with family members. Friends from school were discouraged, and Rao and Sanjay, now 17 and 14, respectively, were expected only to go places with one another, never alone or with friends. Television was tolerated, but monitored by the parents, so that no kissing scenes were permitted in what Mr. and Mrs. Singh believed was an exceedingly permissive American society. When either child objected, the parents reminded them that they were being disrespectful and that, if the "disrespectful" behavior continued, the parents would move them all back to India.

Loyalty, respect, and family obligation were essential parts of the family code. Not unlike other Indian families they knew, extended-family ties were stressed, arranged marriages were the norm, and the children were expected to obey the parents, especially the father. When Rao asked to go to a party with her high school friends, the parents refused, asking instead why she hadn't proposed helping out in the store so they could get some rest. Despite her protests that she did help but also wanted to have some fun, the parents threw up their hands in despair and told the children how miserable their ungrateful behavior had made them.

A thoughtful teacher, observing Rao's distress, talked to her about the problems of biculturalism and suggested that such culture conflict was not uncommon under the circumstances. The teacher suggested family counseling, which the parents first refused to do, expressing shame that intervention by a stranger would be necessary. After the children visited a counselor alone for two sessions, the parents reluctantly came in, and together all four began to deal with resolving generational issues and clarifying future family roles.

❊   ❊   ❊   ❊   ❊

## INTERVENING IN A TROUBLED RELATIONSHIP

In each of the cases just summarized, the counselor needs first to determine which therapeutic mode—individual, couple, or family—is likely to be most effective, cost-efficient, and matched to the family stressors (Worthington, 1989). Beyond such preliminary matching, Sperry (1992) notes that the increasing number of nontraditional couple and family arrangements today require even more individualized and "tailored"[4] interventions. Primarily, such "tailoring" may be done according to client or family diagnosis (Frances, Clarkin, & Perry, 1984), level of relational conflict (Guerin, Fay, Burden, & Kautto, 1987), or a couple or family's level of functioning as a system (Weltner, 1992).

As an example of linking diagnosis to treatment, Frances, Clarkin, and Perry (1984) propose the notion of *differential therapeutics*, tailoring treatment strategies to DSM IIIR diagnostic categories. Particular attention is paid to four factors: *setting* (chronic or acute, inpatient or outpatient), *format* (individual, couple, family), *orientation* (type of therapy), and *duration and frequency of treatment*. The authors match these four factors to the client's diagnosis, systematically studying which combinations best fit persons with which diagnosis. This approach is in sharp contrast to one in which the counselor intuitively imposes his or her particular therapeutic orientation on all clients, regardless of their presenting problems, behavior patterns, individual personality characteristics, or diagnosis.

Another interesting effort at tailoring focuses on relational conflict, assuming that different couples express their marital conflict in different ways, struggle over different issues with different degrees of intensity, and have been involved in such struggles for differing lengths of time. Obviously, a one-size-fits-all counseling approach fails to deal adequately with the nuances that often distinguish successful from unsuccessful counseling in such cases. Guerin, Fay, Burden, and Kautto (1987) propose that intervention plans pay particular attention to the intensity and duration of the marital conflict in treatment planning. More specifically, they contend that couples seeking counseling can be differentiated in terms of four stages of marital discord. Careful evaluation, according to specific behavioral indices, is followed by a tailor-made therapeutic plan in which systems, behavioral, and psychodynamic approaches are combined in varying manners, depending on the couple's stage of marital discord.

According to this analysis, stage-1 couples are likely to be married a short time and to have a minimal level of conflict of relatively short duration, probably less than six months. Stage-2 couples display more serious unrest; however, despite conflict lasting over six months, they are still able to communicate, even if that communication is filled with criticism and projection onto the other partner. Severe marital conflict characterizes couples at stage 3, who have been struggling for a long time without resolution, so that communication, except for blame and sharp criticism, is by and large closed off. Couples who present a stage-4 level

---

[4]*Matching* here refers to deciding on a particular therapeutic approach (for example, behavioral) or modality (for example, couple rather than individual) in planning counseling, in order to increase the likelihood of success. This is typically carried out after the initial interview. *Tailoring,* more likely to be adjusted as counseling progresses, involves flexibly utilizing techniques after a client-counselor relationship has been established, in an effort to enhance the therapeutic alliance and create an atmosphere in which suggestions or directives are most likely to be followed. In Worthington's (1992) analogy, the differences are akin to choosing an appropriate suit from the rack versus making the suit fit the client(s).

|            | Level I                                                        | Level II                                                                          | Level III                                                        |
|------------|----------------------------------------------------------------|-----------------------------------------------------------------------------------|------------------------------------------------------------------|
| *Issue*      | Executive capacity (ego) overwhelmed Cannot nurture Cannot contain | Messing up due to old family beliefs and mandates. Faulty expectations (boundary problems) | Preoccupied with issues of meaning or quality of life  Existential dilemmas |
| *Boundaries* | Who cares?                                                      | Achieve generational and personal boundaries                                      | Already mastered                                                 |
| *Resistance* | No                                                             | Yes                                                                               | No                                                               |
| *Strategy*   | Build a new organization (support the shaky ego)  Enlarge the executive system Build a containing coalition | Find alternate ways to view reality  Help clients to unstick themselves from old patterns and loyalties | Bypass ordinary ways of thinking  Access an inner wisdom, the underground stream |

**Figure 1.4**   Criteria for Determining Level of Pathology
*Source:* Weltner, 1992, p. 39.

of marital conflict no longer are able or willing to communicate with one another, fearing self-disclosure will inevitably lead to further criticism and blame from the partner. By the time a couple reaches this last stage, it is likely that one or both spouses has consulted an attorney.

One final tailoring technique, advanced by Weltner (1992) addresses a family's level of functioning as a system, offering a corresponding set of intervention techniques (based on distinct therapeutic stances) for each of three designated levels. In this formulation, level-1 families are viewed as fragmented and under-organized, their lack of parental competence so severe that they have difficulties managing basic survival tasks (food, medical care, protection and safety of children). Families considered to be functioning at level 2 are rigid and idiosyncratic, filled with self-defeating behavior poorly suited to dealing with the realities of their lives. Unlike level-1 families, where a lack of socialization patterns is the rule, level-2 families have such skills, but are rigid and inappropriate in their application. Level-3 families who seek counseling, a smaller group than the previous two, tend to be well organized, with a determination to give their lives greater meaning and purpose. Figure 1.4 describes the criteria used to determine the family's functioning level.

Since the same counseling approach hardly fits families from all of these levels, Weltner (1992) has devised a continuum that differentiates three therapeutic stances. As indicated in Figure 1.5, the *take-charge* counselor views the family as impaired and desirous of help, and not likely to resist direct intervention by the counselor. Taking charge, the counselor uses his or her personal authority to restructure the family, attempting to organize and build an executive system

| Issue | Take charge | Chief investigator | Fellow traveler |
|---|---|---|---|
| *View of client* | Impaired | Faulty beliefs and expectations | Growing, not fixed or limited |
| | Has assets | Sufficient assets | Has unique, valued life experience |
| | Wants help | Ambivalent about help | In charge of treatment |
| *View of therapist* | Informed and competent | Can recognize pathology | Co-learner |
| | | Can find patterns Object of transference | Facilitator |
| | Responsible for the success of treatment | Co-responsible for outcome | Helps client connect to inner wisdom |
| *Focus* | Conscious Present | Unconscious Past | Underground stream Future (growth) |
| *Tools* | Personal authority | Historical perspective (psychodynamic) (family systems) | Empathy and positive regard |
| | Structural and strategic theory | Transference Paradox | Variety of ways to bypass ordinary consciousness |

**Figure 1.5** Therapeutic Stances and Characteristics for Three Counselor Types
*Source:* Weltner, 1992, p. 40.

that should result in more adaptive behavior. This approach is especially tailored to level-1 families.

The *chief-investigator* counselor, most appropriate in dealing with level-2 families, helps clients understand their misperceptions, unrealistic expectations, and behavior patterns that are not in their best self-interest. Providing insight and utilizing a set of therapeutic techniques that increase awareness of self-limiting thought patterns and self-defeating interactions, the chief investigator helps families move beyond the "stuckness" of the past. The *fellow-traveler* counselor, most applicable to level-3 families, believes the family has the capacity for self-healing, and thus acts as a facilitator to help them access their self-wisdom.

A common goal of these tailoring procedures is to avoid mismatching clients and counselors. Because many counselors have one strong suit that they offer all clients, mismatching is likely unless a schema such as we have described in this section is developed for guiding counselor interventions. Nevertheless, matching and tailoring are at an early stage of development, and procedures must be developed for dealing with very complex variables—the counselor's personality, the clients' personalities, lifestyle differences, individual psychopathology, demographic factors, and many more. While this approach offers a promising beginning, we remain a long way from answering a challenge posed by Paul (1967) over 25 years ago: "What therapy is most effective for what problems, treated by what therapists, according to what criteria, in what setting?" (p. 111).

## MARRIAGE AND DIVORCE COUNSELING

Considering the prevalence of divorce and the fact that counselors must deal with this issue repeatedly in their practices, it is curious that, until the last decade, few published guidelines existed for this form of family intervention. In recent years, however, a spate of books has appeared (Everett, 1987; Isaacs, Montalvo, & Abelsohn, 1986; Rice & Rice, 1986b; Sprenkle, 1985; Textor, 1989), generally offering a systems outlook for conducting conjoint sessions of divorce counseling. We should note here that in some cases—an unwilling or untrusting or geographically unavailable spouse, an uncontrollably angry or violent spouse, a spouse resistant to further contact with an ex-mate—the counselor may be forced to work with only one member of the dyad, although continuing to view the dissolution of the marriage in systems terms may still be appropriate. However, whenever possible, the counselor should make every effort to involve both spouses in any divorce decision-making process, if necessary making a personal appeal to the resistant spouse to attend. By failing to intervene with both partners, the counselor not only hears only one side of the story, but is also open to the charge of aligning with one spouse and thus furthering the polarization already taking place (Rice, 1989).

While the term *divorce counseling* may technically be presumed to mean that the decision has been made to terminate the marriage, so that the procedure focuses on disengaging the couple as easily as the situation permits, in reality the circumstances are rarely so tidy or clear-cut. More likely, marriage and divorce counseling are segments of the same continuum, and where the former ends and the latter begins cannot readily be demarcated. Some couples begin marriage counseling without having raised the issue of divorce among themselves; indeed, they are determined to make the marriage work, and only with great reluctance and a sense of failure may come to realize the impossibility of such a lofty goal. Others come reporting a vague sense of stagnation in their relationship, or perhaps reporting symptoms in themselves or their children that distress them. At the other extreme, couples may seek counseling after determining that divorce is inevitable, perhaps asking for help in minimizing the pain involved in the process for themselves and their children. Thus, couples begin at differing points in the decision-making process, or may drift back and forth while trying to reach a decision; this calls for considerable flexibility on the counselor's part.

Married couples, then, enter counseling with a variety of expectations and hopes, to say nothing of varying degrees of commitment to remaining together. One or both may have concluded earlier that the marriage is no longer satisfying, although they nevertheless are prepared to engage briefly in the counseling process as a last resort, or perhaps to give the appearance of making a final effort before separating and filing for divorce. Others, badgered into coming by an insistent spouse (perhaps with the threat of divorce as the other alternative), may be denying their internal sense of hopelessness about the future of the relationship, and remain fearful even about saying the word *divorce* publicly. Still others think of divorce as a personal failure, or perhaps as something that occurs to other people but not to themselves or their families. For some couples, one partner may attend a joint session in order to announce the decision to divorce in the presence of the counselor, feeling less guilty if a possibly distraught spouse is in professional hands.

Finally, some couples enter counseling together, hoping to improve the relationship. Such improvement is a good possibility, as we have noted (Guerin, Fay, Burden, & Kautto, 1987; Kaslow, 1988), especially if intervention begins early enough in the conflict, when communication is still intact, too much damage has not yet been done, and the partners still wish to strengthen their marital bond. On the other hand, marriage counseling may force them to face the fact that their differences are irreconcilable, their goals unrealistic, and their future together unpromising, despite the positive changes each has attempted. In these instances, divorce may be the most feasible alternative for resolving their relationship conflicts.

Divorce counseling, then, may be the final stage in a sequence of unsuccessful efforts to save the marriage. Or, under other circumstances, divorce counseling may follow the legal divorce proceedings, as ex-mates, individually or conjointly, attempt to cope with unfinished or continuing conflict (for example, over visitation rights with the children). In the former case, in which the couple seeking to repair their marriage is forced to conclude it cannot be done, counseling need not be finished once that decision is reached. Rather, even if the decision to divorce has been agreed upon, the counselor must help educate both spouses about a number of unfinished tasks: understanding why the relationship failed (as insurance against future failure); how best to disengage (and not continue or escalate their conflictual relationship); how to cope with the sense of loss, acute stress, and perhaps temporary disorganization in personal functioning (in one or both); how best to deal with other members of the family system (children, parents, and others); and how to foster autonomy and personal development for each as individual persons (Rice & Rice, 1986b).

In this regard, Salts (1985) makes a useful distinction between three stages of divorce counseling, along with commensurate tasks and goals for the counselor:

1. *The divorce decision-making stage:* helping couples recognize what made theirs an unhappy marriage and aiding them in determining whether their needs can be met within the marriage or what alternative solutions are possible.

2. *The restructuring stage:* if the decision to divorce has been made, providing both spouses with an opportunity to reaffirm its benefits or, in the case of an unwilling partner, to accept its inevitability.

3. *The postdivorce recovery stage:* helping couples rebuild separate lives, deal with loss, develop alternative relationships.

Sprenkle (1990) has outlined a practical set of goals for counselors helping couples cope with the inescapable pain inherent in the divorce process (Box 1.1). Dealing with role loss, loss of a partner, family, or lifestyle, loss of self-esteem, and doubts that one has what it takes to be a good or lovable husband or wife— all this forms part of the rebuilding process.

The decision to divorce is never made lightly, even in mutually destructive marriages, and is almost always accompanied by feelings of anguish, despair, shock, and disbelief that this is actually happening. Frequently the couple vacillates between trying one more time to salvage the marriage and wishing to dissolve it. Of necessity, the counselor may alternate between marital and divorce counseling during this period, and must be especially vigilant to avoid inadvertently taking sides in the middle of the conflict, as one mate insists on leaving and proceeding with the divorce while the other begs for another chance. It is the counselor's task to help the couple consider all options at this predivorce decision-making stage, without being maneuvered into deciding for them whether or not to remain together.

The counselor must also take great care not to become impatient or intolerant with the vacillation and thereby force a premature decision. As Turner (1985) points out, the counselor can expect puzzling decisional behavior at this stage, often marked by seeming irrationality, a great deal of ambivalence, regressive behavior, impulsivity, and frequent reversals.

Granvold (1983) recommends the possibility of a planned structured separation for couples at an impasse, especially if they continue to be doubtful about whether divorce is the best alternative. The therapeutic purpose here, during the

---

### Box 1.1  Goals of Divorce Counseling

Partners need to be helped to:

1. Accept the end of the marriage.
2. Achieve a functional postdivorce relationship with the ex-spouse.
3. Achieve a reasonable emotional adjustment.
4. Develop an understanding of their own contributions to the dysfunctional behavior that led to the failure of the marriage.
5. Find sources of emotional support.
6. Feel competent and comfortable in postdivorce parenting.
7. Help their children adjust to the loss without triangulating them or nourishing unrealistic expectations.
8. Use the "crisis" of divorce as an opportunity for learning and personal growth.
9. Negotiate the legal process in a way both feel is reasonably equitable.
10. Develop physical, health, and personal habits consistent with adjustment for everyone.

*Source:* Sprenkel, 1990, pp. 176–177.

decision-making stage, is to interrupt the heated marital conflict in order to facilitate a more measured, rational decision. Such separation also provides both parties with a glimpse of independent living, a period of value reassessment, and an opportunity for experimentation with other lifestyles. A written contract outlining the length of separation (say, three months) as well as its ground rules (dating others, outside sexual relationships, visits with the children) is common under these circumstances. Typically, the nature and frequency of the partners' contacts with one another is spelled out during this "cooling-off" period, and conjoint counseling on a regular basis is continued.

The counselor needs to be particularly attuned to the stage of the individual, marital, and family life cycle, and to the stage of the divorce process (see Table 1.1) of the presenting clients. Grief, mourning for the failed relationship that once held so much promise, and despair at ever weathering the crisis and going on alone are all to be expected. Denial, feelings of anger and frustration, vengeance, rage, fear of abandonment—these too are familiar to any counselor dealing with a divorcing couple, especially in the early phases of the marital dissolution. Later, sadness, resignation, regret, and remorse are more common. Rice and Rice (1986b) suggest that the counselor, in addition to offering support, be prepared to teach social, interpersonal, and even assertiveness techniques to help individuals regain confidence and learn effective coping skills as a single person.

Particularly when children are involved, parents have the additional task of learning to deal cooperatively with one another. While most divorcing parents try to buffer their children from the impact of adult conflict, some unfortunately recruit their children into taking sides. In the midst of conflict, some parents abdicate their caretaking responsibilities, or perhaps lose confidence in their ability to carry out parenting tasks. Isaacs, Montalvo, and Abelsohn (1986) urge counselors working with such cases of "difficult divorce" to focus on the parents' efforts toward reorganizing their relationships both with each other and with their children. Here the focus is on the *family* getting divorced, not just the parents.

In the following case, a couple has separated but is stalled in the divorce process. What appears to be a request for counseling directed at reaching decisions regarding their 3-year-old child turns out to be an effort to finish up their divorce.

❋  ❋  ❋  ❋  ❋

Harry and Lola, separated for six months, called a counselor for help in making joint decisions regarding Meredith, their 3-year-old daughter. They asked to come in together as a couple, without the child; while the counselor suspected more was involved between them than was apparent, she agreed to their plan, hoping that without Meredith they might more readily deal with what was blocking their proceeding with the divorce.

As expected, the presenting problems—arrangements regarding visitation, overnight stays for Meredith, vacation plans for her stay with each parent—were indeed easily resolved, the couple spending less than one session on deciding these issues. Later in the first counseling session, however, the counselor began to wonder aloud about the reasons their marriage had failed, observing that Harry and Lola showed little awareness or insight into their relationship. It was soon clear to the counselor that they were covering up a number of unresolved issues between them, and that their inability to deal with those conflicts kept them from moving ahead with the divorce. The counselor suggested that they seemed to have some unfinished business between them, and invited them to explore those areas for a session or two. They quickly agreed, and set up the additional meetings with the counselor for the forthcoming week.

As Harry and Lola spoke of their backgrounds, it became clear that they had come a long way, socially, culturally, intellectually, and financially, from their working-class beginnings. Now both successful architects, they had met at school, drawn together by similarities in religion and the shared experience of growing up poor and being the first in each of their families to attend college. Both were ambitious and fiercely determined to get ahead in their profession. They married soon after graduation, struggled together to succeed, and put off having a child until they were closer to their professional goals—academic careers as professors of architecture and urban planning at a major university.

Meredith was born when the couple was in their early 30s, and they both adored her right from the start. However, aside from their devotion to her, they seemed less and less to have their earlier closeness and affection for one another. During the previous decade, each had emphasized work, career, and success and, without acknowledging it, had become highly competitive with the other. While each rarely if ever expressed unhappiness or dissatisfaction to the other, both partners nevertheless realized that something was amiss. Sex between them had become infrequent and, while they blamed it on fatigue, busy schedules, and preoccupation with careers, both had a sense—never put into words—that they had lost much interest in each other over the years. Instead, they viewed their lives as filled with obligations and responsibilities from which they drew little pleasure.

Under these circumstances, it was hardly surprising that Harry met Celeste, a young instructor, and was immediately drawn to her. Astonished by the intensity of his feelings, he became all the more aware of the emptiness in his life at home. Despite a renewed effort to reach out to Lola, he found himself still unable to speak to her about any of his feelings of discontent, nor was she able to do so to him. Thus immobilized in any effort to become more intimate, each pulled further and further away from the painful marital situation. Finally, overwhelmed with guilt—although he and Celeste had not become sexually involved with one another—Harry moved out. Typically, finding himself unable to face Lola, he left behind a note, indicating his unhappiness and despair, and blamed his upset on his "mid-life crisis." Dismayed, dumbfounded, and internally enraged, Lola nevertheless accepted Harry's decision with outward calm.

The couple continued a civil relationship, especially in regard to their daughter. No anger was ever expressed directly, no bitterness was ever shown by either partner. However, their underlying rage at their failed marriage did manifest itself in their inability to agree to the simplest arrangements regarding Meredith. While they never brought up what went wrong or what was missing in the marriage, they continuously disagreed about every detail (school, clothes, activities, lessons) of Meredith's life. While the counselor agreed that the rift between them had gotten too great to be breached, she noted that, if they wanted to help Meredith, which they did, they would have to learn to express feelings more directly to one another (and by implication, to any future person with whom each wished to pursue a serious relationship). The block in their ability to communicate angry or hurt feelings was holding up each of them in moving on with their lives.

Straight talk was alien to their personal styles or cultural backgrounds. Each had been carefully raised only to speak of pleasant things, and to say nothing if one could not say something nice. Nevertheless, the counselor pressed them to get in touch with their feelings, insisting that they learn to put into words what each was experiencing internally and expressing nonverbally through their oppositional behavior. As they did so, the problems they initially presented regarding their daughter were more easily resolved.

The couple terminated counseling after three sessions, as they had originally planned. They continued to practice a more open exchange of feelings and, while it did not seem to come naturally, they did make progress. After two months, they returned, having moved along sufficiently that they were ready to see an attorney and reach decisions regarding child custody and the division of their assets. The counselor encouraged their greater openness, and helped each overcome feelings of anger, sadness, and disappointment. Each seemed more ready to move on in their lives as separate persons who continued to have a relationship because of their child, as well as their common profession.

They divorced a month later. On the day of their court date, and within five minutes of one another, each separately called the counselor to indicate what had transpired and to say they were pleased and relieved. Together they had shared a meaningful experience with the counselor, toward whom they both felt close. Each independently reported that Meredith seemed happy and that the ex-spouses were getting better at working their differences out. Within two years both were happily remarried.

❄    ❄    ❄    ❄    ❄

## DIVORCE MEDIATION

Assuming a couple has decided to divorce, there remain a multitude of practical problems to face, disputes to be resolved, differences inherent in the marriage dissolution to be negotiated. As Stier (1986) reminds us, after the divorcing couple has mourned together in divorce counseling, worked through their feelings of disappointment and anger, and perhaps explored their separate fears and hopes about the future apart, there is an immediate need to work out the terms of their dissolution agreement and their postdivorce family relationship. Divorce mediation with the aid of a specially trained, nonpartisan third party is intended to provide precisely such an opportunity.

Traditionally, during the legal stage of the divorce process, the spouses separately seek the counsel of attorneys and embark on the adversarial procedures of a litigated divorce. Each lawyer sets out to serve the best interests of his or her client, retaining or obtaining as much as possible for that client. While attempting to portray his or her client in the most favorable light, each attorney assumes that the other spouse's interests will be similarly represented by opposing legal counsel. Negotiations are thus primarily in the hands of attorneys or, should they fail to arrive at an agreement, settled by a judge. As Kaslow (1988) observes, the resulting fray sometimes becomes a destructive free-for-all, resulting in "long-term embattlement and embitterment in which relatives and friends take sides, children are victimized by the continuing strife, and everyone is left depleted and feeling like a loser" (p. 87).

On the other hand, divorce mediation, which arose in the mid-1970s, offers an alternative route to resolving potential disputes over custody, visitation rights, the distribution of family assets, and other such issues. Here the assumption is that the couple themselves are the experts in their own divorce, and they know better than anyone else what they need for a satisfactory postdivorce working relationship. Much as in labor mediation, the divorce mediator, knowledgeable about the substantive issues involved in marital dissolution and trained to provide impartial mediation services, acts as a facilitator (rather than a counselor or advocate) helping the couple to cooperatively examine the pros and cons of various alternatives and arrive at a calmer, more equitable, and ultimately more humane set of joint decisions (Neville, 1990).

The mediator's role,[5] according to Stier (1986), a psychologist-lawyer, is to help reorient the disputing parties toward each other, not by imposing rules but by helping them achieve a shared perception of the situation and of their relationship. Ideally, if mediation is successful, the new perception will redirect their attitudes and dispositions toward each other.

Most divorce mediation can be accomplished in 6 to 12 hour-long sessions. Despite the possible examination together of the couple's disputing patterns, particularly as they hamper progress in the mediation process, the approach is not the same as divorce counseling. It does not focus on the interpersonal problems that led to the breakup nor does the approach seek to modify existing individual personality patterns. Although insights and stress reduction may occur, these are fringe benefits, not the major purpose of mediation. Divorce mediation does, however, provide for an airing of emotional issues, something rarely occurring in court proceedings, and thus may help resolve them and avoid their resurfacing later in the form of postdivorce litigation (Folberg & Milne, 1988).

Divorce mediation is a multistage process of conflict management or resolution, with a continued focus on the family system rather than the interests of a particular family member. An impartial mediator (or team of mediators), with no previous counseling relationship with the clients, helps the couple identify

---

[5]An effective mediator, according to Neville (1990), needs the ability to reframe—to take messages of anger, jealousy, hurt, and resentment and place them in a different verbal or emotional context. Thus, negative messages from one spouse are given a positive connotation and relabeled as well-intentioned (for example, really expressing the fear or disappointment underlying the manifest anger), transforming the way in which the message is heard and interpreted by the other spouse.

disputed issues, develop and consider options, and make choices, in order to reach consensual agreements that will realistically meet the needs and concerns of the family. Taylor (1988) distinguishes the following seven stages:

*Stage 1. Creating structure and trust:* The mediator develops rapport with the couple and begins to gather relevant information about each partner's perceptions of conflicts, as well as their goals and expectations; the participants begin to understand the nature of the mediating process.

*Stage 2. Fact-finding and isolation of the issues:* The underlying conflict areas, their duration and intensity, and the expressed and perceived rigidity of positions are identified.

*Stage 3. Creation of options and alternatives:* Both parties are actively involved in assigning priorities to the remaining disagreements, locating stumbling blocks, and together developing new options that may be more satisfactory to both participants.

*Stage 4. Negotiation and decision making:* The couple is encouraged to take the risky step of making choices, accepting compromises, and bargaining; the couple is directed from a competitive negotiation to a more cooperative interaction.

*Stage 5. Clarification—writing a plan:* A document outlining the participants' intentions and decisions is produced and is agreed to in writing by both parties.

*Stage 6. Legal review and processing:* The family system is connected to larger watchdog social systems and institutions, such as private attorneys or judges, in order to verify the agreement's completeness, fairness, and feasibility.

*Stage 7. Implementation, review, and revision:* Outside the confines of the mediation sessions, a follow-up is conducted on the participants' ability to match intentions with agreed-upon action and behavior.

Animosity and rancor are typically reduced as a result of the mediation experience, allowing both partners to separate peacefully so that each might begin building a new life. While the mediation process is not acceptable to all divorcing couples, nor necessarily effective under all circumstances for those willing to participate, it does hold promise for many as a way of lightening the pain of divorce, not only for the spouses but for their children as well. Before we look at the makeup, common problems, and counseling needs of many of today's families, however, we need to provide a theoretical framework for understanding how families function and how and why some become dysfunctional. We turn, therefore, in the next chapter to a view of the family as a social system.

## SUMMARY

In today's changing society, the nuclear family is less common, and certain nontraditional family forms are becoming more evident. The high divorce rate; the rapid increase of women in the professional work force; the choice of singlehood over marriage or the delay of marriage by many Americans; and the sharp rise in the number of childless couples, illegitimate children, single-parent–led households, and stepfamilies—these contemporary phenomena have, together, forced counselors to deal with new sets of lifestyles and family-relationship problems.

Approximately half of those couples who marry today can expect to become divorced, for a variety of social, personal, and interpersonal reasons; relationship problems are probably the major cause of most marital breakups. The process of divorce typically extends over time and goes through certain predictable stages before each of the ex-mates can resume separate lives. Because couples are divorcing at an earlier age than ever before, it is increasingly common for young children today to live with a single parent and, perhaps later, in a stepfamily.

Today's counselors can expect to deal with a variety of family styles in addition to nuclear families. Single-parent–led families, stepfamilies, cohabiting heterosexual couples, gay male and lesbian couples, and dual-career families are increasingly common.

Counselors first must determine in each case which therapeutic mode—individual, couple, or family—is most likely to be effective. Whenever possible, matching and tailoring to client diagnosis, relational conflict, or level of functioning can help maximize counseling benefits. Divorce counseling, an increasingly practiced form of family intervention, may be the concluding segment of an effort at marital counseling, or may follow the legal divorce proceedings as former spouses attempt to cope with unfinished or continuing family conflict. A newer technique, divorce mediation, offers a nonadversarial attempt by mediators, trained in mental health as well as the law, to help divorcing couples together to reach agreements, avoid future conflict, and, ideally, to separate without recrimination so that all family members, children included, may go on with building new lives.

# C H A P T E R

# T W O

# The Family as a Social System

Historically, efforts by counselors and other clinicians to conceptualize the origins and meaning of problematic or dysfunctional behaviors have turned to explanations that focus on the individual, particularly the person's intrapsychic conflicts. Correspondingly, therapeutic endeavors were, for many years, directed at penetrating as deeply as possible into the individual's psyche—that mysterious "black box"—in order to extract those repressed memories, wishes, or thoughts that were, presumably, at the core of the current behavioral or emotional difficulties.

Beginning in the 1940s, however, an alternate view of human problems and their alleviation began to emerge. In part, the shift in thinking reflected a growing dissatisfaction with mechanical or analytical explanations in various branches of science and mathematics. Within the social sciences, more specifically, a number of counselors and other therapists began looking beyond the past for explanations of current, ongoing behavior. Just as their counterparts in biology, for example, were beginning to comprehend the complex ecological system in which different forms of life (people, animals, plants, birds, air, soil) share a common environment, affecting each other so intimately that it would be naive and foolish to consider them separately, so clinicians began to wonder if it might be useful to consider an individual as existing in a similar kind of ecological system, namely his or her family (Segal & Bavelas, 1983). Within such a framework, they reasoned, perhaps the individual can be better understood, and more effectively treated, when the disturbed behavior (anxiety, depression, alcoholism, an eating disorder) is seen as representative of a **system** that is faulty. That person's current difficulties might then be viewed in the context of a family social system in disequilibrium (Minuchin, 1974), rather than as symptoms of some internal conflict.

The systems outlook has profound implications for the ways in which counselors view, think about, and ultimately intervene in human social phenomena (Koman & Stechler, 1985). Systems thinking is not so much directly translatable into specific counseling techniques, but rather provides the counselor with a way of organizing his or her thinking about people and the origins of their dysfunctional behavior; that way of organizing data and conceptualizing problems between people in turn has implications for how most effectively to intercede with troubled families. As Skynner (1982, p. 4) observes:

> The widening of our perspective from its earlier focus on the individual, to an awareness of family and community systems, has shown us clear reasons for the extraordinary difficulty everyone has found in changing individuals separately from their family systems, or in changing families separately from their neighborhood communities, as long as they remain in close psychological contact with, and so are deeply affected by, these larger structures in which their lives are led.

## GENERAL SYSTEMS THEORY

The systems view has come to dominate much of scientific thinking in the second half of the 20th century, as researchers and theory builders in various disciplines are recognizing the commonality of their efforts. Many have come to appreciate that a common thread interweaves much of their work, and that the rules and regulations of one discipline may have counterparts in others. Some scientists from related disciplines such as Bertalanffy (1968) from biology and Miller (1978) from psychology have proposed that general principles are sufficiently discernible to hazard developing an integrative theory that underlies a multitude of scientific disciplines. While it is still too early to suggest that systems thinking is applicable to all sciences in equal measure or even that the systems perspective is entirely relevant or applicable to understanding the intricate transactions within a family, it is a fact that its impact on both the scientific and clinical communities has been significant.

Largely the result of the efforts of Ludwig von Bertalanffy—although by no means his alone, since scientists in various fields were developing similar perspectives—General Systems Theory emerged in the 1940s as a new way of conceptualizing seemingly unrelated phenomena and understanding how together they represent interrelated components of a larger system. As Bertalanffy (1968) later elaborated, a system represents a complex of component parts or interacting elements that may together form an entity. To fully comprehend how the entire unit operates, we must look beyond a mechanistic view of the functioning of the separate parts; indeed, it is precisely the relationship, the interfunctioning, of the parts that make up the whole that requires our attention. The wholeness of the system, how it's organized, the rules underlying how its component parts relate to one another, its repetitive patterns—these are the system's vital signs.

What is the relevance of the systems view to better comprehending what occurs within a family? As Andolfi (1979) notes, family members are studied in terms of their interactions and not merely their intrinsic personal characteristics. More than the sum of what each family member adds to the whole, it is the ongoing relationship between and among the members, their mutual impact, that requires our attention. From a systems perspective, every event within a family is multiply determined by all of the forces operating within that system. Disordered or symptomatic behavior of any individual within the family is understood to be an expression or manifestation of the interactional processes currently taking place within the family system as a whole.

Such a global view, in which the fundamental unit of study is not the individual but rather the system itself, calls for the examination of a family's established behavioral sequences or patterns; families form repetitive patterns over time, and it is this patterning over time that is the essence of the family system (Segal & Bavelas, 1983). As Constantine (1986) points out, the family is a good example of the organized complexity for the study of which the systems view is most appropriate. What, then, constitutes a "problem family" likely to be seen in a counseling situation? According to Constantine, the determining factor is neither the number nor severity of a family's problems but rather their response to the problems and the extent to which their problems disable the way their family system operates.

## LINEAR AND CIRCULAR CAUSALITY

Presystems theories—those that for the most part we have labeled as mechanistic—tended to be reductionistic. That is, they explained complex phenomena by breaking the whole down and analyzing the separate, simpler parts. Thus, ever-smaller units were investigated in order to get a fix on the causes of larger events. In this simple Newtonian view of the physical universe, it made sense to think in terms of **linear causality**: A causes B, which acts upon C, causing D to occur.

Within psychological theory, such an outlook took the form of stimulus-response explanations for complex human behavior. From this perspective, all current behavior is seen as the result of a series of outside forces that build upon one another in sequence and ultimately produce the behavior in question. To the psychoanalyst, such forces are likely the result of childhood experiences; to the behaviorally inclined, the causes are more apt to be found in past and present learning experiences. By attending exclusively to the individual, however, both viewpoints fail to examine the context in which, as well as the process by which, the current behavior occurs. Thus, they fail to understand fully the complexity of what transpires within a family system.

The systems view, by comparison, more holistic and better attuned to tangled interpersonal relationships, stresses the reciprocity of behaviors between people. **Circular causality** emphasizes that forces do not simply move in one direction, each event caused by a previous event, but rather become part of a causal chain, each influencing and being influenced by the other. Goldenberg and Goldenberg (1991) offer the following contrast between statements based on linear and circular analysis:

> *Linear:* A bad mother produces sick children.
> *Implication:* Mother's emotional problems cause similar problems in others.
> *Circular:* An unhappy middle-aged woman, struggling with an inattentive husband who feels peripheral to and excluded from the family, attaches herself to her 20-year-old son for male companionship, excluding her adolescent daughter. The daughter, in turn, feeling rejected and unloved, engages in flagrant sexually promiscuous behavior, to the considerable distress of her parents. The son, fearful of leaving home and becoming independent, insists he must remain at home because his mother needs his attention. The mother becomes depressed because her children do not seem to be like other "normal" children, and blames their dysfunctional behavior on her husband, whom she labels an "absentee father." He in turn becomes angry and defensive, and their sexual relationship suffers. The children respond to the ensuing coldness between the parents in different ways: the son by withdrawing from friends completely and remaining at home with his mother as much as possible, and the daughter by having indiscriminant sexual encounters with one man after another but carefully avoiding intimacy with any of them.
> *Implication:* Behavior has as least as much to do with the interactional context in which it occurs as with the inner mental processes or emotional problems of any of the players. (p. 6)

Gregory Bateson (1979), a cultural anthropologist by training but with broad interest in **cybernetics** (the study of methods of feedback control within a system), provided many of the theoretical underpinnings for the application of systems thinking to human relationships. He labeled the stimulus-response paradigm as a "billiard-ball" model—a model that describes a force as moving in only one direction and affecting objects in its path—and called instead for a focus on the ongoing process and the development of a new descriptive language that emphasizes the relationship between parts and their effect on one another. While A may evoke B, it is also true that B evokes A, as we have just seen. A marital counselor is likely to hear the following exchange in a quarreling couple, where each partner feels put upon and blames the other for his or her feelings of unhappiness:

> **Wife:** You never seem to talk to me and let me know that you notice I exist.
> **Husband:** It's true. You become so heated and intense at times that you frighten me and I clam up.
> **Wife:** You don't get it! The reason I become so upset is that I get frustrated by your withdrawing behavior. The more frustrated I become, the more persistent I become.
> **Husband:** You're the one who doesn't get it! The more you persist, the more intimidated I get and the more I withdraw.

A counselor working with an entire troubled family, many of whose members blame their woes on one another, is even more likely to confront such a circular situation. These examples illustrate the causal chains that tie together family behavior and communication. Shifting to a perspective that emphasizes circular causality helps us conceptualize a family's collective behavior in current trans-actional terms—as a network of circular loops in which every member's behavior impacts on everyone else. People mutually affect one another; there is no specific cause of any single behavioral event. The counselor needs to analyze the various repetitive links that keep the loop locked in place (and thus maintain the mutu-ally defeating interaction patterns) and prevent the individuals who make up the family system from moving on to more productive or fulfilling activities (Koman & Stechler, 1985).

## FEEDBACK, CONTROL, AND HOMEOSTASIS

One of the pioneers in cybernetics, mathematician Norbert Wiener (1967), de-fined **feedback** as a method of controlling a system by reinserting into it the results of its past performance. Stated another way, information about how a system is functioning is looped back (fed back) from the output to the input, thus modi-fying subsequent input signals. **Feedback loops**, then, are circular mechanisms whose purpose is to reintroduce information about a system's output back to its input in order to alter, correct, or ultimately govern the system's functioning.

One frequently cited example of such a system is the familiar home furnace. Setting the thermostat at a desired 70 °F programs the system so that, when the temperature drops below that point, that information is fed back and activates the furnace. When the desired temperature is reached again, that new informa-tion, once again fed back, alters the ongoing state by deactivating the system until such time as reactivation is needed to warm up the house again and keep the temperature stable. Balance is achieved by the inclination of the system to main-tain a dynamic equilibrium around some set point and to undertake operations to restore equilibrium whenever it is threatened. This tendency toward a stable state of equilibrium, called **homeostasis**, is achieved with the help of what cyberneticists call servomechanisms; in a self-regulating system, the servomecha-nisms are feedback loops that return information in order to activate the internal interactional processes that maintain stability and ensure a dynamic but steady state.

The example just cited illustrates **negative feedback**[1], or the use of attenuating feedback loops in order to maintain aspects of the system's functioning within prescribed limits. As depicted in Figure 2.1, negative feedback is corrective, ad-justing the input so that the system returns to its preset, steady state. All of us are

---

[1]Although *negative feedback* and *positive feedback* are terms commonly used in systems literature, some critics have argued that these terms may imply value judgments concerning undesired versus desired outcomes, and therefore may prove misleading. Kantor and Lehr (1975) suggest that we substitute *constancy feedback loops* (loops that promote equilibrium) for *negative feedback,* and *variety feedback loops* (loops that promote change) for *positive feedback.* In a similar vein, Con-stantine (1986) offers *attenuating loops* versus *amplifying loops.* We have adopted the latter suggestion.

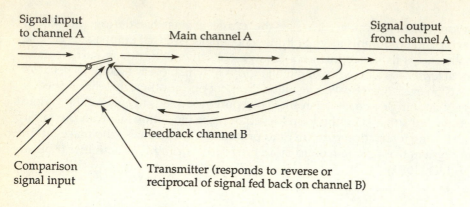

Signal input to channel A

Main channel A

Signal output from channel A

Feedback channel B

Comparison signal input

Transmitter (responds to reverse or reciprocal of signal fed back on channel B)

**Figure 2.1** In this illustration of negative feedback, part of a system's output is reintroduced into the system as information about the output, thus governing and correcting the process. A negative signal from channel A, fed back to the sender through channel B, alters the signal in A. Feedback loops characterize all interpersonal relationships.
*Source:* Miller, 1978, p. 36.

familiar with such error-activated causal events in our daily lives. The attentive driver does not simply hold the steering wheel steady, but in fact continuously makes slight corrections to keep the car traveling in a predetermined direction. Automobiles with cruise-control devices allow the driver to set a desired speed; if a temporary problem arises, say a sudden sharp incline, causing a momentary reduction in speed, that information activates the system, acceleration follows, and the preset speed is once again achieved.

**Positive feedback** (the use of amplifying feedback loops) has the opposite effect: it causes further change by augmenting or accelerating the initial deviation. In some cases it may reach runaway proportions, forcing the system beyond its limits to the point of self-destruction. The furnace explodes; the car is oversteered and goes out of control; the cruise control continues to accelerate to everhigher speeds and disastrous consequences.

Both negative and positive feedback loops abound in families. Negative feedback may occur with a remarried couple like this:

**Husband:** I'm upset at the way you talked to that man at the party tonight, especially the way you seemed to be hanging on every word he said.

**Wife:** Don't be silly! You're the one I care about. He said he had just come back from a trip you and I had talked about going on and I was interested in what he could tell me about the place.

**Husband:** OK. But please don't do that again without telling me. You know I'm touchy on the subject because of what Gina [ex-wife] used to do at parties with other men that drove me crazy.

**Wife:** Sorry, I hadn't thought about that. I'll try to remember next time. In the meantime, you try to remember that you're married to me now and I don't want you to be jealous.

In a less-blissful situation, positive feedback may occur:

**Husband:** I'm upset at the way you talked to that man at the party tonight, especially the way you seemed to be hanging on every word he said.

**Wife:** One thing I don't appreciate is you spying on me.

**Husband:** Spying? That's a funny word to use. You must be getting paranoid in your old age. Or maybe you have something to hide.

**Wife:** As a matter of fact, I was talking to him about a trip he took that we had talked about, but I don't suppose you'd believe that. Talk about paranoid!

**Husband:** I give up on women! You're no different from Gina, and I suppose all other women.

**Wife:** With an attitude like that, I'm starting to see why Gina walked out on you.

While most transactions can probably be characterized by the predominance of one of these two loops—one attenuating a possible conflict, the other amplifying it—both may occur between the same players under different conditions or at different points in their relationship. Despite the potentially escalating impact of the runaway system described in the second example above, not all positive feedback need be considered damaging. Counselors may at times encourage positive feedback to motivate clients to break out of existing, but stultifying, family behavior patterns, such as using one member as a scapegoat in order to hide or obscure other more pressing but unresolved family issues.

Theorists such as Maruyama (1968) and Dell (1982) have suggested that at times it may be advantageous to push a system with untenable behavior patterns beyond its previous homeostatic level. Rather than restore equilibrium, it may be more therapeutic in the long run to encourage family members to make those breakthrough changes that will help the family system function at a new level. The counselor needs to determine whether to help the family return to its former level of functioning (from which they may have deviated because of a temporary stress) or to seize an opportunity to help promote discontinuity and newness. Whatever the choice, Bross (1982) describes the primary aim of family intervention as shifting the balance of dysfunctional interaction patterns among family members in order that new, more effective forms of relating to one another become possible.

## OPEN AND CLOSED SYSTEMS

Systems may be relatively open or closed, depending upon the degree to which they are organized to interact with the outside environment. An **open system** receives input—matter, energy, information—from its surroundings and discharges output back into those surroundings. Theoretically, **closed systems** are not able to participate in such transactions; in point of fact, however, systems are rarely if ever completely isolated or closed off from the outside, hard as laboratory researchers may try to create such a sterile test-tube environment.

Theoretically, for a family truly to be operating as a closed system, all outside transactions and communications would have to cease, hardly a likely prospect.[2] Nevertheless, some families, such as recent immigrants or members of insular ethnic groups, do exist in relative isolation, communicating only among themselves, suspicious of outsiders, and fostering dependence on the family. Children may be warned only to trust family members and nobody else. Characterized by Constantine (1986) as regulated predominantly by deviation-attenuating (negative) feedback, such families seek to hold onto the traditions and conventionalities of the past and avoid change.

In their extreme form, such families may attempt to impose rigid and unchanging behavior patterns, sealing themselves off from exchanges with the outside world. These closed systems tend toward **entropy**—gradually regressing, decaying because of insufficient input, possibly becoming disorganized and destined for eventual disorder. Sauber (1983) describes such families as maintaining strict taboos regarding who and what should be admitted into the house, limiting the introduction of news and certain forms of music, screening visitors, and so on. Beavers (1977) offers this example of an entropic family: the parents have a daughter late in life; out of touch with what parent-adolescent relationships are like today, they may prevent their teenage daughter from behaving as she claims her friends behave. By insisting that she follow rules as they were taught by their parents, without discussion, the parents are inviting family conflict (to which the daughter will no doubt also contribute). We provided a similar example in the previous chapter in describing the generational conflict within an immigrant family.

New ideas, new information, new outlooks are seen as threatening to the status quo in closed systems. As Kantor and Lehr (1975) describe them, closed family systems impose strict rules and a hierarchical power structure that force individual members to subordinate their needs to the welfare of the group. Family loyalty is paramount; rules are absolute; tradition must be observed; any deviation in behavior can only lead to chaos. As White (1978) portrays closed family systems, parents see to it that doors are kept locked, family reading matter and television programs are screened, children are expected to report their comings and goings scrupulously, and rigid daily schedules are kept as closely as possible. Stability in such an arrangement is achieved through the maintenance of tradition.

Open systems use both negative (attenuating) and positive (amplifying) feedback loops. Thus, they are considered to be operating on the systems principle of **equifinality**, meaning that the same end state may be reached from a variety of starting points. (Closed systems, by way of contrast, do not have the property of equifinality and thus their final state is determined solely by their initial conditions.) Within open systems, not only may the same result be achieved from

---

[2]Some religious cults do attempt to close out the world beyond their borders, specifically to halt the flow of information. Those countries that do not permit foreign newspapers or radio or television broadcasts are also deliberately closed systems, in order to better control the behavior of their citizens.

different initial conditions, but the same initial state may produce different results. The major point here is that to appreciate how a family functions, we must study the organization of the family system—the group's interactive process—rather than search for either the origins or outcomes of those interactions.

In open systems, where a variety of inputs is possible, the family's feedback process is an overriding determinant of how it functions. Since a number of pathways lead to the same destination, there is no single "correct" way to raise children, to ensure a happy marriage, and so on. Uncertain beginnings do not necessarily doom a relationship; a shaky start—perhaps as a result of an early marriage—may be compensated for by the introduction of corrective feedback as the relationship matures. By the same token, an apparently congenial marriage of many years may become stale or turn sour for a variety of reasons. As we saw in our discussion of causality, a linear description in which A inevitably leads to B overlooks the central role played by the family interactive process. The concept of equifinality means that the counselor may intervene with a family at any of several points or through any of several counseling techniques to obtain the same desired end results.

In open systems, members are free to move in and out of interactions with one another, with extended family members (such as grandparents, aunts, uncles, or cousins), or with extrafamilial systems such as the school, church, neighbors, or teachers. The family has an impact on the outside environment; the outside environment impacts the family. In contrast to the relatively closed family system, where continuity and tradition are held in high regard, open family systems tend to stress adaptability to unfamiliar situations, particularly if that serves a purpose or a goal that the family finds worthwhile. Because an open and honest dialogue both within and outside the family is prized, disagreement and dissent may be common, and not a threat to the ongoing functioning of the family. Negotiation, communication, flexibility in shifting roles, interdependence, and authenticity—these are the signs of an open system.

Some individuals find relatively closed family systems safe and secure and never stray too far, physically or psychologically. Members may on occasion be called upon to sacrifice their individual needs for the good of the family, but in the long run may get most of their important needs met through participation in the family group. One problem, of course, is that a closed structure may become rigid; family members may run away or otherwise rebel. Or families may feel isolated; for example, a young never-married mother, alienated from her unaccepting parents, may find she has little opportunity for exchange with the outside world. Open family systems, desirable as they may appear to be, run the risk of having free expression turn ugly and perhaps divide the family into warring factions. Incompatibilities may surface—over discipline within a stepfamily, for example—and excessive strains may result.

In gauging the degree of openness of a family system, the counselor needs to evaluate how (and how well) the family deals with new information, particularly if that new input provokes a family crisis (for example, discovering a teenager's drug addiction). To what extent do the family members realistically perceive and appraise the problem? How well are they able to delay closure until sufficient information has been sought and discussed and a family plan formulated? To what degree are they able to coordinate their individual responses so that the best possible family action can be undertaken in this unfamiliar situation?

In systems terms, open systems are said to have **negentropy**—they are organized to be adaptable, open to new experiences, and able to alter patterns and discard those that are inappropriate to the present situation. Through exchanges outside their own boundaries, open systems increase their chances of becoming more highly organized and developing resources to repair minor or temporary breakdowns in efficiency (Nichols & Everett, 1986). The lack of such exchanges in closed systems decreases their competence to deal with stress. Limited or perhaps nonexistent contact with others outside the family may lead to fearful, confused, and ineffective responses to crisis. In extreme cases of rigid systems and/or persistent stress, chaos and anarchy within the family may follow.

## SUBSYSTEMS AND BOUNDARIES

**Subsystems** are the parts of an overall system assigned to carry out particular functions or processes within that system, in order to maintain and sustain the system as a whole. Every family has a number of such coexisting subdivisions, formed by generation, gender, interest, or role and function within the family (Minuchin, 1974). The most enduring are the spousal, the parent-child, and the sibling subsystems.

The spousal (husband-wife) unit is basic; it is central to the life of the family in its early years, and continues to play a major role over the life span of the family. There is little doubt that the overall success of any family is to a large extent dependent upon the ability of the husband and wife to work out a successful relationship with one another. (The absence of one parent, more and more common, may have a particularly damaging effect on the remaining parent as well as the children, as we shall see in subsequent chapters.) Any dysfunction in this subsystem is bound to reverberate throughout the family, scapegoating certain children, co-opting others into alliances with one parent against the other, and so on. The way spouses together make decisions, manage conflict, plan the family's future, meet each other's sexual and dependency needs, and much more provides a model of male-female interaction and husband-wife intimacy that will surely affect the children's future relationships.

The parent-child subsystem teaches children about child rearing; nurturance, guidance, limit setting, and socialization experiences are all crucial here. Through interaction with the parents, children learn to deal with people of greater authority, developing in the process a strengthened or weakened capacity for decision making and self-direction. Problems in this subsystem—serious intergenerational conflicts involving rebelliousness, symptomatic children, runaways, and so on—

reflect underlying family disorganization or instability. The following case reflects dysfunctional behavior extending over several generations:

❊  ❊  ❊  ❊  ❊

Jill Clemmons, now 40, had a history of unstable relationships with men. An only child, lonely and unhappy, she lived in poverty and on welfare with her mother, who was herself bitter at having been deserted by her husband a decade earlier. Finally feeling unable to bear the boredom and frustration of her life, Jill (with the tacit encouragement of her mother) ran off at 16 and married her high school boyfriend. Their marriage—stormy, without much affection or intimacy, filled with daily fighting—lasted several months, before Jill met and ran off with Dave, an older single man of 40, whom Jill was sure would take care of her. Divorced at 17, she married Dave immediately. However, their marriage soon proved to be a nightmare: Dave was verbally and physically abusive and occasionally beat her severely, especially when he came home drunk. On some nights, he would bring home a man he had met at a bar, often insisting Jill have sexual intercourse with the stranger while Dave watched. Jill finally managed to escape after three years, even though she had no place to go.

Drifting from one menial job to the next, Jill managed to survive and live a relatively uneventful life for several years. She dated on and off, and when she met Tom, at 27, she thought her life had finally turned around. He seemed intelligent, caring, and sensitive to her needs. They married after a brief time together, and for a while the relationship was the best Jill had ever known. They had two children together, and seemed to be living a relatively tranquil and conventional existence for several years. However, Jill found herself feeling bored and restless having to stay home with her youngsters. She had few child-rearing skills, her mother had been such a poor model, and more and more she began to view the children as a burden. Correspondingly, as the children grew into adolescents, their conflicts with their parents (especially Jill) increased sharply. Jill and Tom, too, found less and less to do or talk about together; all they seemed to agree about was that something needed to be done about the children, although neither one knew exactly what. Neither had the ability or the experience to work out problems together, nor did they consider getting professional help.

Soon Tom and Jill realized that there was nothing to stay together for, and they separated. Nora, 16, and Tom Jr., 14, remained with their father, and Jill moved to another state to "start life again." However, Nora found that she could not get along with her father and brother and, like her mother earlier, she ran off, ultimately finding her mother and moving in with her. Although she had considerable misgivings, Jill still believed she and her daughter could work things out. Not surprisingly, they could not, and within four months Nora had run away from home and begun living with a series of men in a nearby city, contacting her mother only in emergencies. Occasionally, when Jill was at work, her daughter would return to the house for some clothes or food or whatever money she could find.

❋    ❋    ❋    ❋    ❋

The parent-child subsystem, beginning with the wife's pregnancy, expands the boundaries of the previous husband-wife spousal subsystem. The arrival of children vastly complicates family life, particularly when a first child is involved. With subsequent children, as the family expands, the system multiplies in complexity. Alliances and coalitions—some along age lines, some by sex, some by personality characteristics or attitudes—may make an impact on the spousal subsystem, sometimes to the point of threatening its existence, as parents experience their own conflicts about growing up and taking responsibilities. The relatively sudden shift to child-related issues, as Nichols and Everett (1986) point out, may be especially taxing on young-adult marriages, challenging each spouse's own degree of individuation and dependency. A facilitating effect may result, consolidating their parenting efforts; on the other hand, some may retreat back into alliances with their own parents, or perhaps out of the marriage.

Siblings represent a child's first peer group. Through participation in this sibling subsystem, a child may develop patterns of negotiation, cooperation, competition, mutual support, and later attachment to friends. Interpersonal skills are honed here and, if successful, may develop further in school experiences and later in the workplace. Although the future impact of this subsystem is not always clearly discernible when the children are young, its influence on overall family functioning is to a great extent dependent on how viable the other subsystems are. Especially noteworthy for overall family functioning is the extent to which alliances and intergenerational coalitions exist in the family.

Other subsystems, most less durable than those just described, exist in all families. Father-daughter, mother-son, father-oldest son, mother-youngest child are only some of the common transitional alliances that can develop within a family group. The overdevelopment or protracted duration of any of these to the detriment of the spousal subsystem should signal to the counselor that instability and potential disorganization exist within the system.

Goldenberg (1977) illustrates the possible impact of a father-daughter alliance on family functioning. In this case, the coalition between the two has destructive results for all family members:

❋    ❋    ❋    ❋    ❋

Lisa Ash, a 5-foot, 260-pound, 13-year-old girl, was brought to a residential treatment center by a distraught mother, who complained that she couldn't control her daughter's eating habits and was alarmed about the danger to her health. Lisa, a junior high school student, was the oldest of three daughters in a lower-middle-class Jewish family. Both the father, a moderately successful shoe store owner, and his wife, a housewife, were overweight, as were various other uncles, aunts, and to a lesser extent Lisa's two younger sisters.

The mother-daughter conflict was evident from the intake interview. In particular, both agreed that they battled frequently over discipline or any restrictions imposed by Mrs. Ash on Lisa's eating behavior. Whenever this occurred, Lisa would lock herself in her room, wait for her father to come home, and then tell him how "cruel" the mother had been to her. Usually, without inquiring further or getting the mother's story, he would side with Lisa and countermand the mother's orders. Occasionally he would invite Lisa out for a pizza or another "snack."

Needless to say, the mother-father relationship was poor. They had not had sexual intercourse for several years, and Mrs. Ash assumed that her husband was impotent, although she was too embarrassed to ask him. She had become increasingly unhappy and had seen a psychiatric social worker a year earlier for several sessions, although then, as now, her husband refused to participate in counseling. He also opposed Lisa's hospitalization, and for several months would not speak to any member of the hospital staff about his daughter's progress.[3]

Lisa was placed on the adolescent open ward of the hospital and attended the special school within the hospital complex, remaining there for 12 months. During that period, four coordinated therapeutic programs were introduced: nutritional control (including a careful watch on caloric intake), individual psychotherapy twice weekly, family counseling (which, after much resistance, Mr. Ash agreed to attend), and ward milieu therapy. The picture that emerged was of an emotionally intense and chaotic family existence in which Lisa often screamed, hit, swore, and threatened to break household objects if she didn't get her "sweets." There was no regular mealtime at the Ash house; each member ate when and what he or she wanted. Lisa would regularly visit her father's store after school, and they would go out together for an ice cream soda or sundae. Finally acknowledging, during one family counseling session, that the situation had gotten out of hand, Mr. Ash defended his actions by saying that he could never get himself to say no to Lisa for fear of losing her love. Mrs. Ash quickly conceded her resentment of her husband's relationship with Lisa, her own feelings of isolation, and her sense of helplessness; she was finally able to separate the two by hospitalizing her daughter.

The program of caloric restriction was immediately successful. After two months, Lisa had lost 35 pounds, after seven months, 80 pounds, and by ten months, a full 100 pounds. Family counseling was less immediately successful. Mr. Ash and Lisa continued to play seductive games with each other; he called

---

[3]The detrimental effect of the flawed spousal subsystem on the parent-child subsystem should be clear to the reader here, as should be the similar impact of the latter on the former. For the sake of brevity, we have omitted a description of the influence of both on the other children and the sibling subsystems in general, although the reader can assume that both have a powerfully negative effect on all concerned.

her on the telephone frequently, sent her flowers, and even visited her with a box of candy on her birthday, and she deliberately delayed coming to the telephone or lobby, to make her ultimate appearance more appealing. Finally, Lisa put an end to this kind of transaction, to Mrs. Ash's relief; Lisa learned limits on her behavior largely from milieu therapy on her ward. Eventually, Mr. Ash was able to give up his seductive and overprotective behavior, realizing that if he really wanted to help his daughter, he should limit her self-indulgent, self-destructive behavior rather than encourage it.

Upon her discharge from the hospital, Lisa weighed 140 pounds, had some insight into her eating behavior, and had dealt with a number of other preadolescent problems. She agreed to undergo weekly individual psychotherapy for a while so that she would not regress to her former ways once she was home. A two-year follow-up found her able to control her eating and generally proud that she could take care of herself successfully. (pp. 350–351)

❊  ❊  ❊  ❊  ❊

Lisa's recovery and her parents' being forced to examine their deteriorated marriage were two of the beneficial results of their entering counseling as a family. Strengthening the parental coalition resulted in a clearer delineation of boundaries and a greatly diminished need for parent-child alliances. Lisa's eating behavior was no longer used by all family members to avoid the real issues between the parents. As communication was reestablished between the parents, they were more open to looking at what had led to their deteriorating relationship, of which the lack of a sexual life was but one manifestation. Ultimately, they learned new ways of problem solving and instituted the necessary changes to break out of their old destructive patterns.

Before leaving the general topic of subsystems, we should note that all members participate in several subsystems simultaneously within the family. For example, a 22-year-old woman may be a new stepmother of three, pregnant with her first child, trying at the same time to build a satisfactory marriage, learning to cope with her "instant" family, looking to her own mother for guidance, remembering to check on her aging grandmother and to encourage her younger sister to go to college, and lots more. From a subsystems vantage point, she is at one and the same time a wife, a prospective mother, a stepmother, a daughter, a granddaughter, and an older sister, engaging in perpetual exchanges with those around her, participating in various alliances (with greater or lesser success), and playing different roles in each. Ascendant in one, she may be submissive in another; fulfilled in one, she may be utterly frustrated by her lack of success in another; feeling competent in one, she may feel defeated in another. All the subsystems in which she takes part are interrelated and all perform vital routines necessary for the whole—the family—to grow and change in order to keep the system balanced.

Subsystems within a family stand in dynamic relationship with one another, both influencing and being influenced by the others. All are organized to perform the functions necessary for the family as a whole to go about its tasks smoothly and efficiently.

Family interaction is governed by rules, for the most part unstated, which have typically been developed and modified through trial and error over a period of time. Such rules (for example, who has the right to say and do what to whom; what is expected of males versus females, adults versus children) determine what is permitted and what is forbidden within a family, and thus serve the necessary function of regulating each member's behavior toward the others. The origin of such rules is buried in years of explicit and implicit negotiation among family members; the rules themselves become so fine-tuned in most cases that they are taken for granted by all and only draw attention when an effort is made by a member (an early adolescent in many cases) to change the long-standing "regulations."

An essential way in which the family maintains itself as a self-regulating system is through the constant exchange of information fed back into the system; this information automatically triggers any necessary changes (for example, extending late night privileges to the adolescent) to keep the system fluid and functional. In systems terms, feedback loops (circles of response from which there is a return flow of information into the system) are operating, and information is being processed through the system.

**Boundaries** are invisible lines of demarcation that separate the family from the outside nonfamily environment; they circumscribe and protect the integrity of the system and thus determine who is regarded as inside and who remains outside. Within the family itself, boundaries differentiate subsystems; they help achieve and define the separate subunits of the total system. As Minuchin (1974) notes, they must be sufficiently well defined to allow subsystem members to carry out their functions without undue interference. At the same time, they must be open enough to permit contact between the members of the subsystem and others.

For example, firm but flexible boundaries between parents and children allow for closeness when necessary, while at the same time ensuring that individuality will be honored and protected. Information can be exchanged across permeable boundaries as needed. At the same time, each subsystem is free to carry out its own tasks and responsibilities. Boundaries thus help safeguard each subsystem's autonomy while maintaining the interdependence of all of the family's subsystems.

The clarity of the subsystem boundaries is actually more important than who performs what function. As an illustration, the parent-child subsystem may at times be flexible enough to include a grandparent (or, under special circumstances, an oldest child pressed into service) when both parents are temporarily unavailable, so long as the lines of responsibility and authority remain clear. However, a grandmother who, uninvited, interferes with her daughter's management of a child in ways that undermine the parent-child subsystem (and perhaps the spousal subsystem as well) is overstepping her authority, being intrusive, and damaging family boundary lines. Thus, while boundaries between family members may vary in their degree of permeability, they need to be clearly drawn and apparent to all members. If they are too blurred or too rigid, they invite confusion and increase the likelihood of family dysfunction.

Deviation from subsystem boundaries may occur in one of two ways: through **enmeshment** or through **disengagement**. In the former, the boundary is too permeable, and thus family members become overinvolved and entwined in each other's lives (opening each other's mail, looking in each other's drawers, knowing each other's secrets, continually attuned to each other's feelings). The latter involves overly rigid boundaries, with family members sharing a home but operating as separate units, with little interaction or exchange of feelings or sense of connection to one another. Little support, concern, or family loyalty is evident in disengaged families. At their extremes, enmeshed families run the risk of forbidding separation by viewing it as an act of betrayal, thus making autonomy impossible; by contrast, disengaged families whose members remain oblivious to the effects of their actions on each other may thus preclude their members from ever developing caring relationships with others.

Boundaries, then, are useful, if arbitrary, metaphors for defining the overall system as a functioning unit, an entity. They exist around the family as a whole, around its subsystems, and around individual family members. Without them, there would be no progressive differentiation of functions in individuals or in the separate subsystems and hence, as Umbarger (1983) contends, no system complexity. Without such complexity, a family's ability to create and maintain an adaptive stance in society is weakened. Adaptability is essential if the system is to avoid the forces of entropy and ultimate decay.

## STABILITY AND CHANGE

For an ongoing living system, such as a family, to maintain its continuity, it must be able to tolerate change. Evolution is a normal and necessary part of every family's experience as it goes through its life cycle. However, as Nichols and Everett (1986) observe, a crucial question facing any system is how much change it can tolerate and still survive. Systems theorists use the concepts of **morphostasis** and **morphogenesis** to describe a system's ability to remain stable in the context of change and, conversely, to change in the context of stability. In well-functioning systems, both processes are necessary. A tightrope walker must continually sway in order to remain balanced. Remaining balanced while standing in a canoe calls for making it rock.

Within each system, tension inevitably exists between forces seeking constancy and the maintenance of the status quo, on the one hand, and opposing forces demanding change on the other. Morphostasis calls for a family to emphasize interactions involving negative or deviation-attenuating feedback; it refers to the system's tendency toward stability or a state of dynamic equilibrium. Morphogenesis demands positive or deviation-amplifying feedback in order to encourage growth, innovation, and change.

Systems theorists such as Maruyama (1968) and Hoffman (1981) point out that the survival of any living system depends on the interaction of these two key processes—morphostasis and morphogenesis. Unlike homeostasis, which is the maintenance of *behavioral constancy* in a system, morphostatic mechanisms operate to maintain the system's *structural constancy.* Morphogenetic mechanisms, on the other hand, seek to push the system toward new levels of functioning, allowing it to adapt to changing conditions. The satisfactory ongoing functioning of a couple or family requires a suitable balance between the two processes—maintaining stability, accommodating change.

Umbarger (1983) stresses that both stability and change are necessary for effective family functioning. That is, both stability and change are necessary for the continuity of any family. *Family stability is actually rooted in change.* A family must maintain enough regularity and balance to maintain adaptability and preserve a sense of order and sameness; at the same time, it must subtly promote change and growth within its members and the system as a whole.

Thus, a family is continually subject to inner pressures from the developmental changes in its members (for example, from young child to adolescent; from middle-aged parent to older adult). At the same time, the family must be capable of accommodation to changing external conditions (necessitating the return of the housewife to paid work, for example, or necessitating a school or job transfer). Minuchin (1974), focusing on the family's structural components, notes that responding to these pressures calls for "a constant transformation of the position of family members in relation to one another, so they can grow while the family system maintains continuity" (p. 60). He argues that family dysfunction results from rigidity of its transactional patterns and boundaries when faced with stress, and the corresponding resistance to exploring alternative solutions. Minuchin contends that families that function effectively adapt to life's inevitable stresses in ways that preserve continuity while facilitating family restructuring as needed.

## SYSTEMS THEORY AND FAMILY COUNSELING

As we indicated earlier in this chapter, systems thinking provides the theoretical underpinnings for family counseling. By viewing causality in circular terms, by emphasizing family interrelationships over individual needs and drives, by organizing data according to interpersonal rather than intrapsychic conflicts, and by viewing families as self-governing units attempting to maintain homeostatic behavior, the family counselor has a new perspective for conceptualizing problems between people.

Family counselors typically deal with current, ongoing problems, rather than attempt to recreate the past. Psychiatric diagnoses, developed when the therapeutic focus was on individuals, are downplayed in favor of observing and intervening in those interactional processes that maintain dysfunction. In this context, family counseling becomes a method for exploring dysfunctional family relationships and attempting to shift the balance so that new forms of relating become possible, with the goal of problem resolution (Bross, 1982).

Family counselors, then, help families get "unstuck."

If a family system is as self-regulating as we have been asserting, then what could make it go out of balance for such a long time or to such a degree that the family seeks professional help? Several causes are possible. Operating at either extreme of the morphostatic/morphogenetic continuum may lead to family dysfunction; inflexibility may prevent rule changes, or changes may occur in too rapid or haphazard a fashion. Perhaps the family has achieved equilibrium only as a consequence of a member developing a symptom (for example, **anorexia** or **delinquency**) unacceptable to them or society, compelling them to seek help.

Fishman (1985) asserts that every symptom, regardless of its name, serves a function in maintaining family homeostasis; if the problem did not do something useful for the family organization, it would not be maintained.[4] As an example, he offers the following case, which involves anorexia:

❉   ❉   ❉   ❉   ❉

A family is in crisis. Brother just got married. The identified patient, Bonnie, is a 14-year-old girl who is having trouble with her peers (even though her grades are very good). Mother has just been promoted and now earns more than her husband, who is a truck driver. Husband and wife are fighting a great deal. The system is unstable. Bonnie stays out too long after school and comes home with "pot" on her breath. The parents scold her and continue to fight. A few weeks later, at dinner, Bonnie refuses to eat. The parents are very upset. In this Italian family, food is very important. Furthermore, mother works in a laboratory and is very concerned with health issues. The parents are very preoccupied with the girl's refusal to eat. The more they focus on the problem the more power the symptom has in diffusing the ambient tension in the house. Thus the symptom emerges as the point of family crisis and is maintained by the system. (p. 8)

❉   ❉   ❉   ❉   ❉

Symptoms, in family systems terms, develop to help balance or alleviate stress between the family members. As Friesen (1985) puts it, when a family member's behavior exceeds the normal range of behavior as defined by family rules, a crisis occurs and homeostatic mechanisms are introduced into the system to reestablish equilibrium. Symptoms are one example of such stabilizing devices. As illustration, Friesen presents a case of husband-wife conflict in which one son begins to act delinquent (see Figure 2.2). His behavior turns the attention of the parents away from themselves, relieving the stress in their relationship but increasing the stress on the son. They rally together to help with his problem. As he improves,

---

[4]As we note in the following chapter, the view that maintaining symptoms in one family member thus "protects" the other members, and the family organization as a whole, is not necessarily supported by all family counselors. In the view of some researchers, the mismanaged solution attempted by the family ultimately becomes "the problem."

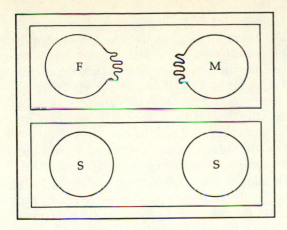

Parents in conflict

Children observe the conflict
and become stressed.

**A conflictual spouse system**

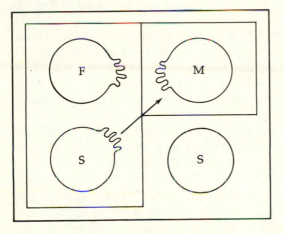

Father and son form coalition
against mother.

Youngest son is isolated
and becomes delinquent.

**Parent–child triangulation**

**Figure 2.2**   A stressful family relationship in which conflict in the spousal subsystem (upper diagram) leads to the creation of family coalitions (lower diagram) and
the manifestation of symptomatic behavior in a family member.
*Source:* Friesen, 1985, p. 46.

the husband-wife relationship once again becomes stressful, retriggering the son's
delinquent behavior.

   The appearance of symptoms is often linked to life-cycle transitions, periods
that call for changes in how a family operates. Expected or normative transitions
might include starting school, getting married, or retirement (Hansen, 1983). Examples of unexpected or nonnormative transitions include divorce, job loss

after many years of employment, or death of a child (Cowan & Hetherington, 1990). Such transition periods cause a temporary disequilibrium in the family system, during which family stability and continuity may be threatened by demands for change. At the same time, the members may be experiencing a sense of loss, confusion, and anxiety (Walsh, 1983). Depending on the effectiveness of their problem-solving style, their flexibility and openness to change, the strength and persistence of the stress(es), and other such factors, the family may become dysfunctional or reorganize and make a successful adaptation.

A symptom may be precipitated by a number of events, some external, some from within the family. As Papp (1983) explains, a change in a larger system (for example, an economic depression leading to the unemployment of the primary breadwinner) may affect the whole family, as part of a cybernetic circuit, and trigger a symptom: the teenage daughter, for example, may develop an eating problem. Or perhaps some internal family event (for example, birth of a handicapped infant, death of a grandparent) shatters the family's customary coping patterns, and a symptom develops as a means of establishing a new pattern. In any case, the symptom now becomes part of the family's ongoing transactions, either as the focus of every member's concern or as an unacknowledged factor that nevertheless insinuates itself in all transactions.

The family seeking to eliminate some problematic, maladaptive, or symptomatic behavior in one of its members (or in relationships between several of its members) may ultimately feel sufficiently distressed to seek help. Viewing the disturbing symptom of one member not as an isolated event but as part of a larger family context, the counselor attempts to alter the broader family system by transforming its structures and customary transactional patterns.

Merely eliminating an individual's symptoms (which constitute a mechanism for maintaining self-regulation within the system) may throw the entire family system into disarray; one part cannot be altered without the whole undergoing change. Instead, the counselor attempts to unbalance the family's established equilibrium and change the overall family context so that changes in individual behavior can transpire. Effective intervention, as we shall see in forthcoming chapters, helps a dysfunctional family to reorganize and create more satisfying interactive patterns as it attains a new equilibrium.

## THE SELF, THE FAMILY, AND THE COMMUNITY

Before leaving our discussion of the family as a social system, it is important to note that families, like all living systems, exist in a hierarchy of levels. Each level is made up of subsystems that have a relationship with other subsystems at the same level and with the systems at other levels. Individuals, themselves complex beings, combine to form a family system; they influence and are themselves influenced by the members of that system. Families, in turn, interact with, and are influenced by, one or more of society's larger systems—health care, church, welfare, probation, schools, the legal system. In the case of longstanding poverty, for example, the relationship may extend over generations. Thus, although we have chosen to emphasize family systems, we need to remind the reader that neither the individual nor the community level can be overlooked in assessing a family's problems and the most effective intervention levels.

By highlighting intervention at the family level, the counselor runs the risk of neglecting relevant intrapsychic problems of individual family members. By staying focused on behavioral sequences, individual perspectives regarding the meaning of recursive family patterns may be overlooked. By insisting on viewing all presenting problems in family terms, the counselor may lose much of the richness and important influence of personal conflict and motivation. Nichols (1987) has argued persuasively against the neglect of the self as a result of the field's early zeal to move away from what was viewed as entrenched but antiquated psychiatric outlooks on mental disorders. Now, the pendulum has begun to swing back, and a number of clinicians (Feldman, 1992; Wachtel & Wachtel, 1986) have led the way in building bridges between the individual and family approaches to therapeutic intervention.

It is important that the counselor heed Nichols' (1987) reminder that, no matter how much individual behavior is related to, and dependent on, the behavior of the others in the family system, family members remain flesh-and-blood persons with unique experiences, private hopes, ambitions, outlooks, expectations, and potentials. As he points out, regardless of the conflicting effects of social relationships, at times a person acts in part from personal habit and for private reasons. The essential message here is to remain focused on family interaction, but not to lose sight of the singularity of the persons involved.

In the same way, attention needs to be paid to issues that involve families and the social institutions with which they deal. Counselors working with poor families, for example, must recognize their sometimes herculean efforts to make life livable, and must be able to assist them in connecting with, and successfully engaging, appropriate social agencies. Hardships, crime, violence, limited mobility, the struggle for survival—these are the daily experiences of inner-city residents. However, economic impoverishment must not be confused with social or emotional impoverishment, although in some cases it may have such a consequence. According to social workers Parnell and Vanderkloot (1989), children growing up in economically deprived inner-city environments also frequently experience unselfish friendships and supportive family networks. They may expect life to be difficult, and these differing expectations may bring different kinds of satisfactions and problems.

These authors point out that working with poor families requires the counselor to be aware of the additional issues of housing, nutrition, and health, as well as the abstract ideas of discrimination and oppression encountered daily. Helping families utilize their resources, and at the same time connect with the resources of the community, can often help them to advocate for themselves and provide better opportunities for their children.

# SUMMARY

The systems view of dysfunctional behavior in an individual looks to disequilibrium in the family system of which that person is a part. General Systems Theory, an increasingly prominent influence in modern scientific thinking, defines a system as a complex of component parts or interacting elements that together form an interdependent entity. A system's wholeness, organization, and patterns are its crucial characteristics; in family terms, ongoing relationships and enduring transactional patterns represent its essential aspects.

Systems thinking stresses circular causality, the cybernetic idea that each element in a system influences and is influenced by every other. Dynamic equilibrium or homeostasis is maintained in a system through a series of feedback loops, which reintroduce information into the system. Negative feedback attenuates deviation and thus maintains the stability of a system; positive feedback amplifies deviation and thus causes change.

Families can be differentiated by their degree of openness to the outside world. Open systems interact with the outside environment; closed systems do not. Closed family systems, which hold onto the traditions of the past and avoid change, are in danger of becoming rigid and isolated. The prospects for open family systems are better, since they stress adaptability, but they too may show strain and break down if open expression results in incompatibilities.

Systems are composed of interacting subsystems, and within a family such subsystems carry out separate functions that together sustain the whole. All family members participate in several subsystems simultaneously, playing different roles in each. Boundaries differentiate these subsystems and have differing degrees of permeability. In enmeshed families, the boundaries are too loosely defined and members may become too entwined in each other's lives. Disengaged families have overly rigid boundaries. In the former case, separation from the family is difficult; in the latter, family members may never learn to develop caring relationships with others.

Families frequently seek professional help because of the appearance of symptomatic behavior in a member. Such symptoms reflect a disturbance in the overall family system, as a result of changes in the larger system of the external world or of some internal family event. Symptoms become incorporated into the family's transactional patterns; merely helping to eliminate them may disrupt the ongoing functioning of the family system. Dysfunctional families need to reorganize and learn new interactive patterns in order to attain a new equilibrium. The counselor, while continuing to focus on the family unit, must remain attuned to relevant intrapsychic problems in individual family members, and must attend to forces in society that enhance or further diminish a family's problem-solving abilities.

# Appraising Family Functioning

From a systems perspective, an individual's personal as well as interpersonal problems must be viewed in the context of the family system of which that person is a part. The family counselor regards any set of presenting problems or symptoms not merely as the manifestation of individual **psychopathology**, but as indicative of a disturbance in the family's relationship patterns. The **identified patient** is thus seen as signaling the presence of family pain or distress.

As we noted in the previous chapter, many family counselors believe that to attempt to relieve the symptom, without helping repair the family system of which the individual (and his or her symptom) is a part, is to ignore that the symptom may serve a protective function—to keep the family stable and functioning. (In this viewpoint, the teenage girl who develops a drug habit may rally her divided parents into uniting in their concern over her welfare, rather than allow them to go through with the divorce that she senses they are contemplating.) From such a perspective, the family may be understood as "needing" the patient to be symptomatic if it is to maintain its balance.[1] It deserves noting here, however,

[1]The notion that symptoms serve functions for the family, enabling them to cope, avoid disruption, and thus maintain the integrity of the family system, has been the cornerstone of thinking among family counselors since the early development of the field. However, this *functionalist* view of symptoms has recently been challenged by adherents of three viewpoints: (1) the **psychoeducational** approach, which argues that schizophrenia, for example, is a biological disease and a family hardship, and that families neither cause the symptoms nor are invested in maintaining them (Anderson, Reiss, & Hogarthy, 1986); (2) members of the Mental Research Institute Brief Therapy Center (Segal, 1987), who contend that family interpersonal difficulties do not cause symptoms; rather, symptoms develop and persist because of the mishandling of normal life difficulties, such that an original difficulty

that symptoms may be maintained for other than protective or distracting purposes in certain cases, and the counselor always needs to address the extent to
which a presenting symptom reveals clues regarding family functioning.

As Wachtel and Wachtel (1986) point out, the systems-oriented clinician might
ask: what would happen to other family members if this person were to change
(become symptom-free)? Is he or she expressing feelings, through the symptoms,
that other members are denying or not permitting themselves to experience? Is
the individual really being "helpful" to others by not functioning well? We might
wonder, too, if other family members need one person to be dysfunctional in
order to assure themselves of their own emotional well-being.

If the person's symptoms or problematic behaviors are not as clearly understood
when separated from the family interconnections out of which they emerge, then
the counselor must examine the family relationship network. To understand a
problem situation adequately, according to Karpel and Strauss (1983), a counselor
should ideally hear it described by each family member from his or her unique,
separate perspective; at the same time, the counselor needs to observe the family
members interacting with each other in characteristic ways. We believe, further,
that a family systems perspective is equally desirable when working therapeutically
with a single client, with a combination of family members, or with an entire
family.

Specifically, the counselor needs to appraise the family as a functioning unit
to determine: (1) whether or not they exhibit dysfunctional interactional patterns;
(2) whether their dysfunctional processes are self-repairing or serious enough to
warrant counselor intervention; (3) what underlying interactive patterns fuel and/or
help maintain the family disturbance and lead to the complex symptoms; (4) if
counseling for the entire family is called for; (5) who are the appropriate members
with whom to work; (6) whether the counselor has the competence, interest,
and motivation to take on the case; and (7) how to plan effective clinical intervention and determine appropriate goals.

Reiss (1980) notes that accurate family assessment is important for precisely the
same reasons that accurate individual assessment is important: (1) to determine
whether family counseling is an appropriate treatment, and, if so, what specific
modification the family in question may require; (2) to develop a short-term and
long-term **prognosis**; (3) to know the strengths and resources the family has and
is willing to commit in order to improve the chances of a favorable therapeutic
outcome; and (4) to establish a baseline so that whether treatment produces improvement or deterioration can be determined. In addition, assessment results
provide an economical and effective way to communicate with clinical colleagues
and interested agencies.

ultimately produces a problem when mismanagement leads to the repeated use of the same flawed
"solutions"; and (3) the **constructionist** approach (White, 1989), which asserts that a family member's
symptoms are oppressive rather than protective for the family, and thus the family needs to unite
so as to externalize and together defeat the burdensome symptom.

While the goals of appraisal are indeed worthy, they are not meant to imply that the family must undergo a full and comprehensive assessment before *any* clinical action is undertaken. Clearly, a certain amount is learned about the family by interacting with its members as a group. Counselors continuously make therapeutic moves on the basis of a partial assessment of the family, and learn more about the family by noting the outcome of their prior interventions.

## THE APPRAISAL PROCESS

Gauging a family's functioning as an ongoing system is obviously a complex undertaking, in which the counselor must consider a complicated tangle of experiences, temporary or semipermanent alliances, family histories extending over several generations, varying degrees of openness to inquiry, shifting roles played by the same individual over a number of years, and many other factors. Where does the counselor begin in trying to make some sense out of this labyrinth of potentially useful data? By what means may essential material be distinguished from interesting but nonessential material?

Reiss (1980) makes the useful suggestion that a number of pathways are open to the counselor in carrying out the appraisal; as yet, no single most valuable approach has emerged. Among the available choices are the following:

   *Whether to adopt a cross-sectional or developmental view:* The counselor may choose to attend to the family as it is currently functioning or to take a more long-term view of its development. Most family counselors choose the former, and attempt to characterize major family patterns and themes at the time of the appraisal. Others adopt a developmental perspective, reconstructing how the family has evolved over time as it has passed through various phases of its life cycle (marriage, birth of the first child, and so on). The choice is likely to depend primarily on how much relative emphasis the counselor gives past versus present factors in understanding family dysfunction or psychopathology.

   *Whether to conduct a family-based or an environmental-based inquiry:* Both perspectives focus on the family's interactions with its social surroundings, differentiating families on the basis of the breadth and quality of their outside relationships (with extended family members, other families, community agencies such as schools). However, the family-based approach views interactive processes within the family as the primary shapers of these transactional patterns. On the other hand, the environmental-based approach emphasizes the examination of the family's external relationships and seeks to discover the impact of these outside dealings in which the family is embedded to better understand the family's internal patterns.

   *Whether to adopt a crisis or character orientation:* Familiar to most clinicians, this distinction is one of emphasis and outlook. Immediate problems and family complaints are the focus of the crisis orientation. Some family counselors go so far as to type family crises according to the diagnosis of the most conspicuously disturbed member (schizophrenic families, depressed families, alcoholic families), although this is less frequently the case nowadays than in the past. More likely, counselors adopt a character orientation, searching for and defining the family's enduring interactive and adaptational patterns. Any attempt at typology of the family follows from how these patterns translate into family rules, role assignments, and so on.

*Whether to focus on family pathology or family competence:* While the search for family disorder or dysfunction is a familiar one to counselors trained in psychodiagnostic methods, a more current view is to seek family strengths and resources along with deficiencies (Karpel, 1986). Reiss (1980) particularly emphasizes those psychological and social resources that a family can call upon to meet crises as well as conduct their daily lives. From this perspective, differences between families—in role relationships, family rules, and interactive patterns—are not judged as to degree of psychopathology, but rather understood as shaped by differences in values, objectives, and long-term family goals.

*Whether to emphasize underlying family themes or observable behavioral events:* This choice is shaped by the counselor's theoretical view of how human behavior is to be analyzed and understood. The thematic position assumes that overt behavior is but a surface phenomenon and that underlying but largely inaccessible unconscious experiences determine the basis for actions. The task, then, is to determine those hidden events and especially unresolved conflicts, typically in the past, that influence the frequency and force of the current behavior. In marked contrast to this primarily **psychoanalytic** view is the **behavioral** position: that maladaptive or problematic family interactional patterns, like all behaviors, are learned, and therefore may become unlearned or extinguished if not reinforced or rewarded. The assessment task, then, is to focus on the frequencies of the undesired behaviors, as well as their antecedent events and consequences, as an initial step in identifying and ultimately eliminating them to reduce family distress.

Beyond these choices made by the counselor, we believe at least four interactive factors influence the appraisal process: (1) the counselor's theoretical framework; (2) his or her personal counseling style; (3) the unique structure and patterns of the family being appraised; and (4) what the appraiser wants to learn about the family. Although these cannot really be separated in practice, we intend in this book to emphasize the last two aspects: how different family configurations elicit different appraisal and therapeutic interventions, and how the purpose of the undertaking determines what assessment methods will be used.

We believe it is most instructive to divide the appraisal process into two distinct parts. The first, the evaluation phase, consists of initial investigations directed at gaining a feel for what the family is all about, why they are seeking help, and whether family counseling is needed or appropriate. The assessment phase is an ongoing process, as the counselor continues to probe and gauge the family's functioning throughout treatment in order to evaluate the effectiveness of various therapeutic interventions.

## THE EVALUATION PHASE

Three conditions must be met, according to Caille (1982), before a first meeting between a counselor and a family seeking help can occur. To begin with, family members need to agree at some level that they have a particular problem (what we have been referring to as a symptom). Second, the family or an influential outsider (a close friend, a trusted doctor) must decide that the problem exceeds the family's capacity to deal with it, so that the family ultimately is persuaded to present the symptom to a counselor to whom healing responsibility is delegated. Finally, the counselor needs to decide whether the symptom falls within his or her domain of competence or whether the family should be referred to others (other counselors specializing in the presenting problem, say, drug abuse; social or legal agencies; the police).

One particular family member, or a coalition of members, usually begins the process by seeking help outside the family. Perhaps their efforts to solve a personal or family problem have been ineffective and psychologically costly to one or more individuals. Note that this initial decision to step outside of the family for help with the problem is influenced by a number of nonpersonal considerations. Social class factors, ethnic considerations, familiarity with and belief in the psychotherapeutic process—all may play a role.

For example, low-income Hispanic Americans are likely to underutilize mental health services, because of a language barrier or because they perceive insurmountable cultural or social class differences between themselves and the counselor (who is likely to be non-Hispanic and either from, or attempting to achieve, middle-class status). Lacking knowledge of each other's culture, both participants in the counseling process often feel dissatisfaction with the interaction (Acosta, Yamamoto, & Evans, 1982). In the case of marital discord, potential Hispanic-American clients may be unaware of the existence of clinics dealing with family problems. Falicov (1982) observes that working-class, immigrant Mexican families are likely to turn inward and seek guidance from designated family members rather than from less familiar professionals.

Thus, the appearance of a symptom in a family member as a sign that the family needs therapeutic help may have a varied outcome, to a large (and often arbitrary) extent dependent on the family's position in society. As Caille (1982) reminds us, it is not unusual to meet families who live with serious problems such as violence, psychosis, or drug addiction without seeking treatment. Even if they are put in contact with a counselor, a fragmented or truncated presentation of their problems may make the problems seem incomprehensible or unsolvable, and therapeutic action may be impeded. The counselor's or agency's point of view regarding the provision of services on an individual or family basis will also structure the evaluation, and ultimately the intervention process.

## The Initial Telephone Contact

All human systems, including families, develop symptoms or find themselves in crisis at one time or another; most relieve the symptoms or resolve the crisis without therapeutic intervention. Even among those who do not, only a relatively small proportion of families call a counselor asking specifically for family counseling. More typically, according to Karpel and Strauss (1983), one adult member calls to arrange an appointment for himself or herself or for another member.[2] In actuality, this seemingly routine initial telephone contact may be crucial in determining the course of the subsequent evaluation and counseling.

This first telephone contact with a counselor is an opportunity for both the caller and the counselor to size each other up and sense something about each other's attitudes and personalities. The counselor gets some idea of how the caller perceives the problem and, perhaps more subtly, how he or she views the family as an interactive system. The caller, too, is making an evaluation, and forming an impression: have I contacted a person who is friendly, understanding, helpful, warm, insightful, has a sense of humor; someone who is willing to listen beyond a moment or two, who is willing and able to find time for me, who gives me hope that finally I have reached the right person who can help with my (our) problem?

In addition to gathering some preliminary information about the caller and his or her reasons for seeking help, the counselor is forming some hypotheses about the family based on the caller's view or explanation of the problem. How much self-awareness does the caller seem to have? What sort of impression is he or she trying to make? What other family members are involved, and will they willingly attend the initial session? Who should the counselor ask to see for this first meeting (the caller alone, both parents if a child is identified as the patient, the child alone, the parents and the child together, the parents and all the children)? How does the counselor best present his or her decision and make an effective opening move in scheduling an appointment?

Generally speaking, most counselors tend to opt for as many participants as possible during the first session, especially if relationship conflicts (between parents and one or more of the children, or between children) are involved. In some cases, divorced parents may need to attend together with a troubled youngster, or grandparents may be key players in the family system and should be present.

The rule of thumb is to ask as many significant persons as are available to attend, whether or not they reside together as a family unit. Although some may resist ("Why do I need to include my oldest child? He's no problem." "My husband

---

[2]This phenomenon may be changing as the general public becomes more aware of the marital and family counseling fields. However, as we have just noted, certain minority or immigrant groups may be unaware of available family-counseling services, or may simply distrust mainstream institutions. McAdoo (1977) observes that black families, regardless of socioeconomic class, are apt to rely on family ties and church groups during times of crisis, rather than seek professional help; this is especially so if they must deal with a white counselor (Jackson, 1973).

can't take time away from work; besides, it's my child and not us who has a problem." "Does my divorced husband [or wife] have to attend? We always end up screaming at each other"), the majority will cooperate, if for no other reason than wanting to appear cooperative. The counselor's matter-of-fact statement that this is the procedure he or she usually follows, emphasizing that all members are necessary in order to fully understand the problem, usually proves to be sufficiently persuasive.

In general, then, how the counselor uses this telephone opportunity to make a mini-evaluation, and take the first step in entering the family system, may be critical in determining if the family makes (and keeps) the appointment, who will attend the first session, and the family's (and each member's) degree of participation in the subsequent counseling process. Even if the counselor must acquiesce to a caller's insistence that the parents attend the first session alone before others become involved, it may be worth engaging the otherwise resistant family and making later modifications in attendance. The counselor, however, must not allow the caller to determine the course of counseling, even if, having stated a desire for the entire family to attend, he or she settles for less for this first session. Allowing the caller to dominate the call takes power and control from the counselor, who may never again be in charge of the counseling with this family. Carl Whitaker (Whitaker & Bumberry, 1988) is particularly adamant about winning this "battle for structure." He believes that the counselor must insist on establishing the rules of the game, and will not begin the counseling until he is convinced that this has been accomplished.[3]

## The Initial Session

Once the initial session begins, the counselor's first task is to establish a relationship with the family, called "joining" the family (Minuchin, 1974) or "building a working alliance" with them (Karpel & Strauss, 1983). At this point, the counselor needs to present, through both verbal and nonverbal means, a picture of being a competent, fair-minded, empathetic, and understanding individual with whom the family can feel sufficiently comfortable to entrust their problems. Framing comments at the family's vocabulary level, adapting to the family's emotional pace, not challenging or contradicting a member's stated views prematurely, perhaps even making small jokes or adding a personal anecdote relevant to the topic under discussion—all enhance the view of the counselor as easy to talk to and unintimidating. In the process, the counselor is gaining access to the system, from within which he or she is better able to direct change.

[3]Not all family counselors insist that the entire family attend. In some cases, one spouse may even be absent in marital counseling. For example, the Brief Therapy Center noted in a previous footnote will, with the client's permission, work with anyone motivated enough to help with the presenting problem (Segal, 1987). Bowen (1978) often worked with one marital partner when a couple sought his help, typically choosing the one he considered more capable of breaking through the couple's old emotional entanglements. Even when the identified patient was a symptomatic child, Bowen might urge the parents to come in without the child, arguing that the family's basic problems emanate from unresolved conflicts between the parents.

With the family seated in a circle, arranged as they see fit, the counselor needs to be free to address all members equally. Deliberately not beginning with the identified patient, in order to avoid going along with possible family stereotyping that he or she is "the problem," perhaps the counselor turns to the father, if the mother has made the initial contact, in order to break any previously established set that the mother is the family spokesperson. An opening gambit such as "I've heard from your wife over the phone about how she sees the problem, and now I'd like to hear your view" is likely to encourage him (and, later, others) to get involved in the process. If this scenario is adopted, the counselor needs to make explicit what he or she has been told, so that no hidden information and/or hidden alliance exists between the counselor and the initial caller.

Of course, no hard and fast counseling rules exist about whom should be addressed first. However, Whitaker (1977), for one, is likely to involve the father by this tactic early in the treatment. Without prior information, his reasoning is that the father is the most likely family member to resist seeking help; moreover, the father usually also has the power to pull the family out of treatment if some rapport is not established with the counselor from the beginning. We should add that, in certain ethnic groups, addressing the father first is a necessary sign of respect, and failing to do so may create an insurmountable obstacle to the counselor continuing to see the family.

In a similar fashion, working with a family where there is an identified problem child or adolescent, Henggeler and Borduin (1990) gather together the parents (or guardians), the identified patient, and the siblings, and offer an opening gambit that asks each person, in effect, "What brought you here?" Their top priority, however, is to obtain the parents' response; the responses of the problem youngster are given second priority; and thirdly, the responses of the siblings are noted. The rationale here is to affirm the parents' authority while simultaneously obtaining each family member's unique perspective. In the process, the counselor might begin to identify additional problem areas of various family members.

In still other cases, the counselor may wait to see who will present himself or herself as the family spokesperson, who will be silent, how free family members feel to talk to each other, and so on. When the identified patient is a frightened child, the counselor may begin with him or her, to reassure the child that it will be safe to speak.

Certain identifying data need to be gathered at the outset from each family member. Names, ages, occupations, current living arrangements, and other such details are, of course, necessary; beyond such basic information, the counselor begins to obtain some face-to-face impressions of each member and to develop some hypotheses concerning his or her role in the overall family constellation. By addressing each member, the counselor establishes that each member's comments are valued, and that each member will be heard, thus starting to develop a connection with each person present. Every member should have an opportunity (if necessary, prompted by the counselor) to talk before the close of the initial hour or hour-and-one-half session.

The reason for being with a counselor occupies the family, and early on in the initial session they will want to talk about the problem from which they are

## Box 3.1 Step-by-Step Guide to the Initial Family Interview

Beginning the first family session properly, without drifting or getting muddled in irrelevant details, is an imposing challenge, especially for inexperienced counselors. To aid the process, Weber, McKeever, and McDaniel (1985) offer a concise, step-by-step generic guide for conducting a problem-focused first family interview. According to these authors, four primary goals shape the conduct of the interview: (1) to join the family, accommodate to its style of interacting, and create an environment in which all members will feel supported; (2) to organize the interview so that the members begin to gain confidence in the counselor's leadership; (3) to gather information about the problem in ways that make family transactions around the problem clearer; (4) to negotiate a counseling contract, emphasizing the family's initiative in defining goals and desired changes.

To accomplish these ends, they break the interview down into 12 separate phases. Both preinterview and postinterview tasks are included.

1. *Telephoning:* To make contact; to contract for first interview (who will attend, when, where); to determine referral source (if not self-referred), reason for referral, and how follow-up information will be given to referring person.
2. *Forming hypotheses:* To develop tentative hypotheses (based on family life-cycle stage, reason for referral, and so on) to be tested in the interview; to plan strategy for gathering data to help test initial hunches.
3. *The greeting* (approximately 5 minutes): To welcome, identify, and greet each member separately; to observe seating arrangement family selects; to orient to counseling format.
4. *The social phase* (approximately 5 minutes): To build nonthreatening setting for the family; to attempt to engage all members; to note each member's language and nonverbal behavior in order to facilitate contact in future sessions.
5. *Identifying the problem* (approximately 15 minutes): To explore each member's view of the problem in behavioral terms, as well as specific solutions that have been attempted.
6. *Observing family patterns* (approximately 15 minutes): To have family describe or reenact examples of the problem; to note repetitive behavioral sequences that occur around the problem.
7. *Defining goals* (approximately 5 minutes): To crystallize treatment goals as viewed by each family member in specific and realistic behavioral terms.
8. *Contracting* (approximately 5 minutes): To reach agreement regarding continuation of counseling and its structure (who will attend, fees, insurance, signing of consent forms for gathering further information from schools, previous counselors, and so on); if family chooses not to continue, to offer referrals or indicate how they might return in the future.
9. *First interview checklist:* To review session so as to determine how well previous goals of each phase were reached.
10. *Revising hypotheses:* To revise and refine preinterview hypotheses and plan the next session.
11. *Contacting the referring person:* To obtain referring person's perspective, and to share initial assessment of the family; to lay groundwork for collaboration in carrying out treatment strategy.
12. *Gathering records:* To obtain all relevant information from professionals or social agencies.

seeking relief. After one member, preferably not the caller, begins, others are encouraged to add individual comments, and silent members in particular are encouraged to participate. As the counselor directs the discussion, perhaps over several sessions, he or she seeks clues to the following (Bross, 1982; Caille, 1982; Doherty & Baird, 1983):

Why is the family seeking help *now*?

What have been the family's attempted solutions in the past?

What are the sources of stress on this family?

Who has the symptom? How severe? Chronic or acute? Why this person?

When did the problem or symptom first begin, and who is most affected by it?

What function, if any, does the symptom serve for family stability?

How often, when, and under what circumstances does the symptom occur?

What are the family members' assumptions about the cause and nature of the problem?

Are interactive patterns discernible that may be related to the onset or termination of symptomatic behavior?

What kind of boundaries or hierarchies exist in the family?

What is the current level of family functioning?

Are noticeable alliances or coalitions operating?

How permeable are the boundaries between subsystems?

In what manner, and with what degree of success, has the family dealt with this or other problems in the past?

Has the family sought professional help before? With what degree of success? What are their current expectations?

How adaptable or rigid is the family? How receptive to help?

What apparent family interactive patterns are related to the perpetuation of the problem?

While these questions may seem overwhelming to the beginning family counselor who is trying to keep them all in mind, several words of reassurance may be in order. They need not be memorized; the counselor will think of those relevant to the current situation as he or she attempts to learn more about the family as an ongoing system. In addition, these questions need not all be addressed in one or even two or three sessions; the data will probably evolve slowly and in stages as the counseling proceeds. We merely offer these questions as a checklist or set of guidelines to help the counselor organize his or her thinking in systems terms when dealing with a new family. They should provide a framework for generating clinical hunches or hypotheses about the family's structure and interactive processes, and thus form the basis for planning more effective clinical interventions.

### History Taking

How much background information does a family counselor need before deciding on and implementing a counseling plan? Histories for each family member? Histories for the family only? Going back how many generations? Does the counselor obtain a formal case history through a series of straightforward questions, as in some forms of individual counseling? How relevant to the present are the facts of the past?

Counselors vary considerably in the emphasis they place on historical information, dependent primarily on the theoretical viewpoint from which they operate. A secondary factor may be the purposes for which the evaluation is being carried out. For example, in a crisis situation following a suicide attempt, the counselor most certainly would deal with immediately precipitating factors and look for family resources to deal with the emergency; in a more long-lasting situation in which parent-child conflict is at issue, the counselor might conduct the counseling at a slower pace and make use of relevant historical data.

At one end of the spectrum, systems theorist Murray Bowen (1978) takes the position that multigenerational patterns and influences are crucial determinants of current family difficulties. Consequently, he investigates the genesis of a family's presenting problems or symptoms by detailing the backgrounds of husband and wife through at least three generations. To aid the process and to keep the record in pictorial form in front of him, he constructs a **genogram** in which each partner's family background is laid out.

In their simplest form, genograms are schematic diagrams, in family-tree fashion, depicting information about several generations of a family. Figure 3.1 illustrates some commonly agreed-upon genogram symbols. Beyond providing a concise and graphic picture of a family's current composition, a genogram reveals relevant data concerning families of origin and extended family networks. Ages, dates of birth and death of key family members, divorces and remarriages, birth order, and other such details may be included, all potentially useful in elucidating relationships and family transactional patterns.

Since the functioning of family members, from a systems view, is profoundly interdependent, and changes in one part reverberate throughout the system, a picture of the happenings over several generations may be very enlightening. McGoldrick and Gerson (1985), strongly influenced by Bowen, believe that families tend to repeat themselves: what happens in one generation will often occur in the next, as the same issues get replayed from generation to generation. Counselors who seek such multigenerational connections for assessment clues are thus more prone to use genograms (and history taking in general) in their quest.

Genograms are typically prepared with the aid of the family during the first session or two. For both the counselor and the family, they help provide a framework for understanding family relationship patterns, and also provide a well-defined structure for families to begin to think in intergenerational terms about themselves. For example, Figure 3.2 is a three-generational map of a family who has contacted a counselor in 1988 because their son, Ivan, is having school difficulties, disrupting class activity, and generally being inattentive. The genogram reveals that his mother, Loretta, was adopted, after her adoptive parents tried unsuccessfully to have a daughter after three sons. She married early, at 20, soon after the death of her adoptive mother. Steve, a middle child whose parents divorced when he was a preteenager, lived in a single-parent household with his

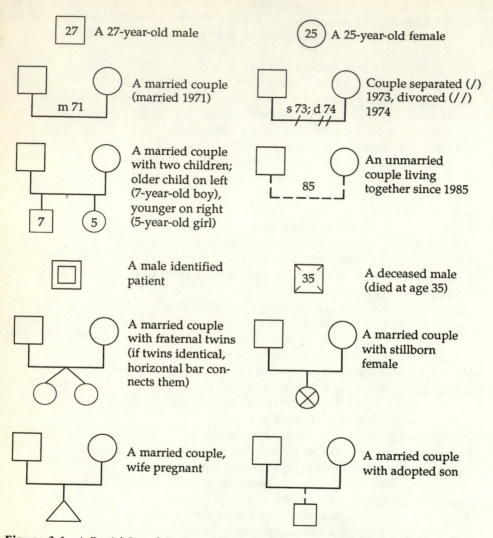

**Figure 3.1** A Partial Set of Commonly Agreed-Upon Genogram Symbols
*Source:* McGoldrick & Gerson, 1985.

mother and two sisters until he married Loretta. Steve and Loretta started their own family before either was 25, perhaps in an effort to create some stability in contrast to what they had known growing up.

The fact that they now have four children (one died at birth) suggests a strong involvement in family life, especially because the children's ages are spread over more than ten years. Are the parents being overprotective, perhaps to compensate for what they felt deprived of as youngsters? What has been the effect of Loretta's pregnancies over the last several years on the other children? To what extent does Ivan feel he is being displaced as the youngest child by the birth of

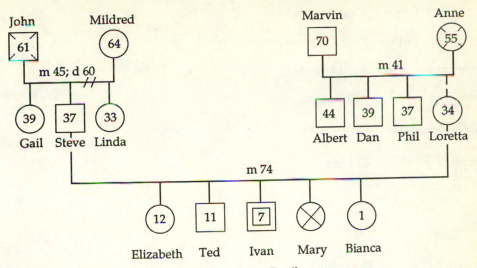

**Figure 3.2**   Genogram of a Three-Generation Family

Bianca? These are some of the issues a counselor might begin to explore on the basis of the genogram data, to be checked out as he or she learns more about the family. The counselor with a systems viewpoint is likely to see symptoms in the identified patient as reflecting the family system's adaptation at this given moment in time. Both historical and current family patterns may point to dysfunctional family structures.

A more moderate position regarding the importance of history taking is offered by **structural** theorist Salvador Minuchin (1974) and **strategic** theorist Jay Haley (1976). Stressing a systems outlook, both attend primarily to more immediate presenting problems and ongoing family transactions and only secondarily to intergenerational patterns. Both also attend to a family's hierarchical structures, especially possible coalitions that cross generational boundaries. While Minuchin concentrates on a family's organizational patterns and Haley on its communication and interactive patterns, both focus on repetitive sequences in the current behavior between and among family members, paying particularly close attention to those sequences that maintain symptoms. Not adverse to dealing with family history as it relates to a here-and-now problem, they may elicit such information, for example, if it helps them understand what may have precipitated a current crisis.

Minuchin (1974) prefers the technique of **family mapping**, another type of family diagramming useful in depicting the structure and patterns of family systems. In particular, he views a family's structure as "an invisible set of functional demands that organizes the ways in which family members interact" (p. 51). Again using symbols (see Figure 3.3), Minuchin is interested in delineating the clarity of current family boundaries (clear, diffuse, or rigid), subsystem operations, and family transactional styles (enmeshment or disengagement). He uses the map as a guide to the family's transactional patterns, and as an aid in developing hypotheses for how best to help change family structures; thus, evaluation and assessment

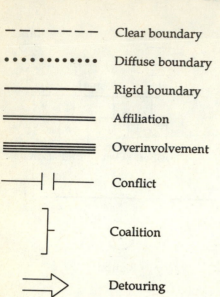

– – – – – – –    Clear boundary

• • • • • • • • • • •    Diffuse boundary

———————    Rigid boundary

═══════════    Affiliation

≡≡≡≡≡≡≡    Overinvolvement

———|  |———    Conflict

Coalition

Detouring

**Figure 3.3**  Minuchin's Symbols for Family Mapping
*Source:* Minuchin, 1974, p. 53.

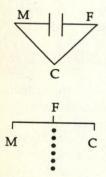

M  |  |  F    Father (F) and mother (M), both stressed at work, come home and
criticize each other, but then detour their conflict by attacking a
child (C). This results in less danger to the spousal subsystem,
but stresses the child.

     C

F    Father criticizes mother, who seeks a coalition with the child
against the father. Note the inappropriately rigid cross-genera-
M     •     C    tional subsystem of mother and child as well as the diffuse
boundary between mother and child; both have the effect of
excluding the father. Minuchin refers to this result as a cross-
generational dysfunctional pattern.

**Figure 3.4**  The Effect of Stress on the Subsystem Boundaries of a Family, as
Depicted by Family Mapping
*Source:* Minuchin, 1974.

are integrated into the therapeutic process. Figure 3.4 illustrates the use of family
mapping to depict parental conflict detoured onto a child (upper figure) and intergenerational coalitions within a family (lower figure).

A family evaluation and assessment model based on structural and strategic
theory has been offered by Friesen (1985). (A case of family triangulation was
described in terms of this model in Chapter 2; see especially Figure 2.2.) Emphasizing interpersonal interaction, Friesen has developed a schema for locating family patterns along a number of dimensions as a guide to the therapeutic

process. Specifically, Friesen has developed the following eight scales for assessing aspects of the family system:

*Scale 1. Family developmental issues:* Each stage in a family's life cycle presents its own developmental tasks and creates a potential crisis event. The view here is that family dysfunction emerges from within the family system itself, and that developmental stages simply color the expression or define the nature of the symptom.

*Scale 2. Family life context:* The concern here is with the extent to which those environmental factors that sustain, enhance, or impair the family's operations are present. Seeing the family within its social context includes its relationships to schools, work, ethnic and religious groups it belongs to, societal expectations, and so on.

*Scale 3. Family structure:* The family "code" regulating relationships, transmitted from generation to generation, is investigated here. The flexibility of boundaries, power and leadership, coalitions, and their impact on how well the system carries out its functions are studied.

*Scale 4. Family flexibility:* Here the focus is on the degree to which the system's rules allow for the adequate exchange of information between systems or within the family system itself.

*Scale 5. Family resonance:* This scale measures the degree to which the family is sensitive to the needs of its individual members. Openness, fluidity, the expression of affect, and the level of tolerance for differing beliefs are important here.

*Scale 6. Family communication processes:* This scale attempts to identify the communication patterns within the family. The assumption is that the manner of communicating will offer clues to the family's underlying interactional patterns.

*Scale 7. Marital system:* The degree of vitality in the marriage and the parents' level of commitment to it provide clues to overall family functioning.

*Scale 8. Individual issues:* Effort is made here to identify individual members' problems within the context of the family and social structure.

Although **behaviorists** such as Stuart (1980) place great reliance on assessment—indeed, a formal assessment procedure (questionnaires, standardized interviews) is often the first order of business, before counseling begins—they are not likely to attend to historical material. Instead, they set out to learn as much as they can about the family's present interpersonal environments that maintain and help perpetuate or reinforce maladaptive or problematic family behavior patterns.

As we have seen, the importance accorded to history taking will be determined by the counselor's theoretical framework. It will also be different for different families: for some families the problems that have brought them to counseling can be stated briefly and succinctly. Typically, their explanations are couched in current behavioral terms: an ongoing extramarital affair; a bad school experience for one of the children, leaving the single mother feeling frantic and in need of guidance and support; a breakdown in communication between a young child and his newly remarried mother; conflict between immigrant parents and their "Americanized" children.

Other families view their current problems in longitudinal terms: a husband and wife grown more distant since the birth of their first child three years ago; a steady deterioration in a marriage since the wife decided to return to school; a recognition that a husband has distanced himself from his wife and children over the years, without knowing exactly why or when it began; a father's heavy drinking and depression since he lost his job over a year ago. Such families offer historical explanations, and insist that the counselor know the background history in great detail. From a counselor's viewpoint, too much emphasis on history may signal an unwillingness to look at the present; such families must be brought back into dealing with why they are seeking help today. Conversely, families who insist on seeing all issues in current terms and suggest any history is irrelevant may be, wittingly or not, covering up crucial details that might play a key role in the counselor's understanding of presenting difficulties. In the latter case, the counselor may need to probe selected areas of the family's past to gain better awareness of the problem's genesis.

History taking has the advantage of giving the family as well as the counselor something concrete and nonthreatening to do early in the evaluation, although there is the risk that the exchange may become stilted and tedious. It may make a family feel reassured that the counselor is learning some essential facts about their past; similarly, it may buy time for the counselor to get his or her bearings with this family. Nevertheless, the process of history taking must not obscure that the family is there to work together, here and now, on a current problem, not merely to answer questions about the past. Even if the counselor has taken a formal history, he or she must at some point signal, through word or gesture, that it is time to shift from a question-and-answer mode to a more interactive one.

## THE ASSESSMENT PHASE

Counselors probably get a better sense of how a family functions by interacting with its members over a period of time than from any initial interviewing in the evaluation phase. Observing the formation of coalitions and family triangles, scapegoating, how subsystems carry out necessary family functions, how differences are negotiated, what forms of communication exist and their degree of effectiveness in dealing with family issues, how the family as a group deals with stress, and other details provides vital information about family structures and ongoing family processes.

As we noted earlier, assessment goes on throughout family counseling, as the counselor broadens his or her understanding, develops, modifies, and discards hypotheses, and makes suitable interventions based upon progressively refined appraisals of the family (as well as continuing assessments of the effectiveness of previous interventions). In other words, the counselor gains knowledge about the family as a result of a continuous interactive process, involving the family's perception of the problem, the counselor's analysis of that perception and subsequent interventions, the family's response to those interventions, and the counselor's response to the family response (deShazer, 1983).

# FAMILY-MEASUREMENT TECHNIQUES

Many clinical practitioners find that planned intervention, whether with an individual client or a family, is facilitated by the precounseling use of appropriate tests and measurements. By selecting instruments and procedures tailored to the situation, and using the results to form a multidimensional "family profile," these counselors feel better prepared to outline treatment goals, devise treatment strategies, and later evaluate treatment outcomes (Bagarozzi, 1985). In the process, they attempt to derive the benefits of obtaining both an "insider" (family members' self-reports) and "outsider" (counselor's observations) perspective on family processes and functioning.

Both approaches have their strengths and limitations. While it is frequently of great value to learn of the inside subjective perceptions of each of the individuals involved, critics argue that family members are often biased (and thus inaccurate) informants regarding their own behavior. On the other hand, an outside observer's inferences may be inaccurate by failing to understand the idiosyncratic shared meanings of events that families frequently develop.

Ideally, counselors interested in improving the functioning of entire family systems should assess families at all levels—at the individual, dyadic, and family-systems levels (Kniskern & Gurman, 1983). In practice, however, such a comprehensive evaluation in most cases is impractical, considering the time, energy, and costs involved. Nevertheless, it is sometimes necessary to assess individual functioning—especially of the identified patient—as part of a family appraisal, in an effort to learn more about how the family functions as a system. Bagarozzi (1985) and Grotevant and Carlson (1989), both adopting a systems perspective, have provided useful guides to test instruments assessing whole-family functioning as well as certain dyadic (for example, parent-child interaction patterns) relationships. Both pay close attention to such psychometric criteria as reliability and validity, as well as ease of use and usefulness to clinicians and researchers. When selecting a test instrument, Bagarozzi (1985) pays particular attention to the extent to which the instrument requires specialized training or expertise to administer.

## SELF-REPORT MEASURES

Self-report measures—typically in the form of standardized questionnaires—can provide the counselor with important information about the ways in which each family member experiences the family system. That person's attitudes, roles, values, self-perceptions, and satisfaction with family relationships can often be gleaned from such results (Huston & Robins, 1982). Self-report procedures usually require less training to administer and score than do counselor observational techniques, and often produce revelations of private behaviors that the counselor may not have an opportunity to observe. Thus, by having family members provide separate, subjective views of family relationships, the counselor gains access to an insider picture related to their behavioral interaction patterns (Grotevant & Carlson, 1989).

Despite the concern of some critics that the nonobjectivity involved may lead to inaccuracies, and thus the results may be of questionable validity or ultimate usefulness, family self-report measures are increasingly popular; they are particularly attractive to those clinicians who emphasize the relationship between cognitive processes and behavior. For the most part, the questionnaires focus on measuring the concurrent attitudes, beliefs, and perceptions of family members, rather than attempting to provide less reliable retrospective information about family functioning.

An outstanding example of a reliable and valid self-report measurement, easy to administer and interpret, is the Family Adaptability and Cohesion Evaluation Scales III (FACES III), based upon the circumplex model of family functioning.

## The Circumplex Model

A useful insider view of two central properties of family life—adaptability and cohesion—can be gleaned from a research-based technique developed by David Olson and his colleagues (Olson, 1986; Olson, Russell, & Sprenkle, 1989). Grounded in family-systems theory, sociological models of family functioning, and concepts concerning family life-cycle changes, these researchers' efforts have been directed at understanding how families cope with various situational stresses and demands throughout the life cycle. Over 1000 families participated in their study, at least 100 at each of seven family life-cycle stages.

These efforts have produced the circumplex model, a family typology based primarily on two dimensions, *adaptability* and *cohesion;* a third dimension, *communication,* facilitates family movement on the primary two. Taken together, the researchers believe, these dimensions adequately describe family functioning. Adaptability refers to the family's ability to permit change—in its power structure, rules, and role relationships—in response to changes in members' life situations or life-cycle transitions. Cohesion is defined as family members' emotional bonding with one another. Steps along these two dimensions are divided into four levels each, resulting in a four-by-four matrix yielding 16 possible family types, as illustrated in Figure 3.5.

A family's placement on each of the intersecting scales is determined by their responses to a 20-item self-report assessment procedure, the Family Adaptability and Cohesion Evaluation Scales (FACES III) (Olson, 1986).[4] Family members complete the test twice; the scores provide a measure of how individuals presently

---

[4]Olson and his colleagues have also developed PREPARE, a reliable 125-item, 12-category self-report that focuses on specific issues within a marriage and is useful in premarital counseling (Olson, Fournier, & Druckman, 1986). We describe the test in greater detail and offer an example of its use in a case discussed in Chapter 6. MACES III (Marital Adaptability and Cohesion Evaluation Scales), a 20-item self-report measure similar to FACES III, has been developed specifically for use with couples (Olson, 1990).

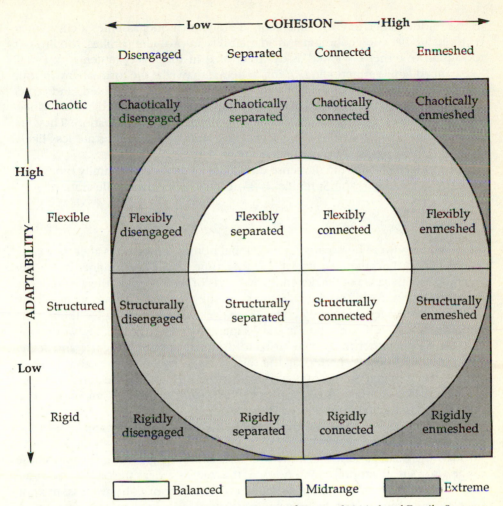

**Figure 3.5**  The Circumplex Model, Representing 16 Types of Marital and Family Systems
*Source:* Olson, 1986, p. 339.

perceive their family system and also their ideal description of family functioning. (The perceived/ideal discrepancy is an indirect measure of family satisfaction; the greater the discrepancy, the less the satisfaction derived from family life.)
Plotted on the circumplex-model grid of the 16 possible family types, the four
central ones are considered most balanced in our society (although other configurations may work best in other societies).

According to Olson (1986), balanced families function more adequately than
extreme families, and they typically demonstrate more positive communication
skills. Families with extremely high scores on both dimensions fall at the outer
extremes; midrange families may have middle scores on one dimension but extreme scores on the other; balanced families are those whose scores place them

in the middle range of each dimension. Thus, this model assumes a curvilinear relationship between cohesion and adaptability in problem families: too little or too much of either is viewed as dysfunctional in the family system.

Balanced family functioning, in this schema, may take the form of any of four types: flexibly separated, flexibly connected, structurally separated, and structurally connected. These types of families combine stability, the ability to change, and sufficiently open boundaries to permit effective communication. They are more resourceful, make use of better coping strategies, and thus are less likely to succumb to stressful events than extreme families.

The model is dynamic in the sense that changes can occur in family types over time. Olson, Russell, and Sprenkle (1983) offer the following illustration:

❊  ❊  ❊  ❊  ❊

Steve and Sally were both raised in traditional homes. Three years after they were married, they became parents for the first time, and Sally resigned from her teaching job. Because of the dependency needs of their son and their own desire for mutual support in this transition period, they developed a moderately high but not extreme level of family cohesion. Also, their upbringing led them to be moderately low, but not rigid, on the adaptability dimension. They were comfortable with a rather traditional husband-dominant power structure and segregated role relationship, preferring the relative security of these established patterns to the ambiguities of continually negotiating them. Using the current model, we would classify their family type as *structurally connected,* an option that seemed to be satisfying to them at the time.

When their son became a teenager, Sally started pursuing a career, and both parents experienced a good deal of "consciousness raising" about sex roles through the media and through involvement in several growth groups. Because of their son's needs for more autonomy at this age, as well as the parents' separate career interests, they began operating at a lower level of cohesiveness, moving from being connected to being more separated.

Furthermore, the family power structure shifted from being husband-dominant to a more shared pattern. Sally exercises much more control in the relationship than previously, and she and Steve are struggling, almost on a weekly basis, to redefine the rules and role definitions that will govern their relationship. Although they occasionally yearn for the security of their earlier, more structured relationship, both find excitement and challenge in this more flexible relationship style. In short, *flexibly separated* best describes their current family organizational pattern. (pp. 75–77)

❊  ❊  ❊  ❊  ❊

Other self-report measures, such as the Self-Report Family Inventory (SFI) based upon the Beavers systems model of family functioning, and the McMaster Family Assessment Device (FAD) derived from the McMaster model of family functioning, have been adapted from two well-regarded outsider views of families that we are about to discuss. We shall return to these self-measuring devices after reviewing those counselor observational measures.

# OBSERVATIONAL MEASURES

Measuring family functioning is a complex but necessary task in any clinical undertaking. Counselors, especially those who view families as systems, typically rely upon observational techniques to investigate family interactional patterns that are considered to be crucial in understanding both psychopathology and competence within the family (Grotevant & Carlson, 1989). Especially appealing to those counselors who distrust family members' ability to report accurately on how they relate to one another, observations may take the form of *interactive coding schemes* (diagramming family interaction patterns along a series of cognitive, affective, and interpersonal dimensions) and of *rating scales* (judging and scoring those overt, observable patterns along predetermined psychological dimensions). The former provide a more molecular level of analysis by trying to capture the moment-to-moment contingencies of the behavior of family members toward one another; the latter, at a more molar level, are more complex and ambitious, and attempt to provide an objective summary judgment of family behavior patterns. Observer competence and training, as well as test manuals, enhance the reliability and validity of the observations, of course, in contrast to self-report tests.

In this section, we elaborate on two leading observational measures, both based on rating scales, since such methods are particularly suited to furnishing objective information on whole-family interdependent relationship patterns.

## The Beavers Systems Model

Robert Beavers and his associates at the Timberlawn Psychiatric Foundation in Dallas, Texas, after years of research, developed a 14-item rating scale for assessing and classifying family functioning, the Beavers-Timberlawn Family Evaluation Scale, which provides an outsider or counselor's view of family functioning. The studies began with an early research effort (Lewis, Beavers, Gossett, & Phillips, 1976) to understand how healthy family systems differed from those in which one or more members required psychiatric treatment or hospitalization. The experimental design involved assigning both groups an identical series of tasks, observing and videotaping the results, and then having trained judges rate the resulting interactions along five major dimensions—family structure, mythology, goal-directed negotiation, autonomy, and family affect—along with subtopics under each rubric. Results indicated that, although differences in style and patterning existed, essentially no single quality or thread differentiated the two groups. Among the key differences were: (1) the family's capacity to communicate thoughts and feelings and (2) the central role played by the parental coalition in providing family leadership and serving as a model for interpersonal relationships.

The Beavers-Timberlawn model (more recently renamed the Beavers systems model) portrays family life as existing on an infinite linear continuum of

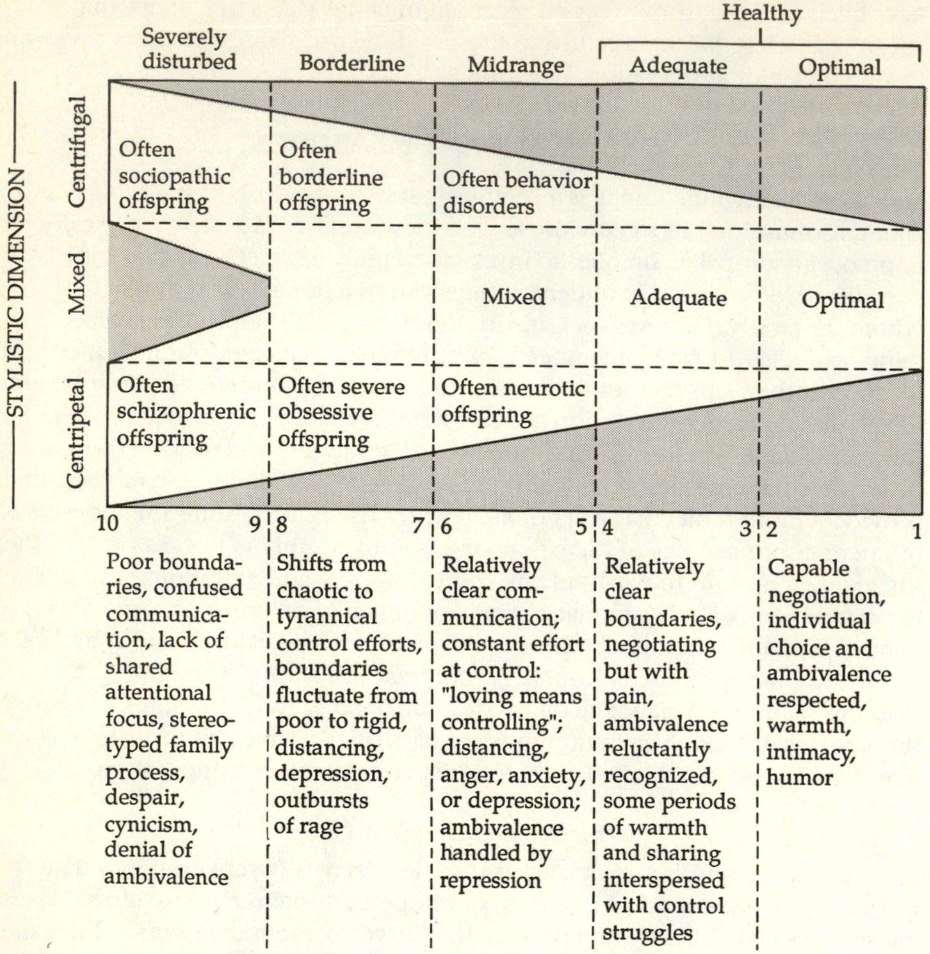

**Figure 3.6** The Beavers Systems Model, in the Form of a Sideways A, with One Leg Representing Centripetal Families and the Other Leg Representing Centrifugal Families *Source:* Beavers & Voeller, 1983, p. 90.

competence, thereby underscoring the Beavers view of a limitless potential for growth (Green, Kolevzon, & Vosler, 1985). At one end are leaderless, invasive, chaotic families, with diffuse boundaries between members. Closer to the mid-point of competence, families show rigid interpersonal control, with frequent distancing, projection, and little consequent closeness. Families at the high end of the scale tend to be better structured; they are composed of autonomous individuals who share intimacy and closeness but also respect separateness (Beavers, 1981; Beavers, 1982; Beavers & Voeller, 1983).

In the Beavers systems model, shown in Figure 3.6, families are classified on a five-point scale according to their degree of functioning. Optimal and adequate families are considered competent or healthy. Midrange, borderline, and severely disturbed families represent progressively poorer levels of functioning. The Beavers systems model is similar to the circumplex model in that it too represents a cross section of current family functioning and makes use of two axes to conceptualize differences among families. In this case, however, the structure, flexibility, and competence of a family and its members are scored on one dimension and their style of interaction on the other.

As formulated by Beavers, the horizontal axis reflects the family's structure and its adaptive flexibility. In systems terms, we might think of it as a negentropy continuum, since the more negentropic (the more adaptive and flexible) the family, the better able the family is to deal effectively with stressful situations and events. In order to remain highly adaptive, the family must have a stable structure but at the same time be able to negotiate changes in its structure, as required to meet the changing needs of its members, without loss of stability. Not only adaptability but autonomy (the family system's capacity to allow or even encourage members to function competently in making choices, each member assuming responsibility for his or her own choices) is called for in competent families. According to Beavers and Voeller (1983, p. 89), "capable families intuitively have a systems approach to relationships, with an appreciation of the interchangeability of causes and effects."

The vertical axis, curvilinear rather than a continuum, reflects the family members' style of interaction. Members of **centripetal** families view most relationship satisfactions as coming from within the family; the world outside is perceived as menacing, and separation in such families is thus threatening and difficult. By contrast, members of **centrifugal** families see far more promise in what the outside world has to offer than in what their family can provide; they seek to distance themselves from their families, often prematurely, and to look outside the family for sources of gratification. The arrow shape of the diagram is intended to convey that extremes in style—whether profoundly centripetal or profoundly centrifugal—are associated with poor family functioning. Thus, as families become more competent, or more adaptive, their excessive centripetal or centrifugal styles tend to diminish, as noted in the diagram.

Families who are at one or the other extreme are most entropic, with the greatest risk of producing disturbed children. Beavers believes that, in a severely dysfunctional family with a centripetal style, a good chance exists that one or more of the offspring will become schizophrenic as adults—socially isolated, progressively withdrawn, and disorganized. Children from severely dysfunctional families with a centrifugal style are more prone to sociopathic behavior—antisocial, irresponsible, egocentric. As Beavers sees it, the sociopath's self-defeating behavior, redefined in family terms, may represent an expression of rage at an uncaring world. In midrange families, both groups are less discrepant, although one tends to behavior disorders and the other to neuroses. Within the healthy category, extremes are rare and the structure aids effective functioning for individuals as well as the family as a whole.

Ratings are made on a 1–5 scale for each of the dimensions listed earlier—*family structure* (with subscales such as overt power, parental coalition, family closeness), *mythology, goal-directed negotiation, autonomy* (subscales include responsibility, clarity of expression, invasiveness, permeability), *family affect* (subscales for range of feelings, mood and tone, empathy, and unresolvable conflict), and a *global health/pathology* rating. An accompanying test manual allows the user to convert the rating scores into placement on the Beavers systems model classification scheme (Figure 3.6).

The Self-Report Inventory (SFI) (Beavers, Hampson, & Hulgas, 1985), still being refined, essentially translates the family-systems constructs and scales just described into a 36-item self-report format. Its reported high reliability and validity make it a potentially useful complementary measure; filled out by the family members about themselves, this measure, together with the rating scales, offers a multimethod, multilevel family-systems evaluation.


## The McMaster Model

The McMaster model of family functioning is perhaps the most carefully crafted of the measurement techniques we have been considering. This model has evolved over a long period of time; it was first reported in the late 1950s at McGill University in Montreal, Canada (Westley & Epstein, 1969). The systems-based research shifted to McMaster University in Hamilton, Ontario, in the 1960s and 1970s, and later continued to be refined at Brown University in Providence, Rhode Island (Epstein, Bishop, & Baldwin, 1982). Throughout its history, the research has focused on the family's structure and transactional patterns, attending particularly to how the family develops and maintains itself by dealing with certain necessary tasks.

Families are assessed in this model with respect to their current functioning in three areas:

1. *Basic task area:* how they deal with problems of providing food, money, transportation, and shelter.
2. *Developmental task area:* how they deal with problems arising as a result of changes over time, such as first pregnancy or last child leaving home.
3. *Hazardous task area:* how they handle crises that arise as the result of illness, accident, loss of income, job change, and so forth.

Families unable to cope effectively with these three task areas have been found to be most likely to develop clinically significant problems.

The McMaster Clinical Rating Scale (Epstein, Baldwin, & Bishop, 1983) translates the research model into specific areas of family functioning in order to determine a family's need for counseling. To evaluate how a family manages the tasks outlined above, six aspects of family functioning are investigated:

1. *Problem solving:* the family's ability to resolve issues that threaten its integrity and ability to function effectively.
2. *Communication:* how, and how well, the family exchanges information and affect.

3. *Roles:* how clearly and appropriately roles are defined; how responsibilities are allocated and accountability is monitored in order to sustain the family and support the personal development of its members.
4. *Affective responsiveness:* the family's ability to respond to a given situation with the appropriate quality and quantity of feeling.
5. *Affective involvement:* the extent to which the family shows interest in and values the particular activities and interests of its members.
6. *Behavior control:* the pattern the family adopts for handling dangerous situations; for handling social interaction within and outside the family; and for meeting and expressing members' psychobiological needs (eating, sleeping, sex) and drives (aggression).

The counselor using the McMaster Clinical Rating Scale is interested in determining how well the family carries out its primary mission of providing an environment in which social and biological development can flourish. Each dimension of family functioning is rated on a seven-point scale, ranging from 1, *severely disturbed,* to 7, *superior functioning.* Ratings between 1 and 4 are intended to suggest that the family needs intervention. Grotevant & Carlson (1989) warn that differentiation between scale points may be difficult to make, however, and that the multidimensionality of each scale is such that a high level of inference by raters may threaten reliability and validity.

As have other researchers into family functioning, Epstein and his associates (Epstein, Baldwin, & Bishop, 1983) have turned their attention to constructing a 60-item self-report questionnaire to evaluate families according to the six clinical dimensions (plus an overall *general functioning* dimension) just outlined. The Family Assessment Device (FAD) is thus made up of seven scales that measure each of the six aspects of family functioning described previously, plus the family's collective health/pathology.

Once again, the assumption here is that family health is related to its ability to carry out certain essential tasks. Each family member responds to each set of items by indicating his or her opinion on a four-point rating scale, ranging from *strongly agree* to *strongly disagree.* (For example, one item to measure problem solving: "We confront problems involving feeling"; an item to measure affective responsiveness: "We are reluctant to show our affection for each other.") Still in an early stage of development, the test at present is probably best used for screening purposes, to quickly identify a family's problem areas, rather than in any more diagnostic ways.

# SUMMARY

Counselors need to appraise the family as a functioning unit to determine whether treatment is in order, which members should be seen, and which underlying interactive patterns lead to symptomatology in one of its members. The appraisal process itself can be divided into two distinct stages: the evaluation and assessment phases. The former begins with the initial telephone call, an occasion for counselor and caller to gain some image of each other's attitudes and personality. For the counselor, it is also an opportunity to size up the situation and direct the caller to bring in as many significant family members as are available to attend the first session. The assessment phase of the appraisal continues throughout the subsequent counseling.

Counselors vary in their reliance on family history, primarily according to their theoretical orientation. Bowen views multigenerational patterns as highly influential in understanding current family difficulties, and constructs genograms to diagram such information. Minuchin, more concerned with learning about ongoing family patterns and structures, relies on family-mapping techniques to depict current transactions.

Two sets of measurement techniques are typically employed in carrying out appraisals of family functioning: self-report measures and observational measures. The Family Adaptability and Cohesion Evaluation Scales (FACES III), a self-report measure based on Olson's circumplex model, stresses a family's adaptability and cohesion as indicative of its overall functioning; the resulting four-by-four matrix yields 16 family types. The Beavers systems model provides the basis for a five-point observational rating scale—optimal, adequate, midrange, borderline, and severely disturbed—for evaluating family functioning. In the McMaster model, three major areas of current functioning (how the family handles basic tasks, developmental tasks, and hazardous tasks) are differentiated. The McMaster Clinical Rating Scale, based on the McMaster research model, investigates six aspects of family life (problem solving, communication, roles, affective responsiveness, affective involvement, and behavior control) and is intended to suggest the family's need for further counseling.

P A R T

T W O

# Counseling Families with Varied Lifestyles

# CHAPTER

# FOUR

# Counseling the Single-Parent–Led Family

While divorce has become a familiar and recognized fact of American life—approximately 1 million divorces occur annually in this country—it is never routine for the family members undergoing the often-agonizing experience and its aftermath. Indeed, for many if not most families, the decision to split up is often a traumatic event filled with uncertainty and perhaps even dread about the future. Moreover, despite its common occurrence, divorce may still frequently be greeted with shock and embarrassment, if not outright hostility, by family and friends (who may find themselves in the uncomfortable position of having to reevaluate their own marriages). According to Ahrons and Rodgers (1987), who urge that divorce be viewed as an enduring societal institution (much as marriage is perceived in our culture), many people still cling to the long-held attitude that divorce is inherently pathological; if two people are unable or unwilling to maintain a lifelong commitment, goes this argument, one or both partners must have some psychological defect or deficit. Divorcing partners, then, especially if young children are involved, must often deal with a sense of failure, of guilt over breaking up a home, of anguish at being labeled by many as socially deviant or morally weak—all at a time when significant life changes are taking place and important decisions about the future must be made.

For a variety of reasons, many of which we discussed in Chapter One, many couples are less willing today to make emotional compromises or remain in an unhappy situation for economic security, for the sake of the children, or for social appearances. No-fault divorce laws make divorce more readily obtainable, with

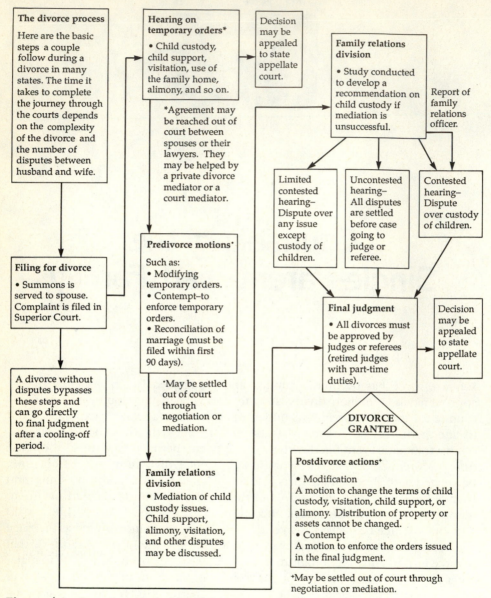

**Figure 4.1**  Steps in a Typical Legal Divorce Process
*Source:* Gullotta, Adams, and Alexander, 1986, p. 240.

less stigma of blame attached. Although most people are generally more accepting of divorce, families led by a single parent continue to be viewed as flawed or imperfect versions of the "normal" two-parent family.

In contrast with this commonly held view, studies by Morawetz and Walker (1984), Ahrons and Rodgers (1987), Mednick (1987), and others challenge the assumption that single-parent households represent some deviant family form; their findings indicate that good adjustment, well-being, and satisfaction with life are possible for single parents. Cashon (1982, p. 83), summarizing the published research of the previous decade on female-headed households, concludes that "the majority of families, when not plagued by poverty, are as successful as two-parent families in producing children with appropriate sex-role behavior, good emotional and intellectual adjustment, and non-delinquent behavior."

Confirmation for this view comes from an investigation of poor, minority-group, single-parent–headed families by Lindblad-Goldberg (1989). Her findings reveal that competence building is possible, and that many of the social/psychological problems often associated with growing up in a single-parent–led home are more a function of family poverty than of an inevitable breakdown in family structure. Viewing the single-parent–led family as an open system in transformation, she and her colleague Joyce Dukes found, in studying 126 African-American female-headed families with incomes well below the poverty line, that successful adaptation was related to the reciprocal processes of three dimensions: family resources, environmental stress, and social-network resources. In this framework, the family's internal resources involve its ability to organize itself and maintain its integration while adapting to changing events; executive hierarchy headed by a mother with a sense of control or mastery, clear boundary functioning, and workable family communication patterns are especially important here. The family's perception of stressful events in the external environment and its subsequent coping patterns also helped determine adaptation. Lastly, the family's ability to call upon outside resources such as friends and family for network support was critical. Overall, despite an absent mate, the single parent's effort to sustain a sense of family structure, while helping children develop coping skills, can develop and maintain family competence and stability, with support from others.

## VARIETIES OF SINGLE-PARENT HOUSEHOLDS

Before considering some of the issues encountered in counseling single-parent–led families, we should define our population. For our purposes, the term *single-parent household* is preferable to either *broken home* or simply *single-parent family*. *Broken home* is pejorative, implying that the family deserves second-class status because of the parental split, and that its subsequent vulnerability makes serious consequences inevitable. *Single-parent family* is misleading, in our opinion, in that it suggests that only one parent is involved after divorce. In point of fact, divorce does not necessarily mean that the family no longer exists, but only that the marital relationship has ended; particularly where children are involved, some form of family relationship with the absent parent or other extended family members probably continues, even if the parents are physically separated. Counseling such families, the counselor must keep in focus the impact of these outside family members (parent, siblings, grandparents) as much as those who live together under the same roof.

Marital disharmony leading to separation and divorce is perhaps the most easily recognized but hardly the only avenue to single-parent status; a separated or widowed parent and an unwed mother who gives birth to or adopts a child also require inclusion. Moreover, although families led by a single parent as a result of divorce have become highly visible in the last decade, such a family structure is not new but actually represents a traditional form of family organization in the United States.

Seward (1978) notes that between the mid-19th century and 1970, perhaps one out of ten families was maintained by one parent, most likely the mother. Especially in the earlier part of this period, death of a spouse and desertion were the most likely causes of parental absence. Only since the early 1970s, as Thompson and Gongla (1983) report, has that pattern changed. The proportion of single-parent–led households in the population has now doubled, to more than a quarter of all families with dependent children at home; separation and divorce are currently the most common causes of such families. As Figure 4.2 reveals, according to census data, the increase in one-parent households has continued to increase every decade since the 1970s. In the case of African-American families, unmarried mothers now outpace separated, divorced, or widowed mothers.

Clearly, single-parent–led families are not a homogeneous group. According to Hill (1986), and as shown in Figure 4.2, the overwhelming proportion are headed by females. This is confirmed by U.S. Bureau of the Census (1991a) findings, which indicate that, following divorce, 85% of children reside with their mothers.[1] These children are likely to spend an average of five years in a single-parent home before their custodial parents' remarriage. Divorced or widowed mothers themselves are not a unitary group, since it is important for the counselor to distinguish between those women who are temporarily single but will ultimately remarry and those who will not. These groups are likely to have different economic lives, different expectations concerning the future, and different sets of problems brought to the counselor.

For example, a temporarily single woman and her children, living for a period in a one-parent household, must later adapt to a stepfamily and to a possible return to childbearing (thus forcing the family to deal simultaneously with an infant/toddler and, say, an adolescent from the previous marriage). She is also vulnerable to a second divorce, and thus new marital transitions and household reorganizations, before returning to single-parent status. The single parent who does not remarry has a shorter period of childrearing, but statistically runs a far greater risk of financial impoverishment, to say nothing of increased feelings of loneliness and despair. She also may very likely find her single life ultimately unrewarding and find herself relegated to a status that is without honor or respect (Weiss, 1979).

---

[1]The primary focus of discussion in this section is on custodial mothers, since they represent the overwhelming proportion of single-parent–led families. However, although only 15% of the children from divorced homes live with their fathers rather than their mothers, the number (1.4 million) is still sizeable and is growing. In addition, fathers who share custody are actively involved in the upbringing of their children, although they do not reside in the same home. We intend to elaborate on custody issues later in this chapter.

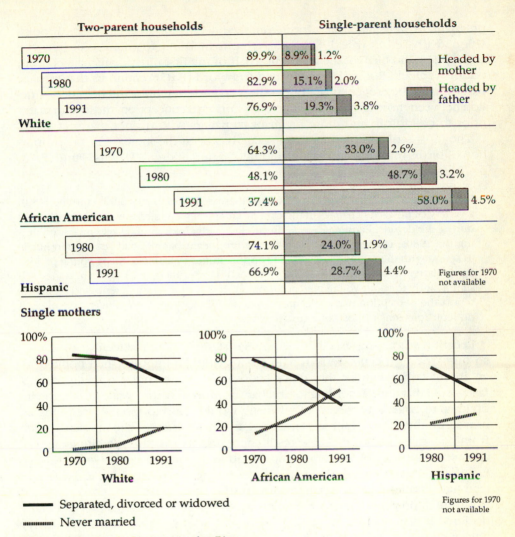

**Figure 4.2** Single Parents on the Rise

Although still a minority overall, never-married mothers are the fastest-growing group of single parents. Morrison (1991) has predicted that, by the year 2000, more than one out of every four children will be born to an unmarried mother. Since unmarried mothers as a group tend to be younger, poorer, less educated, and more dependent on welfare than their married counterparts at the time their child is born, the implications for providing adequate long-term social services and, for our purposes, counseling are staggering.

## TEENAGE MOTHERS

Teenage girls account for almost 20% of all births in the United States. Of these, close to two-thirds of white teen mothers were unmarried when they became pregnant, as were almost all African-American teens (97%) (Furstenberg, Brooks-Gunn, & Chase-Lansdale, 1989). Although one in four marry some time between conception and birth of the child, fully half of the first births to teenagers occur out of wedlock. Roosa, Fitzgerald, and Crawford (1985) remind us that teenage parents are a heterogeneous group, however, and they offer the helpful distinction between those teen couples who marry prior to conception, those who marry prior to childbirth, and those pregnant teenagers who do not marry at all.

The most striking trend in recent years has been the increase in the proportion of births that are to unmarried mothers. The Children's Defense Fund (1993, p. 7) offers the following observation:

> While there is no simple explanation for the increase in teen births during the late 1980s, a variety of powerful changes in the circumstances of teens and their families occurred during the decade. Economic stress on families with children of all ages increased during the 1980s; changes in work and family life meant parents had less time available to spend with their children; economic opportunities available to many young people, particularly those without a college education, declined; and median wages fell significantly for both young men and women. In addition, both parents and teenagers report the perception that social mores and popular culture increasingly have made it difficult for teens to postpone sexual activity.

Recent research suggests that the popular stereotype of the teenage mother—an unmarried African-American who comes from an impoverished home with an absent father and is either doing badly in school or has dropped out—is a false generalization. According to Abrahamse, Morrison, and Waite (1988), the individual teenager's awareness of what she would stand to lose by becoming an unwed mother is an important tempering factor in whether she protects herself from becoming pregnant. These researchers suggest that this inhibiting effect is apparent at all rungs of the socioeconomic ladder and across all races and ethnicity. Especially among young African-American women, those hoping to go to college have dramatically lower nonmarital birth rates than their peers.

Although pregnancy rates for sexually experienced adolescents have gradually declined in the last two decades, the proportion of pregnant teens who marry before childbirth has sharply decreased, so that today the vast majority are unmarried.[2] A reported 40% end their unintended pregnancies through abortion; proportionately, more abortions occur among younger than older teens, and among white than African-American adolescents.

Whites, especially those of higher socioeconomic status, are more apt to marry if pregnant, or to place their child for adoption (Burden & Klerman, 1984). However, no more than 3% of those white (1% of African-American) pregnant

---

[2]This trend toward remaining single and having a child out of wedlock is not restricted to teenagers. Davis (1985) reports a similar antimarriage tendency since the late 1960s among older women as well, in all Western nations. Chilman (1988) points out that the number of births outside marriage is actually higher for adult women in their 20s than for adolescents. The incidence of nonmarital childbearing in this older age group, as in the younger one, is higher for women who are African-American, unemployed, not currently enrolled in school, and have no education beyond high school.

adolescents who carry to term voluntarily choose adoption with unrelated families for their infants; that figure has steadily decreased in the last two decades (Sobol & Daly, 1992). African Americans as a group make greater use of informal adoption, whereby the infant is absorbed into the extended family.

Among all groups who place their infants for adoption, typical reasons given include: providing the baby with a family, feeling unprepared for parenthood, wanting to finish school, or lacking financial funds for proper care of the infant. Family pressures or pressures from physicians or social workers may also contribute to the decision. Although the long-term effect of such an important decision has not yet adequately been researched, Sobol and Daly (1992) note an enduring sense of loss as a recurrent theme; this is no doubt exacerbated by society's blocking of open grieving and the biological parent's restricted opportunities to participate, even indirectly, in the life of the child.

Puerto Ricans residing in the United States mainland show the highest level of households headed by unmarried female adolescents among all Hispanic groups and, correspondingly, have the highest rate of families living below the poverty line in that subgroup. Unexpected teenage pregnancy is likely to precipitate a crisis in the Puerto Rican family, such an event flying in the face of cultural legacies and traditional values. Gutierrez (1987) reports that initial parental rejection is typically followed by intense turmoil (emotional outbursts, threats of murder or suicide), as issues of family honor predominate. Ultimately, especially with the aid of counseling, some accommodation is reached, the inevitability of the situation is accepted, and practical issues of living arrangements and financial support, and later child care, are resolved.

Although younger girls may voice misgivings about becoming a single parent, those who choose to carry the fetus to term, as most do, become increasingly committed to that decision as their pregnancy proceeds (Furstenberg, Brooks-Gunn, & Chase-Lansdale, 1989).

Teenage girls with low academic ability from poor female-headed families are many times more likely to have a child out of wedlock than are those with high academic ability from upper-income intact families (Abrahamse, Morrison, & Waite, 1988). It is not uncommon for the teenage mother to call on parents or siblings for financial support and help with childrearing responsibilities and to rely on public assistance. Furstenberg, Brooks-Gunn, and Chase-Lansdale (1989) contend that early childbirth is a potent predictor of long-term welfare dependency, particularly because high school dropout is common and the probability of finding stable and remunerative employment is slim. Their long-term investigation reveals that adolescent fathers are usually less adversely affected, economically and scholastically, by early parenthood, although as a group they tend to have negative attitudes toward marriage, to doubt their parenting skills, and to drop out of high school.[3] Many never admit paternity and refuse to provide emotional or financial

---

[3]It is not yet clear from this research whether early male or female parenthood precedes or follows school dropout, since some teenagers leave school or show serious school problems before becoming pregnant. In addition, many adolescent mothers return to school after their children are themselves in a school situation. As for teenage fathers, there remains a paucity of research, and it should be noted that major problems may exist but at this point in our knowledge remain unrecognized.

support, even if able, which often is not the case. Others do continue to visit and show interest in the children and their mother, even if remaining unmarried.

Chilman (1988) contends that families of never-married adolescent parents are apt to have a high rate of poverty, a high rate of minority representation, a relatively low level of education, and little status in society. The offspring of teen mothers tend to show developmental disadvantages and to do less well in school; this is not unexpected since they are likely to have had poor prenatal care and to have grown up in disadvantaged neighborhoods, attended low-quality schools, and lived through high rates of family instability. Moreover, their mothers may be less equipped emotionally, or feel overburdened and depressed, or be less informed regarding desirable childrearing practices.

## ASSESSING SINGLE-PARENT–LED FAMILIES

In assessing single-parent–led families, the family counselor needs to explore the following factors:

How single parenthood came about (for example, through death, divorce, desertion, never married).

At what stage in the marriage that parent became single (for example, after 12 months of marriage or after 15 years).

The apparent precipitating factors of a marital breakup (for example, infidelity, chronic quarreling and dissatisfaction, in-law intrusions, immaturity of one or both partners, sexual incompatibilities, financial problems).

The number of children, the age of the children as well as the age of the parent at the time of becoming a single parent, the presence and degree of involvement of grandparents or other parts of an extended family.

The specific pile-up of stressor events preceding family dissolution (for example, constant fighting between parents about to separate, forcing the children to choose sides, threats and counterthreats between parents).

The specific pile-up of stressor events following dissolution and family reorganization (for example, moving to a new location, job, or school; making new friends; establishing a self-identity as a single person or as a member of a single-parent–led family).

The unfamiliar roles family members have been called upon to play (for example, as head of a one-parent household or as a child called upon to take on more adult responsibilities in the absence of the same-sex parent).

The role of the absent parent or other significant adult figures in the current single-parent family system.

The quality of relationships within the nuclear family, between the former mates and the family of origin, prior to the events leading to the dissolution of the marriage.

The nature and effectiveness of the single parent's coping skills, sense of mastery, and ability to organize and lead the family while adapting to new circumstances.

The single-parent family's relationship with broader social systems (schools, church, welfare, or legal systems).

In addition, the counselor needs to be aware that one-parent households led by fathers are likely to experience different sets of problems and different lifestyles from those led by mothers. Although fathers may have more money, as a rule, they too experience a drop in income and are more likely to have to buy housekeeping and child-care services, because they themselves generally have less experience of these tasks and feel less competent to deal with them. Moreover, fathers may need to resume a dependent relationship with their parents for help with raising the child, something many men (and women too) consider regressive and distasteful.

Counselors also need to attend to clients' social class, as well as racial and ethnic heritage, since these may provide clues as to how effectively and in what manner (for example, with extended-family involvement and community support) such families function. Standards for acceptable social behavior vary between social classes, and the counselor needs to be careful not to impose his or her standards on clients from different classes or ethnic groups.

The counselor needs also to appreciate that, while families led by a single parent may or may not share a common lifestyle, the more relevant point is that they probably share certain experiences. For example, families led by one parent, whether as a result of separation, divorce, or widowhood, all have experienced some loss. Thus, feelings of loneliness, sadness, guilt, and anger are inevitably present in some degree and in some combination. Morawetz and Walker (1984) report that women in such situations recount the same sets of problems: feeling overburdened, unsupported, and guilty over not being up to the task of raising a family alone. Finding adequate day care or making dependable babysitting arrangements, especially for very young children, almost always presents a difficult problem and often becomes a worrisome issue. The frequent case of a father severing contact with his ex-wife and his children, perhaps paying child support sporadically or not at all, only adds to the hardship and despair.

However, while the widowed person may dampen or even mute these wearisome feelings in time—indeed, may even comfort herself by exaggerating the positive memories of a previous spouse—the divorced person is far less likely to do so (Weiss, 1979). Part of the reason, of course, is that the divorced couple, especially if children are involved, may continue their conflict (now in the form of wrangles over child-support payments or child visitation) long after the legal divorce is final. In addition, as Getty (1981) points out, if the divorce was initiated by one spouse against the wishes of the other, then the latter, in particular, may be filled with feelings of failure, unworthiness, and self-doubt.

Consider, for example, the differences between the situations of an upper-middle-class, middle-aged widow with adolescent children and a young working-class divorced woman, briefly married and with a 2-year-old child. Whereas both may encounter problems trying to raise children on their own, differences in available resources may greatly influence their adaptation to a single life. The former was part of a reasonably happy, intact, nuclear family before her husband's sudden death, and as a widow, at least initially, can call upon a number of outside resources—family and friends—for support and comfort as she attempts to deal with her grief and loneliness and begins to forge a new life for herself.

❋    ❋    ❋    ❋    ❋

Margaret and Ted were married when they graduated from college. She worked for several years as an elementary school teacher while he continued into medical school and through an internship and residency program in ophthalmology. Once Ted established a practice as an ophthalmologist, however, family income was sufficient and they decided to start a family. Margaret had no hesitation in discontinuing her teaching job, since she had long looked forward to having and raising children. Together they had three children—two boys and a girl—and for 25 years Margaret and Ted lived a generally fulfilling and economically comfortable life. However, sudden disaster struck the family when Ted had a massive heart attack at work one day and died shortly thereafter, at age 50.

Unlike many single-parent–led families, Margaret and her children did not suffer severe economic upheaval, since Ted had provided well for their financial future, although their income was reduced. However, Margaret's loneliness was at times almost unbearable, particularly after the initial period when friends rallied to her side and invited her to their social get-togethers. After six months, few such invitations were forthcoming, and Margaret found herself, at age 49, depressed and alone, not knowing where or to whom to turn. One thing she was sure about, however, was that she must allow her children to lead their own lives, and not make them feel obligated or burdened by taking care of their mother. She did, nevertheless, feel responsible for offering them guidance to the best of her ability, although she often bemoaned the fact that she had to be both mother and father to them, and the strain of solo decision-making was taking its toll on her health.

As she slowly began, at the urging of her children, to socialize with old friends, she found herself being asked out on dates. Quickly she realized that she had had few experiences with men, having married Ted at such an early age, and that changing sexual mores were beyond her ability to accept. After six months, she had not found anyone to match her husband, whom she now missed more than ever.

Despite her good intentions, she did find herself leaning on her children. Concerned about their mother's chronic unhappiness and sudden dependence, and recognizing they too needed to deal with their grief over their father's death, the children suggested that they go together as a family for counseling sessions. With the counselor's help, after several months Margaret resumed dating and ultimately returned to graduate school to obtain training as a school psychologist.

❋    ❋    ❋    ❋    ❋

By way of contrast, now consider the case of Lynne, a young divorcee with few personal or familial resources, little education, and few job skills, with little in the way of social or emotional supports, and with the solo responsibility of raising a young child.

❋  ❋  ❋  ❋  ❋

Lynne, at 22, was the mother of a 2-year-old child. She had married Tom three years earlier after a brief romance, and their relationship had been filled with problems from the start. Ever since high school, Lynne had thought about settling down and being a housewife like her mother. She had just barely managed to graduate from high school, had few marketable skills, and had taken a number of jobs in fast-food restaurants in order to have some way to occupy her time. The work was unrewarding, and she was unable to afford her own apartment. When she met Tom, an auto mechanic, she moved in with him after knowing him one month, and shortly thereafter they were married. Despite their frequent quarrels, they were always able to "kiss and make up"; sex between them was very satisfying and frequently followed one of their prolonged arguments. After a year of marriage, they decided to have a baby. Lynne was sure that a child was exactly what the marriage needed to make it stronger.

Unfortunately, the arrival of Lisa, their daughter, only made matters worse. Tom was more worried about money now and, frustrated, complained that Lynne cared more for the baby than for him. Lynne, on the other hand, could not understand why her husband spent so little time with Lisa, and why he was so impatient when the baby cried or in some way interrupted his plans. The couple bickered more than ever, and their sex life, once a certain way to reduce conflict and drain off tension between them, became infrequent and mechanical. When Tom began staying away from home for hours and then days at a time, it was clear to Lynne that nothing was left in their marriage and she sued for divorce.

Although Lynne was awarded custody (uncontested by Tom) and a small amount of child-support money monthly, she soon realized that she needed to make some immediate decisions—where to live, how to get a job that paid enough so she could become the primary breadwinner, how to get adequate child care on her meager income. Tom soon got laid off from his job, and Lynne's fears concerning Tom's ultimate inability to pay child support soon proved to be well founded: his payments were late for the most part and often nonexistent. His visits with Lisa became less and less frequent, primarily because of his guilt and anger at the situation, and finally stopped after a year or so, leaving Lynne with all the child-rearing responsibilities.

Lisa soon began to show signs of stress, frequently waking at night and demanding she be allowed to sleep in her mother's bed for the rest of the night. When Tom told Lynne he was engaged to another woman and planned to remarry, the blow to her self-esteem was indescribable. The strain on Lynne became unbearable, financially, emotionally, and socially. Within eight months she had moved back home with her parents. Her mother reluctantly assumed daily child care for her grandchild, although she expressed some bitterness over the fact that she had assumed she was done with this stage of her life. Lynne's nighttime job as a cocktail waitress allowed her to be with Lisa during the afternoons; mornings and evenings, Lisa was cared for by the grandparents. Lynne's work schedule made dating all but impossible for her, although she occasionally went out with a customer when the bar closed.

❊   ❊   ❊   ❊   ❊

These cases illustrate some of the major themes a counselor will encounter in assessing a single-parent household:

Single parenthood is not necessarily a transitional stage on the way to remarriage, but rather a probable end point for many of today's families.

The life-cycle stage of the single parent at the time of separation determines, to a significant extent, the problems that are likely to be confronted (for example, an older woman might become widowed or divorced at a time when her children are themselves having family or marital difficulties; a younger woman is likely to be beset with many problems of child care as well as economic survival).

The age of the dependent children strongly influences the family's subsequent response and adaptation to separation. Widows are more likely to be older than divorced women and therefore, in general, are more likely to have older and thus more self-sufficient children; on the other hand, two-thirds of all women who divorce do so before age 30, and consequently most children are under age 7 at the time of divorce (Beal, 1980).

The duration and degree of intimacy of the marriage influences postseparation adjustment. Separation later in life reduces the options, especially for a woman, of developing another close long-term relationship; at the other extreme, very young parents, especially teenage mothers, probably have poorer parenting skills, and are economically and socially burdened in future relationships.

Since three-fifths of all children born today will, according to best estimates (Morrison, 1991), spend at least part of their childhood living with one parent, issues of child custody and visitation rights must be addressed and resolved.

One-parent families have differing resources and differing levels of organization; the single parent's coping skills and sense of mastery of her situation will influence her ability to maintain family integration while adapting to changing environmental stresses and the changing developmental needs of family members.

## COMMON PROBLEMS IN SINGLE-PARENT–LED FAMILIES

After a divorce, as nuclear-family ties are disrupted, various adjustments and rearrangements are called for. Most children, especially those below the age of 12, will live with a custodial mother; they may see their father on a regular weekly (in rare cases, daily) basis, intermittently, or not at all. Inevitably, the divorce and its immediate aftermath is a critical experience that affects the entire family system. No one is immune. The functioning and interactions of all of the members are changed permanently. As Hodges (1991) observes, parents remain under significant stress prior to divorce and immediately thereafter, as they attempt to deal with separation and redirecting their lives; as a result, they may have limited ability to be helpful to their children during this time.

Hetherington, Cox, and Cox (1982) point to two factors that require attention in appraising the impact of the divorce. To begin with, the outcome of divorce will affect each member differently, depending on that individual's personal stresses, support systems, and coping strategies. Parents and children differ in their coping styles and abilities; children of different ages call upon different resources. These authors note that the needs and adaptive strategies of different family members are not always compatible. Indeed, "the pathway to well-being for one family member may lead to a disastrous outcome for another" (p. 234).

Second, Hetherington, Cox, and Cox (1982) remind us that it would be a mistake to view divorce as an event occurring at a single point in time. Rather, an extended transition is usually required, for parents and children alike. Moreover, in some families, the sequelae of divorce (emotional distress, denial, depression, anger, loss of self-esteem) occur immediately following parental separation; for others, these effects may increase over the first year and then abate; for still other families, such signs may not emerge until a considerable period of time has passed. In the long run, however, according to Furstenberg and Cherlin (1991), a child's adaptation to divorce depends primarily on the extent to which the custodial person is seen as a source of support, and on the level of conflict that continues between the ex-spouses.

For pedagogical purposes, we will consider the impact of divorce separately for the various family members—the custodial parent, the noncustodial parent, and the children. In point of fact, of course, the different parts of the family system cannot be so easily separated; each impacts on the other. All changes associated with marital transitions must be considered from the perspective of changes in the entire family system and its various subsystems. Moreover, the responses of all participants will be affected by the larger social milieu in which they function: peer groups, friendship networks, schools, neighborhood, workplace, and extended families (Hetheringon, 1993). There is great diversity in the responses of both parents and children to separation and divorce. Our intent is to alert the counselor to common responses from all family members to the divorce process and its immediate and subsequent aftermath.

## THE CUSTODIAL PARENT

Box 4.1 offers the counselor an overview of some typical problem areas to explore with custodial single parents. As we have noted a number of times, economic impoverishment is more likely than not to be a daily fact of life, particularly for

---

**Box 4.1   A Problem-Appraisal Checklist for Custodial Single Parents**

Custodial single parents may experience problems in the following areas:

- Change in economic status (for most, especially women, this translates into economic hardship)
- Grief, self-blame, loss of self-esteem, and depression
- Role overload (attempting to play a multitude of roles—such as organizing a household, caring for children, producing income—previously divided between both parents)
- Social stigma and disapproval over being divorced
- Disruption of customary living arrangements (may include change in residence, community, school district for children, and return to work force)
- Loneliness, feeling of social isolation, loss of friends (especially married couples), need to develop new social circle
- Lack of adequate support system (formerly provided by mate, in-laws, friends in old community)
- Strain from solo decision-making (taking major or perhaps full responsibility for family decisions, unlike past experiences in which such judgments were likely to have been shared or at least discussed)
- Child-care arrangements (depending on the age of the child or children of the parent working or returning to school, this may require considerable planning, energy expenditure, and flexibility in schedule, particularly in the case of illness of the child or parent)
- Interpersonal conflict (with children, ex-spouse, parents and former in-laws, babysitters, lovers, roommates)
- Sex and dating (new person introduced into family circle, decisions regarding resumption of a sex life, concern over reactions of children)
- Custody and visitation (continued relations with ex-spouse, concern over child's loyalty, upset as children are introduced to new friends or lovers of ex-spouse)

---

women raising young children alone.[4] As Thompson and Gongla (1983) report, considerable evidence exists that low incomes, high rates of poverty, and fewer employment opportunities are characteristic in such situations. They contend that the major problem faced by women in such cases is not the lack of a male's presence but the lack of a male income.

---

[4]Research on custodial fathers has been meager, probably because this situation is relatively new and is just now receiving the attention of social scientists. For the discussion to follow then, we will assume, as we have throughout this chapter, that the mother has physical custody of the children. In those cases where fathers achieve physical custody, it is likely to be decided out of court and by mutual consent of both parents. Nevertheless, it should be noted that, in addition to joint physical custody, some fathers are starting to gain sole custody through court battles, especially if the ex-wife is judged to be incompetent or otherwise unfit to have custody, or if the fathers have remarried and the ex-spouse has not. Greif (1985) found that the father's possibly better financial situation, emotional stability, or personality fit with the child were determining factors in such decisions.

Pearce (1978) has coined the phrase *feminization of poverty* to characterize the typical problems of such women, many of whom are unemployed and on welfare. Even among those who are fortunate enough to have a full-time job, Mednick (1987) estimates that women heading their own families have a poverty rate that is 2.5 times that of the two-parent family. Part-time and unemployed women workers are, of course, even worse off. Sometimes, as we saw in the case just presented, a woman may move back as an adult and custodial parent to her own parents' home, although this makeshift solution may itself add other sources of stress. Taking in lodgers to share expenses or moving in with other women in similar straits are other possible solutions, again with potential problems.

Norton and Glick (1986) summarize the economic circumstances of most one-parent families in general and mother-child families in particular as follows:

By most objective measurements, the vast majority of these families hold a disadvantageous position in society relative to other family groups. They are characterized by a high rate of poverty, a high percentage of minority representation, relatively low education, and a high rate of mobility. In short, as a group, they generally have little equity of status in American society and constitute a group with usually pressing social and economic needs. (p. 16)

Mothers with sole custody (particularly if the father has opted out, or been closed out, of the reorganized family system) are frequently overburdened by responsibilities and become depressed (Brandwein, Brown, & Fox, 1974). Belle (1982) notes that one in three female-headed households lives in poverty; those women who live in financially strained circumstances and who have responsibilities for young children are particularly prone to feelings of hopelessness, loss of energy, and depression. According to Henggeler and Borduin (1990), the financial impact of the divorce may contribute to a number of psychosocial problems within the family, including the mother's depression and withdrawal from friends, the children's relative lack of interaction with their peers, and disturbances in the mother-child relationships. Solo responsibility for the management of child discipline often becomes an overwhelming task for an already-harassed single parent, especially if the child evidences increased behavior problems in response to the stress and conflict surrounding the divorce.

Makosky (1982), a participant in the Stress and Families Project funded by the National Institute of Mental Health, found that low-income mothers with young children represent a particularly high-risk group for mental health problems. This group is constantly confronted with having to adjust to stressful life events, as we have indicated in Box 4.1. The group of women at greatest risk, however, are those who have endured the most difficult ongoing life conditions during the previous two years. According to Makosky's data, the critical attribute in the majority of cases is low income.

It is hardly a surprise to learn that money problems pose a severe stress on people, or that one result is often depression. Of more significance, psychologically speaking, may be the mother's *change* in economic standing and the subsequent fear of losing control over her own life, as well as the lives of children for whom she feels responsible. When Bould (1977) interviewed mothers with sole custody whose situation was long-standing, she found that those women who had developed a stable income, regardless of amount, were more likely to have achieved higher self-esteem than those who stayed at home. As Mednick (1987) notes, the sense of control over income and the feeling of being effective as a self-supporter represent significant predictors of life satisfaction and reduced stress. Together, they help diminish the inevitable sense of powerlessness to which custodial mothers are so vulnerable, particularly in the period immediately following the divorce.

Hetherington, Cox, and Cox (1982) have this to report as the result of their two-year investigation of the impact of divorce on families (the Virginia Longitudinal Study of Divorce):

> The main areas (for the custodial parent) in which change and stress were experienced were, first, those related to practical problems of living such as economic and occupational problems and problems in running a household; second, those associated with emotional distress and changes in self-concept and identity; and third, interpersonal problems in maintaining a social life, in the development of intimate relationships, and in interactions with the ex-spouse and child. (p. 244)

## THE NONCUSTODIAL PARENT

Noncustodial parent roles vary widely, from a cessation of contact with ex-spouse and children (a closed boundary) to remaining a vital part of the family despite living separately (as in the binuclear family). Where any one person fits on this continuum depends largely on his or her previous role in the family system, interest, and availability, and on the freedom of access permitted by the custodial parent.

Generally speaking, if the parent living outside the family retains some sense of influence over the children's upbringing, he (or she) remains involved in visiting them and contributing financially to their support. On the other hand, feeling disenfranchised and without input into how the children are raised, the excluded parent is less likely to continue contributing child support and may ultimately relinquish any emotional involvement with the children (Braver et al., 1993).

In some cases, as Morawetz and Walker (1984) report, the level of fury toward the noncustodial spouse, who is seen as abandoning or betraying the marriage, is so great that the counselor will meet strong resistance when attempting to help family members work through their feelings about the divorce. In such situations, the absent spouse may be kept from the children on one pretext or another, or may be scapegoated or called names ("untrustworthy," "cruel," "crazy") by the custodial parent. The custodial parent may attempt to coerce the children into sharing his or her rage, as a sign of their loyalty. Not only does this place the children in conflict, but it also forces the noncustodial parent into becoming an outsider. That parent's reaction, in defense, is to distance himself or herself from the family, thereby perhaps confirming his or her indifference and irresponsibility in the others' eyes.

Box 4.2 is intended to alert the counselor to the possible problem areas to consider with noncustodial parents. Beyond the divorce itself, which may be a prolonged and often embittering process, the result in a great many cases leaves the noncustodial parent feeling deprived of ongoing involvement with the children. (The negative consequences of the separation for the children will be discussed in the following section.) From his survey of available research, Hodges (1991) concluded that, although women were more likely than men to articulate their distress about marital conflict prior to the separation, men have more difficulty recovering from the divorce than do women.

When Hetherington, Cox, and Cox (1976) studied the effects of divorce on noncustodial fathers, they found that, of all the necessary adjustments, the most compelling was the pervasive sense of loss regarding the children. Many of the men, particularly those who had been highly involved, affectionate parents while

---

### Box 4.2   A Problem-Appraisal Checklist for Noncustodial Parents

Noncustodial parents may experience problems in the following areas:

- Change in economic status (lowered living standard due to contributing to the support of two homes)
- Diminished relationship with their children (pain over loss of day-to-day sense of what's happening in their lives)
- Feeling of devaluation as a parent (no longer feeling important and necessary in the lives of their children)
- Disruption of customary living arrangements (change of residence, feeling of starting over, loss of friends)
- Necessity of learning to cope with new tasks (especially for men, having to provide own care, feeding, cleaning, and other services formerly provided by mother or wife)
- Development of new connections with children (including visitation activities, providing a space for children to spend the night, making purchases unilaterally that may provoke the ex-mate)
- Social stigma and disapproval over being divorced
- Necessity of dealing with recurrent memories whenever returning to pick up children
- Grief, self-blame, loss of self-esteem, and depression
- Loneliness, feeling of being at loose ends, need to develop new social circle
- Interpersonal conflict (with children, ex-spouse, parents and former in-laws, lovers, roommates)
- Necessity of learning to deal with events to which parents in intact families go together (school open house, graduation, weddings, funerals), especially when former partner has new mate
- Sex and dating (decisions regarding resumption of a sex life, concern over child meeting new lover, especially if that person has children)
- Custody and visitation (planning activities may be an unfamiliar experience, being sole caretaker may be difficult if young child is involved)

married, reported that they could not tolerate seeing their children only intermittently. Two years after the divorce, these fathers had diminished the frequency
of their contact with their children in an effort to lessen their own unhappiness.
Nevertheless, they continued to feel depressed and to mourn the loss. Greif (1979)
also found in studying middle-class divorced fathers that many dealt with the
pain of separation by distancing themselves from the children. Many of these men
developed physical symptoms (weight loss, hypertension, headaches) following
separation from their wives, and those who especially experienced the loss of
their children manifested signs of depression (sleeping, eating, working, and
socializing problems).

What of fathers who had limited contact with their children while the family
was intact? Wallerstein and Kelly (1980a) discovered that their predivorce father-
child connection was a poor predictor of their postdivorce relationship. In many
cases they became closer to their children and more involved in their children's
activities than they had been before the family reorganization. For most children,
especially the younger ones, these researchers found such an increase in closeness
to be particularly beneficial.

As we noted for custodial parents, the divorced father is most at risk for
psychological disturbance around the time of the marital separation. **Crisis intervention** by the counselor may be necessary at that time, perhaps followed
by more exploratory forms of counseling after the crisis has abated. Jacobs (1982)
urges the counselor to try to remain flexible, shifting back and forth between
treatment of the individual, the couple, and the entire family as needed. As he
advocates, the counselor must remain aware that, in most cases, it is in the best
interests of all family members that both parents be as actively engaged as possible with the children.

## THE CHILDREN

Every family experiences impaired functioning during and after a divorce. For
many children, parental separation and divorce mean exposure to a series of marital
transitions and household reorganizations that often prove to be disruptive
(Hetherington, Stanley-Hagan, & Anderson, 1989). Although generally speaking
the child's adaptation is related to the adaptation and behavior of the parents,
it should be noted that in some cases the decision to divorce may improve parental
well-being but at the same time have a detrimental effect on their offspring.

Box 4.3 outlines some of the results of the ordeal for children. The emotional
impact of the experience is perhaps most telling for younger children (elementary
school age and below), precisely because they are not able to comprehend the
events unfolding around them, while at the same time they sense the emotional
upheaval in their parents, on whom they depend for their security (Kurdek, 1981).
The most severe reactions are likely to occur in those cases where young children
are not given an explanation regarding the disappearance of their absent father
(Wallerstein & Kelly, 1975). Such distress is liable to continue for a considerable
time, as the parents go through a period of mourning for the lost marriage. Parents

---

**Box 4.3    A Problem-Appraisal Checklist for Children of Divorced Parents**

Children may experience problems in the following areas when their parents divorce:

- Shame, embarrassment, lowered self-esteem
- Diminished relationship with noncustodial parent
- Self-blame for parental split
- Depression, sadness, moodiness, emotional withdrawal
- Conflicting loyalties (upset and anger over being caught between feelings for both parents)
- Continuing fantasies of parental reconciliation
- Anger and rage at both parents (blame of custodial parent for the other parent's absence; blame of noncustodial parent for leaving)
- Anxiety over an uncertain or unfamiliar future
- Parentification (prematurely pressed to act as adult, overattached to custodial parent, and pressed to act as a surrogate parent to younger children)
- Lowered economic status
- Disruption of customary living arrangements (new school, new home, new friends)
- Antisocial behavior, poor school performance
- Adaptation to visitation activities
- Response to parent dating (diversion of parental attention to person outside previous family; fear of being replaced by parent's new friend)
- Fear of loss and abandonment if custodial parent is absent

---

frequently can profit from counselor guidance at this point in telling the children of the parental decision to divorce, as well as receiving help in managing their own grief.

Hetherington, Stanley-Hagan, and Anderson (1989) found that, despite initial distress, most children adapt to living in a single-parent household within two or three years if their new situation is not compounded by continued or additional adversity. Nevertheless, during that period they may display aggressive, noncompliant, acting-out behavior, or perhaps experience academic or other school-related difficulties or disruptions in relationships with peers. Despite these difficulties in some children, however, the researchers found that children overall ultimately adapt better to a well-functioning single-parent—led family or stepfamily than to a conflict-ridden family of origin. Counselors often can help clients decide whether to stay together for the sake of the children by informing them of this fact.

Age at time of separation and divorce offers important clues regarding eventual adaptation in children. In a long-term comprehensive research undertaking, the California Children of Divorce Project, Wallerstein and Kelly (1974, 1975, 1976) studied the reactions of 60 divorced families over a five-year period. In all, 131 children, ages 2 to 18, took part. While preschool children tended to react with denial ("It's not happening to me"; "When is daddy coming home?") and on the surface appeared to be untroubled, many were found on closer inspection to be anxious and self-blaming for the breakup of the family. Fears of abandonment, regression in toilet training, clinging behavior, temper tantrums, and fantasies regarding parental reconciliation were common, although, according to a follow-up ten years later by Wallerstein, Corbin, and Lewis (1988), they had few memories of earlier fears and suffering. Hodges (1991) reports that preschool children of younger parents with fewer resources and lower income are likely to have more difficulty with parental separation and divorce than the children of older or more affluent parents. In many cases this is probably because the latter group has more time and resources to attend to the needs of these youngsters.

Slightly older children (7 or 8 years of age) were more apt to become withdrawn and uncommunicative about their feelings and to become depressed. School problems and difficulties in making new friends were common reactions. Children aged 9 or 10 at the time of family dissolution were more likely to be angry and ashamed and to verbalize blame at the parents for what they felt they were being put through. Adolescents as a group were more successful at making sense out of what had happened and why the marriage had failed; in many cases, they resolved loyalty conflicts and even saw the decision by their parents to divorce as a good one.

In a five-year follow-up of all the children, Wallerstein and Kelly (1980b) discovered considerable differences in how well they had resolved their earlier experiences. In those instances where bitterness and interparental conflict continued (or perhaps even escalated), and where a parent sought alliances with the children against the ex-spouse, postdivorce adaptation was seriously impaired. In such cases, children's disturbed behavior patterns were more a reaction to what was going on at present than what had transpired in the past when the family was intact. For the 37% of the sample who showed clinical signs of depression, the war between the parents had continued into the postdivorce period.

On the other hand, both Wallerstein and Kelly (1980b) and Hetherington, Cox, and Cox (1982), who conducted a two-year longitudinal study of 144 white middle-class families with children (half from divorced families, half from intact families; half girls, half boys), reach the same conclusion: to the extent that acrimony between ex-spouses can be reduced and the noncustodial parent can remain involved and offer support to the ex-spouse, the children can get on successfully with their lives.

Hetherington, Cox, and Cox (1982) found, in a study of mother-custody families, that families in which a divorce has occurred tend to encounter many more stresses than do nondivorced families and, correspondingly, contain members who show more personal signs of disturbance. However, as noted earlier, if the divorce is not compounded by continued postdivorce conflict, both parents and their children (average age: 6 years) are likely to adjust to the new family situation, usually within two to three years.

Counselors, then, need to help single parents identify and develop effective support systems in order to aid in the transitions associated with the divorce process. Data from both Wallerstein and Kelly (1980b) and Hetherington, Cox, and Cox (1982) suggest that, within the family system, a child's adaption to the family reorganization in the postdivorce recovery period is probably more influenced by the nature of any ongoing discord between the parents than by the divorce action itself. Citing such data, counselors may be able to persuade divorced parents to work cooperatively in dealing with their children, precisely because such united action will help in the children's adaptation.

Counselors should note, however, that boys living with custodial mothers typically have a more difficult time adjusting to separation and divorce than do girls. Moreover, compared to boys from nondivorced families, boys living with single divorced mothers have been found to show more problems in their interpersonal relations at home and also with teachers and other children at school. Girls from divorced homes, on the other hand, have been found to function well after the two-year crisis period, and generally experience positive relations with their custodial mothers.[5]

In a follow-up study of family relations six years after divorce, Hetherington (1987) expanded her sample to 180 families, including 124 of the families from the original longitudinal study. In general, she found that custodial mothers who had not remarried had more emotional problems and were less satisfied with their lives than those who had never divorced or had divorced and remarried. Once again, she found that, even after six years, divorced mothers continued to struggle "in intense, ambivalent relationships and in coercive cycles with their sons" (Hetherington, 1987, p. 203), whereas their relationships with their daughters tended to be positive ones. Many boys, now an average of 10 years of age, also showed behavioral problems such as noncompliant, impulsive, aggressive behavior.

## CHILD CUSTODY, VISITATION, AND CHILD SUPPORT

The dissolution of a marriage by no means needs to signal the dissolution of the child's relationship with the nonresident parent. Increasingly, for a variety of legal, financial, and also psychological reasons, the courts have deemed it best for all concerned that a shared or co-parenting custody arrangement be worked out, if at all feasible, between divorcing parents. In this way, the child continues to have the benefit of frequent contact with both parents; bitter, drawn-out custody battles are avoided; the nonresidential parent is more apt to remain involved (and to continue child support) rather than drift away or be kept away from the children; and there is a substantial reduction in the incidence of kidnapping by a disgruntled, embittered parent who acts out his or her anger at the court or former mate by running off with the child.

[5]As Hetherington (1987) acknowledges, there is some indication from other studies that children adjust better in the custody of same-sex parents. Age may also be a factor in sex-differential responses: reports of more severe, long-lasting disruption of behavior in boys than in girls following parental divorce generally come from studies of preadolescent children. Wallerstein (1988) has suggested that boys, especially young boys, may have a more difficult time immediately following a divorce, but girls from divorced homes actually may have a more stormy adolescence and a conflict-ridden entry into young adulthood.

Pressures on an overburdened single parent, possibly leading to child neglect or abuse, can be lessened when the responsibilities for child care are shared. Changing custody arrangements also permit women choices beyond the traditional ones of custodial mothers. The social stigma or personal guilt formerly inflicted on women who chose to give up or share custody of their children is less severe today, but still exists for many women, especially if they choose to yield sole custody to their former husbands.

Historically, before the 19th century, women and children were considered part of a man's property. From the time of early English common law, the father as household head had been awarded child custody after a marriage breakup unless it could be established that he was an unfit parent. Such reasoning was based on fathers' better ability to provide economically for their children (Derdeyn, 1976). That standard began to change in the latter half of the 19th century when the criterion of *tender years* was introduced into custody decisions. Mothers were now considered to be in a better position to provide for their children's welfare, particularly in the case of minor children of tender years. In the United States, the dramatic increase in divorce rates, as well as the corresponding liberalization of social attitudes regarding alternative family lifestyles, led to the altered custody law that in general used the criterion of *the best interests of the child* as a yardstick for such decisions.

By the 1970s, the gender-based bias favoring maternal custody had begun to change once again, and judges began to exert a great deal of discretionary power in determining what custody arrangement was in the child's best interest. These changes came about through two sources: lobbying for men's custody rights by the men's movement; and the widespread passage of *no-fault* divorce laws, first enacted in 1970 in California and now the law in all 50 states. By granting a divorce without imputing wrongdoing or assigning blame for the no longer viable marriage, divorce was acknowledged by the state to be an acceptable part of a pluralistic society, like marriage a matter of individual choice; thus its dissolution need not inevitably lead to finger-pointing (one innocent party, one guilty one) and subsequent acrimony (Emery, 1988). Without accusing either partner of any offense, the marriage is simply declared to be unworkable because of undefined *irreconcilable differences* and then dissolved. Child custody remains based on the now gender-neutral principle of who serves the best interests of the child. However, Bray (1988) contends that, despite these recent changes, many men still insist that a sex bias favoring women as custodial parents exists.

## CUSTODY ALTERNATIVES

Today, there is no uniform child custody law for the entire United States, although the laws in all of the states are similar in that a child's welfare remains the prime factor in determining custody (Howell & Toepke, 1984). As of 1984, the majority of states (28) held that neither parent is to be preferred over the other in awarding custody; the child's wishes were to be considered, although not binding, in 33 states; 22 states specifically provided for joint custody. Clearly, counselors need to be informed regarding choices available to parents in their particular state, and can serve a useful function by helping divorcing couples clarify issues before reaching the more adversarial confines of competing attorneys' offices. Counselors working as mediators, as discussed in Chapter One, can be especially helpful here in helping arrange visitation schedules and support payments.

Custody decisions, along with determinations of child support payments and visitation rights for the nonresidential parent, are made during the divorce process (see Figure 4.1). A number of alternate arrangements, established by parental agreement or judicial decision, are possible. According to Schwartz (1987), they include:

**sole custody**: one parent is awarded total physical and legal responsibility for the children; the noncustodial parent has no legal right to make decisions regarding the children but is usually awarded visitation rights;

**joint legal custody**: both parents share legal responsibilities and together participate in the major decisions regarding their children, such as religious upbringing or choice of school;

**split custody**: each parent is awarded the full legal custody of one or more of the children (for example, girls with mother, boys with father), or the children alternate living with the noncustodial parent on weekends or during vacations.

Sole custody, in most cases by the mother, remains the most common pattern, despite recent increases in some fathers' efforts to participate with their children following divorce (Clingempeel & Reppucci, 1982). Split custody is least probable, since such an arrangement may compound a child's sense of loss of the other children (Hodges, 1991). Under a sole-custody arrangement, fathers have visitation rights, plus any additional rights or privileges agreed upon in the divorce settlement.

Joint custody is an increasingly popular arrangement in which both parents have equal authority in regard to their children's general welfare, education, and parenting. In practice, it may take a number of forms. Generally speaking, the most common plan of joint custody is for the children to reside in one home and for the other parent to have access to them. Obviously, this arrangement works best when the ex-mates are each caring and committed parents, can be cooperative, have relatively equal parenting skills, and are able to work together without renewing old animosities.

In some states, such as California, joint legal custody is presumed in all divorces unless a ruling to the contrary is made. As noted previously, under this arrangement each ex-spouse retains legal rights, privileges, and responsibilities as a parent. However, joint legal custody does not necessarily mean shared parenting on a daily basis. The child's primary residence is likely to remain with one parent, but the child may also live with or have access to the other parent at specified times.

In a variation of joint custody called **joint physical custody** (sometimes confused with joint legal custody), both parents take part in the day-to-day care of their children and all necessary decision-making, although the parents may live separately. The family continues to function as when they were intact, at least as far as the children are concerned. For the children's part, they may move between households every week or every month, or perhaps spend weekdays with one parent and weekends with the other; in some cases, they may even alternate during each week, spending three days with one parent and four days with the other, who usually lives in the same vicinity so that the children are able to attend the same school. In relatively rare cases, the children remain in the family home while the parents take turns moving in or staying at another residence.[6]

According to Hodges (1991), successful voluntary joint physical custody can increase the children's satisfaction because they have access to both parents, both of whom are playing familiar parenting roles. In addition, such an arrangement allows parents to consult a counselor on an intermittent basis to help sort out day-to-day conflicts; this proves particularly successful if the counselor is familiar to the couple from earlier counseling, and trust and fair play have been previously established.

Although legal and physical custody arrangements may be jointly agreed upon, in practice they may not work quite as neatly or be as conflict-free as we have outlined. Such an arrangement can be confusing, particularly to very young children or those with emotional problems, for whom the plan may be anxiety-provoking (Irving, Benjamin, & Trocme, 1984). Not unexpectedly, in some cases the arrangements made for custody, visitation rights, and child support payments simply provide additional arenas for battle between combatants, particularly those who remain intensely angry and bitter over what they perceive to be past injustices. Wallerstein (1986), in a follow-up of the women from her California Children of Divorce Project, reported that anger associated with divorce can persist ten years after dissolution of the marriage, even into remarriage; such chronic bitterness can continue to infuse interactions with the ex-mate in regard to the children. According to her data, the ongoing anger, rooted in a sense of outrage and betrayal, was especially prevalent in those women who had been married to their ex-mate for an extended period of their adult years.

Such sustained antagonism is not inevitable, of course, depending on how well previous problems can be resolved once the couple is apart, or perhaps merely accepted and lived with in order for both people to continue to be effective parents. In a large number of cases, a *declined relationship* (Duck, 1982) exists, with a moderate amount of interaction and shared information about issues related to the children, and perhaps even an element of friendship.

---

[6]The controversy among experts over the relative merits of joint custody compared to sole custody continues today. Those in favor of the former emphasize the importance of the father's contribution to the child's ultimate well-being, citing evidence by Wallerstein and Kelly (1980a) and others. Their influence has been felt particularly on the West Coast; according to Richards and Goldenberg (1985), 45% of all awards in Los Angeles in 1983 gave joint custody, while an additional 7% awarded joint physical custody. East Coast legal thinking is more apt to be influenced by the writings of Goldstein, Freud, and Solnit (1979), who argue that children need continuity of psychological care from one parent and that shared parental decision-making promotes conflict. Data offered by Richards and Goldenberg (1985) indicate that, in New Jersey in 1983, only three reported decisions affirmed joint custody.

Ahrons and Rodgers (1987), referring to the binuclear family (two households, one family), observes five distinct types of relationships between former marital partners:

*Perfect pals:* still friends; jointly decided to live separate lives but retain mutual respect; in earlier generations would probably not have gotten divorced; may have had some anger during separation but now each considers the other a responsible and caring parent; still in some conflict at times, but accommodating to one another overall.

*Cooperative colleagues:* no longer good friends but able to cooperate successfully as parents; may no longer like each other in many ways but recognize need to compromise for the sake of the children and to fulfill own desires to be active and responsible parents; some current disagreements but able to avoid escalating power struggles.

*Angry associates:* still bitter and resentful about the marriage and the divorce process; continuous fights over finances, visitation schedules, custody arrangements; each continues parenting but children often caught in ongoing loyalty conflicts.

*Fiery foes:* no ability to coparent; intense anger, even years after divorce; perceive one another as enemies; each parent may have limited parenting ability; continuing legal battles; children caught in the middle and forced to take sides; noncustodial parent probably sees children with decreasing frequency over the years.

*Dissolved duos:* discontinued contact between former partners after divorce; one partner may leave geographic area; kidnapping by noncustodial parent may occur; truly single-parent family.

These authors offer the following illustration of the reactions of each of the relationship types to a child's high school graduation: (1) perfect pals plan dinner out together, sit together during the ceremony, perhaps give one joint gift; (2) cooperative colleagues both attend the ceremony but, if sitting together, do so under some strain; (3) angry associates celebrate separately with the child, sit separately at the ceremony, and avoid contact as much as possible; (4) in the case of fiery foes, one parent is excluded from the celebration and perhaps from the ceremony itself, and feels hurt and angry; (5) in dissolved duos, the custodial parent does not bother informing the ex-spouse of the graduation; the noncustodial parent would not acknowledge the event if aware of it.

## SOME COUNSELING GUIDELINES

Families headed by one parent are typically formed as a result of crisis—a failed marriage, widowhood, an unexpected pregnancy in the life of an unmarried teenager or young adult. As a result, an early family task frequently involves organizing (or reorganizing) the family unit and beginning the process of stabilization by learning effective coping strategies that may be used to deal with the uncertainty ahead. One central issue apt to require immediate attention is the definition (or redefinition) of family *boundaries,* as family members take on many new and unfamiliar tasks and responsibilities.

The custodial mother must learn to establish family rules, delineate responsibilities, and often learn to impose child discipline singlehandedly and deal with other psychosocial problems almost certain to erupt in the children, all at a time when she herself is in a weakened and perhaps frightened and depressed state. She must learn to live in a society organized around two-parent families (for example, in interactions with schools), cope with the children's often unstated but felt reactions to the separation and the absence of their father, and at the same time try to develop a plan for earning money while providing adequate child care for her offspring. In the case of low-income families, she must endure minimum-wage jobs, learn to initiate and ultimately cope with the welfare system, obtain employment training, and get affordable housing if not living with her extended family. As Hodges (1991) notes, the lack of another parent to serve as a buffer or provide social support means that single mothers are more vulnerable to the hurt and anger experienced by their children. Inevitably this increases the pain associated with parenting and may lead to inappropriate problem solving.

Children living with one parent need to adjust to the often-painful prospect of not seeing one parent on a daily basis. At the same time, an additional series of adjustments may have to be made: to a change of school, new friends, a changed relationship with the noncustodial parent and any possible new mates, self-consciousness about the divorce, reduced money and activity—all at the time of grieving for the breakup of the family as they knew it.

Working therapeutically with a single-parent–led family, the counselor must never lose sight of the psychological presence of the other parent, even if, as is likely, that person is physically absent from the consultation room. To ignore the "ghosts" of the earlier marriage, by focusing on the parent-child dyad alone, is to ignore that the absent person (or the memories of that person) may continue to exert considerable influence on what transpires between those presently attending.

❆    ❆    ❆    ❆    ❆

After a bitterly fought divorce, in which Linda would settle for nothing less than sole custody of Craig, their 12-year-old only child, she soon found that the boy was simply adding to her unhappiness. He was a constant reminder, in appearance, mannerism, voice, and behavior, of his father. To make matters worse, the more she vilified her ex-husband, the more Craig defended him and complained about not having him near anymore. Whenever Craig was with his dad, his dad told him what a miserable person his mother had been to live with, attempting to justify his departure to his son. The pressures from both parents for his undivided loyalty began to take their toll on Craig, who became sullen, angry, and withdrawn. Soon a battle began to rage between mother and son; he became increasingly defiant and she continued issuing gloomy forecasts to him about how he would turn out to be just like his father. Counseling for the two focused on working through previously unexpressed feelings about the divorce on both their parts, and creating a less bitter home environment. The father attended several sessions and, while his relationship with his ex-wife was no more loving, they were able to tolerate one another better and not use Craig to get back at one another.

❃ ❃ ❃ ❃ ❃

On the other hand, the ghost may be the spouse who met an untimely death:

❃ ❃ ❃ ❃ ❃

Hilda and Charles had had a solid and loving marriage for 14 years when he succumbed to cancer. Although the death was by no means sudden—his dying stretched out over a year and a half—Hilda felt devastated when it actually occurred. Beyond missing him terribly and trying to cope with life without him, she felt unprepared to manage by herself. Charles had made few demands on her, and seemed to take care of everything—the car, paying bills, banking, repairs around the house, vacation planning, and so on. Now all decisions were up to her. However, fearful of facing the world on her own, she began to rely more and more on her 12-year-old son, Paul, as a partner, often blurring generational boundaries and burdening him with decisions far beyond his capacity or experience to make. In one sense, she was keeping her husband's memory alive, behaving as though nothing had changed from before Charles's death. At the same time she was not allowing Paul to grow up and pursue a life of his own nor herself to learn to become self-sufficient. Finally, Hilda's sister, a social worker, recognizing the evolving problems, was able to intervene, recommending that Hilda attend a counseling group for widows run by a psychologist at the local clinic.

The counselor understood the sudden burden thrust upon Hilda, and also the fact that the father's death had somehow brought mother and son closer. However, he also helped her to see some negative consequences from their enmeshed behavior patterns. Both needed to complete their mourning and get on with their lives; parent-child boundaries needed to be clarified; remaining intertwined hampered the process. With the help of the group, composed of other widows who had lived through the adjustment necessary after their husbands' deaths, Hilda began to gain self-esteem and take on responsibilities as family head that she previously had avoided.

As a result of her family leadership, she and her son were able to let go of one another sufficiently so that they could remain available to offer support and encouragement to one another but at the same time begin to pursue separate lives.

❃ ❃ ❃ ❃ ❃

The first case illustrates how some formerly married couples may be legally and physically separated, but are hardly finished fighting with one another. As we can see, the children of these angry associates often feel caught in the middle—loyalty to one means disloyalty to the other—and are in a no-win situation until the parents resolve or at least diminish their conflicts. Otherwise, the children may remain the long-term recipients of any unfinished business between their parents, and years after the divorce may find themselves still caught up in the middle of their parents' conflicts. In other cases, they choose sides, isolating themselves from the other parent, often for many years.

In the second case, we are dealing with a pseudo-mature **parentified child** forced to give up his chance to be a child and to take on parental executive responsibilities without the knowledge or ability to carry them off successfully. He may become overly serious and prematurely burdened, overworked and undervalued, the recipient of confidences inappropriate for his stage of development, alienated from peers at school, missing a childhood in which to learn to have fun and engage in age-appropriate activities.

These cases also point up the fact that the counselor is most likely to see a custodial mother and her child when the latter is in trouble (with the school, the police) or becomes symptomatic (sullen, withdrawn) or when parent-child conflicts become chronic and seemingly unresolvable. Otherwise, the woman's everyday life may be too burdened with work, child-care arrangements, and domestic as well as financial pressures to allow her the luxury of counseling.

In addition to a single mother's lack of motivation, money, or simply energy for counseling, a number of other roadblocks hinder easy entry by the counselor into the family system. With an intact two-parent family, as Fulmer (1983) points out, the family counselor can rely on the inherent strength or excitement of a revived or reunited parental dyad to alter the rules of the family system. Here, however, no such relationship exists. Instead, a rebellious adolescent, mistrusting adults, may be difficult to reach at first, while a younger child has fewer resources to call upon. Neither is helpful in facilitating a therapeutic atmosphere at the start of the experience. So, more often than not, according to Fulmer, the counselor must begin any clinical interventions with the mother, who has little inclination or wherewithal to take on new (counseling) projects outside the home. The mother's exhaustion and depression noted earlier in this chapter thus become a problem to be addressed early in the counseling if progress with the family is to be made.

Adolescent mothers deserve special attention here. As a group they rarely seek out available counseling or other services on their own, tending to isolate themselves from others during and after pregnancy and confining their social contacts to family-of-origin members at home. Weatherley and Cartoof (1988) maintain that traditional counseling strategies are likely to be less effective with pregnant and parenting teenagers than a combination of supportive counseling, home visiting, and offers to help with concrete tasks. For those who are amenable to counseling, Jemail and Nathanson (1987) suggest the rationale advanced by Weltner (1992), which we described in Chapter One, in which a counselor's interventions are tailored to a family's level of functioning. Level-1 interventions might be directed at a teenage mother and her infant, both of whom lack the basic necessities of food, shelter, and medical care; the goal might be to mobilize family members, friends, agencies, or community helpers in an effort to support, teach, and act as advocate for the ill-prepared young mother. Correspondingly, level-2 families might require interventions providing structure, limits, and safety for the child, while helping the mother to continue her education and learn to once again socialize with peers. If a teenager-headed family is functioning at level 3 but still seeks counseling, the interventions can focus on strengthening family boundaries and promoting clarity between generations.

A number of specific approaches to counseling a single-parent—led family have been proposed: brief strategic family counseling (Bray & Anderson, 1984); structural family counseling (Weltner, 1982); a combined psychodynamic/strategic approach (Morawetz & Walker, 1984); and a skills-building psychoeducational approach (Levant, 1988). Bray and Anderson contend that a brief technique is especially applicable to single-parent situations because their problems usually represent difficulty in making a transition from one family life-cycle stage and structure to another. Because finances are usually limited, short-term treatment is particularly cost-effective. They offer several examples (for example, overburdened families, families with unresolved divorce issues) of successfully **reframing** family problems in a more constructive and acceptable perspective to change the family's perceptions of the presenting problem.

Weltner (1982) points out that the single mother faces numerous problems, as we have noted throughout this chapter, and that their combined weight may overburden her, undermining her competence and sense of self-esteem. Thus, he argues, the counselor's first concern must be to make sure that she adequately performs her executive function as family head. Recognizing that her countless tasks (providing family meals, maintaining family routines, protecting the children, managing the budget, disciplining and guiding her offspring, and so on) may collectively be beyond the energies of a single parent (particularly if, as is likely, she must work outside the home), Weltner urges that supportive help be directed at aiding her to expand the executive function.

In the following case, an ex-client of the counselor contacts him again several years after the termination of counseling:

❇  ❇  ❇  ❇  ❇

Rosemary and Jack met at church when each was 20 years old, and after going steady for a year they married. Both had few social experiences with others, and seemed to be drawn to one another primarily because each was unhappy at home. Jack lived with a widowed mother who drank and was physically abusive to him. Rosemary's parents were together, but were hard-working blue-collar workers, often working extra shifts, who had little time for her. Whether by design or because of their demanding schedules, they neglected her and provided poor models for her regarding parenting. Jack and Rosemary had a brief and conflict-ridden marriage. Each had an insatiable need for attention, and neither knew how to give attention or much love back. By the time they contacted a counselor, their relationship had deteriorated to the point where little was left of the marriage, and after five sessions they agreed to separate and obtain a divorce.

The counselor did not hear from either of them for two years, at which time Rosemary called to say she had met someone at work (both were newspaper reporters) whom she wanted him to meet. James, 30, turned out to be an intelligent, hard-working, driven person who seemed to neglect his appearance and, for that matter, his health. Although he seemed to care a great deal for Rosemary, he admitted to her and the counselor that he had a drinking problem and, while he had stopped drinking for the last six months, he could not guarantee that he would not start again. Rosemary claimed that it made no difference, that his love was all she cared about, and that because they loved one another she was sure the drinking would not become a problem. Despite efforts by the counselor to get them to explore some of these issues further, Rosemary insisted she had met the man she wanted to marry. The drinking issue, to plague their marriage later, thus never got resolved. The counselor, recognizing the counseling was unfinished, left them with an open invitation to keep in contact.

Rosemary sent the counselor Christmas cards and, over the years, announcements of the birth of her two children, Joey and Max. In one note she mentioned that James had tired of newspaper reporting and, in order to pursue his interest in fine wines, had bought a liquor store that he would run. Several years passed, and the yearly notes stopped. The counselor lost touch with them, although he continued from time to time to wonder what had happened to them, and especially if James could handle being around liquor all day.

A full ten years passed before Rosemary once again called for help. She seemed to have aged considerably over that time—not surprisingly, considering the story she had to tell. She had endured a number of hardships, but two in particular were devastating. The first concerned the death of Max, at age 4, when a babysitter failed to stop him from running into the street after a ball and he was hit by a car. While this had happened six years earlier, it was clear from her telling of the event that she had never fully recovered from the loss, and continued to grieve. James's periodic drinking became more serious after Max's death. Their marriage, already weakened by James's drinking and neglecting his business, could not survive the death of their child, and several months thereafter James moved out. By this time, he was unable to control the drinking, nor was he able to hold a job. He lived with various friends or family members for several days at a time and held odd jobs for short periods between bouts of drinking.

Rosemary's presumed reason for calling was to bring the counselor up to date, and to seek help for her loneliness. She was desperate for companionship, but at the same time fearful of involving herself with a man again. She blamed herself for her situation, and said she could understand if no man would ever want to be with her. She felt very much alone in raising Joey (now 16), and had few friends to turn to for support. Her parents, with whom she had never repaired her relationship, were now elderly and ill and even less available than before. With the counselor's help, she did begin to socialize by attending Parents Without Partners meetings. While the depression seemed to lift, she began to tell of her problems with Joey, especially her feelings that she did not know how to raise him by herself, did not have sufficient parenting skills, and wished James or someone (the counselor?) would rescue her.

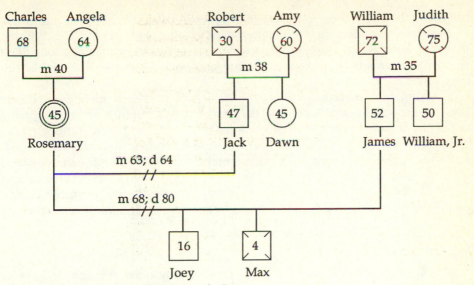

**Figure 4.3** Genogram of Rosemary's Case

Joey evidently was a school truant, spending countless days looking for his father along Skid Row. He had also been in trouble with the police over numerous speeding tickets he had failed to pay. Rosemary insisted it all was beyond her ability to cope, and that Joey could drop out of high school and go off on his own if he wanted to, as long as she did not have to take care of him. The counselor wanted Joey to attend the sessions with his mother, but he refused. He stayed away from home some nights, took money from her purse, emptied his bank account to spend money on his friends. Rosemary felt incompetent to control the situation.

The counselor began by helping her explore her relationship with her parents, in an effort to gain some understanding of why there was a deficit in the parenting she received growing up. As counseling proceeded, it became clearer that the parents, like Rosemary herself, lacked nurturing skills but were not uncaring, as she had believed. Caught up in the same situation, she was able to understand them better, and to begin to forgive them. On a more practical note, she was also able to call on them to help her in small ways with Joey, especially when she was away from home on a work assignment. Her newly enhanced relationship with them made her feel less alone.

The counselor thus focused his efforts on building family resources and helping Rosemary develop a support network, while also providing aid in reestablishing her as family head. He and she worked on improving her coping skills and gaining a sense of control or mastery over what was happening to her and Joey. As she began to reorganize the family, she began to monitor his activities more closely, to demand that they do more things together, that they eat their meals together every night, and that she go to school to determine just what was happening there. She no longer left her purse out for him to open and remove money, as she had done before. She talked to Joey about her new social life, and brought her new boyfriend for him to meet. She encouraged Joey to talk to her about his problems, to go with her to meetings for children of alcoholics, to bring his friends home if he so wished. For the first time she told him about her life with James, something she had deliberately kept from him before, and invited him to tell about his feelings about their divorce.

As Rosemary assumed an executive function as family head, she began to divide family responsibilities with her son. However, she was careful to maintain generational distinctions and not cross generational boundaries with him. Although there were only two of them, a hierarchical structure was established and maintained. Her newly developed sense of empowerment seemed to help Joey understand the new family organization and his place in it. Each learned to respect the other's privacy and not to intrude. After eight months of counseling, the workable alliance established between Rosemary and Joey was holding, and counseling terminated.

✳ ✳ ✳ ✳ ✳

In this case, as in others, the single mother may need therapeutic help in developing a functioning support system. She might, like Rosemary, be encouraged to restructure the family by assigning her children certain supportive tasks or chores around the house, under her guidance, each according to age and appropriate skills. Other restructuring, as in this case, may involve extended-family members such as grandparents, who may also be pressed into service, once again under the mother's direction and periodic surveillance. In both cases it is essential that blurred generational boundaries be clarified. This may be especially difficult if working mother and children live in grandmother's house, where the mother may run the risk of losing her executive function to the more available person. Under these circumstances, it is often beneficial for the counselor to include the grandparents in some family sessions, to help define roles and place the mother back in charge of her children.

The mother-led family also should be encouraged to seek the help of resources beyond the family. Friends, social service agencies, school-related organizations, members of church congregations, co-op babysitter groups, single-parent groups such as Parents Without Partners,[7] employer-sponsored child-care groups, and various women's organizations may all offer exactly the kind of aid a beleaguered single mother needs. An even minimally involved ex-spouse who helps out in emergencies or on weekends or one weeknight can offer considerable comfort and support.

In their work with single-parent–led families, Morawetz and Walker (1984) begin by attempting to involve all those present in the counseling process. One early task is to assess the family structure (who is the spokesperson, who is silent, who seems resistant, what coalitions appear to exist, and so on). As they carefully join

[7]A number of organizations offer social as well as educational events for divorced parents and their children. The largest is probably Parents Without Partners, with over 1000 chapters in all 50 states and a number of foreign countries, and with a membership of 200,000 single parents.

the family, they begin the process of reorganizing family interaction patterns. The family members, who come to counseling with their own linear explanations of the problem (A happened, which caused B to occur), have to be taught to think in terms of circular causality, in which the problem stems from input from the family as an interacting unit. Helping the family to begin to think in systems terms may facilitate later interventions aimed at specific structural changes necessary to alleviate the symptomatic behavior in a family member.

In the matter of conflict between custodial parents and children, Morawetz and Walker (1984) suggest a number of possible scenarios requiring therapeutic intervention:

When a child is seen as the embodiment of the absent parent, either as a reminder of the denounced parent or as a permanent memory and symbol of the deceased parent. (See the two cases earlier in this chapter that refer to ghosts from a previous marriage.)

When a parent "marries" his or her child. (In an effort to compensate for the loss following dissolution of a marriage, single parents frequently replace their marital partnership to some extent by developing a closer partnership with their children, sometimes leading to confusion over hierarchical boundaries. Children may be treated as intimate confidants by a lonely mother one moment and as disobedient children the next.)

When a child is seen as an overwhelming burden (particularly in the case of a custodial parent who is unable or unwilling to let go of anger, grief, or self-pity, and who perceives any effort by the child to gain attention or be comforted as an intrusion that is resented).

When perspective is lost in the struggle for survival. (In this case, unreasonable and excessive demands may be made on the child—to grow up faster than his or her peers and to understand just what the parent is experiencing. Under such circumstances, the child's appropriate feelings of sadness, anger, or divided loyalties may be hidden or disguised, and an unhappy and uncommunicative child may present problems, as in the case of Rosemary, earlier in the chapter.)

When the burden of guilt (for having put the parent's desire to end the marriage ahead of the needs of the children) impedes effective functioning. (Unresolved difficulties in disciplining may lead to family turmoil.)

When reentry into the social scene is experienced as a return to adolescence (particularly difficult if one's own teenager is at a similar developmental stage, causing an unstable parent-child hierarchy).

When the single parent becomes dependent on the family of origin (reawakening old conflicts between dependency needs and wishes to be independent).

Under these or other circumstances, the counselor's role may go beyond traditionally defined counseling, sometimes extending into intervening on the parent's or entire family's behalf with a school, camp, or welfare counselor. Here the counselor must proceed cautiously, for two reasons: (1) to avoid permanently weakening and thus undermining the parent's executive activities; (2) to avoid being drawn into the family's neediness and willingness to listen by assuming the permanent role of the absent parent. The family needs to be helped to reorganize in order to reduce stress; the counselor must then return control to the mother, encouraging her to seek other adult relationships and the children to spend time with their peers.

Single-parent families pass through a number of predictable stages, according to Morawetz and Walker (1984): (1) the aftermath of the divorce; (2) the family regrouping or realignment; (3) the reestablishment of a social life; and (4) successful separation of parent and child. In their therapeutic work with single-parent–led families, these authors found that families who seek help in the wake of their divorce frequently experience rage, despair, overwhelming anxiety, and a sense that they will not be able to cope with the problems they must suddenly confront. The counselor can offer some first aid in stabilizing the family system at this point, by joining the system temporarily as it regroups. (The risk of the counselor's stepping in as family rescuer is greatest at this phase of counseling; nevertheless, intervention of this type is sometimes necessary.) Morawetz and Walker suggest that the counselor is most helpful here in assisting the family members as they attempt to make sense out of some of the issues that led to the marital breakup and begin the mourning process for the loss of the family.

The success with which the family can deal with its grief and bitterness in the aftermath of the divorce and the speed with which it can be helped to develop self-esteem and overcome feelings of helplessness set the stage for phase 2, realignment. Now, with the counselor's assistance, the family must learn to adjust to the new reality brought about by the absent parent. The counselor can play a key role at this point, usually a stormy period, as the family members are helped to accept that the painful and unwelcome dissolution of the family as they have known it is permanent. Morawetz and Walker describe as common the surfacing of anger and violence, often on the part of the children, during this therapeutic phase; this may perhaps provide a symptom that serves to pull the custodial parent out of a depression or to signal to the noncustodial parent that the family needs his or her return.

By now, if counseling is successful, the children have learned to live with one parent or to accommodate to two households, and the custodial parent has abandoned any prior hope of reconciliation. In phase 3 of counseling, the family begins to look toward the future, and to seek new social relationships. Dating by the single parent may prove disruptive to the children, who are apt to view this new development as a further loss of parental availability and possibly as behavior disloyal to the absent parent. By phase 4, the counselor is likely to be attempting to expedite the successful separation of parent and child from the bonding that followed the divorce, so that each may move on with their lives. This relinquishing of parent-child attachments may lead to an unbalancing of the family system, and the counselor may expect a period of intense feelings. Morawetz and Walker warn that truancy, delinquency, and perhaps even teenage pregnancy may occur; these are all efforts to disrupt change, delay separation, and ensure a return to the earlier parent-child involvement.

In a somewhat different therapeutic approach, a number of counselors such as Levant (1988) have designed psychoeducational and skills-training programs to remediate specific family problems and, in the process, enhance aspects of family living. Generally brief or time-limited, didactic/experiential programs such as the Fatherhood Project at Boston University aim to promote family functioning by teaching fathers, often single custodial parents, how to improve their communication skills with their children. In particular, men wishing to develop a more nurturing role, but with few previous experiences or with poor role models from their own fathers, are offered an opportunity to enroll in courses where they learn various communication skills such as listening and responding to their children's feelings, and expressing their own feelings in a constructive manner. A basic understanding of child development and child management is also taught, from the perspective both of the child and of the father.

Levant (1988) employs a skills-training format, in which participants role-play situations from their own family experiences, are videotaped for instant playback and observation, and fill out workbook exercises at home with their children. The program is voluntary, offered as an educational experience for men who wish to improve their empathic sensitivity to what transpires in their interactions with their children. The Fatherhood Project thus provides a combined didactic/experiential series of group meetings in which, if successful, fathers undergo a cognitive restructuring regarding their views of ideal family life. The program is currently being expanded to include single parents of either sex, divorced parents with joint custody, stepparents and their spouses, and those couples about to become parents.

In our final example of counseling a single parent, an unwed working-class mother calls for help:

❋   ❋   ❋   ❋   ❋

Tammy contacted a counselor in the small university community in which she lived, ostensibly for guidance with her stepchild, Jolie. The counselor suggested that both Tammy and her husband come in together, and after some hesitation Tammy agreed. Although she and Brad gave different last names, it was not until ten minutes into the interview that the counselor realized that the couple was unmarried. The "stepchild" referred to over the telephone turned out to be Brad's daughter, Jolie, 7, from a previous marriage, who visited them during summer breaks from her school. In addition, Tammy and Brad had a child together, Rebecca, 4. Before the close of the first counseling session, it was clear to all three participants that Tammy had a more serious problem in mind than the one regarding Jolie; she was forcing a showdown with Brad regarding his degree of commitment to their relationship, especially whether he intended to marry her.

Subsequent sessions revealed that Tammy's and Brad's backgrounds could hardly have been more dissimilar. She was from a large, working-class family from West Virginia, had dropped out of high school after one year, and had travelled to California on her own at age 17 to get away from an abusive father. After a series of odd jobs, she found work as a waitress at a restaurant near the university. Brad, on the other hand, came from an upper-middle-class northeastern WASP family, had been educated in private schools, and was now about to receive his doctorate in public health. Soon after they met at the restaurant, they began dating, and within three months were living together. Rebecca was born about one year later.

Although Tammy and Brad had now been together for five years, his parents knew nothing of Tammy's existence, nor of their grandchild. Brad had also taken great pains to hide her from all but his closest friends at school, telling himself that he was embarrassed by her poor grammar, her lack of sophistication, and what he considered to be her tendency to sound ignorant and uninformed. While Tammy did complain from time to time about such treatment, she was not some-one who expected very much from life, and seemed more than willing to accept Brad's explanation that he was trying to work things out, and that it was only a matter of time before they married.

Tammy was able to express her anger and resentment early in the counseling sessions. She was furious and hurt that Brad denied her existence to his family and friends, and that he never publicly claimed Rebecca as his daughter. Although she loved Brad, she expressed her bitterness over feeling tricked into having a baby when he apparently had no intention of ever marrying her. Brad responded somewhat intellectually at first, trying to appear modern and thus not hampered by marriage certificates since "they were nothing more than useless scraps of paper." However, he did acknowledge his love for Tammy, but expressed his bewilderment over how to satisfy her as well as his family. After two months of joint counseling, Brad did finally agree to marry Tammy and to tell his parents that Rebecca was his child, despite his anticipation that they would never approve. Tammy, however, by now was sufficiently angry and disappointed by his behavior and past unkept promises that she insisted they separate.

Tammy lived alone with Rebecca, and the counselor saw them together for two sessions. Rebecca, who carried her father's name, did not seem to feel too stigmatized, especially since they lived in a community where divorce was fairly common and she was not the only child in her class without a father at home. She did not know that her parents had never married. Brad did send money to support her, and visited her regularly before he graduated and took a job at a midwestern university. Within a year, however, he had met a woman with two children and married her, and his money to Tammy and Rebecca became sporadic.

Tammy continued to see the counselor from time to time, and eventually was encouraged to return to school. She obtained the equivalent of a high school diploma before registering at a local junior college to become a Licensed Voca-tional Nurse. She did expand her social life, and did manage to place Rebecca in a good child-care facility after school, but life for Tammy continued to be hectic. She had periodic bouts of depression, and felt particularly alone and desperate at these times. Despite the counselor's support and encouragement, Tammy found herself with few options, little money, and no apparent prospects for a brighter future. She eventually moved to North Carolina, where her cousins lived, and found a job at the local hospital. She never told anyone that she had never married, nor did anyone appear to assume this to be the case. Although her life was far from being fulfilled, she was managing—according to the periodic letters sent to the counselor—to support herself and her child and had regained some sense of self-esteem.

✳  ✳  ✳  ✳  ✳

In this case, the counselor initially helped the clients determine the real problems they were having, which was necessary before they could begin to resolve their conflicts. By offering support and understanding, largely absent in Tammy's life, she joined the family system and provided some model for self-sufficiency. Such support seemed essential to the counselor if she was to help Tammy think out important life decisions. The counselor encouraged Tammy to develop marketable skills in order to help her build self-esteem. Finally, Tammy was helped to reconnect to another family system that would offer the support of an extended family. The overwhelming survival issues faced by many single parents are such that counseling may at times be primarily supportive, while the parent gains the wherewithal to reunite with a more real and more permanent support system.

## SUMMARY

Despite the fact that divorce has become a familiar phenomenon of American life, it is still viewed as representing a failure by many members of society, and single-parent–led families are often seen as flawed, although many are as successful as two-parent families. Families headed by single parents are not necessarily a homogeneous group; they are formed by death, desertion, and birth out of wedlock, as well as separation and divorce, although in recent years separation and divorce have become the leading causes for the formation of these families. Teenage mothers, who account for one out of five births in the United States, are likely to have a high rate of poverty and a low level of education, and to be from minority groups. The counselor needs to understand the manner in which single parenthood occurred, the stage in the marriage at which it took place, and the number and age of the children involved.

Divorce is, by definition, disruptive to all family members. The custodial parent, still most likely to be the mother, faces a wide range of practical problems (finances, role overload, child-care arrangements), as well as emotional distress connected with loss of self-esteem, grief, and loneliness. The noncustodial parent must cope with many changes surrounding his or her customary living arrangements, although the most probable adjustment difficulty revolves around a sense of loss of the children, loneliness, and loss of previous social supports. Impaired functioning of children is common following divorce, with elementary school–age or younger ones most vulnerable to distress. Boys living with custodial mothers tend to have a particularly difficult time adjusting after separation and divorce.

The extent to which the parents remain involved and offer support to one another largely determines the extent to which the children make a successful adaptation to the divorce and get on with their lives.

Child-custody decisions today increasingly favor shared parenting arrangements as being in the child's best interests. Joint custody allows both parents equal authority in raising their children; such an arrangement may or may not involve joint physical custody.

Counselors must help newly formed single-parent–led families establish boundaries, as different members take on new tasks and responsibilities. In addition, such families must come to terms with the psychological presence of the absent parent, whether dead or divorced. Otherwise, they run the risk of creating a parentified child as an absent parent's substitute. The counselor may also have to deal with the single parent's depression and fear of reentering the world outside the home. Several counseling approaches (brief strategic family counseling, structural family counseling, and a skills-building psychoeducational program) have been proposed for working with single-parent–led families. In general, they attempt to strengthen the executive function of the family head, to restructure the family by helping the children take on supportive tasks, to help develop an outside support group, and to teach custodial and noncustodial parents alike new skills aimed at remediating specific family problems. Teenage mothers, if amenable to counseling, can most likely benefit from interventions tailored to their specific level of functioning.

# Counseling the Remarried Family

Overall, as Ihinger-Tallman and Pasley (1987) observe, Americans seem to demonstrate an inherent "marriage bias." They enter first marriage at a greater rate than people in most other countries; they also appear to have higher expectations of the marital unit, so much so that they are prepared to abandon the relationship if it proves unfulfilling and to try again to find satisfaction, as evidenced by a higher remarriage rate than couples in other Western nations. In what Furstenberg (1987) refers to as American society's general acceptance of "conjugal succession," many couples today expect to stay together only as long as their marriage is emotionally gratifying. If one or both mates find that no longer the case, the partners are permitted—or sometimes even encouraged (particularly when the couple is childless)—to break the marriage contract and search for someone who might provide greater emotional gratification. Most marriages (about three out of five) do involve children, however, and, according to Furstenberg's calculations, probably a third of all children growing up today will be part of a stepfamily before they reach adulthood. Glick (1984c), a demographer, goes as far as predicting that stepfamilies will be the predominant American family form by the turn of the century.

Because mothers continue to be awarded physical custody in the overwhelming number of cases, stepfather families are the most prevalent form of stepfamily arrangement. Contrary to television-inspired expectations that stepfamilies resemble *The Brady Bunch* (young children from both former marriages residing together), most stepfamilies are likely to be composed of a father living with his wife and her children from a previous marriage. If he has children from an earlier marriage, according to a recent California survey (Weitzman, 1985), his visitation with them may become steadily less frequent and irregular after his remarriage (and decrease even more dramatically after his former wife is remarried). Despite possible joint-custody responsibilities and initial involvement, there is a one-in-four chance that eventually he will cease all contact with them.

Beyond the simple stepfamily structure just portrayed, Cherlin and McCarthy (1985) describe the less common complex structure in which children from both spouses, whether they reside together or not, are considered to be, and treated as, family members. According to Pasley and Ihinger-Tallman (1988), about half of all remarriages include children from one partner's prior marriage, and 10% or so include those from both previous marriages. In perhaps the most complex family structure—and also the least frequent—only 3% of remarriages involve his children, her children, and their children (Bernstein, 1990).

As for the experience of living as a single parent (see the previous chapter), it is temporary for many divorced people, especially in the middle class. Three out of five eventually remarry (three-quarters of divorced women and five-sixths of divorced men); about half do so within three years of their divorce (Glick, 1980). Remarriages after divorce are most likely to occur between the ages of 25 and 44, the median period being somewhere in the early 30s. Not surprisingly, remarriage after widowhood occurs considerably later—between the ages of 45 and 64, more probably in the early 60s. One of the interesting findings of Glick's research is that, for both men and women in early middle age, the odds of remarrying are greater if the earlier marriage ended in divorce rather than through death of a spouse.

According to Cherlin and McCarthy's (1985) analysis of census data, there are between 9 and 10 million remarried households in the United States. In approximately a third, the wife had been married before; in a third, only the husband had been previously married; and in the remaining third, both spouses had previously been married and divorced. Glick (1980) discovered that better educated and financially well-off men were most likely to remarry quickly; on the other hand, the higher a woman's educational level and income, the less likely she was to remarry. (Perhaps, as we noted in the previous chapter, in some cases the divorced woman trying to raise her children alone may feel the financial pinch without the support of her husband's income and may seek to remarry to regain that support; on the other hand, autonomous and economically self-sufficient women may not feel that need, and for that reason choose not to remarry.) According to data offered by Hernandez (1988), only slightly more than half of today's children live together with both their biological parents.

Remarried families or stepfamilies are neither inherently problematic nor necessarily a poor substitute for an intact or "natural" family unit (Walsh, 1991). Well-functioning families—as well as dysfunctional ones—can be found in either type of family structure. Although born out of a series of disruptive transitions to a family system—from intact family to single-parent–led to remarried—that inevitably generate a series of structural and relationship shifts and role changes, reorganization and adaptation are possible, and successful marriage is achievable.

If successful, remarriage has a great deal to offer adults and children alike. For adults, the experience can help rebuild self-esteem and a sense of being a worthwhile person capable of loving and being loved. Wiser as a result of the earlier failed experience, the adult has a second chance to form a more mature, more stable relationship and, as Crohn, Sager, Brown, Rodstein, and Walker (1982), point out:

> an opportunity to parent and to benefit from a supportive **suprasystem**. . . . Children can learn to appreciate and respect differences in people and ways of living, can receive affection and support from a new stepparent and the new suprasystem, and can observe the remarried parent in a good and loving relationship, using this as a model for their own future love relationships. (p. 162)

After witnessing a destructive marital relationship, children may now observe positive and mutually enhancing interactions between adults.

On the other hand, a failed second try can lead adults to a renewed sense of defeat, self-blame, and frustration. Children may confirm for themselves that good and caring relationships are short-lived if they exist at all. Without a doubt, many adults enter a second marriage with fewer illusions or romantic expectations, and presumably experience some internal pressure to work harder to make the marriage work this time. Yet, despite a personal familiarity with the possible anguish and family upheaval brought about by the dissolution of a marriage, remarrieds divorce at a somewhat higher rate than partners in first marriages (Glick, 1980).

In an effort to convince others (and themselves) of their sexual desirability as well as their ability to be successfully married, divorced people may choose new partners who turn out to be all too similar to their ex-mates (for example, alcoholics) or, more accurately, partners with whom they develop and maintain similar interactive patterns. Perhaps they have been psychologically fortified by their earlier experience to go through with what must be done to dissolve an unhappy union, or perhaps they are unwilling, having forged a sense of independence between marriages, to relinquish or compromise their position or accede to the demands of a new mate for too little in return. In many cases, the higher probability of divorce simply reflects the complexities involved in adjusting to a family structure that includes stepchildren and adults who must deal with two households (Jacobson, 1987). In other instances, financial burdens aggravated by the need to help support two households, including alimony and/or child support payments, may prove the ultimate undoing of a remarried relationship. For whatever reasons, remarriers are about 10% more likely to get redivorced (56 out of 100) than are those who are divorcing for the first time (49 out of 100) (Weed, 1980).

# VARIETIES OF REMARRIED-FAMILY STRUCTURES

Remarriage following divorce has become a familiar marker event in the lives of many people in recent years. Although remarriage itself is hardly a new phenomenon, in the past its main purpose was to mend families fragmented by the premature death of a parent, restoring the domestic unit to its original nuclear or intact structure. Today, as Furstenberg (1980) contends, most remarriages follow divorce rather than death, and thus the surrogate parent augments rather than supplants the biological parent. In most cases, minor children are part of today's remarried families (Bumpass, Sweet, & Martin, 1990).

One consequence of this relatively new structural change, according to Furstenberg (1980), is that we have not as yet developed an adequate set of beliefs, a language, or rules for this family form in which there are "more than two parents," despite the fact that more than 40% of all new marriages today involve at least one partner who has been previously married.

The blending together of two families is a complex and difficult process at best; the absence of clear-cut ground rules (for example, how to discipline stepchildren, whether loyalty to one parent means disloyalty to the other, what to call an absent parent's new spouse) vastly complicates the merger. Addressing this issue, Bray (1992) observes that:

> The structure and membership of stepfamilies create important differences from first-married families. These include a lack of socially defined role relationships, problems with defining and maintaining family boundaries, developing affection between new family members, and the challenge of negotiating relationships within the binuclear family system. (p. 60)

Remarried families (variously referred to in the literature as Rem, blended, second, or reconstituted families, or stepfamilies) come in a variety of forms (see Table 5.1), although for simplicity's sake we can divide them into three major types: those in which the wife becomes a stepmother; those in which the husband becomes a stepfather; and those in which both occur. It is important for the counselor to understand that remarriage connotes far more than joining a simple dyadic relationship. On the contrary, as Sager, Brown, Crohn, Engel, Rodstein, and Walker (1983) point out, each adult entering such a developing dyadic system brings a plethora of attachments and obligations. That person's gender, previous marital status, and custodial and/or noncustodial children must be considered. For example, as noted in Table 5.1, the previously single woman who weds a formerly married man with children (combination #10), and is thus thrust at once into the unfamiliar role of stepmother, undoubtedly has considerably different expectations, experiences, and possible areas of conflict than does a previously married woman with children in the same circumstances (#12).

The following example illustrates combination #10. We present a case of a father who divorces, obtains joint physical custody of his minor children, and then remarries, although this is still more the exception than the rule.[1]

---

[1]As we noted in the previous chapter, father-only households, while still small, are beginning to grow and are now approaching a sizeable portion (1.5 million or 15%) of today's one-parent–led families (U.S. Bureau of the Census, 1991a). The likelihood of remarriage is actually substantially greater for a custodial father (41%) than for a custodial mother (23%), but it is not clear from census data what percentage of remarried custodial fathers obtained custody of their children before or after they remarried (Meyer & Garasky, 1991). In many cases, fathers may wait until they have remarried and established a stable home before seeking physical custody of children living with their ex-wives.

**Table 5.1  Twenty-Four Possible Remarried-Family Combinations**

|  | Woman Previously Single | Woman Previously Divorced or Widowed, No Children | Woman Previously Divorced or Widowed, Custodial Children | Woman Divorced or Widowed, Noncustodial Children | Woman Divorced or Widowed, Both Custodial and Noncustodial |
| --- | --- | --- | --- | --- | --- |
| Man Previously Single | n.a. | 1 | 2 | 3 | 4 |
| Man Previously Divorced or Widowed, No Children | 5 | 6 | 7 | 8 | 9 |
| Man Previously Divorced or Widowed, Custodial Children | 10 | 11 | 12 | 13 | 14 |
| Man Divorced or Widowed, Non-custodial Children | 15 | 16 | 17 | 18 | 19 |
| Man Divorced or Widowed, Both Custodial and Noncustodial Children | 20 | 21 | 22 | 23 | 24 |

*Source:* Sager et al., 1983, p. 65.

❋  ❋  ❋  ❋  ❋

Alan had been married for nine years to Joy and together they had had two children, Deidre, age 5, and Todd, age 2, by the time they consulted a marital counselor. Married in their senior year—they had both attended a large midwestern university—they had continued for several years after graduation to live relatively unburdened lives not unlike their student days. Alan, the more serious and scholarly of the two, had soon tired of his job as an accountant, however, and with Joy's encouragement had begun graduate studies leading to a Ph.D. in economics. Joy had worked at assorted jobs before signing on as an assistant to the head of an insurance agency, a position that took her away from home for long hours each day. After the birth of their children, Joy, advancing in her job, had continued her work, sometimes barely managing to come home for dinner before returning to see clients in the evening. More and more, Alan had taken over the care of the children, a task he found he did successfully and enjoyed. By the time they saw the counselor, they had grown apart sufficiently—emotionally, intellectually, socially—that little if anything was left of their marriage and they decided to get divorced. By mutual consent, reflecting their previously agreed-upon living arrangement, they shared custody of the children, but Alan retained physical custody. Over the following five years the children saw less and less of their mother, although she would occasionally call them and promise to see them as soon as her busy schedule allowed. As the children learned to predict, it was a promise that was rarely kept. However, she did not disappear entirely; rather, she would arrive at their home occasionally, usually unannounced, arms loaded with expensive gifts.

When Alan met Sara, a fellow doctoral student, they discovered that they shared many values in common. As their relationship blossomed, they found too that they were emotionally compatible, and soon they decided to marry. The children, now 10 and 7, liked Sara well enough at first, and Sara was enthusiastic about having a ready-made family. She was good with children, and since she was a bit younger than Alan and herself childless, she was anxious to prove to him that she could cope. However, she found it particularly hard to adapt to this instant family despite her efforts to be a good mother. She resented their demands, their intrusions, their possessiveness of their father. Without a honeymoon period in which to develop greater intimacy with her husband, Sara felt thrust into a series of childrearing tasks for which she had no experience, and from which she received little reward. Her husband expected her to relieve him of some parental responsibilities, and could not understand her resistance to becoming an instant parent. The children, on the other hand, soon refused to listen to any rules she might impose, insisting she was not their parent and therefore did not have any rights to discipline. Sara felt that she was on the receiving end of all the abuse from children who resented her closeness to their father, without any of the pleasures, satisfactions, or displays of affection due a parent. Although Alan and Sara both had believed she would make a wonderful mother—she actually had very good success with caring for their needs early on—all four family members were soon involved in considerable turmoil.

Recognizing that the new family system was in trouble, Alan sought out his previous family counselor, and along with Sara, Deidre, and Todd began a series of visits as a family. In the process, Alan learned to offer support to his wife and to help her out of the no-win situations in which she often found herself. By relinquishing some of his ideas about what constituted a good parent, he learned to reduce whatever rescue fantasies he had been experiencing of marrying someone who would be another perfect parent. Before the family counseling sessions, he had believed that only if she were perfect, according to his definition, could he relax and entrust the children to his new wife.

Through counseling, Sara was able to acknowledge and ultimately express her frustration and resulting bitterness, often directed toward Alan, at his insistence that she be the mother he would have liked Joy to have been. As this unreasonable expectation became clear to them—they both had bought into it—Alan relaxed his demands in this regard and Sara made an effort to stop competing with the children's natural mother to win their love. She slowly began to recognize that affection and acceptance from the children would come out of their daily living patterns, and that the verbal expression of such feelings from children the ages of Deidre and Todd is commonly limited, even in intact families. Particularly if the boundary around her and her husband became stronger, the children would respond to their father's feelings for her, and would start to treat her as their parent.

The children were helped to deal with their loyalty conflicts regarding their own mother, and to accept that, while Sara was not their biological mother, she was in fact the person who was willing to carry out the day-to-day tasks of mothering. As the children became aware that loving Sara did not mean abandoning the tenuous hold they had on their natural mother, the relationship with their stepmother became closer and the family overall became a more cohesive unit.

The counselor held two closing sessions with Alan, Sara, and Joy, but without the children. Together the trio, in a relatively calm way, first dealt with Joy's intermittent extravagant behavior toward the children. Joy acknowledged her guilt feelings over neglecting the day-to-day parenting, recognizing that she attempted to compensate periodically for these feelings by lavishing expensive gifts on the children. Alan and Sara, although resentful of Joy's indulgent behavior, came to understand it better, and themselves recognized that they ignored Joy's ideas regarding childrearing, and could be more open to her suggestions. A more inviting attitude on their part led to an arrangement for more regular and more consistent visitation schedules on her part. As Joy began to be treated by them as a mother entitled to be in on decisions affecting her children's lives, she felt more a part of their daily lives. When she planned on giving a particularly expensive gift, she discussed it beforehand with the other two parents. Over several months, the relationships began to improve for the children, parents, and stepparent alike.

❋　　❋　　❋　　❋　　❋

A remarried family into which both partners bring children from previous marriages (#12) presents a different set of problems. Especially when each child has lived in a single-parent arrangement for a period of time, that child's role and position in the family is usually severely altered when his or her parent remarries. Building a stepsibling relationship in the case we are about to present was complicated further in that each was an only child, and thus accustomed to a special intimate bond with the previously single parent.

❋  ❋  ❋  ❋  ❋

Both Marlene, 29, and Dan, 32, had been married briefly before terminating their first marriages. Each had ended that marriage with a joint-custody arrangement in which they were awarded physical custody—Marlene of her 2-year-old son Robert, Dan of his 3-year-old daughter Christine. Each adult had remained a single parent for several years, until they met at a church social, fell in love, and decided to marry. In their haste to connect with another adult in a loving relationship, however, they neglected to talk through any differences in childrearing values, expected household rules, remaining financial and emotional ties to a former spouse, and a host of related issues involving the transition into the new family structure. As one indication of their lack of planning, the children, now aged 7 and 8, respectively, did not meet each other until two weeks before the wedding ceremony.

The early period in a remarried family's life is usually a time of considerable reorganization and inevitable disequilibrium. In this case, chaos would be a more accurate assessment. The children, in particular, fought over space in the new house, which previous family routine (dinnertime, bedtime) was to be followed, and who could be disciplined by whom. Each child aligned with his or her own parent to the point of seeming at times to represent two warring camps. Robert was vigilant in measuring how much attention Christine was getting, and Christine was equally on the lookout for any special benefits that might come her stepbrother's way. Needless to say, little bonding took place between the children, nor between each child and his or her stepparent. Marlene and Dan were dumbfounded, both having wanted to believe that, because they loved their new spouse, they would automatically love (and be loved by) their spouse's children. For the first hectic year, nothing seemed further from the truth.

Nor was the conflict restricted to the children. The parents often found themselves defending the action of their own child against the other, and exchanged open criticism about the childrearing practices of the other. On occasion, usually after a visit by a child with his or her noncustodial parent, that parent would call to criticize or complain about the child's alleged mistreatment; this typically had the effect of stirring up old conflicts between the ex-spouses. By the end of the second year of marriage, both Marlene and Dan had many doubts about the possibilities of ultimate success of their marital union. Their earlier plan to have a child together was put on hold and, as a last resort, they sought the help of a family counselor.

The counselor saw all four family members together, and helped them to redefine their conflicts in interactional terms as a systems problem to which each participant contributed. Instead of factions, based on earlier experiences living as single-parent households, he emphasized their wholeness as an expanded system in which each person's needs as well as responsibilities had to be addressed. Rather than clinging to earlier parent-child patterns, the counselor suggested, here was an opportunity for creating new family guidelines and traditions. For example, both children could now give up being partners to their respective parents and return to being children again, something each seemed to desire. Family boundaries were slowly redrawn, and the children began to refer to one another with their friends as brother and sister, this despite some awkwardness over different surnames.

After two months, the counselor began working with Marlene and Dan alone, strengthening their bond and helping them work as a parental unit. At several sessions, the ex-spouses were brought in to help reduce friction, as well as better coordinate activities with the children. After six months, Marlene announced that she was pregnant and that she and Dan were ready to terminate treatment.

✳   ✳   ✳   ✳   ✳

Despite their seeming differences, both cases illustrate that the basic integrative tasks for stepfamilies, as Visher and Visher (1988a) point out, are twofold: (1) redefining and maintaining existing parent-child and ex-spouse relationships, but in a new context; and (2) developing new relationship patterns to build trust within the household as a means of achieving a solid identity as a new family unit. Figure 5.1 depicts an intact functional nuclear family (top), a new stepfamily (middle), and a mature stepfamily (bottom). If successful, the new stepfamily progresses from its early formation, in which little connectedness exists between members, to the mature stepfamily where links between all members are strong and binding. As these authors note, the process of establishing themselves as a viable and integrated unit is often a lengthy one for most stepfamilies, since they usually have to overcome a combination of built-in parent-child alliances, problematic generational boundaries, influences outside the household, and a lack of family history or loyalty.

In a study of 88 remarried couples, Duberman (1975) found that stepfamily integration was facilitated if: (1) the previous spouse had died rather than divorced; (2) the new spouse had divorced rather than never having been previously married; and (3) the remarried couple had children of their own together. She found further that parent-child relationships were helped when the wife's children from her previous marriage lived with her and her new spouse. On the other hand, men who left their children with their ex-wife tended to deal less well with their live-in stepchildren. Acceptance by the in-laws and other extended family members helped strengthen the remarriage. One noteworthy finding was that stepmother-stepdaughter relationships tended to be the most problematic of all stepfamily interactions.

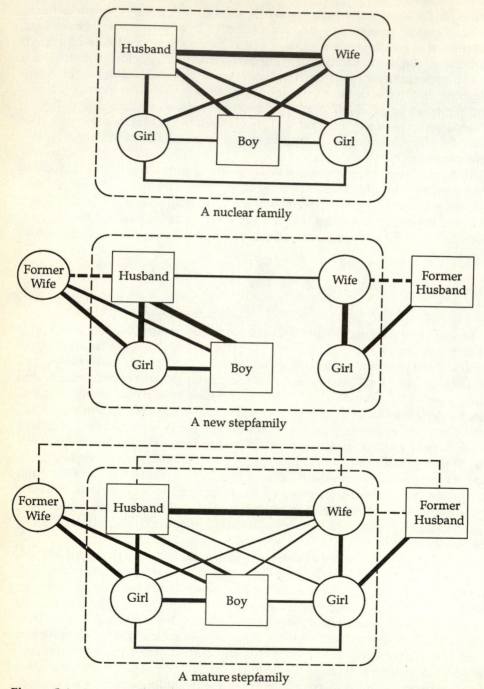

**Figure 5.1**   Interactive Networks in Three Family Configurations
*Source:* Visher and Visher, 1988a, p. 13.

# STEPFAMILY LIVING ARRANGEMENTS

A remarried family has been defined by Sager and associates (1981) as

> one that is created by the marriage (or living together in one domicile) of two partners, one or both of whom has been married previously and was divorced or widowed with or without children who visit or reside with them. The couple and the children (custodial or visiting) comprise the Remarried family system. The "metafamily" system is composed of the Remarried family plus former spouses, grandparents, step-grandparents, aunts, uncles, and others who may have significant input into the Remarried system. (p. 3)

Jacobson (1987), in an effort to break away from an approach tied to conventional terms such as *nuclear, intact,* or *broken* families, prefers to conceptualize stepfamilies as *linked family systems.* She believes the term *linked* more accurately reflects the web of interrelationships and the dynamic complexities occurring in such families. Her formulation goes beyond the common phenomenon of a child living with a custodial remarried parent and his or her spouse (usually the biological mother and stepfather). Instead, Jacobson views the child as likely to be related to two households—the custodial or lived in, and the noncustodial or visited—each of which represents a subsystem of the dual-household or binuclear family system. In such a setup, the child is a link influencing and being influenced by those in both households.

Of particular relevance to counselors is the clinical observation made by Visher and Visher (1979) that in such linked families virtually all members have sustained a recent primary relationship loss with which they must cope. One implication we might draw, then, is that the prospect of making a new commitment is likely to provoke fear and apprehension for adults and children alike. Adults may hesitate out of a feeling of vulnerability due to pain from past intimate experiences. Children, too, may pull back from trusting new adults in their lives. Not unexpectedly, they are likely to use the rules and roles of the earlier family life as guidelines for current behavior. Satisfactory stepfamily integration, then, is likely to take years to achieve.

McGoldrick and Carter (1988) adopt the useful premise that interactions in the restructured remarried family are likely to be complex, with conflicting and ambiguous roles played by all members. As we illustrated earlier in the case of Sara, an unmarried woman marrying a man who had custody of his children, the formation of the new family does not follow any ordinary step-by-step progression; instead, a previously single young adult is often expected to plunge into instant multiple roles as wife and stepmother, for which she has had little if any preparation and in which she cannot expect to be welcomed wholeheartedly.

Unstable and poorly defined boundaries may cause dissension and struggle; and intense conflictual feelings on the part of all participants in stepfamilies must be expected, particularly during the early period in the life cycle of any blended family. As McGoldrick and Carter (1988) note, such boundary difficulties often involve issues of

- membership: who are the "real" members of the family?
- space: where do I belong? what space is mine?

- authority: who is in charge of discipline? of money? of decisions?
- time: who gets how much of my time and how much do I get of theirs?

Disequilibrium is inevitable, despite the wishes or even the good intentions of all of the members of the new family. Ultimately, at least two tasks must be accomplished before the participants can be anchored in a truly blended family: (1) the new partners must accept each other as executives in the new family hierarchy, and (2) the children must accept the new partner, having worked out the problems of territory or turf that arise from unclear or dysfunctional boundaries (Isaacs, 1982).

The successful renegotiation of boundaries in a stepfamily is essential. Counselors need to help such families restructure their roles within the new unit (biological parent, new parent, and child) and at the same time make certain they do not neglect a similar renegotiation (relinkage) within the larger family unit that includes the former spouse (the child's other parent). The way the process unfolds—it should be started as early in the relationship as possible, even before marriage—can facilitate or impede successful blending.

What problems should the counselor especially screen for? Box 5.1 outlines some of the typical interpersonal difficulties likely to restrict, obstruct, or foil efforts of a remarried family to develop into a functioning unit. As noted, one area of frequent intergenerational conflict involves developing and maintaining rules—a crucial area because these rules help determine the effectiveness with which the stepparent can assume a parenting role. Rules regarding discipline, manners, the delegation of tasks and responsibilities, eating and sleeping habits, the form and intensity with which feelings (both positive and negative) are expressed—all need to be established as ongoing family patterns (Ganong & Coleman, 1987). In most cases, such rules can be established only after any underlying fear, anger, and resentment have been cleared up.

Since roles and boundaries are almost certain to be unclear, especially during the new family's formative stages, confusion and disorganization seem inevitable as the family seeks to establish some equilibrium. Einstein (1982) points out the importance of delineating

- physical boundaries: shared space, property, activities;
- psychological boundaries: the degree of intimacy, authority, and affection the family members share;
- roles: the rights and duties that determine family behavior patterns.

A new stepmother of an adolescent, for example, learns soon enough that such efforts may require considerable tact, thick skin, and the ability to tolerate frustration and rejection. (The same virtues may, of course, be expected in a biological parent dealing with his or her own adolescent.) Her desire to please her new spouse by rushing to be a much-loved substitute mother is almost certainly doomed to failure, and will likely be accompanied by a sense of personal defeat, rejection, and often, despair.

Under ordinary circumstances in an intact family, sibling attachments play a key role in helping children form a sense of identity, a self-concept. Ihinger-Tallman

---

**Box 5.1    A Problem-Appraisal Checklist for Remarried Families**

Remarried families may experience problems in the following areas:

- Difficulties of stepparent in assuming parental role
- Rivalry and jealousy between stepsiblings
- Boundary ambiguity
- Unfinished conflict between ex-spouses
- Competition between biological mother and stepmother (or biological father and stepfather)
- Idealization of absent parent
- Lack of intimacy between parent and nonbiological child
- Loyalty conflicts in children between absent parent and stepparent
- Loyalty conflicts in parent between absent children and stepchildren
- Children's surname differences
- Effects of birth of child from new marriage
- Financial obligations (alimony payments to ex-spouse, child support payments)
- Adolescent issues—change in custody requests; loosened sexual boundaries

---

(1987) points out further that "siblings also serve as defenders/protectors of one another; they interpret the outside world to each other, and they teach each other about equity, coalition formation, and the processes of bargaining and negotiation" (p. 164). They may at times serve as buffers against their parents. As contributors to the family "culture," they share common experiences, help establish a family history, and play an essential role in intergenerational continuity. Despite occasional disputes and rivalries, they generally feel positively bonded to one another.

In stepfamilies, such a history is missing, making attachments and eventual bonding all the more tentative and difficult to achieve. Relationship problems among stepsiblings may actually promote increased systemic problems within the family. As Henggeler and Borduin (1990) observe, adolescents may resent child-care responsibilities for younger stepsiblings; same-aged siblings may resent unfavorable comparisons regarding grades, appearance, or friends. Thus, integrating stepsiblings into the new family is a major task in most cases, especially (as in the case of Marlene and Dan cited earlier) when they have been part of established single-parent homes for any length of time. In these circumstances, where a special bond with the solo parent has developed, particularly when the child assumed the role of the absent spouse, it is understandable that the child feels betrayed at the very suggestion of remarriage. Data from Wallerstein and Kelly (1980b) on the children of divorce indicate that older children are especially resistant to accepting stepfathers, and often require several years before they come to terms with the realities of the remarried situation. In certain cases, it seemed unlikely that such acceptance of the stepfather as a family member would ever occur.

On the other hand, a stepfather who enters a family when a daughter is reaching puberty may, under certain circumstances, find himself in a situation ripe for triangulation between the husband, wife, and adolescent. While such mother-daughter competition is common, as is some form of triangulation, the competition may take on the character of sexual acting-out in families where problems exist. Without the normal incest taboos that act as powerful injunctions in an intact family, sexual boundaries may be loosened, leading to sexual abuse between a nonbiological parent with poor impulse control and a vulnerable child seeking closeness (Keshet & Mirkin, 1985). Sager et al. (1983) observe a range of responses in such an unstructured situation: pleasurable fantasies; repressed thoughts and distancing behavior; angry and violent fighting as a defense against sexual stirrings; and the extreme of sexual relations between stepparent and stepchild. Similarly, sexual involvement between stepsiblings is possible, particularly if they meet at adolescence, when no prior rules are yet in place regarding their relationship.

Generally speaking, according to Visher and Visher (1979), children do not welcome remarriage[2] for at least two reasons: (1) they may feel split in their loyalties to two sets of parents, and (2) they may continue to harbor the wish that their divorced parents will reunite, a fantasy that is undermined by the remarriage to someone else. As Keshet (1980) contends, a stepfamily by its very structure inevitably has strongly bounded subsystems to which members remain loyal. Unless such conflicting loyalties can be worked out, however, stepfamily integration will remain incomplete. In a study of 7- to 11-year-olds, followed up five years later, Baydar (1988) found that children in a remarriage often showed an increased number of emotional problems, had trouble concentrating, tended to withdraw, and (especially boys) showed signs of restlessness. Working therapeutically with children, counselors can hardly ignore the possible sources of stress from parental conflict or adjustments in the case of remarriage.

Children's initial assessment of their potential gains and losses from the formation of the new family (and the acquisition of new siblings) helps determine future stepsibling relationships (Ihinger-Tallman, 1987). Whether required to share attention and affection from his or her own parent, or friends and possessions (rooms, toys, pets) with a stepsibling, each child may feel short-changed, as though the loss exceeds the benefits of living in a new family. Conversely, in some cases, the children may perceive a mutual set of benefits without excessive personal costs, and strong emotional bonds may develop between them. There is certainly a very strong correlation between the ease with which the new parents form a close union, and the stepsiblings form a close union, since one process impacts on the other.

Residues from the former marriage of either or both newly united persons may afflict a remarriage, especially in its early stages of greatest vulnerability. As we have noted a number of times, divorce may represent the end of a marital affiliation, but most often it does not terminate the parenting relationship between

---

[2]There are exceptions to this statement that should be noted by counselors. Some children are delighted when a single parent remarries, feeling relieved of the burden of offering adult-style companionship. In some cases, the parent's depression may lift with remarriage, there may be more money available, and so on. Such children, however, may be particularly distressed when they sense a new divorce on the horizon.

ex-spouses. Thus, remarriage may cause previously agreed-upon custody arrangements, visitation schedules, or financial support payments to be renegotiated, thereby reopening old wounds between ex-combatants. Or conflict may develop between the stepfather and the biological father—for example, over discipline; sometimes the child's mother joins in; the child usually adds fuel to the resulting conflagration. In addition, a biological parent's jealousy about the new spouses and their more permanent living arrangement with his or her own children may be a threat.

As Westoff (1977) notes, "living ghosts"—photographs, furniture, laundry marks, monograms, habits—are a part of every remarriage, and thus a constant reminder of the time one's partner has spent with another in an intimate relationship. It is not surprising, then, that some divorced couples return to court, sometimes repeatedly, over issues ostensibly involving the children, when in reality they are continuing the battles that led to the divorce in the first place. Particularly when the unmarried ex-spouse did not want the divorce to take place and is now jealous over being displaced by the new marital partner, bitterness may linger and attach itself to any cause justifying litigation and a chance at revenge.

The counselor should be alert to various other potentially conflictual relationships in stepfamilies. In an early work, Bernard (1956), a sociologist, outlined six such relationship areas: (1) between the child's biological parents; (2) between the new parent and the biological parent of the same sex; (3) between the old in-laws and the new spouse; (4) between the new father and the children; (5) between the new mother and the children; and (6) between the children. Einstein (1982) points out that all of these conflict areas involve competition for the affection of the children.

Finally, all remarried families must come to terms with a number of persistent myths regarding stepfamily living. For example, the stereotype of the "wicked stepmother" plagues many women married to men with children. The term *stepchild* is a metaphor for neglect and abuse in many societies, and the stuff of endless fairy tales (Snow White, Hansel and Gretel, Cinderella) usually involving an uncaring or abusive stepmother and an uninformed or deceived or busy father. The myth no doubt originated at a time when stepfamilies were the result of death of a parent rather than divorce, and a stepmother was expected to raise her husband's child without much attention from her mate. In many cases, women were married by widowed fathers for the express purpose of raising the children, something men were not thought to be equipped for or expected to know how to do.

One consequence of these negative sexist stereotypes is the greater stress found in families with stepmothers than in corresponding stepfather families (Clingempeel, Brand, & Ievoli, 1984). Increased tension in such families is at least in part a function of increased social pressures on stepmothers and the general societal failure to fully accept this family form. For a variety of reasons, society expects more from a woman in her relationship with children than it does from a man with children. This seems to hold true whether the children are hers by birth, adoption, or remarriage. A man is expected to provide support or money (less so if his stepchildren are receiving child support from their father); whatever else he provides—and it may be significant—is all to the good, but not essential in the eyes of many people. Visher and Visher (1988a) suggest that many women still derive much of their self-esteem from their role as good parent, and this in turn may help account for more tension between mother and stepmother than between father and stepfather, contributing to increased stress in stepmother families.

Pasley and Ihinger-Tallman (1987) indicate that, compared to stepfathers, stepmothers tend to be less satisfied in their relationship with stepchildren, to feel more often that their marriage is negatively affected by their spouse's children, to be more dissatisfied with their role, and to feel more often that the relationship between them and the biological parent of the same sex is difficult. These researchers also found that, compared to stepfathers, stepmothers tend to be less involved with their stepchildren and to have more conflict with them; and children in stepmother families are at greater risk than their counterparts in stepfather families.[3] As we indicated earlier in reporting Duberman's (1975) findings, relationships between stepmothers and stepdaughters seem especially conflictual.

## THE DEVELOPMENTAL STAGES OF REMARRIAGE

Remarriage is more than a discrete event; it is a complex interactive process, extending over time, in which a group of individuals without a common history or established rituals or behavior patterns attempts to unite and to develop a sense of family cohesion and identity. Such a conversion or redefinition, which must be viewed as going back at least to the disintegration of the first marriage (McGoldrick & Carter, 1988), typically proceeds through certain predictable developmental phases, from the decision to separate, through the legal divorce and custody arrangements, to the remarriage and possible shifts in custody of one or more children, and ultimately to forging an integrated stepfamily unit. Counseling a family that is about to be remarried, we need to help them understand as best they can the reasons for the failed earlier marriages, the development of the separate family members since the divorce, and the future directions they anticipate as a new family. Above all they need to be counseled not to expect instant stepfamily unity, but instead to work together to slowly build a lasting identity as a family unit.

As Whiteside (1982) conceptualizes the process, the developmental sequence passes through several key stages: the initial married family, usually with children;

---

[3]Many family counselors believe that the quality of the relationship between stepparent and stepchild may actually be a better predictor of the family's ultimate adaptation to the remarriage than the quality of the marital dyad. It is entirely possible for a remarried couple to experience marital satisfaction while encountering dissatisfactions within the family regarding stepchildren. In many cases, such chronic problems may ultimately erode the marital bond. In other cases, however, the stepparent-stepchild interactive pattern may simply reflect the degree of connection and dedication of the marital couple to the remarriage.

a period of parting, as couples separate, divorce, and establish two households; a courting period with plans for remarriage; early remarriage, and finally, if successful, established remarriage. Each stage entails different forms of family organization in terms of boundaries, roles, legal ties, and emotional relationships. Each transition too requires significant disruption and change, and Whiteside has suggested that counselors can help normalize the process by informing members of common transitional dilemmas:

> Without clear expectations for what is needed or expected in roles such as single parent, non-custodial parent, stepparent, and stepchild, family members cannot easily employ available coping skills, solutions to problems can be less easily reached, and the situation is more likely to be felt as a crisis. (p. 60)

Whiteside's distinction between early and established marriages is significant for the counselor. The former concerns a transition into marriage and typically involves dealing with residual issues from the first marriage and the one-parent period, along with the challenges of forming a functional remarried system. Having just recently worked together to establish stability in the one-parent period, the family is likely to require help from the counselor in dealing with the disruption of that new-found stability. Families in the later stage of remarriage, although established in their interactive patterns, commonly seek counseling because of chronic distress regarding a never-resolved divorce, or because a noncustodial parent suffers from being cut off from a biological child, or because the stepfamily feels isolated from the family of origin; in some cases, a satisfactory remarriage structure may have been established but, as in nuclear families, life transitions or unexpected external traumas can strain the family's resources and produce symptoms in one or more members (Whiteside, 1989).

Bradt and Bradt (1986) provide the following colorful description of the stages of remarriage, beginning with the remarriage ceremony and proceeding, optimally, to the emergence of the new, integrated family structure. Progression from one stage to the next is made easier by the successful completion of the prior stage.

1. *Go back!* "What have I gotten myself into?" "Is this a mistake?" "I never thought it would be like this." The couple may be filled with doubt and apprehension; the children may protest in various ways and attempt to undermine the remarriage; friends and relatives may withhold support.
2. *Making room:* The family members learn to share physical territory and emotional space with others, delineate work/home allocations, and avoid a sense of being an intruder.
3. *Struggles of realignment:* Loyalty conflicts, power struggles, protests, and negotiation occur as former relationship alliances break down and are restructured.
4. *(Re)commitment:* A family identity is established as a budding of family feeling occurs, family mythology and ceremony evolve, shared experiences are created and defined, rituals regarding celebrations or vacations or family meetings are developed.

5. *Rebalancing relationships:* Once recommitment is achieved, the family members can freely move back and forth between the old and new households, defining different membership in each and maintaining loyalty to each, based on the present rather than the past.
6. *Relinquishing feelings of deprivation and burden:* Previously held feelings of being isolated, untrusting, overresponsible, unwilling to collaborate, and so on are given up as each member better defines obligations to self and others.
7. *Growth toward integration:* Having accepted differences, addressed challenges, acknowledged complexity, established commitments, and relinquished feelings of deprivation and burden, the family emerges with an identity and cohesiveness much like any other functioning family.
8. *Moving on:* Members are free to move into complex networks of relationships focused on problem solving, growth, and interaction with broader systems outside the family.

In each of the stages just outlined, major dislocations must be attended to and major adaptations made. Each stage evokes stress; each provides an opportunity for further growth and family consolidation, but also the risk of relapse and family disruption.

Carter and McGoldrick (1980) regard remarriage as one of the most difficult transitions a family is ever called upon to make. Because most members have experienced recent loss, pain, and a sense of ambiguity, they may wish prematurely for a feeling of closure, without understanding that they must confront the built-in complexities of the remarriage process. In most cases, what lies ahead before stepfamily integration can occur, according to Visher and Visher (1982), is mourning the losses of past family relationships, developing new family traditions, forming new interpersonal relationships within the new family, renegotiating ties with the absent biological parent, and, for children, learning to move satisfactorily between two households. It seems hardly surprising that the remarried family, especially when children are present, may be a fragile entity for a considerable period of time, highly vulnerable to a wide variety of interpersonal, generational, and emotional stresses.

Adopting a developmental point of view, Carter and McGoldrick (1988) contend that separation, divorce, and remarriage each represent significant dislocations in a family's life cycle, calling for additional restabilizing steps before the family can resume their ongoing development. Tables 5.2 and 5.3 represent their step-by-step outline of the process. In their view, the attitudes listed in column 2 of both tables are prerequisites for families to work out the developmental issues regarding divorce and postdivorce adjustment (column 3). The counselor who presses families to resolve the developmental issues without first helping them adopt the appropriate attitudes is, in the opinion of McGoldrick and Carter, wasting effort. These authors note further that restabilization calls for an additional ingredient, namely the passage of sufficient time. The counselor needs to communicate this point to families who feel harassed and impatient for change.

**Table 5.2 Dislocations of the Family Life Cycle Requiring Additional Steps to Permit Restabilization and Further Development**

| Phase | Emotional Process of Transition Prerequisite Attitude | Developmental Issues |
|---|---|---|
| *Divorce* | | |
| 1. The decision to divorce | Acceptance of inability to resolve marital tensions sufficiently to continue relationship | Acceptance of one's own part in failure of the marriage |
| 2. Planning the breakup of the system | Supporting viable arrangements for all parts of the system | Working cooperatively on problems of custody, visitation, finances<br>Dealing with extended family about the divorce |
| 3. Separation | Willingness to continue cooperative coparental relationship<br>Work on resolution of attachment to spouse | Mourning loss of intact family<br>Restructuring marital and parent-child relationships; adaptation to living apart<br>Realignment of relationships with extended family; staying connected with spouse's extended family |
| 4. The divorce | More work on emotional divorce: overcoming hurt, anger, guilt, and so on | Mourning loss of intact family: giving up fantasies of reunion<br>Retrieval of hopes, dreams, expectations from the marriage<br>Staying connected wih extended families |
| *Postdivorce Family* | | |
| A. Single-parent family | Willingness to maintain parental contact with ex-spouse and support contact of children and ex-spouse's family | Making flexible visitation arrangements with ex-spouse and ex-spouse's family<br>Rebuilding own social network |
| B. Single-parent (noncustodial) | Willingness to maintain parental contact with ex-spouse and support custodial parent's relationship with children | Finding ways to continue effective parenting relationship with children<br>Rebuilding own social network |

*Source:* Carter and McGoldrick, 1988, p. 22.

**Table 5.3   Remarried-Family Formation: A Developmental Outline**

| Steps | Prerequisite Attitude | Developmental Issues |
|---|---|---|
| 1. Entering the new relationship | Recovery from loss of first marriage (adequate emotional divorce) | Recommitment to marriage and to forming a family with readiness to deal with the complexity and ambiguity |
| 2. Conceptualizing and planning new marriage and family | Accepting one's own fears and those of new spouse and children about remarriage and forming a stepfamily<br>Accepting need for time and patience for adjustment to complexity and ambiguity of:<br>• multiple new roles<br>• boundaries: space, time, membership, and authority<br>• affective issues: guilt, loyality conflicts, desire for mutuality, unresolvable past hurts | Work on openness in the new relationships to avoid pseudomutuality<br>Plan for maintenance of cooperative coparental relationships with ex-spouses<br>Plan to help children deal with fears, loyalty conflicts, and membership in two systems<br>Realignment of relationships with extended family to include new spouse and children<br>Plan for maintenance of children's connections with extended family of ex-spouse(s) |
| 3. Remarriage and reconstitution of family | Final resolution of attachment to previous spouse and ideal of intact family<br>Acceptance of a different model of family with permeable boundaries | Restructuring family boundaries to allow for inclusion pf new spouse-stepparent<br>Realignment of relationships throughout subsystems to permit interweaving of several systems<br>Making room for relationships of all children with biological (noncustodial) parents, grandparents, and other extended family<br>Sharing memories and histories to enhance stepfamily integration |

*Source:* Carter and McGoldrick, 1988, p. 24.

If the future spouses come from different life-cycle phases (for example, an older man with adult children marrying a young woman with no children or with pre-teenage children), their differences in experiences and approaches to current responsibilities may delay stepfamily integration still further. The joining of partners at discrepant life-cycle phases calls for a process in which both learn to function in different phases simultaneously. Becoming a stepmother to a teenager before a honeymoon or before becoming an experienced wife or mother is disconcertingly contrary to normal life sequences. In the same way, the husband who is called upon to return to a life phase passed through years earlier—beginning a marriage or raising young children—may find the experience unappealing, especially if his previous marriage had difficulties during this phase. (He may, of course, find it rejuvenating, just as the out-of-sequence experience for the younger wife may prove enlightening and enriching.)

# SOME COUNSELING GUIDELINES

Remarried family life is unique, stepfamily dynamics complex, and the counselor who insists on dealing with such families as though they resembled intact biological families has undoubtedly started with a false set of assumptions that require correction. Counselors working with stepfamilies need to be aware of numerous and important structural differences between this family form and intact biological families, bearing in mind that each of these differences may be accompanied by specific stresses and tasks.

## COMMON THEMES AND COUNSELOR TASKS

The counselor attempting to deal effectively with a remarried family will most likely need to provide help in one or more of the following sets of problem areas:

1. *Mourning for losses.* A stepfamily is born of relationship losses, through death or divorce, and the relinquishing of hopes and dreams in the previous family. Special childhood positions in one family (for example, only child) may be lost with remarriage, and special household roles (for example, parent confidant to a single mother) surrendered. Adults must deal with finding or changing jobs, making new housing arrangements, and relinquishing some old friends and neighbors. Thus, counselors must help stepfamilies address these losses, psychologically disengage from the past, and begin to direct their lives toward future relationships. As an example, a session where the new family listens while the counselor explores the last six months before a mother died of cancer, encouraging the children to express what they experienced during that period and what a loss they continue to feel, may have a significant cathartic effect.

2. *Living with differences.* The stepfamily is made up of members with separate family histories and traditions. In addition, each family may come together at differing points in their life cycles (for example, late adolescent children and preschoolers) and with ways of doing things that seem incompatible. Thus, they are likely to have experiences and expectations significantly different from one another, and the counselor will need to help them negotiate differences that lead to interpersonal conflicts and direct their efforts toward building a new family system. A counselor may, for example, help a 12-year-old girl who feels she should have the same curfew time as her 15-year-old stepsister, or perhaps a 17-year-old boy who sorely resents a 3-year-old entering his room and messing with his things.

3. *Resolving loyalty issues.* Parent-child relationships precede the new couple bond, and adults may feel loyalty conflicts between love for their child and

love for their new marital partner. Children in stepfamilies often experience loyalty pulls between their natural parents, while at the same time feeling little loyalty to the stepfamily, especially in its early stages. The counselor may need to direct attention to helping all members learn to trust the new group and develop an identity as a remarried-family member. For many children, this may mean relinquishing the fantasy that their biological parents will reunite. Helping the remarried parents strengthen their marital bond (without feeling they are somehow betraying an earlier parent-child bond) may go a long way toward helping the child relinquish the fantasy. In this regard, counselors are accustomed to helping a child who was used to a close relationship with his or her mother before remarriage and now laments their lost closeness ("I could always come in and sit on your bed and talk to you, but now you are always with *him* and the bedroom door is closed.").

4. *Acknowledging the absent parent.* An absent biological parent exists in the case of divorce and, if the previous struggle between the biological parents remains unresolved, the children will likely be torn between the parents. The counselor must further help the family to avoid fostering an adversarial relationship between the new parent and the biological parent of the same sex. Continuing contact with the absent biological parent may actually aid the child's ability to form a relationship with the stepparent. The counselor's responsibility here is to help the family confront the problem; if necessary, the counselor may bring the absent father physically into the stepfamily sessions in order to help resolve the conflict.

5. *Living simultaneously in separate households.* Children often are members of two households, frequently with different rules and expectations and different parenting styles. Thus, transitions between the two may be stressful for all concerned, and stability may take time to achieve. Counselors may need to help children understand that a relationship with the noncustodial parent continues to exist despite periodic separations. In general, children should be encouraged to remain in contact with both parents, especially if the ex-mates can work out the details in an amicable fashion. Encouraging each set of parents to allow for tension on reentry into their household is often therapeutic for all concerned.

6. *Developing a family identity.* There is no legal relationship between stepparents and stepchildren (although later adoption is possible), and adults may therefore have reservations about getting involved emotionally with someone who may disappear from their lives at some future date. The counselor needs to be aware that stepfamily integration—especially stepparent-stepchild bonding—takes time, perhaps years. To attempt to fit the stepfamily into a biological family mold is doomed to failure, with the possible rare exception of stepfamilies forming when all the children are very young.

7. *Overcoming boundary problems.* Successfully disengaging from previous marital systems and forming a boundary around the new couple and their household can often be an arduous task, what with regular visitation schedules and the presence of the noncustodial parent. Children may impede progress in the

disengagement, which is necessary for forming a new, integrated stepfamily. Counselors need to guide stepfamilies to make the separation, as well as create boundaries within the new stepfamily where new roles and new rules can be worked out together.

8. *Learning coparenting.* In most cases, the counselor should encourage the maintenance of an open system with permeable boundaries between current and former spouses and their families. An open coparental relationship is extremely desirable, especially if the former mates have worked out their emotional divorce and any lingering bitterness between them is kept to a minimum. Children should never have the power to decide on remarriage, custody, or visitation, since that would violate the parental boundaries and responsibilities; however, their input into such parental decisions does deserve attention.

## STEPFAMILY STAGES AND COUNSELOR INTERVENTIONS

Recognizing that the stepfamily's ultimate goal is greater self-definition as a new family unit, counselors need to appreciate that stepfamily cohesion and ultimately integration require time and occur in stages. Each stage in the process of solidifying a remarried family's attempt to achieve an identity calls for the renegotiating and reorganizing of a complex and dynamic network of relationships. Thus, at each juncture, there is risk of unresolved issues from the previous stages reemerging and old feelings flaring up, especially if these have been covered over in the rush to form a united remarried family.

Counseling efforts, in addition to persistently supporting the growth and integration of the new family, must address the relationship problems specific to the stage of the family's development. Early on, this may mean directing therapeutic attention to helping members successfully relinquish lost dreams and relationships.

Stepfamily members may also require help in learning new roles or perhaps in beginning to examine boundary realignments now that a new family entity has been formed. Perhaps new conflict-resolving mechanisms can be encouraged by the counselor and new decision-making structures set in place. Bray (1992) suggests that three key developmental issues are likely to require resolution during the first years of remarriage: arranging for discipline and parental authority for children; forming a strong marital bond; and developing a workable relationship with the noncustodial parent.

Later in the history of the remarried family, relationship rules may need revision, or a child born to the remarried couple may need to be incorporated into the boundaries of the family. Whatever brings the family to the counselor, problems related to the phase of the family's development and integration must be scrutinized. McGoldrick and Carter (1988) draw special attention to the impact of remarriage in the two possible family life-cycle combinations:

*When spouses are at different life-cycle stages:* Family members may experience greater difficulties in making the necessary transitions, and thus are likely to take longer to integrate into a working family.

*When spouses are at the same life-cycle stage:* Stepfamily integration is generally easier, in that family members are dealing with similar life-stage tasks. On the other hand, problems may arise if family members feel overloaded by such tasks as coping with stepchildren, ex-spouses, in-laws, and others.

The early stages of remarriage require interventions that help the new family gradually develop new shared rules and values that feel right to all the members (Whiteside, 1983). Strengths carried over from the previous family need to be acknowledged, and feelings of tension, confusion, and frustration accepted as normal and to be expected. Later in the remarriage, unhappy coalitions within the stepfamily may challenge family stability and equilibrium, or perhaps normal life-cycle events (the birth of more children, shifts in custody arrangements at adolescence, children growing up and leaving home) may cause disruption in family functioning. At each transition, Whiteside urges that the counselor help the family reach back into its history, review its past solutions, and clarify and construct relationship patterns to meet the current challenge.

## COUNSELING ON MULTIPLE TRACKS

Sager et al. (1983) argue that the precursor of remarriage has been the simultaneous disruption in three aspects of the life cycle—the individual, the marital, and the family—and that the counselor must consider dislocations in all three in order to obtain a comprehensive picture of what transpires in the transition to remarriage. The focus here is on the suprafamily system, composed of functionally related subsystems such as the marital couple, the wife and former husband, and also aunts, uncles, and grandparents. At the beginning of counseling, all members of this suprafamily are seen together, thus forming a therapeutic relationship with all concerned; later, various subgroups are seen, as called for by the stage and content of counseling.

According to the formulation of Sager et al., the conflicts in remarried families are generated in that each spouse has to operate along multiple tracks, dealing simultaneously with possibly incongruent individual, marital, and family life cycles. For example, as a consequence of divorce and remarriage, individual life cycles are lived out over the course of two or more marriages. As these authors observe, husbands and wives may be simultaneously biological parents and stepparents; conflicts may exist in a father, for example, between loyalty to his natural children and to the stepchildren with whom he resides on a daily basis. With remarriage, the man must cope with the complexities of not only being part of an old family life cycle and perhaps of an old marital cycle with an ex-wife but also beginning a new marital cycle and a complicated new family cycle with stepparent-stepchild relationships! The counselor needs to remain alert to the array of tracks on which the systems and their members are likely to be operating, and to ascertain if developmental needs are being sufficiently met in the different systems.

By the time a man or woman contemplates remarriage, he or she has gone through a number of powerful structural life changes in all three life-cycle areas.

Sager et al. (1983) offer as illustration the case of Amy Greenson (Table 5.4) as she separates from her family of origin, marries, has children, separates, divorces, lives as a single parent, and then remarries, beginning a new family life cycle. Note how previous and new marital and family cycles are current and overlap, and how new life-cycle tracks are added to her life, rather than merely replacing old ones.

Reading the table vertically provides a longitudinal view of her life along each life cycle; horizontally, the reader gets a cross-sectional view of what is transpiring simultaneously in her individual, marital, and family life cycles. For example, we see at ages 45 to 50 that by remarrying she has added an additional marital-cycle track to her existence, not merely moving from one marriage to another. Hence she must deal at one and the same time with difficulties allowing herself to love again (individual cycle), coparenting her daughters from her first marriage through adolescence as well as entering a new marriage (marital cycle), and restructuring her family to now include a stepson as well as her new husband, in addition to caring about her aging parents (family cycle). As is undoubtedly clear from this example, and as Sager et al. (1983) point out, the conflict and stress felt by many dysfunctional remarried couples arise from attempting to deal with the multiple tracks that are by definition part of the remarried-family suprasystem.

Counseling such often-multiproblem families starts by involving as many members as possible, establishing a working alliance with each, and beginning the process of making each feel safe in the counseling environment. Sager et al. (1983) strongly recommend the early use of three-generational genograms, as do McGoldrick and Carter (1988) as well as Visher and Visher (1988a). Since such a large amount of data needs to be organized, the schematic drawing provides information about previous marriages, the length of any single-parent–household periods, and possible shifts in children's living arrangements. A clearer picture of the complexity of the suprafamily system is likely to emerge, offering some basis for understanding why the members are experiencing current stress and confusion. Later, sessions with various subgroups can be arranged for further assessment purposes, and a treatment plan directed at specific problems in the individual, marital, and family life cycles of the particular remarried family is developed. Overall, the process is intended to refocus and redefine the family's problems in terms of the whole remarried system and its needs and individual responsibilities.

## WHOM TO SEE AND WHEN

Visher and Visher (1988b) argue that, although the type of problem or specific characteristics of the remarried family are important in determining what combination of members to see, the major determinant is the remarried family's stage of development. Families are unlikely to contact a counselor during an early fantasy stage (see Table 5.5), preferring other informational or self-education sources for help. Should they seek counselor aid during the following three stages (pseudo-assimilation, awareness, and mobilization), it is likely that the stepparent has begun

**Table 5.4   The Individual, Marital, and Family Life Cycles in a Remarried Family**

| Age | Individual Life Cycle | Marital Life Cycle | Family Life Cycle |
|---|---|---|---|
| 18–21 | Pulls up roots. Develops autonomy. (Amy M. moves out of family's home and attends college in another city.) | Shift from family of origin to new emotional commitment. (Amy meets George Greenson and they begin to date exclusively.) | During college, Amy still financially dependent on her family of origin; her old room is kept for her at home. |
| 22–28 | Provisional adulthood. Develops occupational identification. (Amy graduates and works as a teacher; shares apartment and then lives alone.) | Provisional marital commitment; stress over parenthood. (Amy and George engaged when Amy is 23; marry at 24.) | Self-sufficient vis-à-vis family of origin; her room at home is converted to study. |
| 29–31 | Transition at age 30; decides about commitment to work and marriage. | Commitment crisis. (Married six years, George is questioning the relationship. They receive marital counseling.) | Pressure from her family to stay together and have children; her father retires. |
| 32–39 | Settling down, deepening commitments. (Amy feels committed to George and desires children; she stops working with birth of first child.) | Productivity: children, friends, work for George. (Their daughters are born when Amy is 32 and 34.) | Family with young children: need to accept new members, take on parenting roles. |
| 40–42 | Midlife transition; searching for fit between aspirations and environment. (Amy questions homemaker role, is restless and dissatisfied. After an impetuous sexual misadventure, she avoids dating.) | Couple is summing up; success and failure evaluated. (Amy and George again receive counseling; George has affair; decision to separate is made when children are 6 and 8 years old.) | Postseparation family: two households are set up. Amy returns to live with her parents; there is a resurgence of dependence on her family of origin as she returns to the job market. She has custody of children, who visit father. Grandparents very involved with children while Amy works and begins to date. |
| 43–45 | Middle adulthood: restabilizing and reordering priorities; struggle to reestablish autonomy from her family of origin; dealing with work advancement. (Now begins to desire a loving relationship with a man.) | Continuing coparenting relationship although marriage is dissolved. Beginning to date. Testing out new ways of relating to men. | Double single-parent stage: girls are now 11 and 9 and are part of both parents' households. |

| | | |
|---|---|---|
| 46–50 | Tasks of middle adulthood continue. Emotional divorce from George sufficiently complete for her to contemplate idea of marriage again. (Difficulty allowing herself to trust again as love relationship develops.)<br><br>Remarries to fulfil coupling needs. Simultaneously continues coparenting of her children with first husband while taking on coparenting role with second husband. | *Marriage #1*<br>Need to coparent the girls through their adolescence. Dealing with ex-husband on issues around the girls such as dating and their desire to visit father less often.<br><br>*Marriage #2*<br>1. Entering new relationship with Steve.<br>2. Planning and conceptualizing new marriage.<br>3. Remarriage.<br>4. Making new commitment.<br>5. Commitment crisis: questioning choice.<br>6. Resolving conflicts and stabilizing remarriage. | *Old Family*<br>Allowing adolescent children to individuate.<br><br>Launching children and moving on.<br><br>Dealing with aging and illness of her parents.<br><br>*Rem Family*<br>Restructuring family to include new spouse and stepson (age 10) who lives with Rem couple.<br><br>Providing a nurturing environment to prepubescent child. Dealing with Steve's ex-wife.<br><br>Family with adolescent child. (Cycle repeats what Amy experienced with her girls.)<br><br>Launching child and moving on. |
| 51–59 | | *Marriage #1*<br>Coparenting relationship is less important. Establishing a workable relationship with George around their adult children.<br><br>*Marriage #2*<br>7. Supporting and enjoying friends and activities as children begin to leave home. | |
| 59+ | Looking ahead to enjoying the later years. Dealing with her own aging process. | *Marriage #1*<br>Little contact with George except for milestone events of children and grandchildren.<br><br>*Marriage #2*<br>8. Continuing support; retirement, pursuit of interests, individually and together with Steve. | *Old Family*<br>Relating to her children's spouses and children.<br><br>*Rem Family*<br>Relating to stepson's spouse and children. |

*Source:* Sager et al., 1983, pp. 51–53.

**Table 5.5  Determination of Whom to See in Therapy**

| Stage | Characteristics | Productive Therapeutic Contacts |
|---|---|---|
| I. Fantasy | Adults expect instant love and adjustment. Children try to ignore stepparent in hopes that he or she will go away and biological parents will be reunited. | 1. Couple<br>2. Stepfamily household (unlikely to see anyone except for education) |
| II. Pseudo-Assimilation[a] | Attempts to realize fantasies. Vague sense that things are not going well. Increasing negativity. Splits along biological lines. Stepparents feel something is wrong with them. | 1. Couple seen individually and/or conjointly<br>2. Children if disturbed |
| III. Awareness | Growing awareness of family pressures. Stepparent begins to perceive what changes are needed. Parent feels pulled between needs of children and new spouse. Groups divide along biological lines. Children may observe and exploit differences between couple. Usually takes outside push—reading, stepfamily group, support from a friend, therapy—to get to stage IV. | 1. Couple seen individually and/or conjointly.<br>2. Children if need help urgently |
| IV. Mobilization | Strong emotions begin to be expressed, often leading to arguments between couple. Stepparent clear on need for change. Parent fears change will bring loss. Sharp division between biological groups. Stepparent with no children is in isolated position and lacks support. | 1. Couple seen individually and/or conjointly.<br>2. Children if need help urgently |
| V. Action | Couple begins working together to find solutions. Family structure changes. Boundaries are clarified. Children may resist changes. | 1. Emphasis on couple<br>2. Appropriate subgroups<br>3. Suprasystem subgroup combinations |
| VI. Contact | Couple working well together. Closer bonding between stepparent and stepchild and other steprelations. Stepparent has definite role with stepchildren. Boundaries clear. More ability to deal with suprasystem issues. | 1. Any suprasystem grouping (depends on issues) |
| VII. Resolution | Stepfamily identity secure. When difficulties arise, family may regress to earlier stages, but moves ahead quickly. Usual difficulties are around nodal family events involving the suprasystem. | 1. Any suprasystem grouping (unlikely to come in now) |

[a]Papernow uses the term *assimilation*. Visher and Visher consider *pseudo-assimilation* to be a more accurate description of this stage.

*Source:* Visher and Visher, 1988b, p. 237.

to recognize that something is wrong and changes are required. Here the authors recommend the counselor see the couple alone in order to strengthen their relationship; if counseling is successful, children may not need to be seen or can be seen, if necessary, after the couple relationship becomes viable.

Once the couple has formed a cohesive unit, various combinations of family members working conjointly with the counselor are possible. During the action stage, appropriate subgroups may meet together with the counselor in order to manage specific family problems. If working well, relationships between all stepfamily relatives may deepen (contact stage) and resolution may be reached as the stepfamily strengthens its sense of identity.

The counselor's immediate task, according to this formulation, is to assess the stepfamily's stage of development, as a preliminary to determining which subgroups should be seen first, and whether certain individuals or subgroups need to be seen at once or can wait to join the counseling after the couple has achieved adequate stability.

## THREE CASE STUDIES

First, we consider a remarried family with a stepfather:

❋    ❋    ❋    ❋    ❋

Juan and Maria had known one another growing up in a poor, rural part of El Salvador, but were not close friends. Both were members of large families, and both lived among large extended family networks. Since the families needed their help in making a living, both were taken out of school after five or six years and worked alongside their parents and siblings as farm workers.

When Maria's parents realized that more money was needed to support the family of six children than they could possibly earn, her father headed north, crossing the border illegally in California and making his way to the Central Valley to earn cash as a farm worker and send the money back to his family. Hoping to find work since there were few opportunities in El Salvador, Maria joined him when she reached 16, and together they shared a small apartment near the fields. When she was 18, hoping to escape life with her controlling father, Maria married a Mexican laborer, Luis, and a daughter, Isabella, was born the following year. However, the marriage was shaky from the start—Luis drank heavily and frequently became sexually involved with other women. Moreover, when drunk, he was physically abusive to Maria and Isabella. When he left one day to take a job in another part of the country, Maria felt relieved to be rid of him, and drifted into a series of relationships with men, in part to relieve her loneliness and also to gain some financial support. She became the mother of Elvira as a result of one such union.

Juan too had migrated to the United States as soon as he was 17. For the most part he worked at odd jobs—parking lot attendant, busboy, delivering new telephone directories—until he was told by a friend about a job as a carpenter's assistant at a construction site. Applying himself to the work, which he enjoyed, he stayed with the construction company, ultimately joined the union, and now worked on a more or less regular basis depending on available work in the home-construction business.

When Juan and Maria met at a friend's house, they remembered one another and immediately began dating. After several months, Maria divorced Luis and she and Juan were married. He seemed willing to take on the role of stepfather to the two girls, and they felt happy finally to have a "real" family with a mother and father. However, consistent with his cultural background, but also due to his lack of experience with raising children, he disciplined them in a heavy-handed manner. Problems between them soon developed, and Juan complained that the children did not accept his strong authority.

Maria and Juan were reasonably happy for a short period of time, although they did quarrel from time to time over what she perceived as his need to control her. He was jealous of her contact with other people, and suspicious of her whereabouts if she was late coming home from marketing. While he insisted that she have no secrets from him, he refused to tell her how he spent his paycheck. Whenever she complained that their 700-square-foot house was too crowded—besides the parents and children, Juan's brother now lived with them—he shouted at her, threatened to hit her, and told her to get a job if she wanted more money. Ridiculing her religious beliefs, he sarcastically told her on more than one occasion to pray for a job, that perhaps that would help.

When Maria learned about the availability of counseling from a neighbor, she asked Juan to go with her, but he refused. However, after the initial session with her, the counselor called Juan on the telephone and persuaded him to attend joint sessions, which he agreed to do only if it would help Maria to stop complaining about him. Together they attended six counseling sessions.

Realizing that their number of visits would be short, the counselor tried to help them redefine their relationship as a partnership in which each could benefit. Maria was urged to support and back up Juan in taking on coparenting authority with the children, which he desired, and Juan was advised that Maria would be more responsive to his needs if she did not feel so controlled and imprisoned by him. They were urged to listen to each other's suggestions about the children's problems. Together they were counseled to strengthen their marital bond by defining the boundary between themselves and the children. With no interference from Maria's former husband Luis, whose whereabouts they did not know, they were able to proceed to build and strengthen the stepfamily structure. While by no means problem-free, at the conclusion of counseling they left better prepared for working together as a family.

❋    ❋    ❋    ❋    ❋

Unlike the stepfather family just described, in the following case a newly formed stepmother family runs into trouble almost from the beginning:

❋   ❋   ❋   ❋   ❋

Joyce and David Oliver had been married only eight months when they contacted a family counselor as a last resort. Both in their late 20s, Joyce had never been married, establishing a career in business, while David, previously married, had been divorced for about a year when they met at a ski resort. They had a great time together and, after seeing each other daily for several months when they returned to the city, they decided to marry. David had spoken briefly of Kiri, his 4-year-old daughter who lived with his ex-wife in another state, but Joyce did not see the child as having much to do with her since Kiri lived with her mother. She had met her future stepdaughter only once before the wedding ceremony.

The family problems began shortly after the wedding, when Rhonda, David's former spouse, announced that she was having some personal problems, including some with Kiri, and was sending her to live with David and Joyce. For David, who took his parental responsibilities very seriously, this was a welcome opportunity to see Kiri on a regular basis and take an active part in her upbringing. At last he would have the perfect family he had always dreamed of, the perfect harmony that he had failed to achieve in his previous marriage. Having had no experience with children, Joyce wasn't sure what to expect but was eager to share parental responsibilities if it would make her new husband happy.

Unfortunately, David's dreams failed to materialize, in no small part due to his own behavior, as well as Kiri's. She was not an easy child to live with, having been suddenly whisked away from an overclose mother. Confused and frightened, she clung to her father, quickly becoming overattached to him, and excluded her stepmother. David, in turn, feeling guilty over his child's obvious upset, became very attached to Kiri, so much so that at times it felt to Joyce that he preferred the child's company to hers. Instead of learning to live with her new husband, Joyce soon felt she was saddled with an instant family in which she felt like an outsider in her own home. David would call Kiri daily before coming home from work, to see if she needed him to bring anything home. When his wife objected and complained of feeling "frozen out," he defended himself as merely acting as any concerned parent would, adding that Joyce's jealousy forced him to do even more for Kiri than he might have if Joyce had done more.

Evenings, David would put Kiri to bed; if he stayed more than the 10 minutes he had promised Joyce, she would get depressed, withdraw, and not talk to him the rest of that evening. According to David, Joyce was a spoiled child herself, competitive with a 4-year-old, and he was losing respect for her. During their joint sessions with a family counselor, he spoke of being raised by a widowed mother as an only child, and how central to his life was the feeling of family closeness. Joyce, on the other hand, insisted that David did not allow her to develop a relationship with Kiri, expecting her to instantly love someone because he did, but doing nothing to instill in Kiri that they had to reorganize the family to include all three of them. She herself had been raised by a divorced mother in a relatively disengaged family where all three children lived relatively separate lives.

The conflict between them had reached the boiling point by the time the couple contacted the counselor. David labeled his wife a "wicked stepmother," whom he threatened to leave unless she "corrected her behavior." She, in turn, accused her husband of having a "romance" with his daughter, strongly implying that there might be more to the father-daughter relationship than was evident. Neither was willing to listen to what the counselor was saying, each apparently eager to win his favor and favorable judgment regarding who was right. Joyce would hear of nothing short of sending Kiri back to her mother; David insisted he would not be given an ultimatum regarding how to deal with his own child. While the counseling was in its early stages, Rhonda announced that she had gotten remarried, to Mel, and that she was pregnant.

The counselor began by indicating he was not there to judge who was right, but to help them gain some tools for understanding what was happening to them. It was clear both were miserable, as Kiri undoubtedly was also. If they continued this way, they would almost certainly get divorced, an unfortunate circumstance for both of them since their marriage had not had a chance.

In order to reduce the white heat between them so that counseling might proceed, the counselor attempted two early interventions. One was to reduce the tension by asking them to describe their own histories of childrearing. The information would be useful later, and for the moment would help each begin to grasp that they had come into parenting with different experiences and expectations. As another initial intervention ploy, he asked whether they would be willing to listen to what the other had to say, without condemning it or getting defensive or resorting to name calling. The counselor thus appealed to their rational selves and, since each was anxious not to be labeled the difficult or unreasonable one, they agreed.

Each proceeded to discuss his or her view of childrearing. They had clear disagreements based on different experiences of their own, and the counselor helped each to listen and try to understand. Joyce's rejecting behavior toward Kiri was relabeled by the counselor as inexperience rather than wickedness; David's overinvolvement was relabeled as eagerness to be a good father. Joyce acknowledged she could learn from David, since she had known little parental attention and affection growing up; however, she insisted he would have to try to be less critical of her if he really wanted her to make the effort. David acknowledged he might be overdoing the parenting, since he had not had a father of his own as a model. The counselor helped him understand that fathers who obtain custody often have unrealistic expectations of how a stepmother should behave. In this case, he was willing to relinquish some parenting chores as he became convinced that she was willing to try. He was encouraged to avoid any coalitions with Kiri against Joyce.

The next phase of the counseling dealt with reestablishing boundaries. The counselor explained that stepfamily blending does not come automatically or instantly, but only through a gradual rearrangement of the new family's structure.

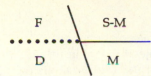

F                    S-M          The diffuse boundary between father and daughter indi-
                                  cates they have formed an overinvolved or enmeshed
                                  relationship; the stepmother is isolated and excluded, as
D                    M            is the absent biological mother.

Precounseling

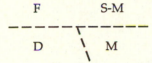

F                    S-M          A restructuring has occurred, and a clear boundary  now
                                  exists between the united parents and the daughter, as
D                    M            well as between the daughter and her biological mother.

Postcounseling

**Figure 5.2**   Pre- and Postcounseling Structural Mapping of the Oliver Remarried Family

It was agreed that David would allow Joyce to do more of the parenting in the best way she saw fit—even if it differed from his way—and that he would explain to Kiri that Rhonda was still her mother, but Joyce would be taking over the day-to-day job, with his approval, when Kiri lived with them. That is, Kiri was told that Joyce was not replacing her biological mother, only supplementing her while Kiri remained with them. Kiri could visit her mother whenever it could be arranged, something she expressed an interest in doing, especially after her stepsister was born. Kiri was told by David and Joyce together that she was a member of two households; she could feel free to move between the two without loyalty conflicts.

David and Joyce had their own loyalty issues to resolve. As he came to understand that he had given his daughter his first loyalty, primarily out of guilt over the impact of his failed marriage on Kiri, he recognized that he was contributing to the diminution of his marital relationship. Joyce too recognized that, because she felt in a secondary position, she struggled against the child excessively, forcing David to defend Kiri; thus, she too contributed to the deteriorating marriage. The counselor helped them untangle these difficulties, focusing them on working to strengthen their separate identity as a couple and their primary loyalty to each other. They were encouraged to spend more time alone as a couple, sharing activities that did not include Kiri. As this occurred, their bond grew; differences between the couple, although still present, began to be negotiated in a more open fashion rather than through a father-daughter vs. stepmother conflict. New rules and happier solutions followed, as David, Joyce, and Kiri began to develop their own traditions and to define themselves as a family.

❀   ❀   ❀   ❀   ❀

Note the counselor's goals in this case:

1. Reduce the accusations and blame-fixing between the adults.
2. Reframe or relabel the behavior each finds objectionable in the other as well-intentioned, thereby diffusing some of the self-righteous rage and indignation.
3. Appeal to each adult's wish to be seen as reasonable and fair in hearing out the spouse's contentions.
4. Define the problem as a systems one to which each member, including the child, is contributing.
5. Strengthen the spousal subsystem, encouraging their loyalty to each other and their common purpose and family identity.
6. Consolidate parental authority and unity in regard to the child without her experiencing loss of her biological mother.
7. Help reduce loyalty conflicts for the child and adults.
8. Keep the remarried system an open system with permeable boundaries, so that the child derives a sense of security from the home where she lives, but also retains membership in her other household.
9. Help the family members to tolerate differences among themselves or from some ideal intact family model.
10. Encourage the development of new rules, behavior patterns, and family traditions.

With the Oliver family, as with all stepfamilies, the counselor's overall task is to help the fragmented family become more cohesive and better integrated. In addition to helping family members develop a sense of identity as a family unit and strengthening the new marital bond, the counselor needs to pay attention to fortifying the sibling bond where stepsiblings exist. Pasley (1985) advises that helping stepfamilies build generational boundaries within the new stepfamily system rather than supporting original family boundaries will facilitate stepfamily integration. She recommends further that counselors invite both households to participate in the counseling process, in order to provide greater clarity regarding the roles and responsibilities of the various members in the enlarged stepfamily suprasystem.

In the following joint-custody case, the counselor meets with all four main adults in the suprasystem—the custodial parent, the noncustodial parent, the spouse of the custodial parent, and the spouse of the noncustodial parent—despite the fact that the identified patient is one of the preadolescent children:

❊    ❊    ❊    ❊    ❊

Kevin, aged 11, was doing extremely poorly in school. The teacher complained that he was hyperactive in class, and seemed unable to sit still or attend to class activity for more than three or four minutes at a time. The older of two children, Kevin, along with Mark, 8, lived in a joint-physical-custody arrangement, generally

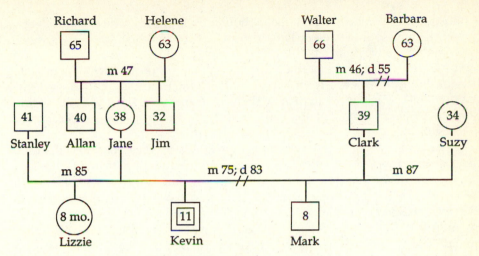

**Figure 5.3** Genogram of Kevin's Suprafamily

staying at his remarried father's home three days a week and at his remarried mother's four days. When the teacher contacted both parents, each angrily blamed the other for the problems Kevin was having, but ultimately their physician persuaded them to take him to a university-affiliated pediatric clinic for an evaluation.

It was clear almost immediately to the pediatrician who worked on Kevin's case that more was involved than simply what was going on inside the boy. He was aware that the continuous fighting between both sets of parents was having a damaging impact on Kevin, so before he prescribed medication (in this case, Ritalin) for the hyperactivity, he recommended that the four adults seek family counseling. Although they initially resisted the idea, he finally insisted that he could not go ahead with treating Kevin until the family conflict had been reduced. After two weeks of further bickering between the couples, they agreed to see a family counselor the pediatrician had recommended. However, each couple expressed doubts about the wisdom of working together, since their prior efforts in conciliation court (over issues regarding finances, visitation schedules, and custody changes) had proved pointless and unsuccessful.

The counselor made it clear from the start that she would only see them as a foursome. When she greeted them in the waiting room, she could see that they were poised to fight, an impression that was confirmed as soon as they entered the consultation room. They immediately attempted to set the counseling agenda along the lines of their previous conciliation court experience, each couple pulling out divorce settlements to back up their claims. The counselor spent some time dissociating herself from the legal process, and the current counseling from their past experiences. The first session was spent identifying the players—Suzy had recently married Clark, Kevin's father; Stanley and Jane (Kevin's mother) had been married for four years and had a newborn child—and filling out a genogram.

Subsequent sessions revealed that, although each former spouse believed that the other's new spouse had initiated the trouble between them, the truth seemed to be that the new spouses had simply empowered their mates to stand up and fight—Clark to limit his financial contribution to the support of the two children, previously given generously, now that he had remarried; Jane to demand that the boys' father help more in picking them up from school and take them more often on holidays, now that she had the additional responsibility of caring for her newborn, Lizzie.

Rather than deal with these difficult issues right away, the counselor refocused their attention on the presenting problem of Kevin's school performance, asking each couple how they understood what was happening to him at school. As each spoke, they began to be aware that Kevin showed similar behavior at home and that, what was more, each experienced him in the same way. He was obstreperous, irresponsible, fidgety, and forgetful about doing his assigned chores, and he frequently fought with Mark. Whereas each couple had assumed previously that they were burdened with his problematic behavior and that the other couple was spared, they now began to recognize that both sets of parents were having identical experiences, and neither was being handed a problem created by the visit to the other, as each had assumed.

The counselor's strategy of getting them to work together on solving their common problem seemed to pay off. Each ex-spouse started to view the other's new spouse as a real person—someone who did indeed create some difficulties but, contrary to what had been assumed, was not responsible for certain other problems. With greater insight came greater sympathy and less scapegoating. Rather than remaining angry with one another, they started tentatively to work together on helping Kevin. As they spoke together in the counselor's office weekly, they recognized that each set of parents was alternating between being too rigid in their demands on Kevin—asking for more than he could give and thus creating an inevitable failure situation—and then giving up in defeat and frustration and becoming too lax and undemanding. The counselor helped them work at being consistent, offering specific suggestions ("You are asking him to perform too long a chore"; "Make sure he is expected to do the same thing in both homes") that, coming from a neutral authority, all four seemed to accept.

The consistency was not lost on Kevin either. Instead of getting a weekly bombardment in each home about the shortcomings (or evil intent or craziness) of the other set of parents, Kevin now heard the parents talk in more supportive terms about one another's efforts. His relationship with Mark improved, as he became less competitive with him for parental approval. Both sets of parents seemed less tense with one another and better organized, and that was comforting to Kevin. He became less confused at school and less agitated, although his short attention span continued to be a problem.

By strengthening the coparental coalition, the counselor had helped create a more secure set of home environments. Kevin was sent back to the pediatric clinic, where he was put on a trial run of Ritalin. Although it was dramatically effective at school, all four parents were frightened of keeping him on drugs, and began to compete at home over which set of parents was able to keep him off the medication longer while he resided with them during the week. After consulting with the pediatrician, the counselor persuaded the parents to accept the drug use, since it helped greatly in focusing Kevin's attention first at school and later at home.

All four parents were thrilled by Kevin's progress, as well as their ability to discuss issues about the children with one another without quarreling. Slowly they ironed out the final issue to be resolved—their financial differences. The counselor asked them to come a half hour early for their next appointment and to meet in the waiting room to work out solutions to practical issues (for example, scheduling the time and place of pickup) between them. They did so successfully and, when the counselor was away on vacation, they met at the neutral territory of a local recreation center to continue talking.

The counseling dealt with such powerful issues as competitiveness and jealousy between the biological mother and stepmother, as well as economic and social conflict between the father and stepfather. The system in which both sets of parents participated remained open and the boundaries permeable. The parents felt an increased sense of self-esteem, considerably different from their earlier feeling of anger and helplessness regarding childrearing. Together they learned negotiating skills, vital in remarried-family situations.

Some issues remained unsettled. Anger surfaced occasionally over money, and both of Kevin's parents continued to feel some injustices left over from the original marriage. However, they did agree to put aside their differences in the service of their newly developed family stability. Kevin became increasingly attached to his stepsister, Lizzie, and helped out with her when he could. Suzy and Clark, having survived a crisis over a stepchild that nearly wrecked their marriage, were feeling more optimistic about the future, and were planning to adopt a baby.

❀　❀　❀　❀　❀

## PSYCHOEDUCATIONAL PROGRAMS

Beyond family counseling, stepfamilies can often profit from reading about the experiences of other stepparents and stepchildren (for example, Einstein, 1982). Another important information resource is the stepfamily-awareness movement, led by the Stepfamily Association of America. This national nonprofit organization founded by Emily and John Visher has state and local chapters that offer a variety of educational programs (training for professionals; referral to counselors who work with stepfamilies) and provide a network of mutual help services (survival courses in stepfamily living). Its quarterly publication, *Stepfamily Bulletin,* is intended to act as an advocate of stepfamily life, while keeping the readers, many of whom are themselves stepfamily members, informed on the latest studies and events that affect the stepfamily. Visher and Visher (1986) have developed a stepfamily workbook manual (an excerpt from which is shown in Box 5.2) to aid in discussion groups aimed at structuring new suprafamily systems.

**Box 5.2   Tasks That Must Be Completed to Develop a Stepfamily Identity**

1. Dealing with losses and changes
2. Negotiating different developmental needs
3. Establishing new traditions
4. Developing a solid couple bond
5. Forming new relationships
6. Creating a "parenting coalition"
7. Accepting continual shifts in household composition
8. Risking involvement despite little societal support

1. Dealing with losses and changes
   * Identify/recognize losses for all individuals
   * Support expressions of sadness
   * Help children talk and not act out feelings
   * Read stepfamily books
   * Make changes gradually
   * See that everyone gets a turn
   * Inform children of plans involving them
   * Accept the insecurity of change
2. Negotiating different developmental needs
   * Take a child development and/or parenting class
   * Accept validity of the different life-cycle phases
   * Communicate individual needs clearly
   * Negotiate incompatible needs
   * Develop tolerance and flexibility
3. Establishing new traditions
   * Recognize ways are *different*, not right or wrong
   * Concentrate on important situations only
   * Stepparents take on discipline enforcement slowly
   * Use family meetings for problem solving and giving appreciation
   * Shift "givens" slowly whenever possible
   * Retain/combine appropriate rituals
   * Enrich with new creative traditions
4. Developing a solid couple bond
   * Accept couple as primary long-term relationship
   * Nourish couple relationship
   * Plan for couple "alone time"
   * Decide general household rules as a couple
   * Support one another with the children
   * Expect and accept different parent-child and stepparent-stepchild feelings
   * Work out money matters together
5. Forming new relationships
   * Fill in past histories
   * Make stepparent-stepchild one-to-one time
   * Make parent-child one-to-one time
   * Parent make space for stepparent-stepchild relationship

**Box 5.2   (continued)**

- Do not expect instant love and adjustment
- Be fair to stepchildren even when caring not developed
- Follow children's lead in what to call stepparent
- Do fun things together

6. Creating a "parenting coalition"
   - Deal directly with parenting adults in other household
   - Keep children out of the middle of parental disagreements
   - Do not talk negatively about adults in other household
   - Control what you can and accept limitations
   - Avoid power struggles between households
   - Respect parenting skills of former spouse
   - Contribute own "specialness" to children
   - Communicate between households in most effective manner

7. Accepting continual shifts in household composition
   - Allow children to enjoy their households
   - Give children time to adjust to household transitions
   - Avoid asking children to be messengers or spies
   - Consider teenager's serious desire to change residence
   - Respect privacy (boundaries) of all households
   - Set consequences that affect own household only
   - Provide personal place for nonresident children
   - Plan special times for various household constellations

8. Risking involvement despite little societal support
   - Include stepparents in school, religious, sports activities
   - Give legal permission for stepparent to act when necessary
   - Continue stepparent-stepchild relationships after death or divorce of parent when caring has developed
   - Stepparent include self in stepchild's activities
   - Find groups supportive of stepfamilies
   - Remember that all relationships involve risk

*Source:* Visher and Visher, 1986, pp. 235–236.

Finally, a word about the positive benefits of remarriage and stepfamilies. Clearly, the heavy burden of single parenting is reduced. Not only are economic pressures on the single parent lightened, but the presence of another adult provides essential feedback information on child-rearing procedures. Further, the danger that a child may be pressured into assuming a spousal role with a single parent is lessened. The participation of grandparents and other extended family members in a remarried situation typically is a plus for the children. A stepfamily also provides an opportunity for parents to have a larger family; this is especially a benefit if one spouse is childless or has fewer children than he or she desires. An only child is certain to benefit from mingling with stepsiblings. A functioning remarried family elicits all the respect and social acceptance that an intact family does. Last, doing something helpful and beneficial for someone you love, such as helping raise their children, is rewarding in and of itself.

# SUMMARY

Remarriage is an increasingly common phenomenon; three out of five previously divorced persons remarry, usually within three years of their divorce. Perhaps 40% of all marriages in the United States today involve at least one partner who was married before. Such remarried families come in a variety of structural forms, depending on whether one or both spouses were previously single, divorced, or widowed, and whether children (who may or may not live with them) are involved. Each pattern brings with it a separate set of problems for the counselor to consider.

In general, all members of a remarried family have sustained a recent primary-relationship loss. New interactive patterns are likely to be complex and prone to stress, as unfamiliar roles and rules are worked out and boundaries stabilized. Disequilibrium and conflict are the norm, especially in the early stages of a remarried family, and particularly so when children are present. Unfinished conflict between ex-mates adds to the overall turmoil, as does the presence of stepsiblings living under one roof. Loyalty conflicts in both children and adults are frequent. Early in a remarriage is also often the time for rearranging custody, visitation, or financial affairs between ex-spouses, sometimes reopening old wounds; this is a special problem because the newly married couple is at its earliest and thus most vulnerable point.

Remarriage is a process that proceeds through a number of distinct phases. Each has its potential for dislocation; each provides an opportunity for family consolidation. Counselors need to remain aware that disruptions may be occurring simultaneously at three levels—individual, marital, and family—for each member of the remarried family. Thus, members may need help in completing mourning for their earlier losses, in working out new relationship problems, and in forging boundary realignments as they attempt to form a stable, integrated family structure.

Counselors need to remain aware that remarried or stepfamilies are structurally different from intact biological families. They are likely to be far more complex, as two distinct families, with different experiences and traditions, attempt to blend into a stable system with an identity of its own. Counseling efforts must address the numerous relationship problems specific to the suprafamily's stage of development. Psychoeducational programs directed at stepfamily life may provide useful help in achieving stepfamily integration.

C H A P T E R

S I X

# Counseling Cohabiting Heterosexual Couples

One alternative or unconventional lifestyle that came into prominence in the 1970s is that in which two adults of the opposite sex live together in a sexual relationship without the formality or sanction of being legally married. According to U.S. Bureau of the Census (1980) population data, close to 2 million unmarried couples shared such a living pattern by the end of the 1970s, some perhaps having lived through several such arrangements over varying periods of time. More recent census data indicate that the overall number continues to rise, although at a somewhat slower rate. The latest available count (U.S. Bureau of the Census, 1986) estimates that 2.2 million unmarried couples shared households in 1986. Although still representing little more than 4% of all American couples living together at any one time, the number of people who have *ever* cohabited without marriage is thought to be considerably greater, because many married couples today have experienced previous phases of unmarried cohabitation.

On the basis of data collected from a large national representative sample aged 19 and over, Bumpass and Sweet (1989) found that about one-sixth of the respondents cohabited before marriage, and about one-quarter had done so at some time in their lives. These findings reveal further that, by their early 30s, almost half the population has lived together unmarried at one time, and the proportion is two-thirds among separated or divorced persons under the age of 35. Taken together, cohabiting couples were found to be a heterogeneous group, their choice of living arrangement likely to reflect a variety of attitudes and motivations. For some, marriage is definitely planned, although the precise time of the ceremony is uncertain. For others, marriage is a real possibility, and cohabiting represents an opportunity to check out the relationship before making the big decision. Still others have no interest in marriage, preferring the freedom of the cohabiting arrangement.

For those uncertain about their relationship but considering marriage, cohabitation, then, represents a late stage of courtship. For others, anxious to marry but delayed by whatever practical restraint, it represents an early stage of marriage. Neither of these interpretations is true, of course, for those who see living together as an end point in the relationship, and do not seek to go further with a commitment to marry. According to the results of this survey, cohabitors, overall, decide soon enough about marriage: one-quarter marry within a year, and half have married within three years.

In an effort to gain a field-work estimate of cohabitation, Gwartney-Gibbs (1986) compared the marriage license applicants between 1970 and 1980 in Lane County, Oregon, and discovered that the same address was given by 13% of the brides and grooms in the earlier period, but by 53% a decade later. Thornton (1988) notes that similar increases in cohabitation have occurred in other parts of the Western world.

Clearly these findings illustrate a dramatic increase in both prevalence and public acceptance of a heretofore little-noticed and infrequently practiced type of heterosexual union; this increase is particularly striking among college students and better educated middle-class adults. Buunk and van Driel (1989) suggest that nonmarital cohabitation gradually is becoming an institutional part of the mate-selection process in the United States and elsewhere. For many couples, because of its timing, cohabitation actually may represent more of a landmark—a transition into an intimate relationship with a member of the opposite sex—than does marriage, which may or may not follow such a living arrangement.

Cohabitation itself is not exactly a new occurrence—common-law and other nonlegal unions have long been accepted in many societies, particularly among low-income persons—but what *is* new is its increased prevalence in a broader segment of American society, the fact that the participants do not consider themselves to be married or necessarily in a permanent relationship, and the increasing acceptance of this dyadic structure by the majority culture (Macklin, 1983). Where such a living arrangement between unmarried couples once was likely to cause strong social disapproval (and still does among some segments of society), in no small part because the persons involved were flaunting their sexual intimacy, the issue today has become largely irrelevant since sexual relationships are commonplace regardless of living arrangement (Bumpass & Sweet, 1989).

It appears likely that much of the current decline in the rate of marriage, as well as the marriage delay noted in Chapter One, may be offset by the increased prevalence of cohabitation; conversely, divorce rates might be even higher except for breakups among cohabitors before marriage occurs. Observing both the high divorce rate and the increased prevalence of cohabitation, Axinn and Thornton (1992) suggest that the increase in cohabitation may be a response, at least in part, to the burgeoning divorce rate, leading couples increasingly to view marriage as a fragile relationship and to question the institution of marriage. Instead, many opt for nonmarital cohabiting unions, without children or the legal implications of marriage, while they spend time living together and testing out the chances of a successful marriage.

Because cohabitation is still considered unconventional by the majority of society, few guidelines are available, and thus roles, interactive patterns, and styles of conflict management are often forged between partners on an individual trial-and-error basis, often at the cost of considerable interpersonal distress. Whether one or both partners have been married previously, whether children are included in the living arrangement, whether financial pressures are experienced, whether families of origin know of and support the arrangement—all these factors influence the kinds of stressors and levels of satisfaction experienced by each partner in the cohabiting relationship. Without question, counselors can expect to see some couples who live in a cohabitational arrangement seeking help in resolving relationship problems, others attempting to settle conflicts over differences in commitment to a shared future, some perhaps desiring premarital counseling, and others reaching out for therapeutic aid in the emotional upheaval accompanying the pair's breakup.

## CHANGING MORES, CHANGING LIFESTYLES

Public media awareness of the phenomenon of two young people, more often than not college students, living together without being married began in the latter half of the 1960s, a time of social ferment, changing sexual values, and a willingness to experiment with unorthodox lifestyles. As Macklin (1983) observes, prior to that time

> only the most avant garde or the most impoverished, or those otherwise considered to be on the social periphery of society, were to be found openly cohabiting outside of marriage, and unmarried persons known to be living together could be expected to be referred to derogatorily as "shacking up." (p. 52)

Since that time, growth in the prevalence of cohabitation in all age groups has spurted; as Glick and Spanier (1980) note, rarely does social change relating to marriage and family life occur with such rapidity. College students and middle-class young adults, in particular, have gravitated toward cohabitation in large numbers, although that living arrangement is more familiar to poor people. According to Bumpass and Sweet's (1989) analysis of their survey data, growing up in a family that received welfare is associated with a 40% higher rate of cohabitation before marriage.

Perhaps those from poorer families experience a push from parents to leave home, accompanied by a desire to have a home of their own, but a lack of financial resources places a damper on the couple's ability to marry. In some cases, welfare laws may place a burden on marriage, making a live-in arrangement more economically feasible. Regardless of the reasons, cohabitors are most likely to be people who did not finish high school, grew up receiving welfare, and were not raised in an intact family. The family-of-origin context is clearly related to the likelihood of cohabiting as a young adult.

In a typical scenario, an unmarried couple cohabits for a brief period, during which decisions regarding marriage are made. Somewhat less frequently, a person who has been through marriage and divorce chooses to live with someone, sometimes with, but often without, a plan for future marriage. In addition, older people, widowed or divorced, may choose to live together without being married; in the case of senior citizens, the primary motivations often are companionship and the opportunity to informally merge financial resources without risking the loss of retirement or Social Security benefits or jeopardizing inheritance for their children as a result of remarriage. Later in this chapter we present clinical examples of various cohabiting relationships, together with a discussion of their interpersonal dynamics, the problems confronting the counselor, and recommended solutions.

Counselors should certainly concern themselves with what sorts of individuals choose this living pattern, what motivates them, and why they choose cohabiting rather than dating or marrying. Are specific attitudes—for example, regarding male-female roles or the wish to delay commitment or retain a sense of independence while relating to another—likely to be typical of people in this lifestyle? Are cohabitors more unconventional, more defiant of traditional values? Do they as a group have more liberal attitudes toward sexual behavior? Clearly, the counselor needs to look at the specific dyadic relationship of the presenting couple, but we mention certain common patterns as guidelines in organizing an appraisal.

Why the sudden change in social values and behavior, not only on the part of young people, which might be more expected, but also on the part of their elders? Several factors, some of which we have touched upon in previous chapters, seem to be operating here. More openness regarding sexual behavior, increased availability of effective contraception, and a growing acceptance of sexual involvement before marriage all seem to be pertinent. Moreover, a growing demand on the part of women for equal rights and the abandonment of the double standard vis-à-vis men is clearly a factor. An emphasis on a meaningful relationship and on the continued growth of both partners probably has played a part, as people of all ages explore new ways to achieve fulfillment and escape the many games involved in dating.

Increasingly, the fear of AIDS or other sexually transmitted diseases has prompted many people to seek a single partner, although they may not yet feel ready to commit to marriage. Delaying marriage in order to establish professional and economic identities has become of paramount interest to many women, as well as men, and cohabiting may well be an important interim solution. The high divorce rate that we have noted has probably led many to proceed cautiously— to try out an intimate relationship before making a more permanent commitment.

The counselor needs to explore the precise reasons for this particular couple's choice of cohabiting over marrying, being careful not to make premature assumptions that may later prove to be incorrect. One further note of caution: the factors that one or both individuals cite, early in counseling, as the reasons for choosing or remaining involved in a live-in arrangement may turn out, on closer examination, to be only a small part of the whole story.

Are personal, social, and attitudinal differences likely to be identifiable between those who choose to cohabit and those who do not? Unfortunately, the little research data available are not sufficiently clear, perhaps because people in these relationships do not represent a unitary entity. Rather, as we have noted and as a number of authorities (Macklin, 1978; Newcomb, 1983; Peterman, Ridley, & Anderson, 1974) point out, *cohabitation* is really a general term for a cluster of heterogeneous relationship types (discussed in the following section)—some temporary or simply convenient, others more committed and permanent; some casual, others a "trial marriage"; some preparatory to marriage, others a substitute for it—whose only commonality is their living situation.

As for discovering a single path to cohabitation, once again none is likely to fit all participants. Although some couples may carefully plan the move only after considerable deliberation about the pros and cons, others seem to drift into living together without a great deal of forethought or formal joint decision-making, as a natural next step after a period of steady and exclusive dating. In the latter case, staying over at the other's apartment on an increasingly regular basis gradually leads to the accumulation of clothes and other personal possessions there as a purely practical matter. Perhaps a job loss or other financial pinch, a lease that expires, a job offer in a new location, an offer to help in child care, or acceptance in a graduate program in another city may then become the precipitating factor leading to the decision to move in together.

## THE MYTHOLOGY OF COHABITATION

A variety of myths exist around cohabitation, depending on the viewer's outlook. For some younger people, learning that an unmarried couple shares living quarters conjures up an image of two loving and caring individuals—both independent and fearless, indifferent to convention, liberal at least in their attitudes regarding sexual behavior—who opt for a monogamous relationship but reject the more traditional ideas concerning marriage. Not hampered by the bonds of matrimony, goes this romantic notion, they are free to explore an intimate relationship while maintaining a sense of independence. They stay together because they choose to, not because they are bound by some legal marriage document.

From another perspective, cohabitors are viewed as rebellious, defiant, and immoral people, without legal responsibilities to one another, unwilling to make a lasting commitment, but instead choosing a temporary alliance that is doomed to failure and that will leave both parties feeling heartbroken and guilty when the inevitable breakup occurs. If they really loved each other as much as they claim, goes this argument, they would get married and raise a family, something they are afraid to do.

Neither of these views is entirely accurate—or entirely inaccurate. Like most human relationships, living together outside of marriage involves a complex arrangement that is entered into for a variety of reasons, some of which may not be fully understood by the participants or their critics. In any specific cohabiting dyad (or triad, where a roommate or perhaps a child shares in the living arrangement), multiple motivations no doubt are operating, including a combination of factors described in the two previous chapters.

The counselor needs to be aware that, despite the statements of the couple seeking help regarding their attitudes and values, other hidden agendas may be at work, as we have noted, and the clients may need help in uncovering them. With even minimum probing, it is common to find clear but unstated disagreements just below the surface. For example, one partner may want to get married but be afraid to say so, believing that such a view reneges on their no-strings-attached agreement. In another case, one participant may no longer wish to abide by a previously agreed-upon monogamous sexual relationship but be reluctant or fearful of broaching that subject. Or, conversely, he or she may wish for a rule change to make a previously open relationship into a monogamous one, but not know how to go about implementing that desire. The counselor has to guide the couple in unmasking and attending to these underlying but unexpressed conflicts.

The counselor must also be careful not to take statements at face value or assume that because the couple live in a cohabiting relationship they fit some preconceived stereotype. For instance, couples who may appear unconventional because they live in an atypical marital structure may actually live fairly conventional lives, dividing their responsibilities (for example, who does which household tasks) and priorities (whose career development takes precedence) along traditional sex-role lines.

It is important, too, that the counselor be in touch with his or her own values regarding what is still an unorthodox living arrangement between unmarried adults. If that viewpoint is antithetical to this lifestyle, it may bias the therapeutic process, and in such cases the clients deserve a forthright and explicit statement of the counselor's views on cohabitation. For example, it is only fair for a religious counselor who believes the couple is living in sin to impart that outlook at the start. If the couple, having this knowledge, nevertheless chooses to continue counseling, then they do so bearing that counselor's view in mind. Thus, it is essential that the counselor have an explicit, articulated understanding of his or her own values, and how they might differ from the clients'. Effective counseling requires not imposing counselor values on other people's lives.

## TYPES OF STUDENT COHABITATION

As we have noted, cohabitation is not a unitary entity, but rather an unmarried heterosexual living arrangement that may take a variety of forms, serve different functions, and come about for a multitude of reasons. Among college students, for example, at least four patterns have been differentiated: the Linus-blanket, emancipation, convenience, and testing types of cohabiting patterns (Ridley, Peterman, & Avery, 1978).

In the Linus-blanket type of cohabitational setup, named after the Peanuts comic-strip character who is never too far from his security blanket, the counselor can expect at least one of the partners to need a relationship so badly that it hardly matters what kind or with whom. The primary goal here seems to be the avoidance of loneliness and insecurity.

The following cases, abstracted from our files, illustrate some of the transactional forces at play:

❊ ❊ ❊ ❊ ❊

Josh and Nicole met one day at the Student Union of the college both attended. Nicole, 18, was a freshman with an undeclared major, living in the college dorm, away from home for the first time, 1000 miles from her family. Josh, 20, a junior business major, also lived several hundred miles from home, but in his own apartment. Nicole was immediately attracted to Josh's good looks, his intelligence, and especially his seemingly high sense of self-assurance. Josh, on the other hand, in addition to finding her physically attractive, was immediately taken by Nicole's sweetness, vulnerability, and apparent need to be taken care of. They dated for several months, developed a sexual relationship—Nicole's first, it turned out—and soon Nicole was spending more and more time at Josh's apartment. Midway through the spring semester, Josh's roommate moved out, and Nicole moved in. However, she retained her dorm address, because the school required dorm living for freshmen and because she tried to hide the living arrangement from her parents.

Problems began soon after they became roommates. Nicole, very dependent on Josh for her emotional security, was jealous of his friends and of any time he spent in activities where she was not invited. She worried about whether he was sexually faithful, despite his repeated reassurances. Also, she lived in constant fear that her parents would discover the living arrangement, would certainly disapprove, and might insist she not return to the school the following year. Josh was bothered by her overdependency, her immaturity, her seemingly few coping skills, and her poor self-esteem. Although he agreed to see a counselor together with Nicole, it was clear from the first session that he was simply going through the motions and wanted an excuse to end the relationship. They separated after three sessions, but Nicole continued on an individual basis with the counselor to work on her personal insecurities.

❊ ❊ ❊ ❊ ❊

The emancipation type of cohabiting relationship presents the counselor with a different configuration. Here the young person seeks escape and freedom from parental restraint; the decision to cohabit represents a statement of liberation and independence.

❊   ❊   ❊   ❊   ❊

Denise, 18, raised as a devout Catholic, had had few close relationships outside her family before going away to a college with a strong religious orientation. Growing up in a well-to-do large family and attending the best parochial schools in her community, she had been sheltered from most everyday problems of living. Her parents were protective and doting and, despite her being the oldest child, expected little of her except that she earn good grades, not smoke, and stay away from bad company. Denise did not disappoint them, since she was a top student, always had her assignments in on time, and never caused anybody any trouble. When she was ready for college, she consulted her parents as well as her school counselor, and together they decided on a nearby school with a reputation for a religious student body and serious dedication to scholarship.

Denise was driven to the campus by her parents, who expressed pleasure at the dormitory accommodations. They were pleased, too, by her roommate, Alice, also 18, who seemingly had a social-class and religious background similar to their daughter's. By the time they left to return home, some 75 miles away, they felt Denise was in a safe, protected environment conducive to personal development.

Trouble began when Denise, now on her own, soon found herself caught in a conflict between internalized pressures from her religious upbringing, her own emerging need to develop an identity, and peer pressures from her classmates, especially Alice. Although raised as a Catholic, Alice had secretly rebelled against the teachings of the church, and in high school had had considerable experiences with drugs and sexual experimentation with several boys. At first, Denise was horrified—and somewhat intrigued—by Alice's accounts of her past exploits. As Alice began to bring some of the college men to the room, Denise became increasingly involved, and soon found herself particularly interested in Randy, a young African-American student from another part of the country.

Randy, 19, a bright, serious, hard-working student, also Catholic, came from a lower-middle-class background. He was interested in going on to law school, and had spent the year after graduation working in order to save up enough money to supplement the support from his parents. In Denise he found a quiet, unassuming, but caring person with whom he felt comfortable. He and Denise recognized they both lacked sophistication or a great deal of previous dating experience, and that was a plus to their way of thinking. Both were shy and modest, and since neither was the kind to use a friend's apartment for a sexual liaison, Randy and Denise soon found an apartment near campus to which they retreated several nights each week and on the weekend. However, when Denise's parents decided to surprise her with a visit one Sunday, they were able to track her down and soon, dumbfounded, discovered the situation their daughter had kept from them. Although they protested that racial issues were not involved, but that Denise was too young for such a living arrangement, it was clear that there was nothing about the situation to their liking. They refused to recognize the new relationship, insisted their daughter return home immediately, and that she not bring Randy or ever see him again. Denise refused, told them she loved Randy, and that if they persisted they would never see her again.

It was the parents who consulted a family counselor. Their dislike of the situation was accepted, but they were directed to examine what issues most incensed them. The racial issue called for special scrutiny, suggested the counselor, because it was essential that they be clear in their own minds just how they truly felt. They also were urged to deal with what was involved for them in letting go of Denise and allowing her to make her own judgments about her life. True, they disapproved of the situation and, yes, they had every right to let their daughter know in no uncertain terms how they really felt. But beyond that, how much risk were they willing to take of alienating her to the point that she might marry him out of spite? Perhaps by accepting the situation and getting to know the couple, they might remove the heated, rebellious motive that might exist in Denise's behavior. In such a case, they might influence the outcome in the direction they desired, instead of forcing the opposite resolution. Denise might or might not continue with Randy, but at least they would not lose contact with their daughter, and Denise and Randy could decide what to do on a more rational basis.

When these issues had been successfully dealt with in the opinion of the counselor, he suggested all four players come together for a joint family session. Denise spoke of her anger at her parents; she accused them of dishonesty regarding their racial attitudes, and of unwillingness to let her grow up out of their control. Because the parents had previously worked through the issues regarding their feelings about Randy's color with the counselor, they were not defensive. Instead they did discuss some of the complications of an interracial marriage, but insisted that was not the primary basis for their opposition. Rather, they were more concerned by her inexperience in other relationships, as well as Randy's. Denise made it clear that she and Randy were far from making any permanent commitments, and that actually they had decided to live separately next year precisely because they too recognized that each needed opportunities to explore new relationships.

The counselor had helped the parents to see Denise's behavior as transient and a necessary part of her development. Bringing parental attitudes regarding the racial issue into the open helped clarify for Denise that certain ordinarily unspoken but powerful feelings could be addressed. By not making the conflict one over power, with one side forced to back down, any need to be rebellious or punitive was reduced and the young people were allowed to get on with their lives. By keeping down the uproar and emphasizing the need for clear and honest communication, the counselor had made it possible for Denise to confront her parents with normal late-adolescent issues, and for all four persons to benefit from the encounter.

❊    ❊    ❊    ❊    ❊

Turning now to an example of a cohabiting arrangement based on convenience, much like a marriage of convenience, we find the couple entering a knowingly temporary arrangement but one that offers stability and the safety of a single sex partner:

❊ ❊ ❊ ❊ ❊

Terri, a college sophomore, answered an ad for a roommate in the college newspaper soon after the new school year began. She had decided during the summer break that she would live with a girlfriend from high school, but when that plan failed to materialize—the friend transferred to another school at the last minute—Terri sought other living arrangements. In responding to the ad, she found one to her liking, living in a three-bedroom apartment near campus with Nancy and Eric, two people she did not know before but seemed to like at first glance.

Nancy and Eric, old friends but not lovers, had a lot of friends who visited them frequently, and Terri enjoyed living with them very much. She and Nancy would talk at great length with each other, but Eric tended to be more reserved and aloof. He definitely was not her type, she thought; he was three years older, too serious for her tastes, and the fact that he was Jewish made any long-term involvement with him too complicated. Nevertheless, to some extent because of their proximity on a daily basis, within six months they had drifted into a sexual relationship. Nancy was aware of what was happening and did not object, since she was not romantically interested in Eric and was glad two people she liked liked each other. When Nancy decided to move to her own apartment, Eric and Terri remained without getting a new roommate.

Together they were sexually compatible, and enjoyed the luxury of domestic living without the responsibilities of a deeper or more permanent commitment. However, after two months, Eric began to find fault with Terri: she was too immature, and she was not serious enough about her studies. She, too, found fault with him: he was too involved with term papers, had little time for her, and when they were together he would find fault with her "childish" behavior in front of his friends. Both expressed resentment over feeling "tied down" and not able to pursue interests in other people to whom they might feel attracted.

When they went together to the school counselor, she pointed out that they had drifted into their living together at least in part because of convenience, and that they had not really made a commitment to one another. Each indicated a lasting fondness for the other that each was afraid to jeopardize, but the counselor observed that they could remain friends while living separately. Reassured that they had profited from the domestic experience together without too much pain, they acknowledged that there were no hard feelings and that each was now ready to go on alone.

❊ ❊ ❊ ❊ ❊

As indicated by these examples, the Linus-blanket, emancipation, and convenience types of live-in formats are not conducive to fostering a long-term nonmarital relationship. They are, however, characteristic of cohabiting arrangements among college students, in that they tend to be short-lived, typically terminating after several months or at the end of the school year. In that sense, they can be thought of as more a courtship phenomenon (perhaps the next step following steady dating for many couples) than an alternative to marriage.

In a smaller number of cases, cohabitation is a temporary alternative to marriage. Both partners tend to be older, more mature, and more ready to make a permanent commitment to marriage. They may have decided to live together because it is more convenient until some roadblocks have been overcome (graduation, better income, parental disapproval). However, they are prepared to enter an intimate relationship with someone they love with an eye toward eventual marriage. Testing whether a conjugal experience will confirm their shared beliefs regarding their future together, this living arrangement has the best potential for both personal development and the achievement of interpersonal fulfillment.

❊ ❊ ❊ ❊ ❊

Patti and Michael met during their last year at college and immediately started dating each other exclusively. Both had had a number of earlier dating experiences, and Michael had lived with a female student during his sophomore year. Despite Michael's urging, Patti resisted the suggestion that they move in together, since they had only known each other for four months and she feared it would cost her some sense of independence, which she cherished. They discussed the matter at great length and agreed that they would see each other every night for dinner at his apartment or hers, and one would often end up staying the night, but it would be best if they retained their own separate lifestyles for the time being. In that way they could build the relationship slowly and determine whether a long-term living arrangement, perhaps ultimately marriage, made sense.

When Michael graduated, he went on to medical school in another part of the country. Although he wanted Patti to accompany him, he was aware that she had her own career plans, so he did not pursue the matter strenuously. Besides, he said to himself, medical school was demanding, and it would not be fair to Patti or himself if she lived with him during the first year or two. Patti too went on to graduate school in rehabilitation counseling, a two-year program that required a great deal of time and dedication. They did agree to speak together by telephone at least once each week, and to fly to each other's cities to see one another about every three months. Although each was lonely, and also somewhat apprehensive of losing the other because they no longer were in daily contact, the relationship continued to grow and be strengthened.

Upon graduation, and by mutual agreement, Patti found a job in the city where Michael was attending medical school, and they moved in together. Both worked hard at building the relationship, since the time apart had convinced them both that they wanted to spend their lives together. Cautious to the end, they contacted a counselor for some premarital counseling, more a kind of checkup to make certain that no hidden feelings would mar their future together. Satisfied that they could each retain a sense of independence while gaining much from relating to one another, they made plans to get married the following June.

✳  ✳  ✳  ✳  ✳

# ADULT COHABITATION:
# TRIAL MARRIAGE OR SUBSTITUTE FOR MARRIAGE?

In considering unmarried students living together and sharing a bedroom, we were dealing with only one portion of the adult cohabiting population. What of the other portion? Some have opted for a permanent or semipermanent alternative to marriage, which may even include having children together, sharing a joint bank account, buying a house, and so on. For a variety of philosophical or practical reasons, these couples commit themselves to a long-term relationship very much like a marriage, but without the legal or religious sanctions.

Cohabitation tends to be more familiar and acceptable among poor people than others, probably because sharing a household makes economic sense, a priority when money is scarce:

✳  ✳  ✳  ✳  ✳

Carmen, a 24-year-old Puerto Rican woman, had become pregnant at age 15, and under extreme pressure from her family married Roberto, 17, who had recently dropped out of high school. With Roberto working at odd jobs—he really wanted to be a hairdresser but could not afford the necessary schooling—and with whatever money their working-class families could spare, the couple and their child, Alicia, managed for several years, although the strain of continuous financial pressure inevitably took its toll. Since neither had completed high school, available work was scarce and what was available was typically at minimum wage. Although both Carmen and Roberto worked hard, and allowed themselves few if any indulgences, they were constantly in debt. What money was available, perhaps as an occasional gift from their parents, would go into clothes or a toy for Alicia. The strains of the marriage left little time or room to work at building their relationship, which deteriorated and ultimately collapsed. When Alicia was 7, Roberto moved out to another city to look for work, although he continued sending them money whenever he was able. He wrote to Alicia several times a year, and would call her on her birthday and at Christmas time, but beyond those occasions there was no contact between Roberto and his wife and child.

Attempting to cope with the solo task of raising a child by herself, Carmen worked as a teacher's aide in a neighborhood Head Start classroom while Alicia was at school. In the evening, her mother or father, her primary support group, would come by to look after Alicia, so that Carmen could finish high school and be in a better position to provide support for herself and her daughter.

At school she met a number of other women with similar stories, and together they offered each other support and comfort. In addition, Carmen was introduced to Raul, a handyman, by one of her women friends, and they became friends, occasionally going out after class for coffee and conversation. Raul had recently separated from his wife and two children and, after knowing Carmen six weeks, he expressed his loneliness to her and asked if he could live with her—no sexual pressure intended, he vowed. Worried about the effect on Alicia, but lonely herself for adult companionship, she reluctantly agreed. While she was not looking for a roommate in her small apartment, and was not interested in Raul in any romantic fashion, she could use his physical help around the house and he promised to help out financially by paying his share of the rent and food.

The relationship, as it evolved, was not without problems, but the affection each began to feel for one another grew. Both, having experienced failed marriages, felt vulnerable and were guarded, especially during the first few months. Carmen expressed the fear that she was not worth loving, and that Raul would tire of her and abandon her sooner or later, as Roberto had done. She worried too about the effect of another breakup on Alicia, toward whom she felt guilty over her broken marriage. Raul too was fearful of commitment and worried that he would not be able to financially support his new family while still helping his wife and children as best he could.

Despite these doubts and misgivings, the cohabitation arrangement seemed to flourish. Alicia, now 9, had gotten to know and like Raul, and was happy; together, the three formed a blended family that resembled a remarried family, particularly after Raul divorced and he and Carmen began a sexual relationship. However, they did not marry, since neither saw a particular advantage a marital state might offer that they did not already have. They tried talking to a counselor at a nearby clinic for several sessions, to ascertain whether their decision was in everyone's interest, Alicia included. Satisfied that the choice of living arrangement offered the best of both single and married lives, they continued to live together and thrive.

❄   ❄   ❄   ❄   ❄

Middle-class women in such an arrangement may also opt for cohabitation in place of remarriage, since many may be receiving alimony and child-support payments from an ex-spouse, and thus may not be in a hurry to marry and relinquish such payments, especially if they do not intend to have additional children. As we noted earlier, middle-aged or even elderly persons also may choose to live in a conjugal relationship, sharing expenses, providing companionship and a social partner to one another, but not willing to marry again, nor particularly interested in doing so.

In the following case, a widow, aged 70, chooses a nonmarital live-in arrangement with a man rather than the more orthodox way of marriage in which she was raised:

❄   ❄   ❄   ❄   ❄

Minna and Milton, her husband of 45 years, lived what appeared to be a perfect existence to their friends and family. They were in good health, had three happily married children and two grandchildren, and were financially comfortable as a result of Milton's successful wholesale produce business. They were both active people, enjoyed being with friends, and loved traveling as Milton's business permitted. When Milton died of cancer, at age 75, Minna, feeling suddenly alone at 70, was devastated, and with the encouragement of her children moved into a condominium retirement community so that she could be with other people her age, but without the responsibilities of keeping up her large older home.

Soon after her arrival, Minna met Reese, 72, himself a recent widower, who had moved into the community several months earlier. A retired furrier, Reese too had been happily married and the father of three before his wife's sudden death in an auto accident. Both lonely and unaccustomed to leading a single life, they began to see more and more of one another, and soon moved in together in Minna's apartment. Minna enjoyed fussing over a man again, and Reese adored the attention and opportunity to love someone again, since his wife had been taken from him so suddenly.

However, when her children learned of the arrangement, they objected violently, arguing with their mother that she would soon end up caring for a sick and aging man from whom she would receive little in return. When Minna revealed to her daughter, Margo, that "sex had never been better," the daughter became even more upset, said she didn't want to know about it, and dropped the conversation. Reese's three sons also seemed to feel threatened about his new relationship, finally voicing the fear that any money he had when he died would go to Minna and not to them.

Minna and Reese, living up to the cultural expectations of their generation, would probably have married under normal circumstances. However, both sets of children applied such pressure on their respective parents not to marry that, contrary to their upbringing, they decided to live together instead, sharing expenses but keeping their individual monies and investments separate.

Still dissatisfied with the arrangement, and fearing her mother was "acting crazy waiting on a man hand and foot, which she had never done to my father," Margo prevailed upon Minna to go with her to see a counselor. After three sessions, in which such issues as their evolving mother/daughter relationship, sex among the elderly, and the memory of Minna and Milton's happy years were explored, the counselor was able to help them begin to work out their new relationship.

When Minna relayed these topics to Reese, he recognized that his children probably had similar concerns, and he proceeded to talk to them without a counselor. Although the children continued to have reservations about the wisdom or propriety of their parents' cohabiting union, they learned to accept it, and Minna and Reese remained living together unmarried.

❈   ❈   ❈   ❈   ❈

People of any age, busy forging careers and not ready for children, or established in careers but divorced or widowed and not interested in expanding their families, may look at cohabitation as less demanding than formal marriage (although breaking up after many years together can be just as painful as a divorce). Finally, as Newcomb (1987), Eidelson (1983), and others have pointed out, for many people, traditional marriage simply does not represent the ideal way to achieve an amalgam of independence and relatedness. Particularly for this last group, long-term cohabitation offers a structure for achieving the often-conflicting goals of autonomy and affiliation with another person.

The dramatic increase in cohabitation in recent years, then, can be explained in a number of ways, and the counselor needs to zero in on which set of factors is at work with any specific couple. Does this couple live together instead of marrying because they lack the readiness to make a complete commitment? Because they are immature and fearful of the responsibility of making a marriage work? Because one or both fear being alone, but do not have the wish or sense of security to form a strong partnership or achieve real intimacy? Because, unless children are involved, they both believe marriage is irrelevant or unnecessary? Because they feel unable to predict how they will feel in the future and thus want to keep open all options? Because they know few if any really happily married people, and want to avoid the legal entanglements and expense of a divorce? Because they can combine all the benefits of both an unencumbered single life (autonomy, independence) and married life (intimacy, sexuality, companionship) by living together?

Do they plan to marry? Does one partner want marriage and the other not, or not now? Is their present living arrangement temporary? Are they in a trial marriage because they seriously contemplate a permanent commitment and first want to check out their compatibility and the quality of their relationship? As we have indicated, an increasing number of marriages today are preceded by cohabitation, perhaps indicating a wish to test out the strength and durability of the union before making the final commitment.

Cohabiting couples marry for different reasons. Some may be trying desperately to repair a failing union, probably hoping that the added commitment of a marriage contract will rescue their troubled relationship. (Couples in such a situation typically get divorced soon after their marriage, discovering that the conflicts they experienced as cohabitors are likely to remain unresolved despite the marriage vows.) Others, still of childbearing age, are ready to settle down and have children; conversely, some marry in response to an accidental pregnancy. Some young people may want to make their relationship legal to please a dying parent. Perhaps a landlord or employer insists, or the Army requires a soldier to be married if he wants to live on the base. Tax deductions for married couples offer an inducement to some couples. Some are possessive or fear the consequences of an open relationship. Others are finally ready to make the commitment to someone they cannot live without.

Do cohabiting couples establish successful marriages? Since cohabitors try out an intimate relationship before deciding to marry and end seemingly unworkable ones before tying the knot, and since they delay marriage by living together and thus are older and presumably more sure of what they want in a marriage after the cohabiting experience, we might suspect that marriages following cohabitation would be more stable. Actually, marriages preceded by couples living together are much more likely to break up than are unions initiated by marriage. According to the Bumpass and Sweet (1989) survey, the proportion separating or divorcing within ten years is a third higher among those who cohabited than among those who did not.

Does the premarital cohabiting experience weaken commitment to the institution of marriage, thereby diminishing the probability of subsequent marital success? Or is cohabitation initially selected by hesitant people ready only for tentative or trial relationships, or with more liberal attitudes toward divorce, and thus more accepting of the termination of an intimate marital situation? Some authorities (Bennett, Blanc, & Bloom, 1988) argue that cohabitors are drawn disproportionately from the ranks of the divorce-prone, who view divorce as an acceptable alternative, and that this susceptibility to divorce rather than their cohabiting experience accounts for the high rates of marital instability. Another possibility, of course, is that cohabitation produces relationships, attitudes, or values that impact negatively on marital stability (Booth & Johnson, 1988).

As part of a longitudinal investigation of families, Axinn and Thornton (1992) studied the relationship between cohabitation and divorce using sophisticated statistical analyses. They found that nonmarital cohabiting relationships indeed are selective, and that those who choose this lifestyle tend to be least committed to marriage and most accepting of divorce. Moreover, they discovered the important intergenerational effect of maternal commitment to marriage and approval of divorce; that is, mothers' attitudes toward marriage and divorce influence their children's subsequent attitudes and behavior. These results suggest that cohabitation may change the way individuals view marriage, perhaps reinforcing the notion that relationships are temporary and need not be expected to last a lifetime. These researchers argue that, just as high divorce rates may have led to a declining commitment to marriage and nonmarital cohabitation as a substitute, so the rise in cohabitation itself may have a feedback effect, increasing acceptance of divorce and thereby increasing the likelihood of actual divorce.

## ASSESSING COHABITING COUPLES

Cohabiting couples rarely consult a counselor about whether or not they should live together. When they do seek help from a counselor, they are far more likely to present problems common to all troubled couples (for example, poor communication, sexual difficulties, erosion of their previous love and compatibility). Cole (1988) refers to these areas of potential conflict as relationship-maintenance struggles; they may be interpersonally induced (as in the examples in the previous sentence) or situationally evoked by outside forces (for example, emotional cutoff from parents or other relatives). Therapeutically, the counselor needs to treat them as similar to problems occurring between marriage partners.

However, living together unmarried also presents a unique set of challenges. Box 6.1 alerts the counselor to common problems most cohabiting couples must

---

**Box 6.1   A Problem-Appraisal Checklist for Cohabiting Heterosexual Adult Couples**

Cohabiting heterosexual adults may experience problems in the following areas:

- Social stigma
- Term for cohabiting partner
- Unequal commitment between partners
- Lack of legal safeguards
- Dealing with families of origin
- Differing views of roles and lifestyle patterns
- Monogamous vs. nonmonogamous sexual relationship
- Division of labor, money, resources
- Parenting of other's children
- Differing views of autonomy and connectedness
- Differing expectations regarding future
- Terminating the relationship

---

address as they enter into and attempt to advance an evolving relationship. While the social stigma, for example, may be minimal in the couple's own subgroup (such as among college students), that often is hardly the case in the larger social structure, public media to the contrary. Parents, other family members, fellow employees or employer, even friends may be kept in the dark about the live-in arrangement, all pointing to the couple's self-consciousness. Frequently the couple maintains two telephones in their apartment, each prepared only to answer his or hers, to keep up the illusion that they are living alone. In more extreme cases, the pretense goes as far as retaining two apartments while living together in one, in a further effort to avoid detection. If one partner's parents are visiting, the other may move out temporarily, to evade parental disapproval. If the arrangement is discovered, parents may urge a breakup, or in some cases may press for an early marriage. The counselor assessing the strengths and weaknesses or perhaps the durability of the relationship must certainly attempt to help the partners evaluate the degree of discomfort they feel in what is still an unconventional lifestyle.

Another likely area of difficulty is what to call the cohabiting partner. Meet my live-in boyfriend (girlfriend)? The person with whom I share an apartment (bed)? My fiance? My housemate? My lover? My significant other? My domestic partner? According to U.S. census jargon, the man and woman are POSSLQ (People of the Opposite Sex Sharing Living Quarters)! Meet my POSSLQ? The confusion, embarrassment, and discomfort at not knowing precisely how to describe the relationship reflect society's lack of clarity about how best to conceptualize what is occurring between and within individuals who have committed themselves to one another, but in a nontraditional way.

Legal complexities and potentially damaging legal consequences may arise from an unmarried union. A bitter noncustodial father, for example, may demand that the court overturn an earlier custody ruling because the child is living with a mother who is cohabiting, arguing that such a living arrangement is detrimental to the child's moral and emotional well-being. Thus, the counselor may need to alert a divorced client with a live-in lover to the possible threat to custody, and may need to urge the client to evaluate his or her situation regarding conceivable legal action by an avenging or otherwise outraged ex-spouse.

In a similar way, a divorced custodial mother, particularly one who has been left by her husband in favor of another woman, may retaliate by restricting the father's visitation rights, claiming she wants to shield her child from visiting him because he is living with a woman to whom he is not married. Unfinished fighting between divorced parents often erupts over this emotional issue, as they repeatedly drag one another into court (or the counselor's office, where the former mates need to be seen jointly).

As we have noted, the emotional trauma of separation after a live-in arrangement, particularly one of long duration, may be every bit as painful as after a long-standing marriage. The termination of a relationship that has been intimate and binding is never casual, as any marital/family counselor can attest. Losing the emotional closeness, the mutual sharing, the daily involvement in one another's lives is always accompanied by considerable anguish and a sense of failure, no matter how far the relationship has deteriorated. Cohabitors may reject traditional ideas regarding marriage, but that is not to say they survive the breakup with any greater equanimity than do divorcing spouses.

In addition to their lives having become entwined, the unmarried couple may have accumulated property together, and promises of marriage may have been made. In the widely publicized 1976 case of *Marvin v. Marvin,* involving the cohabiting couple actor Lee Marvin and Michelle Marvin (who legally changed her name although they remained unmarried), she sought court action to divide the considerable property accumulated by the couple during their unmarried years together. The California Supreme Court finally ruled that a cohabiting couple can make a contract—a prenuptial agreement—affecting their property rights, as the Marvins had done, as long as sex is not part of the consideration for signing the agreement. That is, before moving in together, a couple can sign a contract regarding their earnings and property rights, as long as the contract does not involve pay for the performance of sexual services, which would in essence be an unlawful contract for prostitution. Not all states have followed the California ruling, although all recognize that legal remedies are often needed to divide property obtained by unmarried cohabiting couples. As Huber and Baruth (1987) suggest, some counselors working with cohabiting adults recommend that relationship interests be formalized, if not by marriage then by binding contract, in the best legal interest of both parties.

Additional legal entanglements, often the source of considerable distress, occur if the cohabiting partners have children together. Beyond that, cohabiting men and women continuously face social discrimination in matters such as buying a house together, obtaining a bank loan, and becoming eligible for the partner's health insurance benefits. Despite increasing judicial recognition of the cohabiting lifestyle, society does not yet grant full recognition of such unconventionality.

## COUNSELING UNMARRIED COUPLES

Although we have focused our discussion on cohabiting couples, the counselor should not lose sight of the fact that these pairs are a part of a larger group of unmarried couples who seek counseling; at the Marriage Council of Philadelphia, for example, unmarried couples represent 13% of all couples requesting help with their relationships. According to Berman and Goldberg (1986), such couples typically present a wide range of problems: from college students in a relationship that they acknowledge is transient, to couples who have lived together for several years and are undecided about splitting up, to common-law marriages of many years' duration. Berman and Goldberg's survey reveals that those seeking premarital counseling are likely to be couples in their late 30s, one or both of whom have been previously married and have children from the former marriages. Kaslow (1985) has presented a detailed account of counseling a mid-life cohabiting couple as they attempted to cope with the future of their relationship.

While any couple, married or unmarried, must deal with similar relationship problems, being unmarried often adds an uncertainty to the character of that relationship. If the couple has been together for a long time, the counselor is bound to wonder what functions are being served by remaining unmarried, and, conversely, what would be changed by the couple getting married. Although the couple may live together in a marriage-like manner for many years, there remains an inevitable nonbinding and temporary quality to their union. Berman and Goldberg (1986) suggest that the lack of a public announcement implies to themselves as well as to others that they wish to retain the potential of availability and lessened interdependence. In many cases, however, as we have seen, although remaining unmarried may preserve the illusion of freedom and autonomy, such relationships often are as fused and highly dependent as any long-term marriage.

Marital counselors experienced in working with unmarried couples are accustomed to the pair presenting differences in their levels of commitment, one partner wanting to marry while the other is uncertain or resistant. Aside from marriage, conflicts over commitment may take place over whether to live together (or continue to live together) or split up. Regardless of the married or unmarried state the couple wishes for, Cole (1988) argues that the couple must develop interpersonal commitments to the maintenance and growth of each other's individuality and of the relationship.

In the case of nonmarital cohabitors in particular, counselors can expect ambivalence from one or both partners—wishing for security, attachment, togetherness, commitment, and dependence on the one hand, while simultaneously wishing for autonomy, freedom, independence, and personal growth on the other. Too much of the former can lead to feelings of being trapped in a relationship; too much of the latter, and there is danger of feeling alone, unprotected, and insecure. Counselors who aid the couple in finding a mutually satisfactory balance can help resolve what for many is a pivotal and recurrent problem (Buunk & van Driel, 1989).

# PREMARITAL COUNSELING

Cohabiting couples frequently consult a counselor when they are at the point of contemplating marriage, often as a kind of checkup on the health of their relationship. At other times, however, their motivation is different: one or both fear that some underlying conflict remains unresolved and may lead to a future deterioration of their relationship. Where one or the other (or perhaps both) has been divorced, such caution is especially apparent, in the form of vigilance to spot flaws that may impair their future happiness together. Some states make premarital counseling mandatory for all couples seeking marriage licenses where at least one partner is under 18 (Bagarozzi, 1986).

Where a couple seeks a professional's help in assessing their relationship, one counseling tactic is to spend four to six conjoint sessions (each an hour to two hours in length) guiding the couple in examining their interactions in some depth. Here the aim is to provide an experience that will enhance and enrich their future married lives together. In the process, the counselor may occasionally ferret out some previously undiscovered but potentially problematic transactional patterns, make the couple aware of them, and try to repair them.

How long have the partners known each other? How long have they lived together? Why have they decided to marry now? Does one of the partners have a stronger wish to marry than the other? How do they think marriage will be different from living together? How well do they communicate? Do they experience any discomfort when they attempt to be intimate or emotionally close to one another? How do they manage areas of disagreement? How deep is each partner's commitment to the marriage? Do they agree about having children, the division of labor around the house, handling money, friends of each, vacations, further schooling and/or career moves, where they want to live, and so on? Are they sexually compatible? How temperamentally suited to one another are they? Do they have any strong religious or political conflicts?

How similar are their socioeconomic backgrounds? Their educational levels? Their ages? Their value systems? Their racial and ethnic backgrounds and religious affiliations? Their life experiences? Does either have any previous history of medical or emotional problems? What kind of parental models did each have? Were their parents divorced? Any signs of potential in-law problems?

Time is needed to explore these and other factors influencing the likelihood of a stable and satisfying marriage. There probably will be some degree of conflict over one or more of these issues, but by itself this does not necessarily rule out the possibility of a happy and long-lasting union. An early identification of potential problems may actually head off future disharmony if addressed and resolved. On the other hand, significant and irreconcilable differences may be uncovered, and the couple may decide to postpone the marriage while they work out these problems, or even to cancel their marriage plans for an indefinite period.

As Stahmann and Hiebert (1987) point out, the purpose of premarital counseling is not to resolve all conflict, but rather to help the couple become aware of significant issues between them, to give them a new way of understanding those issues, and to teach them some skills in dealing with them. One of the counselor's major functions may be to raise questions the two have not raised between themselves, to open up areas they have neglected or avoided, and especially to expand their thinking about the nature of their relationship. Lewis and Spanier (1979) advise that "the greater the likelihood that the motivation to marry is independent of problematic circumstantial factors, including internal or external pressures, the higher the marital quality" (p. 278).

While some degree of conflict is an inevitable part of any ongoing interaction, certain seriously conflicted unmarried couples deserve the counselor's special attention. Stahmann and Hiebert (1987) identify the following transactional patterns that should alert the counselor to potential trouble:

*The uncommitted partner:* One or both partners may present an underlying inability or hesitation to make a firm commitment to marriage at this time, despite appearing verbally agreeable to doing so.

*The passive-inactive partner:* In this profile, one partner appears socially inactive, repressed in expressing feelings, passive and dependent in the couple's interactions.

*The unresponsive and insensitive partner:* Here one person is inhibited and overly restrained, and is typically insensitive, unfeeling, and often hostile and critical in dealing with the partner.

*The apprehensive and pessimistic partner:* One partner is excessively tense, hyperemotional, and periodically discouraged about the future of the relationship.

*The angry and aggressive partner:* In this transactional pattern, one or both are intense, argumentative, and frequently verbally or physically abusive.

All the patterns we have just identified should be looked at as part of a transaction with another person, rather than as a personality trait or characteristic in one or both individuals. The counselor is trying to determine if certain potential trouble spots or destructive interactive patterns exist, the extent to which they intrude on the stability of the relationship, and whether, if uncorrected, they contain the seeds of eventual marital unhappiness and breakup.

## PREPARE: A PREMARITAL INVENTORY

Counselors doing premarital counseling often use one or more assessment devices or instruments to appraise the couple's compatibility and look for areas where there is potential for interpersonal dysfunction. David Olson, who was instrumental in developing the circumplex model for identifying types of family functioning (see Chapter Three) also has produced a useful and reliable inventory for evaluating a couple's preparation for marriage (Olson, Fournier, & Druckman, 1986). Aptly entitled PREPARE (PREmarital Personal And Relationship Evaluation), this computer-scored 125-item inventory is intended to identify and measure relationship strengths and areas where work is necessary in 11 interactive categories:

- realistic expectations
- personality issues
- communication
- conflict resolution
- financial management
- leisure activities
- sexual relationship
- children and marriage
- family and friends
- equalitarian roles
- religious orientation

Each partner separately rates each item on a five-point scale, from *strongly agree* to *strongly disagree*. Typical items in the realistic-expectations category are "After marriage it will be easier to change those things about my partner I don't like"; "Some of my needs for security, support, and companionship will be met by persons other than my partner." In the personality-issues category: "Sometimes I am bothered by my partner's temper"; "At times I think my partner is too domineering." In the communication category: "It is very easy for me to express all my true feelings to my partner"; "When we are having a problem, my partner often gives me the silent treatment."

In addition, the instrument contains an idealistic-distortion scale, an effort to correct for any tendency on the part of either potential spouse to respond to items in an idealistic rather than realistic manner.

For each scale, an individual score is obtained (revised as necessary by the idealistic-distortion score), as is a positive-couple-agreement score measuring their degree of consensus on the issues raised in that category. Olson, Fournier, and Druckman (1986) contend that the scales are designed to promote couple dialogue and relationship enhancement. Fowers and Olson (1986) emphasize the inventory's ability to identify high-risk couples, as well as its preventive value in guiding the couple to potential problems that require attention, perhaps through more intense premarital counseling. In a recent follow-up of their work (Fowers & Olson, 1992), working with a sample of over 5000 couples, these authors were able to use PREPARE to statistically differentiate between four types of premarital couples:

*Vitalized couples:* a high degree of overall relationship satisfaction, comfortable in discussing feelings and resolving problems together; satisfied in their sexual and affectional exchange; interest in religious activity; strong preference for egalitarian roles.

*Harmonious couples:* a moderate level of overall relationship quality; relatively satisfied with each other's personality and habits and able to discuss and resolve differences; did not tend to be religiously oriented; had not yet come to a consensus on child-related issues such as number of children or projected parenting roles.

*Traditional couples:* moderate dissatisfaction with their relationship but with strengths in areas involving decision-making and future planning; somewhat unhappy with partner's personal habits and uncomfortable discussing feelings or dealing with conflict; not entirely satisfied with sexual relationship; quite religiously oriented; agreed on children and parent roles.

*Conflicted couples:* revealed distress on all PREPARE scales; dissatisfaction with partner's personality, habits; poor ability to discuss relationship problems, including sex and how to deal with friends and family; not religiously oriented but endorsed traditional role patterns.

Conflicted couples tended to have the fewest resources: they were younger, less well educated, and in occupations of lower income and status. Their parents and friends tended to view their marriage plans less favorably than did those in the other couple types. Racial and religious differences between the man and woman were more common than elsewhere. More often than in other couples in the study, the woman was pregnant. Together, these demographic characteristics are usually associated with lower marital satisfaction and stability (Fowers & Olson, 1992).

The PREPARE scale is often used in conjunction with the circumplex model, assessing information from each partner about his or her family of origin, as in the following case:

❋   ❋   ❋   ❋   ❋

Marian, 38, had a successful career in publishing and had not really wanted to marry until now. She had lived briefly with men on two occasions in her late 20s, but those relationships, while they had had a sexual aspect that was satisfying to her, had not really provided much in the way of emotional closeness. Each had lasted for approximately eight to ten months, and then had split up at her insistence. In both cases, Marian, an intensely emotional person, had periodically expressed doubts about continuing the relationship, each time finding fault with her partner and concluding that they had no future together and should separate. Only after the man pleaded that they continue would she relent, but it had taken little time before her dissatisfactions resumed.

For the last two years, Marian had lived with Paul, a 46-year-old, previously married land developer. In background as well as temperament, Marian and Paul could not be more different. She was from a lower-middle-class family with a Jewish father and a Protestant mother converted to Judaism, and grew up in a large city in the West. He, on the other hand, was from a small Tennessee town, raised as a Baptist (but no longer a practicing one) in a well-to-do family, and had never left his home state until he was inducted into the Army during the Korean War in the early 1950s. Paul had married his high school sweetheart when he returned from the service, and that marriage, an unhappy one almost from the beginning, had produced two children, now aged 23 and 20 and living on their own on the East Coast. Unable to verbally express his dissatisfactions directly, Paul had slowly withdrawn from his wife, having less and less contact with her over the years. However, they had stayed married for 24 years, at which time Paul, at the urging of his children, had initiated divorce proceedings and soon thereafter moved to the West Coast. He met Marian at a party, they dated for several months, and after knowing one another a year they moved in together.

Marian called a pastoral counselor, in this case a rabbi, in what seemed to him an urgent voice one day, and after she had explained her situation, the counselor set up a joint appointment for her and Paul the next day.[1] Marian was in tears soon after sitting down, explaining that they needed to work out right away whether they should continue together. Paul was quiet, seemed to be listening, and when Marian became upset reached for her hand to comfort her. He indicated that he loved Marian and wanted to marry her, but that she was unsure and was continuously changing her mind in what he called a "she loves me, she loves me not" fashion. She stated that two issues were urgent: she wanted children and believed he did not; she worried too that marrying a non-Jew would be unacceptable to her family and friends.

The counselor noted Paul's passivity and Marian's apprehensive style. After hearing each tell of previous relationships, he suspected that there surely were reasons why Paul had stayed in an increasingly unhappy marriage for so long, and also why Marian had found fault with all previous relationships and seemed to be doing so again. The counselor's working hypothesis at the end of the first session, possibly to be modified or corrected later as he came to know them better, was that Marian had a fear of commitment and possibly of trusting a man in an intimate, sustained relationship; however, she did seem to have access to her feelings and that would be helpful as the couple probed more deeply into their interactions in later sessions. The counselor speculated too that Paul was far less aware of his feelings and motives, probably because he felt they were often hostile and therefore unacceptable to others. Paul was someone who wanted very much to be liked, and it probably would be difficult for him to own up to feelings or motives he thought Marian would find objectionable. Sensing discomfort with one another but not knowing why, perhaps they had seized upon their differences in background or the issue of children because these seemed tangible and thus reasonable explanations for their growing uneasiness as they approached marriage. In order to check out some of these hunches, the counselor had each take home and independently fill out a PREPARE inventory, to be returned the following session.

During the next meeting the following week, the counselor observed that the couple seemed closer. They spoke of wedding plans and, at the conclusion of the session, the counselor pointed out to Marian that the two issues that had seemed so urgent to her the previous week were not even mentioned today. Were

---

[1]In fact, pastoral counselors provide more premarital counseling in the United States than do physicians or mental health professionals.

they merely a smokescreen on her part to cover up her discomfort at getting close to marriage? She acknowledged that their previous session had made her realize that their difference in religious background was a minor factor, especially since neither was particularly religiously oriented. As for children, she said, she had been thinking that perhaps her earlier statement represented more a response to reaching the end of her fertility period than any strong wish to have a baby. Paul, on the other hand, had also been thinking about that first session, and had concluded that, although he thought his parenting days with young children were over, he would agree to have a child if that was what it would take to make the relationship work. The counselor urged Paul to fully examine how he really felt, and not simply to tell people what he thought they wanted to hear, as he had done in the past. As for their transactions with one another, the counselor pointed out that Marian's intensity frightened Paul away, keeping him from expressing what he was feeling. Thus, it had the opposite effect from what she claimed she wanted to achieve. Paul, on the other hand, by withholding feelings, especially when he was annoyed or irritated, forced Marian to pursue him in the only way she knew, by expressing her feelings in no uncertain terms. He, too, through his passive behavior, was drawing out of Marian the opposite of what he wanted. The counselor's efforts were thus directed at helping them focus on their interaction, rather than individual personality traits in one or the other. If they could modify their ways of dealing with one another, and if each took responsibility for his or her own reactions, as well as some responsibility for what he or she drew out of the other, then future interactions between them would proceed more smoothly.

The following week, the couple and the counselor discussed each of their families of origin. Filling out the brief Family Adaptability and Cohesion Evaluation Scales (FACES III) (see Chapter Three) separately, each saw his or her family as reasonably well balanced (see Figure 6.1); Marian viewed hers as structurally connected and with good communication, Paul saw his as flexibly separated but with less-effective communication patterns. She believed hers was strongly bonded—highly cohesive—but not entirely able to accept change. In Paul's view, his family's rules and relationships were more flexible and adaptable to change. Separation from the family had been easier for him than for her. Exploring their families of origin helped each understand that while some differences existed in their backgrounds, the differences were more apparent than real, and thus not likely to be the source of conflict they, especially Marian, had feared.

By the following session, the PREPARE profile had been returned from computer analysis; its printout confirmed that no serious or insurmountable differences existed. Both had realistic expectations regarding marriage; they agreed on the personality issues that required attention, and were generally satisfied with one another's personality and habits. Test results indicated that the couple were congruent in their views regarding finances and their preferences for dealing with leisure time. Marian wanted family to play a larger role in their lives than did Paul, but the differences were not irreconcilable. They enjoyed spending free time together and were comfortable discussing sexual preferences and interests. They could be classified as a harmonious couple.

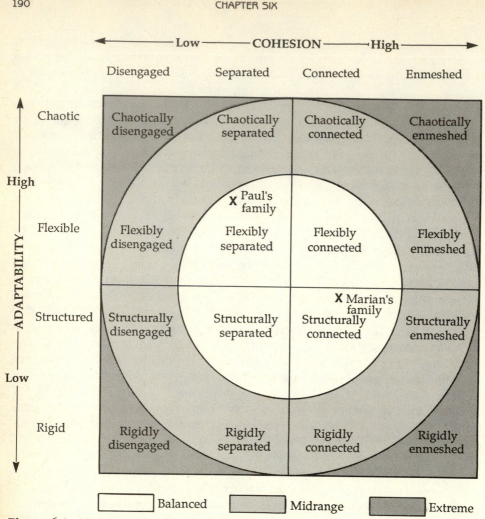

**Figure 6.1**   Marian and Paul's Circumplex-Model Scores
*Source:* Olson, 1986.

Major areas requiring further work involved communicating thoughts and sharing feelings more easily. Paul especially had to work on this, but Marian could help by listening more patiently and by being more aware of the effect on Paul of the intense expression of her feelings. Paul needed to be more prepared to deal with differences between them as they arose, instead of tending to deny or minimize problems. Trust was still an issue for Marian, but the counselor believed that problem would be reduced as she came to have faith that Paul was being honest with her and saying what he felt. They still were somewhat apart in their attitudes regarding the place of religious activity and values in their marriage, but once again the differences were negotiable.

The final session reviewed their outlooks regarding the future together, emphasizing that, while some understanding of the issues between them had been gained, considerably more needed to be accomplished. Each needed to continue what had been started, openly sharing thoughts and feelings and clarifying what each believed, even if some resulting conflict then needed resolution. They needed to have a clearer picture of the attitudes and beliefs of the other, and of the issues between them brought up in counseling that were delicate and still unresolved. Marian and Paul left the counseling feeling closer than they had before, determined to continue on their own what they had started with the counselor. They still had differences and conflicts to resolve, but they felt now that they knew better what those differences were and how to start working on them.

✳  ✳  ✳  ✳  ✳

## SUMMARY

Cohabitation, the situation in which two unmarried adults of the opposite sex live together in a sexual relationship, has increased sharply in recent years among all age groups. Greater public acceptance of this phenomenon reflects changing public attitudes regarding sexual behavior among unmarried adults; increased availability and effectiveness of contraceptive devices; a greater demand for equal rights for women; efforts to abandon the double standard; a trend toward delayed marriages; and a new emphasis on the development of a meaningful relationship between a man and woman where both feel independent while relating to one another.

Cohabitation is not a unitary entity; it takes the form of a variety of relationships: some temporary or convenient, others more committed and permanent; some a trial marriage, others a substitute for marriage. Moreover, it is entered into for a multitude of reasons, many frequently unknown to the partners, despite their stated motives. Cohabitation among college students, perhaps the most conspicuous participants, generally is of four types: the Linus-blanket type, where the primary quest on the part of one or both is for security and the satisfaction of dependency needs; the emancipation type, where one or both are seeking freedom from parental or societal restraints; the convenience type, usually of short duration, allowing a regular sexual outlet and domestic living without commitment; and the testing type, where both are more mature and are seeking a satisfying intimate relationship while maintaining autonomy.

Despite the common view of cohabitation as college-student behavior, however, the highest cohabitation rates are found among the least educated people. Cohabitation tends to be more acceptable among poorer parts of the population, probably for financial reasons. Elderly couples may live together in order to share expenses or to offer each other support and reduce feelings of loneliness. Overall, contrary to popular expectations, marriages preceded by cohabitation are more likely to dissolve than are unions initiated by marriage.

Counselors working with unmarried couples may need to help them deal with issues concerning commitment, social acceptance, relatives, the lack of legal safeguards, the decision whether the relationship is to be monogamous, division of responsibilities, expectations about the future, and in many cases termination of the union.

Couples seeking premarital counseling either want to check on the state of their partnership in light of their forthcoming marriage, or are concerned that some underlying conflict may mar their future marriage. In the latter case, typically there is an uncommitted partner, a passive-inactive partner, one who is unresponsive and insensitive, a partner who is apprehensive and pessimistic about the couple's future, or an angry or aggressive partner. In addition to focusing on key elements of their backgrounds and their current interaction patterns, the counselor often helps them examine their communication styles, their motivations, their attitudes regarding marital responsibilities, and their management of conflict. The purpose is less to resolve all conflict than to help the couple become aware of issues between them and learn some skills for resolving them. Four to six sessions are commonly required, with the counselor sometimes using assessment devices or test instruments as aids in the appraisal.

# Counseling Gay Male and Lesbian Couples

Cohabiting homosexuals[1] have much in common with the cohabiting hetero-sexuals we considered in the previous chapter. Both are part of small social systems in which couples seek satisfaction of their erotic and affectional needs in an un-orthodox living arrangement, usually but not necessarily without children. Both face stigmatization from the larger social system and often feel a need to keep the sexual nature of their relationship secret from others whom they perceive as hostile and disapproving. Both lack most legal safeguards, since they are not considered by society to be part of a lawfully recognized marital union.

Similar as these situations may be, however, they differ in significant ways that the counselor must recognize before attempting to understand gay male or **les-bian** clients. Despite the fact that homosexuality has existed throughout recorded

---

[1]For the remainder of this chapter, we will use the popular terms *gay* and *lesbian* instead of the more common term *homosexual* for several reasons. The latter has a clinically negative connota-tion, suggesting either psychopathology or immoral behavior, or possibly both. By emphasizing sexual-ity, the term *homosexual* unfairly excludes or minimizes all other aspects of the gay lifestyle. The prejudice persists, in the use of the term, that interpersonal love, sensual pleasure, or erotic expres-sions of affection and intimacy must be achieved in a heterosexual form or they are unnatural, in-ferior, or sinful. *Gay* and *lesbian* are more neutral terms used more frequently by those persons themselves who are involved in a preferred erotic relationship with a member or members of the same sex.

history and is present in virtually every society in the world, the idea of two people of the same sex, particularly men, sharing an intimate erotic life together evokes a more negative reaction in many people than does the identical behavior by unmarried heterosexuals.

Thus, the counselor can expect same-sex couples not only to have experienced social prejudice imposed by a hostile and unaccepting society, but also to themselves share, consciously or unconsciously, many of these condemning attitudes, as a result of having grown up in the same society. Weinberg (1972) has documented the ubiquitous nature of **homophobic**[2] beliefs (excessive fear and hatred of same-sex intimacy and sexuality and of homosexual individuals) within contemporary social mores and cultural attitudes. As Malyon (1982) points out in discussing some of the therapeutic issues involved in working with gay males, these clients have likely internalized such attitudes, contributing to a sense of guilt and a desire to punish themselves. Thus, he argues, they require a gay-affirmative viewpoint from the counselor. This is in sharp contrast to what Harrison (1987) observes to have been the attitude of most counselors as recently as the early 1970s: namely, that they should attempt to change their gay clients' sexual orientation.

The term *homosexuality* refers to a sexual orientation or form of interactive behavior—seeking and receiving sexual pleasures with a same-gender partner—and not to a clinical or pathological condition. Nevertheless, men or women suspected of engaging in such behavior typically are labeled as being a certain type of person. It is as though their sexual orientation alone described them fully. This is a mistaken idea, as mistaken as judging a person's entire life by the fact that he or she is heterosexual. Calling someone *heterosexual* or *homosexual* may say something about his or her sexual practices but little if anything about the broader issues of that individual's personality, ways of relating to others, and so on. Still, the label *homosexual* historically has stigmatized the individual or couple, often arousing private snickers as well as public ridicule, and may instantly discredit the person(s) unless the stigma can be hidden. Until very recently, it was only by concealing his or her private life that the homosexual could hope to pass as acceptable in society, and thus not be open to scorn and ostracism.

That situation began to change in the last decade, as laws and public policies that discriminated on the basis of sexual preference were successfully challenged in the courts by gay-rights advocates. As part of the gay-rights movement's emphasis on gay pride, more and more gay persons, particularly in urban centers, opted to "come out" (of the closet) and assert their gay identity, insisting on greater social acceptance. However, the advent of AIDS (Acquired Immune Deficiency

---

[2]Homophobia manifests itself in a variety of ways in our culture. Externally, it is visible in antigay felony statutes in many states and local communities, as well as in "gay bashing," in which vulnerable gays and lesbians are considered legitimate targets of violence because of their sexual preferences. Internalized homophobia, more subtle, represents homophobic values incorporated by individuals—gays included—socialized in a homophobic culture such as ours (Brown & Zimmer, 1986). Internal homophobic beliefs may serve to mask any same-sex erotic feelings in some men.

Syndrome)—once referred to as the "gay plague"—has once again had a disenfranchising effect on the homosexual population. In many cases, antigay heterosexuals have seized on the AIDS scare to practice overt discrimination and even sexual violence and assault on homosexuals (Anderson, 1982; Harry, 1988).

## SOME BASIC CONCEPTS AND TERMINOLOGY

Homosexual behavior can be found worldwide, at all socioeconomic levels, among all racial and ethnic groups, and in rural as well as urban areas. Some individuals who engage in homosexual behavior are married to someone of the opposite sex but have occasional homosexual affairs. Others live together in long-term relationships with a same-sex partner, while still others engage in casual "pickup" sex. Some are contemporaneously **bisexual**, engaging in intimate sexual relations with both a man and woman. Others are sequentially bisexual in a series of sexual relations with people of both genders. Clearly there is not one type of homosexual union or homosexual lifestyle.

Precise census data are, of course, unavailable, considering the danger of exposure experienced by many gays and lesbians, but some reasonably accurate assessments can be made. Marmor (1980) estimates that the prevalence of exclusively homosexual behavior in Western culture is 5% to 10% for adult males and 3% to 5% for adult females. If bisexual behavior is included, these figures may be doubled. According to more recent, but conservative, estimates (Buunk & van Driel, 1989), there are approximately 5 million men and 2.5 million women in the United States alone who have a predominantly homosexual orientation. If these guesses are correct (if anything, they are likely to be underestimates, since many gays and lesbians still avoid disclosure), homosexuality is a widespread phenomenon, even in a society such as ours that strongly condemns the behavior, even among consenting adults.

Research on homosexuality—largely a taboo topic until Evelyn Hooker's (1957) pioneering studies—confirms that no essential difference exists in the incidence of mental problems between homosexual and heterosexual populations.[3] No single personality profile covers all gay persons (Bell & Weinberg, 1978), and the sexual orientation, once established, is not readily subject to change (Storms, 1986). As for etiology, Warren (1980) cites two opposing viewpoints: (1) homosexuality is an acquired taste (therefore the result of choice and, by implication, morally blameworthy); (2) it is inborn (therefore the gay person is not subject to blame). She notes that gays favor the inborn-preference theory, while anti-gays tend to support the acquired-taste explanation (thereby justifying the firing of openly homosexual teachers, for example, because as role models they may unduly influence

---

[3]The American Psychiatric Association did not get around to declassifying homosexuality as a mental disorder until 1973. Even then, that decision was at least as much the result of political prodding from gay activists as it was the result of research such as Hooker's investigations. Prior to that decision, a man or woman whose sexual preference was not exclusively for a member of the opposite sex was diagnosed by psychiatric experts as abnormal.

young people to make the arbitrary moral choice). Most psychiatric or psychological research (for example, Hooker, 1967) favors the view that both biological and social causes are operating: a predisposing homosexual orientation is present at birth, and psychosocial factors, including family dynamics, operate early in childhood to determine the ultimate homosexual disposition.

Gay people tend to face special problems regarding self-disclosure in rural or religious communities, where they are often forced to pretend to others—or even to themselves—that they are heterosexual so as to be accepted in the nongay world. To remain exclusively gay in such communities is to live in daily fear of discovery, to secretly seek out other gay individuals or couples, and to remain segregated from heterosexual marrieds. Since the number of gays is usually limited, it is common to feel socially isolated and to solve the problem, if possible, by moving on to larger communities such as the Castro district of San Francisco, the West Hollywood section of Los Angeles, or West Greenwich Village in New York City. Here gays are far more apt to meet other gays through homophile organizations, bars, or gay churches. As Harry (1988) observes, a number of gay and lesbian organizations devoted to socially integrating the newcomer into the gay world have sprung up in most large American cities within the last 20 years. Among other functions, these organizations provide a social network for meeting other gays, offering an alternative social setting to the often highly sexual context of the gay bar. The point, in keeping with the effort to make the gay life more than simply a sexual encounter or series of encounters, is to emphasize social and cultural, rather than predominantly erotic, opportunities.

The preceding is not to say that "gay scenes"—organized efforts to arrange erotic contact, often between strangers—do not exist. Casual sex has long been a part of gay life, at least for men, and, as Humphreys and Miller (1980) note, nearly all American towns have at least one homosexual scene. Bus terminals, freeway rest stops, isolated park bathrooms, stylish resorts, or athletic clubs—all have served as places for men to establish contact for instant and impersonal sexual liaison.

"Cruising" in public parks or restrooms, far more frequent among gay males than lesbians, constitutes yet another form of searching for brief sexual activity with strangers where no interpersonal commitment, intimacy, or responsibility is required. However, the common belief that such promiscuous behavior characterizes all gay unions is erroneous, according to Bell and Weinberg (1978). These researchers, studying 686 homosexual males and 293 homosexual females in the San Francisco area, found that close to 40% of the respondents either did no cruising at all or did it no more than once per month. Those seeking casual encounters were more likely to visit bars or bath houses catering to homosexual clients rather than run the risk of arrest by cruising in public places. In fact, the study found that most sexual activity was conducted in the privacy of homes. More recently, the AIDS epidemic has prompted many men to reevaluate their sexual practices, and to discontinue pickup activity in favor of forming a committed couple.

Even in cities where casual contacts are easily available, the majority of gay men, like most people in general, seek the comfort of a more stable union with a loved partner. Typically, most of these extended relations last up to three years or so, although some continue for decades. Possibly these same-sex relationships, which are similar in many ways to cohabitant heterosexual unions, end more easily than heterosexual marriages because no legal restraints bind the couple together, and no children keep them involved once problems develop.

## BEING GAY IN A NONGAY WORLD— THE COMING-OUT PROCESS

On September 22, 1975, in San Francisco's Union Square, a woman moved out of the crowd, raised her arm, leveled a chrome-plated gun, and pulled the trigger. A man standing nearby saw the movement and pushed down on the gun barrel. The bullet missed its target by five feet. Oliver Sipple had just saved the life of the President of the United States. His quick action made him an instant hero. The President wrote him a letter thanking him. Over 1000 other people wrote to him praising him. It should have been a moment of triumph for Oliver. Instead it was a nightmare.

"Within 24 hours, reporters had also learned that the ex-Marine was involved in the San Francisco gay community, and the story became page one—and wire service—copy" (*The Advocate*, Oct. 22, 1975). The *Chicago Sun-Times* called him a "Homosexual Hero" in a headline. The *Denver Post* referred to him as a "Gay Vet." Oliver went into seclusion to avoid the media. He was so distressed at the prospect of his mother in Detroit reading about him as a gay hero that he all but declined to take credit for saving the life of the President of the United States! (Berzon, 1979, p. 88)

This excerpt poignantly illustrates not only what apprehension some gay persons experience about the unintended discovery of their secret, but also how that fear of disclosure must permeate much of their daily behavior. As Berzon (1979) notes, nearly every gay person with a family is concerned about disclosure to his or her family. Since only about half the men in Bell and Weinberg's (1978) survey had told their parents of their gayness, the remainder attempted to conceal the fact by developing a series of obfuscating strategies. Gay lovers, especially in their 20s, may maintain separate residences or, if they live together, may pose as roommates. They are likely to discourage parental visits, and, should a visit take place, will maintain the fiction that as roommates they sleep in separate rooms. Repeated visits, sometimes extending over several years, serve to reinforce the illusion that the two are simply very good friends who enjoy being together. Ultimately the pretense wears thin, though, and the parents become aware their child is gay. (In some cases, the parents continue to deceive themselves, even if they suspect, denying to themselves what their eyes tell them.) In either case, the term *gay* or *homosexual* is studiously avoided. The couple can never openly express physical affection toward one another in front of the parents and never make explicit reference to their union (Harry, 1988).

In another scenario, the couple may decide, early on or later in the relationship, to come out to their parents. Here they risk alienation or long-term—perhaps permanent—rejection. In the case of gay males, according to Bell and Weinberg's (1978) data, mothers are most often informed before fathers, presumably because, like most heterosexual males, fathers are more apt to be threatened and to refuse to accept the news. If the parents are strongly religious, both may find the revelation intolerable. If, as is happening increasingly, the parents learn simultaneously that their son is dying of AIDS and has been living a gay life without their knowledge, the shock may be doubly devastating.

Coming out—openly acknowledging and describing oneself as gay—is a process that occurs over time and in front of different audiences. "I came out with my parents" may be followed by "I told some of the nongay people at school" or perhaps "I finally came clean with the boss today." First, of course, the gay person must come out to himself or herself, establishing a positive self-definition. In the following case, a young adult struggles with his self-definition:

❋  ❋  ❋  ❋  ❋

Sheldon, 29, came to a counselor with a vague assortment of physical and psychological complaints. He reported experiencing anxiety attacks several times a week, without knowing what exactly was disturbing him. He felt dizzy at work and couldn't seem to concentrate on his job as a bookkeeper for a large furniture manufacturing firm. He had gone out with one woman for several weeks, but now found himself restless and not really interested in pursuing the relationship much further.

After two sessions of reporting a variety of symptoms of distress, he finally told the female counselor that he had something "awful to confess." He then proceeded to describe a series of experiences—beginning in high school—of visiting bath houses and public parks in a neighboring town in order to engage in impersonal sex with other men. However, he insisted to the counselor that he was not gay, that he actually disliked homosexuals and their "swishy" behavior, and that he wanted one day to marry and lead a conventional life. He had been sexually intimate with several women since high school, he contended, and, while the experiences had ranged from neutral to unpleasant, he remained certain that through counseling he could learn to enjoy heterosexual relationships.

As Sheldon spoke of his growing-up years, the counselor recognized Sheldon's early patterns of difficulty with his family of origin. He was the youngest of four boys, living in a lower-middle-class family with what he described as a strong, domineering, and difficult mother and a weak, inadequate, and unconnected father. Growing up, Sheldon felt disengaged from both parents, as well as from his brothers. The household was filled with tension among the family members, there was a great deal of confusion, and communication was poor or nonexistent.

The counselor recognized Sheldon's struggle over his gay identity, and consulted a gay psychologist from the local Gay Counseling Center over how best to help Sheldon resolve his conflicts over who he was. The consultant urged caution in helping Sheldon come out, pointing out that the client was exhibiting distortions of reality as he fought to deny the object of his sexual urges. The counselor continued to explore Sheldon's past and present homosexual behavior, including an ongoing romance with an alcoholic young man that Sheldon insisted was not significant. She also continued to direct Sheldon's attention to family issues from the past as well as the present.

When Sheldon went back home to another state to visit his family, he was urged by the counselor to talk to his brothers about their sexual experiences. Not unexpectedly, it turned out that two of the three boys were gay but not openly so. The visit seemed to clarify a great deal to Sheldon regarding their upbringing, and he returned to counseling more accepting of himself, although not yet ready to reveal his gayness publicly.

When his parents came to town several weeks later, the counselor recommended that Sheldon invite them to join him in the next session. He expressed considerable discomfort over doing so, afraid something would slip out about his homosexual behavior. However, after the counselor reassured him that she would not reveal his secret, he finally consented to their presence. The mother's opening words, as she sat down, were "I wanted Sheldon to be a girl when he was born, since I already had three boys." By this statement she seemed to be acknowledging at some level that she understood why she had been called to the session, that Sheldon was struggling with his sexual identity. The counselor made no attempt to discuss homosexuality, but instead asked questions about the family's early years. Sheldon's father remained relatively quiet throughout the two-hour meeting, answering questions in a brief manner, and only when asked.

In subsequent sessions with Sheldon, the counselor helped him recognize that his parents "knew" and that he need not waste so much energy in hiding the truth from them. At first, of course, he needed to be truthful to himself, facing who and what he was. After two more meetings with the counselor, Sheldon terminated the sessions. He had accepted his gayness, and had come out on a limited basis, telling his woman friend and some colleagues at work. He never spoke of it with his parents, but he assumed they knew and were able to live with it without acknowledging it in so many words.

✼　✼　✼　✼　✼

Most gay men, in spite of the popular stereotype, are not obviously effeminate in appearance or behavior. Since they pass as heterosexual, giving up the security of anonymity by coming out may be fraught with anxiety. As Harrison (1987) notes, "Every gay man, whatever his age, must decide when to stop asking permission to be himself and to go public about his sexual identity" (p. 226). For lesbians, the secrecy may be somewhat easier to maintain, since society tolerates open physical affection between women far more readily than between men, and women living together generally raise fewer eyebrows than do cohabiting men. Both minority groups learn to avoid disclosure and to pass as "straight" within nongay settings by adopting the manner and dress of the majority. Part of that impression management is to remain silent in the face of jokes or other slanderous remarks about homosexuals if they wish to avoid drawing attention to their gay selves (Ponse, 1980).

The process of coming out has usually begun before the gay person contacts a counselor. That is, while no public disclosure has been made, the individual (young or old, single or married), has begun to acknowledge same-sex erotic feelings and fantasies to himself or herself. This self-recognition stage may last for a considerable period of time, during which the person may feel confused and may or may not act upon the feelings by having one or more homosexual experiences. In most cases this stage leads ultimately to the next stage of self-acceptance: risking rejection by telling carefully chosen others. (We saw in the case of Sheldon just presented that this may be a painful and drawn-out process.) As the individual sets about exploring his or her new sexual identity, there is increased mingling with others with similar sexual interests. (The amount of sexual experimentation differs between men and women; men are more likely to engage in a series of one-time sexual contacts, although some lesbians may do so also.) As the newly found freedom to sexually explore becomes less intriguing and the need for intimacy becomes stronger, a more stable and committed relationship with a single partner is likely to follow. As we observed earlier, the union may be relatively short-lived, and may simply be the first of a number of such coupling experiences. In what Coleman (1982) calls the stage of integration, the gay person has forged a gay identity and incorporated both the public and private images into one unified self-presentation.

As for the counselor, it is essential to understand the significance of these stages of the coming-out process. As with heterosexual clients, having relationships with a series of partners may well represent experimental dating and not necessarily failed relationships. We should note here too that the process is often more rapid and more complete if the client's current significant others—including, when appropriate, members of his or her family of origin—participate in the counseling sessions. Exchanging feedback information, exposing family secrets, and dealing more effectively with interlocking problems often has a catalytic effect on hastening the emergence of a gay identity.

## GAYS AND LESBIANS: SIMILARITIES AND DIFFERENCES

While we have for the most part written of gay male and lesbian couples as though they shared the same characteristics and concerns, the counselor must understand the ways in which these relationships also differ. Since societal reaction to male and female homosexuality has historically been different, and members of each group are subject to different socialization experiences and gender-role expectations as they grow up in heterosexual families, it follows that lesbian and gay lifestyle patterns are likely to differ significantly, and that each group lives in markedly different types of subculture (Buunk & van Driel, 1989).

First the similarities: Both types of couples must face the choice of remaining hidden (denying their true identities to others, losing self-respect and a sense of control over their lives) or lifting the mask and revealing the secret (thereby risking loss of love and support from family and friends, forfeiting jobs or curtailing promotions, and possibly facing police arrest) (Toder, 1979). In avoiding disclosure of "the love that dare not speak its name," gay males and lesbians both frequently find themselves, in Rochlin's (1979) words, participating in the popular homophobic game "I-know-they-know-and-they-know-I-know-they-know-but-let's-all-pretend-nobody-knows" (p. 162).

As we reported in the case of Sheldon, a gay male may engage in homosexual acts but deny to himself that he is gay, thus pretending that he measures up to the community standard of "maleness" and ensuring that he will not be viewed by society as a lower-status female. Similarly, as Toder (1979, p. 45) reports, a woman in a same-sex love affair may fear being labeled homosexual by a rejecting society, and thus may deny the implications of the relationship ("I'm not a lesbian, I just happen to be in love with this person and this person just happens to be a woman").

Role playing in both gay and lesbian lifestyles may defy stereotypes. The popular "butch/femme" notion of a gay male couple emulating a traditional male-female married relationship (one partner masculine, dominant in sexual activity, providing the financial support; the other engaged in complementary household activity) is an improbable one. Rather, as Harry (1983) points out, gay relationships are more likely to be patterned after a best-friends/roommates model than a heterosexual role model. While butch/femme patterns do characterize some gay male relationships, especially those based on inequality, Harry (1983) contends that masculinity in appearance and behavior is likely to be highly valued in oneself and one's partner, suggesting a "butch/butch" pattern may be even more likely among gay male couples.

The counselor would do well to recognize that both gay men and lesbian women lack any role models of how a happy, healthy homosexual couple operates on a day-to-day basis. Unlike members of other minorities, apt to grow up among members of their own reference group where culture and tradition can be transmitted in a positive manner, gays and lesbians have heterosexual relationships as their sole paradigms. Many internalize the prevalent concept that same-sex relationships are by definition brief, devoid of deep feelings, and based primarily on sexual attraction. Growing up male is often to learn to dominate and control and to move to gain power, but not to be nurturant or emotionally expressive; this is often a problem for a gay male couple learning to work at relationship maintenance. Both socialized as women, lesbian couples may have problems expressing anger or asserting power or initiating sexual activity, all usually associated with male activity. It is essential that the counselor comprehend the effects of gender-socialization experiences in understanding differences between gay male and lesbian relationships (Brown & Zimmer, 1986).

Homosexual women are more likely than their male counterparts to strive for stable, extended relationships (Saghir & Robins, 1980). While one-night stands or casual encounters do occur, they tend to be infrequent. Lesbians, much like their female heterosexual counterparts, are more likely to establish affectionate bonds with partners over a period of time before becoming sexually involved.

In those same-sex love affairs, they tend to value equality, emotional expressiveness, and a similarity of attitudes between partners (Peplau & Amaro, 1982). Long-lasting relationships of more than a year's duration, with an emphasis on faithfulness, tend to be the rule. Thus, the total number of sexual partners is usually few compared to gay men. While sexual fidelity may be desired by gay male couples, it may also occasionally be breached by a casual sexual pickup experience by one or the other partner. Among homosexual women, casual or impersonal sex is the exception, although, once again as with heterosexual women, affairs may occur and may lead to a breakup of the relationship (Blumstein & Schwartz, 1983).

While a small minority of lesbians do engage in traditional gender roles (the butch/femme pattern), most are likely to divide household tasks and responsibilities according to talent and interest or by turns, since both are likely to be employed. Socializing is often done at home, usually with other lesbian couples or perhaps gay male pairs. In systems terms, as Rice and Kelly (1988) observe, it makes sense that a subsystem (the couple) trying to relate to a larger system (society) that either ignores or criticizes them will attempt to tighten the partner boundaries, fusing with others like themselves and adopting a tight, self-protective posture against the outside world.

Generally speaking, according to Harry (1983), the social world of lesbians tends to be a world of couples, whereas the world of gay men is one of singles and couples. As we just noted, among lesbians a sexual relationship may arise from an evolving affectionate relationship, while for gay men, in keeping with the socialization of men in general in our society, the sequence is likely to be reversed. Blumstein and Schwartz (1983), reporting on a large sample of heterosexual cohabitors, heterosexual marrieds, gay couples, and lesbian couples, found lesbians to have sex far less frequently than other types of couples, often expressing a preference for physical closeness—hugging, touching, cuddling—over genital sex. According to their findings, such activities are likely to become ends in themselves for many lesbian couples, rather than foreplay leading to genital sex activity.

❈   ❈   ❈   ❈   ❈

Evelyn, 24, and Anne Marie, 26, both assistant professors of music at neighboring universities in the same large western city, met at a music educators' conference and were immediately attracted to one another. They spent several days together, at mealtimes and between sessions, sharing work experiences and talking over their pasts. They found that they had lots in common—both were raised Catholic but no longer practiced their religion, both were brought up in small towns, both had had an early love of music—and when the conference ended they agreed to continue seeing each other. It was only after six months or so that their relationship became a physical one, primarily cuddling and caressing, and only occasionally involving genital play.

As they learned about one another, it turned out that Anne Marie had been a lesbian since her teenage years. A tomboy with an early aversion to girls' activities, she had had her first homosexual experience at 15 with another girl at a summer camp. Anne Marie had never been attracted to boys, or later to men. Instead she had had a number of romantic "crushes" on teachers growing up, and one long live-in arrangement with a woman when she was 21.

Evelyn, on the other hand, had had several love affairs with men, beginning during her adolescent years, but had found them unsatisfactory. For four years prior to meeting Anne Marie, she had not dated and had been celibate. Socially she was extremely shy, and felt inadequate at conventional feminine tasks, such as cooking, decorating, and choosing clothes. From the start she was fascinated by Anne Marie's sense of style as well as her confidence in social situations.

Together, the women bought a house and settled into a "married" lifestyle. They shared expenses, took turns cooking and doing various chores around the house, traveled to Europe on vacation together, and seemed in general to enjoy their life as a couple. Their friends were primarily people from work, mostly heterosexuals, although they also had gay male and lesbian couples to the house for parties. They were not obviously homosexual, nor did they ever bring the issue up before the university administrators, faculty, or students. While they did not deny their lesbian relationship, neither did they affirm or flaunt it publicly. Monogamous, they seemed to friends like a childless couple where both partners were oriented toward furthering their careers. As for family, Anne Marie, an only child, had been cut off from hers since she left home for college. Evelyn's parents were dead, and her two brothers rarely contacted her. When she did hear from them, they pretended Anne Marie did not exist.

After 14 years, Evelyn, now 38, and Anne Marie, 40, began to drift apart. They quarreled more often, seemed to have developed different interests from one another, found they had less and less to talk about, and finally decided to split up. Anne Marie revealed that she had found herself interested in a younger woman at her school and wanted to be free to pursue that new relationship.

Since no strong family or social ties kept them together, they separated, with a counselor's help, without too much bitterness. Evelyn remained by herself in the house for several years, and then she too found a young woman of 26 who moved in with her as her lover. Both "married types" who needed the comfort, support, and intimacy of a coupled relationship, Evelyn and Anne Marie, after their "divorce," each ultimately sought and found another long-term relationship.

❋   ❋   ❋   ❋   ❋

## ASSESSING GAY/LESBIAN COUPLES

Gay men and lesbians seek professional counseling at about the same rate as the general population (Woodman & Lenna, 1980). Although the problems inherent in being gay in a society rejecting of that sexual orientation may lead some to

**Box 7.1   A Counselor Checklist of Common Myths Regarding Homosexuality**

Do you believe these statements?

- Most gay men are effeminate and most lesbians are masculine in appearance and behavior.
- Most gay couples adopt male/female (active/passive) roles in their relationships.
- All gay men are sexually promiscuous.
- Gay men believe that they are women in men's bodies and gay women believe that they are men in women's bodies.
- Most gay people would have a sex-change operation if they could afford it.
- Most gay people are child molesters.
- People choose to become homosexual.
- Most gay people are unhappy with their sexual orientation and seek therapy to convert to heterosexuality.
- Counselors report high success rates in converting homosexuals to heterosexuals.
- Most gay people are easily identifiable by their dress and mannerisms.
- Homosexual behavior is unnatural because it does not occur in other species.
- Homosexuality is the result of a hereditary defect.
- Homosexuals have hormone abnormalities.
- All homosexual males have dominant, overbearing mothers and weak, passive fathers.
- Homosexuality threatens the continuity of the species.
- All male hairdressers, interior decorators, and ballet dancers are homosexuals.
- Homosexuality is an illness that can be cured.

*Source:* Gartrell, 1983, p. 396.

the counselor's office, it is more likely that they come looking for ways to combat external and internal stereotypes of homosexuals, and not for "treatment" for their homosexuality per se (Gartrell, 1983). All of us, those who grow up to become homosexual as well as those who become heterosexual, are exposed at an early age to myths that produce negative stereotypes, particularly about male homosexuality (see Box 7.1): they are sexual perverts, queers, sinners against the natural order of life, faggots, child molesters, possibly criminals. It is hardly any wonder that those who become gay are often filled with self-hatred. As Malyon (1982) points out, that negative self-image, along with an inevitable internalized homophobic attitude, is bound to have serious negative consequences for a person's overall self-identity. A common solution is to develop a false identity by suppressing homoerotic promptings and taking on a heterosexual persona.

It is hardly surprising, then, to find gay persons who secretly struggle with themselves as they grow up, sometimes believing their sexual impulses mean they are mentally ill. For these individuals, accepting society's label that they are abnormal is often less painful than exploring the possibility of adopting a gay identity (Woodman & Lenna, 1980).

---

**Box 7.2   A Problem-Appraisal Checklist for Gay/Lesbian Couples**

Gay couples may experience problems in the following areas:

- Coming out—concealment vs. openness
- Self-acceptance of gay identity
- Family estrangement
- Church acceptance vs. condemnation
- Sexual exclusiveness vs. nonexclusiveness
- The AIDS crisis
- Long-term vs. short-term relationships
- Aging and later-life problems
- Gay fatherhood and lesbian motherhood
- Lack of legal safeguards
- Gender-role patterns in the relationship

---

# ACHIEVING A GAY IDENTITY

Closeting themselves helps homosexuals avoid facing the emotions of shame and guilt over who they are. Coming out, as we noted earlier, is risky, and often there is no turning back once a gay life is exposed. As indicated in Box 7.2, the process of coming out is of major significance, not merely because of the public disclosure, but because it represents self-recognition and the start of gay self-identity. The counselor needs to assess how successfully and how fully this is accomplished and should not be too surprised if further hesitation and stalling follow the initial disclosure to significant others. Also, the counselor should note in working with gay couples whether one of the partners is further along than the other in affirming his or her gayness, since greater concealment by one may have detrimental consequences for the relationship and the couple's social behavior with family and friends.

Estrangement from the family of origin, emotionally, financially, and interpersonally, is especially painful. Gays sometimes report feeling like minority-group members or second-class citizens in their own families, often feeling the need to explain, defend, apologize for, or hide their gayness or else risk ridicule or ostracism. On first learning that their child is gay, parents are apt to be rejecting, perhaps blaming themselves and wondering what they did wrong in raising their child. Some parents seize the opportunity to blame one another for the "aberration." In extreme cases, as Harry (1988) reports, more violent or forceful solutions are sought by despairing parents: kidnapping and homosexual deprogramming, usually of lesbians; pressures to seek psychotherapy in the hope of turning the person into a heterosexual; threats to cut off support, if their child is in college; and threats or attempts to take away a gay person's children, should they exist, unless the homosexual behavior ceases. Ultimately, especially with the aid of counseling, some parents may accept their child's gayness; many do not.

The person coming out is seeking external validation that he or she is a worth-while, socially acceptable human being in the eyes of those individuals from whom such approbation is particularly important. In addition to family and friends, some gays may look to their church for affirmation that their sexual orientation need not be in conflict with their religious beliefs. Unfortunately, until recently, all American churches condemned homosexuality, causing a sense of alienation from organized religion on the part of most gays.

As noted by McNaught (1979), himself a Catholic, growing up gay and Catholic may be akin to living in Northern Ireland with a Catholic mother and Protestant father. Loyalty to one seems to preclude loyalty to the other: the Catholic church censures homosexuality, while other gays castigate those who retain ties to an oppressive church. The Judeo-Christian tradition throughout history has been highly critical of same-sex acts, assuming that heterosexuality is natural and that those who engage in homosexual activity do so willfully. While some conser-vative theologians continue to retain that viewpoint, others (for example, Nelson, 1982) believe that gays as well as the church will benefit from the liberation of gays from oppression. Harry (1988) reports that in recent years a number of inter-denominational churches for gays have sprung up in most large American cities, thus reducing the alienation felt by many religious gays. Moreover, some liberal churches, again in large cities, now permit affiliate fellowships for gay individuals and couples who prefer to remain in the church in which they were raised. For the counselor, the therapeutic task may often include reattaching an isolated gay client or gay couple to a larger system such as the church, which in the past may have provided comfort and faith.

One further consequence of society's unwillingness to confront the fact that people of the same sex may love one another and wish to spend a lifetime together is the inability to legally marry a same-sex partner. Similarly, with few exceptions, health insurance companies will not permit gay men or lesbians to add their long-term partners as cobeneficiaries, although married heterosexual men and women do so. Since they are not considered to be members of each other's families, gay or lesbians may be excluded from visiting such partners in the event of serious illness, either by hospital authorities or because of the wishes of the sick per-son's parents. In the event of death, not a far-fetched possibility in the age of AIDS, family members of the deceased may purposely keep the homosexual part-ner away, again denying to others (and perhaps themselves) that the person they are burying was gay.

## SEXUALITY AND THE AIDS EPIDEMIC

The fear of AIDS has affected coupling between gay men, regardless of age, prior relationship, or history of sexual activity. Sexual exclusivity between partners, including those who previously sought sexual experiences outside of the rela-tionship, has now become more common, placing additional expectations on the relationship. Some experience the loss of extrarelationship sex with sadness and anger and may resent being forced into a heterosexual model of monogamous coupling. Others see exclusivity as adding an expression of positive self-regard, and thus as an important force in the couple's development.

Coming to an agreement regarding the sexual exclusiveness of the relationship is often the single most important decision faced by gay couples (Silverstein, 1981). The point to look for here is not so much whether monogamy or nonmonogamy exists, but rather the extent to which the couple can agree on this point. Gay male relationships, in particular, lack the norms built into heterosexual marriage or other long-term male-female coupling, so that infidelity is not necessarily considered a serious offense or deviation. Since sex with a variety of partners is a fact of life in gay male relationships (Blasband & Peplau, 1985), the counselor should not apply heterosexual norms in evaluating the effect of such behavior on the couple's ability to stay together. Rather, it is important to determine whether the casual pickup or affair has violated one of the couple's expectations, and, if so, the extent to which the violation impairs their future together.

Casual or impersonal sex has had to be reevaluated by gays (as well as nongays) in the light of the AIDS epidemic. AIDS is an infectious disease in which the body's immune system is damaged in varying, often progressive, degrees of severity, with the result that the body is vulnerable to fatal opportunistic infections such as pneumonia or tuberculosis, opportunistic tumors and malignancies such as Kaposi's sarcoma, and in some cases AIDS-related dementia caused by central nervous system damage (Green, 1989). Homosexual and bisexual men are among the highest-risk groups. By 1985, AIDS was the primary killer of men aged 20 to 50 in New York City and San Francisco (Fradkin, 1987).

Fear of AIDS has led to changing sex practices between long-term partners ("safe sex"), the closing of certain bath houses, fewer casual pickups, and sometimes the adoption of celibacy in an effort by gays to protect themselves and their partners. For couples, the discovery by one person that he has AIDS not only is personally terrifying, but also leads to fear that he may become a dependent burden on his lover or, conversely, that the partner may reject him by leaving. Whatever that outcome, the infected person may have to reveal previously hidden casual experiences with other men to his unsuspecting partner, and also to face the disturbing possibility that he has transmitted the disease to his partner. Disclosure of AIDS may also lead to job loss, loss of health insurance benefits, demands that he vacate an apartment, or rejection by family, friends, or work associates. In some cases, the gay person may feel deserving of the AIDS disease, particularly if he still has not fully accepted his gay identity.

Counselors can also anticipate gay couples who seek help with problems concerning sexual intimacy but who insist they are not frightened that one or the other partner may be HIV positive—that is, infected by the human immunodeficiency virus (HIV) that causes breakdowns in the immune system and ultimately leads to AIDS. Walker (1987) suggests that these individuals are most likely in denial, and thus are seeking a less-threatening explanation for their current difficulties. She argues that, unless the counselor working with the couple faces his or her own fear of AIDS and also is knowledgeable about the defense mechanism of denial occasioned by the threat of any fatal disease, the counselor may unconsciously collude in the couple's denial and not raise the issue in assessing their presenting problem. (We'll return to the important topic of AIDS counseling for the entire family system of which the couple is one part later in this chapter.)

# GAY MALE AND LESBIAN PARENTING

Gay fathers and lesbian mothers, according to one estimate (*Not All Parents Are Straight,* 1987), care for between 12 and 15 million children in some 5 to 6 million homes in the United States alone. While such estimates may seem high, a large number, perhaps the majority, are closeted and thus "invisible," with few neighbors or others realizing there is a homosexual parent. Although parenthood may at first glance seem antagonistic to being gay, the facts are otherwise. Gay men marry for a variety of reasons: they may find their homosexuality personally unacceptable; they may use the marriage as a socially acceptable cover behind which to hide their gayness; they may marry to avoid continued family pressure. In addition, they may prefer male sexual partners but develop affectionate feelings for a particular woman or simply feel more comfortable around women. Compounding all these factors may be a genuine desire for children (Bozett, 1982).

Lesbians too may marry and bear children because they wish to have them or because it is expected of women by society. Some may make a transition over time from a self-identification as a previously married heterosexual to a lesbian identity and retain custody of their children.[4] Crawford (1987) argues that lesbian-headed families must deal with the special challenges to their fitness for motherhood that arise in a homophobic society (and in their own internalized homophobia). Among the myths they themselves must overcome regarding a lesbian's suitability to be a mother, Sachs (1986) lists the following fictions:

> Lesbians are women who act like men, hate men, and do not fit the feminine role; motherhood requires a high degree of altruism and nurturance, and lesbians cannot fill the maternal role because they are oversexed, narcissistic, and pleasure-oriented; lesbians are masculine and aggressive, so they cannot assume the feminine task of raising children. (p. 244)

Bozett (1985) differentiates five marker events that typify a gay father's career: (1) a heterosexual dating period; (2) a marriage during which the man assumes

---

[4]While homosexuality no longer disqualifies a parent from custody, judges retain considerable discretion in the matter. Despite the changes brought about by the American Psychiatric Association's declassifying homosexuality as a mental disorder two decades ago, many courts remain concerned about the possible stigma for the child, the possibility of peer ridicule, the possibility that the child might grow up to be homosexual, and the likelihood that the child might learn inappropriate sex-role behavior (Hodges, 1991). Available research (Nungesser, 1980), however, reveals that most lesbian mothers are committed to nonsexist child rearing and make an effort to provide adequate male role models. Recent evidence (Patterson, 1992) suggests that children of gay or lesbian parents are no more likely to become homosexuals and are just as well adjusted as other children raised under more conventional circumstances.

the role of husband; (3) becoming a father; (4) alteration in the spousal relationship (usually separation and divorce); and (5) the activation of a gay lifestyle. Concurrent with these benchmarks, of course, is the man's growing awareness and acceptance of his own homosexuality.

Most gay males do not disclose their homosexuality to their prospective mates, although some do. In some cases, rather than being deceptive, it may be that these men do not consider themselves to really be gay, even if they have had one or more homosexual experiences. It may even be the case that the future wife, if informed, responds positively, perhaps because she believes the gay life is a thing of the past or, more rarely, she prefers nonheterosexual men (Bozett, 1982). Homosexual experiences during marriage may be hidden, or again may be tolerated by the spouse for reasons of her own (the couple has grown apart; she does not enjoy sex with him; she likes the social respectability of being married and wants to keep the marriage intact; she wants to protect the children from knowing; she too is having an affair; and so on).

Most marriages in which the husband is actively and openly gay will likely end in divorce, since the man will not be able to continue finding satisfaction in a heterosexual marriage and/or his wife will not be able to live with his homosexual patterns, according to Bozett (1982).

Premarital counseling with couples where past homosexual liaisons have been admitted needs to explore both the immediate and long-range effect this behavior is likely to have on the integrity of the future marriage. The counselor needs to help both persons honestly explore their abilities to sustain an intimate heterosexual relationship once united. If married, the couple needs help in exploring their options if they wish to continue together (for example, permitting the husband to continue periodic sexual liaisons with men). If children are involved, issues over informing them or issues of custody require exploration.

Being a gay man does not preclude being a good husband and father. In the following case, a conventional middle-class professional man, married for twenty years and the father of three children, finally confronts his desire for a gay lifestyle:

❊   ❊   ❊   ❊   ❊

Andrew S., M.D., was a practicing physician with an excellent reputation in the professional community. At 44, he was financially successful, had a happy marriage, and was the proud father of three children—all girls—whom he adored. But Andrew also harbored a secret: since high school he had engaged in a number of casual homosexual encounters in school restrooms and at public parks.

When he met Allison at college, Andrew found her very attractive and dated her off and on for two years. After he graduated and before going on to medical school, they married. He never told her of his gay past, nor did he ever mention it to anyone else, including some gay friends he had known all his life. After twenty years of marriage, Andrew and Allison appeared to be the ideal couple: they were outgoing, intelligent, sophisticated, well traveled, excellent hosts, and they had three loving children to whom they appeared to be devoted. If Allison felt neglected at times and thought Andrew seemed less interested in sex than she thought he should be, she concluded that he was busy with his career as a doctor and a member of the university hospital attending staff, rather than that anything was wrong between them.

Nevertheless, when Allison decided to return to graduate school after her children did not seem to need her as much as they had earlier, she met a young man 15 years her junior whose company she thoroughly enjoyed. Since her husband was away from home for long periods, she became more and more attached to her new friend, and soon they became sexually intimate. However, she soon felt guilty, knowing Andrew would not do such a thing to her, and she told her husband. At her insistence they decided to see a family counselor.

Andrew was surprisingly nonchalant about the affair. Although he stated that he himself would not do such a thing, he understood that perhaps he had neglected Allison too much recently. Between his practice, his hospital work, and his workouts at the men's gym at the university four nights a week, he recognized that he had not been available for her. They seemed to deal with what had happened in a way that appeared to be acceptable to both of them, and after three sessions they terminated counseling.

The male counselor did not hear from them for six months, at which time Andrew called for an individual appointment. He said Allison knew about the call, and accepted that there were some personal matters he wanted to explore with the counselor. Andrew began by saying that he had not been exactly honest in the joint sessions when he said he had been completely faithful. Actually, he now admitted, he had been sexually intimate with some female patients over the years. He seemed to gain some relief from this disclosure, especially from the counselor's apparent acceptance of his secret behavior. He did not make another appointment at the end of the session, but two weeks later he returned. This time, he appeared agitated, finally disclosing that he had lied during the previous meeting to test whether the counselor would be nonjudgmental. Now satisfied, he was prepared to tell the truth: he had been having impersonal homosexual experiences since early in their marriage. His workouts at the gym were really excuses to be with men and to have homosexual contacts in the gym's shower room.

Andrew was now torn by his desire for a more open gay life and his responsibilities to his wife and children. He was certain that he was some kind of "freak" because married men should not feel or behave as he had. By coincidence, he spotted an ad in the college newspaper inviting married men who experienced homoerotic feelings to join a weekly discussion group off campus. Thus reassured, and with the counselor's encouragement, he met with the group, feeling much relieved to find others in similar circumstances. With their support and the support of the counselor, he finally told his wife, who seemed to receive the news with some understanding and acceptance. Next, he made plans to move into an apartment and begin to associate with openly gay men to see if indeed he preferred a gay lifestyle. To help him with his children, he sought out the local gay fathers' support group.[5]

Soon Andrew began to integrate a gay identity, feeling more whole and less fragmented than he had in 20 years. As he no longer felt torn by leading a double life, he now appeared more tranquil, and as a result more available to his children. Although they were rejecting at first, refusing to have anything to do with a gay father, they gradually learned to accept the truth of their father's sexual orientation. With the counselor's help, Andrew became more disclosing about his homosexuality to them, despite his fears of losing their love and respect. When he moved into a long-term relationship with Harold several months later, he did not introduce him to his daughters for a brief period of time. With support from his gay parents' support group, however, Andrew encouraged regular visits by his children, who now seem to appreciate their father's happy relationship.

❊　❊　❊　❊　❊

Counselors assessing lesbian couples typically confront a different set of parenting problems, since such households are far more likely than those of gay men to contain children. Several factors probably are operating here: lesbians far more frequently have been married before turning to same-sex relationships; and they tend to come out later, increasing the likelihood of having borne children while married. Moreover, despite the hesitations by some judges noted above, courts in general tend to award custody to a mother, particularly if her homosexuality has not been a contested issue in the divorce proceedings (Maddox, 1982).

It is not at all uncommon for one or both lesbian partners to have their children residing with them. Thus, they face many of the same problems as any blended family (see Chapter Five) where children from different households must reorganize their lives into a coherent new family unit. Here that reorganization is complicated by the fact that the union between parents may be temporary or short-lived, and may involve more than one such alliance during the children's growing-up years. Coparenting by two lesbians also must proceed without any legal safeguards—regarding custody should the natural mother die, for example—a further roadblock to involvement by the nonparent. Family counselors may anticipate working with the children along with their parents, since living with openly gay parents is more likely than not to expose children to barbs and harassment from their peers (Moses & Hawkins, 1982).

One final scenario regarding gay and lesbian parenting deserves attention: two men or, more commonly, two women who choose to coparent and thus form families within the context of their established relationship rather than bringing children from a previous marriage (Pies, 1985; Pollack & Vaughn, 1987). Many

[5]The International Gay Fathers Coalition in Washington, D.C., maintains a list of support groups in various cities, along with the names of gay fathers in each area willing to offer assistance and guidance in dealing with children.

lesbians reject the notion that they must engage in sexual intercourse with a man in order to bear a child, preferring adoption or donor insemination as more acceptable choices. Since lesbians cannot adopt as a couple, the nonadoptive partner often remains invisible as her mate goes through a lengthy adoptive process (in which the person seeking to adopt as a single parent may or may not reveal her lesbianism). Such going back "in" after coming out is frequently a painful process for both partners, who in addition are denied the support customarily offered heterosexual couples during adoption agency home visits (Shuster, 1987). Nevertheless, gays and lesbians are adopting with increasing frequency, particularly in large cities and with hard-to-place youngsters. Only two states, Florida and New Hampshire, explicitly prohibit homosexuals from adopting.

If donor insemination is chosen, the counselor may need to help the woman decide in advance whether she wants to be impregnated by the sperm of a donor known to her and, if so, whether or not to have him as an involved father who is not a member of the lesbian family. If she opts for an unknown donor, the woman may need counselor help to explain to the child in later years the reasons for her choice of an absent father and to deal with the child's possible upset about his or her origins in early adolescence and later.

Whatever the choices—adoption or donor insemination—the lesbian mother or gay father must help the child, especially as adolescence approaches, to deal with the likely stigma and homophobic slurs from peers and to develop coping strategies for survival in a society that remains unaccepting. Sometimes conflict develops between a teenager's self-conscious need for secrecy (about not being like everybody else) and a gay parent's insistent openness about homosexuality as a political statement. Whatever the particular set of pressures, the counselor, in dealing with gay parenting, must be prepared to examine his or her basic notions regarding what constitutes a real family.

## SOME COUNSELING GUIDELINES

Most authorities (Harrison, 1987; Krajeski, 1986; Malyon, 1982; Woodman & Lenna, 1980) agree on the absolute necessity, as a minimum, of helping gay clients to accept and value their sexual orientation and to achieve, embrace, and integrate a gay identity. Counselors who feel uncomfortable doing so, despite paying lip service to this goal, would do well to work through any interfering internalized homophobic feelings. Common manifestations of such counselor-internalized homophobia range from a failure to value the couple's commitment ("Gay/lesbian relations never last"), on the assumption that their problems are insurmountable compared to those presented by heterosexual couples, to overglamorizing the same-sex relationship as inherently romantic (the myth of automatic intragender empathy) and courageous in the face of rejection by the heterosexual world. As Brown and Zimmer (1986) observe, denigrating homosexual relationships and placing them on a pedestal have equal potential for harm.

In the event that the counselor, having carefully examined his or her internalized homophobia, cannot overcome prejudicial values regarding same-sex intimate relationships, clients should be referred to some other counselor or community group (for example, a gay counseling center) whose attitudes and outlooks are more consistent with facilitating a positive self-identity. Gay or straight, the counselor must continually appraise his or her own feelings toward the client(s) throughout the counseling, especially as certain erotic, prejudicial, or homophobic **counter-transference** feelings intrude on the counseling process and the personal world of both clients and counselors (Silverstein, 1991). To attempt to force gay clients to rid themselves of their homosexuality is a miscarriage of the counselor's mission.

In some cases, a gay person may insist on seeing a gay counselor, much as a woman client may feel more comfortable with, and better understood by, another woman; or an African American may prefer another African American; or a couple experiencing conflict with their children may only be willing to talk to a counselor who is also a parent. While such a request may simply mean that the client wishes to speak to someone who has had similar experiences, it may also mean a great deal more. In the case of gay clients, it more probably reflects a distrust of straight counselors as members of a rejecting, oppressing group, or perhaps indicates the clients' incompletely worked-through feelings of self-acceptance. Fear of exposure of their secret, loss of privacy, and concern that confidentiality might be broken also may play a part. In the situation where one member of a gay couple is far less open than the other about his or her sexual orientation, and restricts social contacts primarily or even exclusively to other gays, distrust and suspicion may be so great that working with a nongay counselor is ruled out.

Regardless of the particular set of circumstances, the first phase of counseling gay or lesbian couples is to grapple with issues concerning trust. As Malyon (1982) contends, the clients must come to regard the counselor as a person of special knowledge, competence, and good will who cares about them, if counseling is to proceed. Values must inevitably be addressed; the counselor's therapeutic bias with respect to homosexuality must be revealed along with the goals of the treatment. For effective counseling to occur, counselor disclosure of attitudes is every bit as important as that same declaration by clients.

As we have observed a number of times, most gay couples who come for professional help are not there to seek guidance in changing their sexual orientation. Rather, for the most part they come with problems quite analogous to those presented by nongay couples: sharing power, communication difficulties between partners, differences in commitment to the relationship, handling money, balancing work and home commitments, managing time together, dealing with children, coping with in-laws, infidelity, jealousy, sexual problems, intimacy concerns, breaking up, and so on.

However, beyond these issues common to all couples are those unique to the experiences of gay partners. These include dealing with: (1) their own overt or covert homophobic attitudes, leading to low self-esteem and lack of self-acceptance;

(2) the degree to which as individuals and as a couple they are out in the open with gay and nongay friends, family, employers, and colleagues; (3) the paucity of role models for their relationship, leading to uncertainty or to the adoption of inappropriate male-female patterns; and (4) communication difficulties, especially overzealous communication of feelings between partners, causing relationship fatigue and distress (McWhirter & Mattison, 1982).

Lesbian couples, in particular, often struggle over distance regulation and boundary maintenance (Roth, 1989). Achieving a range of behaviors that allows sufficient closeness but also enough distance to maintain a sense of individuality is difficult for many couples, gay or straight, but may become especially acute for a female pair in a society such as ours, in which women typically learn to define themselves in relation to others. Lesbian relationships are susceptible to what Krestan and Bepko (1980) describe as *fusion* feelings; they may vacillate between extraordinary closeness and unbreachable distance, as the exhilaration of intimacy gives way to fear of the loss of self.

Sometimes a gay male couple may also need help to negotiate separateness and closeness. In the following case, two men, both with previous gay experiences, turn a casual sexual encounter into a more extended relationship lasting five years. They contact a family counselor when that union develops signs of dysfunction.

❊　❊　❊　❊　❊

Simon and Alf would probably seem mismatched to most casual observers. Simon, at 45, had established himself as an executive in a large pharmaceutical company, where he was considered to be among the three or four men likely to become chief executive officer in the near future. Alf, ten years younger, worked as a salesman for a small printing company, barely earning enough to support himself. They had met at a gay bar, and after some brief embracing had gone to Simon's house for what they both assumed would be a one-night stand. However, they found themselves attracted to one another, and both wanted to continue the liaison. About three weeks into the relationship, Simon asked Alf to move in with him. Devoid of friends and looking for a safe place to live, Alf readily accepted.

Although living together appeared to work reasonably well from the start, both were aware of major differences in background, education, and financial stability. Their social experiences and degree of gay identity also differed. Simon had a large social circle of prominent gay and nongay men and women. His homosexual behavior was whispered about at work, but neither denied nor admitted by him. He had had two previous live-in arrangements with men prior to living with Alf.

Alf, on the other hand, had had numerous recent homosexual bath-house experiences, but had not been in any but casual relationships until he met Simon. He had not attended college, but instead had joined a cult right after high school, probably in an effort to avoid dealing with his sexual urgings, particularly his homosexual feelings. When Alf's parents had had him kidnapped from the cult and deprogrammed, he had protested at first, but soon had submitted to their wishes. His impersonal sexual experiences with men began soon after returning home, and became a regular part of his weekly routine after work. He never discussed his homosexuality with anyone at work, and most of his co-workers thought of him as interested in women. Alf was essentially a loner before joining with Simon.

Not surprisingly, Simon dominated Alf, who took on his familiar passive role. The older man supplied most of the money, the friends, the travel opportunities. Alf was expected to cook, work in the garden, and in general take care of Simon after his hard day at the office. Their butch/femme pattern thus resembled a traditional male/female one. Simon was always the sexual aggressor, a role he demanded. Alf enjoyed being desired and valued, and felt safe and secure in the relationship.

Before living together, Simon had had extensive individual psychotherapy, and as a result felt secure about his gay identity. Alf continued to struggle with his, and after they had been together for several years he too decided to seek individual therapeutic help. His straight counselor encouraged Alf to find new friends on his own, and to develop a stronger sense of self independent of Simon. In addition, Alf was urged to go through a normal adolescence, which he seemed to have skipped, including exploring other relationships in the gay community.

As a result of counseling, Alf got in touch with previously suppressed feelings of resentment over his subservient position with Simon. He recognized and became bitter over both his emotional and financial dependence on his lover. Alf did not own anything himself, he realized, and now he wanted something in his name from Simon. Also, he felt he had been taken advantage of long enough, having to go to bed when Simon decided, having to socialize when and with whom Simon decided, and so on. He now wanted to meet new men, something Simon opposed, ostensibly because of the danger of AIDS, but more personally because Simon feared Alf would leave him for a younger, more attractive partner.

The couple now was fighting more than ever before. Simon contended that Alf should either contribute more money or, if not, be more willing to contribute more toward housekeeping responsibilities. With increased struggles over sex outside their relationship, in addition to the conflicts over money, the two decided to seek counseling from a family counselor. Both preferred a woman counselor, because they felt there would likely be less prejudice against gay men. When Simon called her for an appointment, he said, "My friend and I are seeking couples therapy. He's free after 5 P.M. Are you interested?" Thus providing a clue that the counselor would be working with gays, Simon seemed to be asking whether, as a nongay, she was comfortable enough to work with them. Assured that she passed the initial test, they set up an appointment for the next day.

At the first session, both men presented, in graphic detail, a description of their favorite sex positions. Once again reassured that the female counselor did not appear startled or repelled, they went on in subsequent sessions to discuss relationship issues. For several weeks they discussed issues of power and control, in addition to their differing views of money. After this first phase of counseling,

Simon put one-half ownership of their summer home in Alf's name, and agreed to a more equitable distribution of responsibilities at home. During this phase, the counselor helped Alf, in particular, work on his homophobic feelings, especially his concern that nobody in the nongay world could accept him.

As Alf developed a stronger sense of his gay identity, he was more willing to come out with his family, as well as friends at work. In particular, the counselor helped both men assert their rights as a couple. Visiting Alf's parents, who knew they were both gay, they no longer pretended merely to be close acquaintances. When Alf's Aunt Georgia came to town, Simon was no longer identified as Alf's landlord, but rather as his gay partner.

The sexual issues were more difficult to resolve, and they took up most of the next phase of counseling, lasting two months. Despite Simon's expressed fear of AIDS, Alf continued his casual homosexual contacts. He did agree, however, to join a small discussion group, called Safe Sex, where gay men frankly talked over their sex habits. While there was no sex per se in the group, Simon was alarmed, especially when he discovered that some group participants had tested HIV positive.

As Alf turned more and more to the group for role models, he began to question whether a woman counselor could really understand him or help him with his conflicts with Simon. Although Simon protested that they still needed to work on the issue of sexual exclusiveness, Alf insisted that he would no longer attend the sessions, and they terminated counseling.

Two years later, still fighting but still together, they once again briefly contacted their former counselor. They were at the point of separating, and asked for some guidance to make the final split-up as painless as possible. Alf now wanted to try living by himself, something he had never done before. Simon opposed the idea, but reconciled himself to remaining friends, to which Alf agreed. After five years as a couple, they let go of one another and went their separate ways.

❀   ❀   ❀   ❀   ❀

As this case illustrates, working with gay couples does not call for any specific counseling techniques per se, but rather a set of attitudes toward homosexuality and a level of knowledge that help gay clients accept themselves and their life choices. Because internalized homophobic feelings are present in everyone, gays need help in uncovering and working through their own antihomosexual biases as a first step toward achieving a sense of self-worth and acceptance of a gay partner. Each partner may be at a different stage of self-acceptance as a gay person, and here the counselor can help bring previously hidden differences to the surface for clarification, reducing dissimilarity and conflict between the pair. As they achieve a better balance between their attitudes, the underlying rejection of self and partner is minimized and resistance to coming out as a gay couple reduced.

Understanding how the couple define themselves and where they are in the coming-out process is one of the counselor's first tasks. Their self-definition always requires counselor exploration, not merely counselor acceptance. The issue of whether to make their gayness as a couple public may or may not be as important. As in most couple relationships, heterosexual or homosexual, the members' feelings regarding public exposure may differ, and these differences need examination and resolution.

The counselor needs to act as a facilitator, offering support and encouragement as gay clients affirm their gay identity. To be of maximum help, the counselor should be acquainted with community support systems and local resource services (mental health programs, health clinics, gay parents' groups, church programs, AIDS projects, gay newspapers, gay political organizations) available to gay clients.

In assisting gays to affirm their sexuality, counselors may need to help them find ways to do so responsibly and safely. The emergence of the AIDS health crisis[6] demands the learning and practice of safe sex. In most gay communities, casual encounters and oral sex have been discouraged, and the use of condoms, spermicidal jellies, and other safety measures has been undertaken, as awareness of the risk of AIDS has become more widespread. Most gays know all too well, by experiencing the death of many of their gay friends, the dangers to themselves and others involved in unsafe sexual practices. Some, however, may need help from the counselor in facing the risks, so that they do not simply deny or avoid possible consequences. It is vital here to ensure that the counselor's own anxiety does not prevent any discussion or acknowledgment of the risk to one or both partners.

## AIDS COUNSELING

Considering the impact of the AIDS epidemic on the functioning of gay couples, it would be safe to say that no counseling with gay men would be complete without a full examination of their attitudes and behavior regarding this issue. AIDS testing is simply a fact of life in the gay community, although some may choose to deny it and believe they are invulnerable or else fear the implications of a positive test result.

In most countries of the world, the incidence of HIV in the population has steadily risen over the last decade. Theoretically speaking, to ensure accurate diagnosis and prompt medical treatment, each gay man who is at risk should avail himself of HIV antibody testing. Practically speaking, however, the decision to be tested is a personal choice in which factors regarding medical treatment and legal protection must be considered (Marks & Goldblum, 1989). That is, while acknowledging that medical intervention is facilitated when the physician knows as much as possible about the patient's health, many gays worry that antibody

---

[6]The crisis, of course, affects not only gays but also heterosexuals, and therefore in no way should AIDS be considered an exclusively gay disease. However, sexually active gay males do make up the largest AIDS risk group in the United States. Others at risk, in decreasing order, include intravenous drug abusers, homosexual males who are also intravenous drug abusers, persons with hemophilia or other coagulation disorders, heterosexuals, and recipients of blood transfusions.

testing may reveal an HIV infection that will stigmatize them and expose them to discrimination in employment, housing, insurance coverage, and even medical care by health workers who seek to avoid contact with such patients. Each individual thus must evaluate the cost to himself of the disclosure, and weigh that cost against the potential benefits of longer survival as a result of early treatment.

Counselor intervention typically takes one of two forms: pre–AIDS-test counseling and posttest counseling. In pretest counseling, the counselor needs to help gay clients explore the degree of risk in their sexual behavior patterns and to define for themselves their areas of concern. Since testing is a crucial decision, often accompanied by depression, sleep disturbance, and even suicidal thoughts, the counselor must limit his or her input regarding the wisdom of proceeding with testing, although providing accurate and up-to-date information about the tests is in order. Whether the client elects to be tested or not, the counselor needs to provide him with necessary risk-reduction information so that he may lower the chances of either acquiring the HIV infection or passing it on to others (McCreaner, 1989).

In the following case, a 47-year-old psychologist, previously unknown to the counselor, asks for help with certain family issues:

❉    ❉    ❉    ❉    ❉

Jay, a successful behavioral psychologist, had had extensive individual psychotherapy over much of his lifetime, starting when he was an adolescent. Although he later recalled that the issue of homosexual feelings did come up in some sessions, he had refused to deal with such impulses, preferring to deny and repress them. Married at 24, he was the father of two daughters within three years. Receiving his doctorate around the time of the birth of his second child, he immediately began a series of part-time jobs in several mental health clinics and eventually opened his own practice, dealing primarily with behavioral problems. The marriage developed a number of seemingly insurmountable problems for Jay and his wife, he told the counselor, and after ten years of marriage they divorced. What he was seeking now, he confided, were suggestions from a family counselor about how best to deal with his children, now grown into young adulthood, with whom he was having problems.

Although he described his marriage as "reasonably happy for the first five years" to the counselor during the second visit, he did report occasional affairs with men during out-of-town trips during that period. As he slowly recognized his sexual preference for men, his marriage deteriorated, he reported, and soon he moved out and found a male lover with whom he shared an apartment. Over the years, he had lived with a number of men, usually for months or even a year or two at a time. He expressed satisfaction that he had come out when he did, and that overall his life as a gay person had been gratifying.

The counselor found Jay intelligent, witty, and sophisticated, but she was unclear as to the exact reason he had sought her services. He did bring up a number of topics over a month of counseling—interpersonal problems with another psychologist with whom he shared an office, conflicts with his children, a decreased sex drive with the younger partner with whom he had shared his home for the last two years. However, if his life seemed to be what he said he wanted it to be, why was he really here?

After six weekly sessions, Jay tangentially mentioned that he was afraid of AIDS and sensed he might be HIV positive. Although he had no obvious symptoms, and had begun to practice safe sex, he was worried about occasional cold sores around his mouth that were slow to heal, and persistent stomach upset. The worry was ever present, he confessed, and he was frightened he might die. When the counselor casually brought up the issue of AIDS testing, wondering if that would reduce his uncertainty and also reduce his distress, he became agitated. There was no cure, he insisted, nor was one on the way, and medication such as AZT would only prolong his life but reduce the quality of that life significantly. If the results were negative, he continued, he would only feel guilty as a survivor, after so many others had died. No, he would have no part of AIDS testing. He had worked so hard to put his life together and deal with his gayness, and now this had happened. As he continued discussing testing during several sessions, he cursed at the unfairness of it all. He and the counselor were able to discuss reducing high-risk behavior with his partner. However, when she suggested he bring in his current lover, so that all three could discuss the issues together, he said he was not ready to do that. After several more sessions, Jay terminated counseling and never contacted the counselor again.

About a year later, still bothered that their sessions together lacked closure, the counselor wrote Jay a follow-up note inquiring about how he was doing. He replied in a long, newsy letter, covering the areas discussed in counseling. Relations with his ex-wife, daughters, and lover were all going well. The one area he avoided was AIDS testing.

Approximately three years later, the counselor came across an obituary item in the newspaper announcing that Jay had died of AIDS.

❈    ❈    ❈    ❈    ❈

Posttest counseling in general concerns itself with helping those found to be infected with the HIV virus (Green, 1989). AIDS is not the same as an HIV infection, and many people with an HIV infection may feel fine, although they are at risk for developing AIDS. Counseling gays who test positive for the HIV virus or with full-blown cases of AIDS involves helping them deal with fears of all of the following: loss of independence, becoming helpless, rejection by a lover, financial problems, disclosure to family or others of being homosexual, punishment by society for being gay, contaminating partners, and their own ultimate death. Harrison (1987) urges counselors to empower gay clients in every possible way: to confront people who withdraw from them, to affirm their right to receive support, to assert themselves in hospital settings, to demand being treated with respect and not as freaks or lepers, to express their anger and frustration, and so on. Even those persons who seem to have fully accepted their gay identity may regress, feel contaminated, become seriously depressed, or fear negative judgment from others. They may blame their illness on their sexual orientation, and thus feel deserving of the disease. The counselor may need to coordinate efforts with other health workers in monitoring the client's condition and in supporting increasingly direct discussions of death.

Counselors should understand that the diagnosis of AIDS is typically catastrophic, the nature of the illness is turbulent, and patients can look forward to repeated hospitalizations and recurrent bouts of illness. Nichols (1986) describes the usual reactions of shock, denial, bargaining, fear, guilt, anger, sadness, and ultimately acceptance—all stages of a grief process similar to those used by people with cancer or other life-threatening illnesses. In addition, AIDS evokes cultural taboos regarding homosexual behavior and thus attaches an additional stigma of an immoral person, a pariah, contagious, dangerous, threatening to one's own existence.

The family counselor needs to remain flexible, perhaps seeing the person with AIDS alone to explore feelings he is not yet ready to share, before bringing in the partner. Similarly, members of the family of origin may require separate sessions as preparation for a conjoint session with the AIDS patient alone or with his partner.

AIDS counseling also involves caring for survivors of the dying person, helping them grieve the loss. Not just gay partners but also families of origin who have lost someone to AIDS may need help with bereavement. The social stigma attached to the disease may deprive them of the social support they would normally expect to receive when a family member dies. As Walker (1987) notes, what individuals, couples, and families with AIDS problems have in common

> is that they all have a member who suffers a uniquely stigmatized fatal illness, one where issues of contagion reverberate through the family and into the larger culture. Most families and individuals are wrestling with issues of guilt and shame, blame and anger, betrayal and fear, helplessness and impotence. They are afraid of contagion, of social ostracism, of pain and death. They must care or be cared for in situations where they meet hostility, contempt, fear and inadequate care. They must fight endless red tape for potentially life saving medicine and perhaps be denied it. (p. 2)

Finally, the counselor must sort out and deal with his or her own feelings regarding death and dying. Attitudes toward sexuality in general and sexually transmitted diseases in particular require self-examination. Working with dying AIDS patients can be a devastating experience in itself, and it may be desirable to arrange for some supportive counseling or networking with other AIDS workers for assistance in mourning and to avoid counselor burnout. The counselor must guard against overidentifying with clients (particularly if the counselor himself is gay), judging them, or becoming demoralized by their demise. The experience may also be humbling and richly rewarding, as the counselor explores his or her own feelings regarding illness, loss, death, and dying, his or her own lack of omnipotence, and at the same time makes someone's last days more bearable.

# SUMMARY

Gay couples have much in common with cohabiting heterosexual couples, but also some major differences: greater rejection by society, self-condemnation, more determined efforts at concealment, internalized homophobic feelings, and fear of disenfranchisement as a result of the AIDS health crisis.

Homosexuality is present in all societies, at all socioeconomic levels, and among all racial and ethnic groups. Gays typically gravitate toward larger communities, from whatever place of origin, since meeting other gays is easier there and disclosure is less likely to lead to social ostracism. Gay subcultures exist in most large communities, easing entry into the gay lifestyle.

The majority of gay men seek extended relationships, but casual sexual encounters, particularly among younger gay men, are common. Coming out as a gay person can cause considerable apprehension and typically is a process that extends over time and in front of different audiences. Lesbians are more likely than gay men to strive for stable, extended relationships.

All gays and lesbians must struggle with achieving self-acceptance in a society in which homosexuality conjures up negative stereotypes and rejection from family, church, and nongay friends. Couples must reach an agreement on sexual exclusiveness, especially in light of the AIDS crisis. Gay fathers and lesbian mothers, who care for approximately 12 to 15 million children in the United States, must deal with integrating children into their gay lives; lesbians in particular often have their children residing with them. Increasingly, gay and, especially, lesbian couples may form families within the context of their relationship, either by adoption or, in the case of women, through donor insemination.

Counseling gays requires providing them with help in achieving a gay identity. In some cases, gays may insist on seeing a gay counselor, especially if they distrust a straight one or if they have not sufficiently accepted their own sexual orientation. Gay couples rarely come for counseling to change that orientation, but rather to deal with relationship issues much like their nongay counterparts. In addition, they typically attempt to grapple with such issues as their own homophobic feelings, problems with coming out, and the paucity of adequate role models.

AIDS counseling may take one of two forms: counseling gays before AIDS testing or after testing has found them to be HIV positive. The former involves helping them assess the risk in their sexual behavior patterns and examining the benefits of AIDS testing versus the cost in possible future discrimination. Posttest counseling requires teaching safe sex practices, and helping HIV-positive gay men, their partners, and their families of origin deal with the ultimate loss through death.

# Counseling Families with Special Characteristics

C H A P T E R

E I G H T

# Counseling Ethnically Diverse Minority Families

American society is in a state of flux, as rapid social changes add complexities and often turbulence and uncertainty to our lifestyles and value systems. We are, increasingly, a diverse society, a pluralistic one made up of varying races and multiple ethnic groups, as millions of people migrate here seeking a better life. One in every four Americans today is a person of color (Homma-True, Greene, Lopez, & Trimble, 1993).

The notion made popular around the turn of the current century, when many European groups flocked to the United States, was that America is a "melting pot," in which immigrants from different places of origin mingle and blend into one. In this view, a new and unique American culture continually emerges as each new immigrant group impacts on the existing culture. However, growing awareness in the 1960s and 1970s of the lack of civil rights for some minorities led to the recognition that the melting-pot principle had bypassed certain groups, such as African Americans, who only had minimal impact on a changing America. Furthermore, new immigrant groups, expected to culturally assimilate, were under pressure to relinquish their traditional ethnic values in order to adopt those of the dominant culture, which many found unacceptable.

Together, these realizations led to the view of cultural pluralism: that individual ethnic groups retain their cultural uniqueness while sharing common elements with the dominant American culture. Rather than a melting pot, Atkinson, Morten, and Sue (1989) liken the cultural-pluralism viewpoint to a cultural stew, in which "various ingredients are mixed together, but rather than melting into a single mass, the components remain intact and distinguishable while contributing to a whole that is richer than its parts alone" (p. 7).

Cultural pluralism and diversity add vitality and need not lead to irreconcilable divisions between various segments of our society, although differences between groups may lead to misunderstanding and conflict. The rapid assimilation of immigrant groups into the majority culture, accompanied by the elimination of differences among such groups and between them and the majority culture, poses the risk of the breakdown of subculture identities and the abandonment of ethnic heritages, which, in turn, results in severe strain to family structures and increased vulnerability to future family dysfunction. Retaining aspects of their separate cultural identities, subgroups can adapt to (and, in the process, help change) American society without various subcultural norms being lost or destroyed. The degree and quality of that adaptation or acculturation is likely to be a function of how long ago newcomers arrived, the circumstances of their arrival, the support system they found upon arrival, and the degree of acceptance or prejudice and discrimination they found here.

The relevance of this for family counselors is that they must be culturally sensitive to the values and traditions of their clients, develop a respectful attitude toward the family's ethnic identity, and take great care before using norms that stem from the majority cultural matrix in assessing the attitudes, beliefs, and behavior patterns of those whose cultural backgrounds differ from theirs (Sue, 1988). Lau (1986) presents a fascinating example of the relevance of cultural values to family relationships by describing a stone tableau in a public park in Singapore:

> Haw Par Villa was built by a rich Chinese philanthropist who felt that the people needed a public park in which moral parables could be portrayed in stone. One such stone tableau illustrated the cardinal virtue of filial piety. At a time of famine in China, a young woman is confronted with a moral dilemma: does she offer her breast milk to her old mother, who is starving, or does she save her remaining child, given her other child is already dead on the ground? Despite her maternal instincts, she turns away from her crying baby and offers her breast to her mother. Thus, for traditional Chinese, the prescriptive rule is one of unquestionable filial piety, where responsibility to one's parent is paramount and transcends responsibilities to spouse and children. (pp. 234–235)

Most Western readers are likely to be uncomfortable with the young mother's choice, thus reinforcing the point that we are all bound by the cultural patternings of our reference group; we are not free agents but rather, no less than the young woman in the parable, we are ourselves culturally constrained persons.

Lau (1986) reminds us that a counselor may not possess the same world view as his or her clients, and thus may be unaware of the cultural norms for those persons: what belief systems are sanctioned by the group of which the client is a part, what is idiosyncratic, and what is indicative of individual or family dysfunction. Adding to the dilemma of working with families of unfamiliar background, the counselor may not understand what norms govern appropriate sex-role or family-role behavior, what interactive communication styles are appropriate for the culture, or in general how that culture organizes the family's experience of itself, which may differ from the counselor's cultural perspective or life experiences.

In order to provide the counselor with some guidelines regarding the cultural relativity of family life, we have attempted in this chapter to outline the lifestyles and common family patterns of three sets of minority families: African Americans, Hispanic Americans, and Asian/Pacific Americans. Our descriptions are hardly exhaustive, but rather are intended to alert the family counselor to be attentive to cultural differences, and to seek consultation or do further research when cultural issues become paramount. At the same time, we wish to note that many significant ethnic groups are not included here, but need to be approached by the counselor with the same diligence and open-mindedness regarding cultural patterns.

Beyond that, we wish to help the counselor expand from an exclusive focus on the transactions within the family to a broader approach that also pays attention to the larger sociocultural contexts that influence family behavior (Falicov, 1988). Counselors make more global interventions when they see families as embedded within the context of larger human-service systems (welfare, educational, legal, health, probation) in which many poor, minority "multiproblem" families often are caught up. Imber-Black (1990) urges the counselor planning to work with such families to adopt a macrosystemic perspective, attending not just to who are the key actors in the family, but also to what larger systems interact with the family and what labels, stigmas, and ethnic myths such systems may adopt or impose when working with these families.

All families are the same and all families are different. To make effective interventions with families, counselors must try to distinguish between universal, transcultural, culture-specific, and idiosyncratic family behaviors. That is, they need to discriminate between those family situations where cultural issues are clinically relevant and those where cultural issues are tangential (Falicov, 1988). To be effective, as Ramirez (1991) contends, counselors need to remain especially sensitive to cultural as well as individual diversity when working with ethnic-minority clients, encouraging the development of diverse coping skills as needed. Moreover, as McGoldrick, Garcia Preto, Hines, and Lee (1991) point out, family counselors who appreciate the cultural relativity of family life (including how families identify, define, and attempt to solve problems, as well as seek help) are likely to adopt a broader perspective, and thus improve their chances to intervene successfully with families. At the same time, counselors must never lose sight of how their own ethnicity and subsequent cultural values and assumptions influence the helping process.

According to best estimates, by the year 2000 ethnic minorities will comprise 30% of the total U.S. population (Serafina, Schwebel, Russell, Isaac, & Myers, 1990). Migration, especially from Central and South America and from the Asian/Pacific area, accounts in large part for the rapid population changes we are experiencing. Sluzki (1979) points out that migration may involve many families together from a particular country, region, or culture, or perhaps be an isolated experience for a single family. Some families may choose to migrate by their own decision or be forced by the decisions of others or by natural cataclysms; they may leave with truckloads of household items, or in many cases no more than a bundle of essentials. They range from those families who arrive by jet airplane to those who sneak under barbed-wire borders at night. Some look forward with hope; others look backwards in fear. Some are thoroughly familiar with, and others completely ignorant of, the situation on arrival in the new land: its language and customs, where they will live, or what work will be available. Migration may represent the last hope of asylum for a religious or political refugee, or the doomed move from poverty in the home country to poverty in the new land. Whatever the reasons for migration, the process inevitably is disruptive for the family; before adaptation is complete, the family must go through several stages that are bound to influence its outlook and test its coping skills. In some cases, that adaptation may take several generations.

**Ethnicity**, comprising the unique characteristics of an ethnic group, is a fundamental determinant of how families establish and reinforce acceptable values, attitudes, behavior patterns, and modes of emotional expression. Beyond race, religion, and national or geographic origins, important as these are, ethnicity refers to a group's "peoplehood" and provides a sense of commonality transmitted by the family over generations and reinforced by the surrounding community. Ethnicity affords an historical continuity, and as such plays a decisive role in shaping our individual and family identities. A powerful force, retained and conveyed over generations, our ethnic background influences how we think, how we feel, how we work, how we relax, how we celebrate holidays and rituals, how we express our anxieties, and how we feel about illness or life and death. The sense of ethnicity unites those who think of themselves as alike by virtue of common ancestry, real or fictitious, and who are so regarded by others in the society in which they live (McGoldrick, Garcia Preto, Hines, & Lee, 1991).

Ethnic origins, whether acknowledged or not, typically play a significant role in family life throughout the life cycle, although their impact may vary greatly between groups, as well as within a group itself. In some families who hold onto traditional ways, clinging to cohorts from their religious or cultural background, ethnic values and identifications may be particularly strong and are likely retained for generations. In such cases, as McGoldrick (1982) suggests, second-, third-, and even fourth-generation Americans often differ from the dominant culture in values, lifestyle patterns, identifications, and behavior. In the case of groups who have experienced serious prejudice and discrimination, insularity may be especially pronounced: remaining in ethnic neighborhoods, working and socially mingling almost entirely with others of similar background, fearful and often suspicious of the dominant culture. (Many families remain in ethnic neighborhoods, of course, simply because economics and racial barriers thwart their efforts at upward mobility.) Other families may attempt to deny or reject ethnic values and past identifications, eager to become a part of the dominant American value system, particularly as they move up in social class and into heterogeneous neighborhoods.

Clearly, just as an individual cannot be fully understood when viewed in isolation from his or her family context, so a comprehensive picture of a family requires a consideration of the cultural system of which the family is a part, its shared history and traditions. Rather than reinforce racial or ethnic stereotypes, we hope to alert counselors to the effect of cultural patterns on family lifestyle that they might otherwise fail to recognize or, worse, label as deviant or dysfunctional. For example, in working with African-American clients, as Thomas and Sillen (1974) observe, for white clinicians to be insistently "color blind" to racial differences is no virtue if it means denial of differences in experiences, history, and social existence between themselves and African-American client families. This myth of sameness in effect denies the importance of color to the African-American clients, and closes off an opportunity for therapist and clients to deal with sensitive race-related issues.

For most counselors, working with ethnic minority families represents a cross-cultural experience. As Ho (1987) points out, such clients are more likely than not to be relatively powerless, politically and economically, to receive unequal treatment in society, and to regard themselves as objects of discrimination. He argues that to treat their family problems using generalized white middle-class American family standards is to be ethnically insensitive to their unique existence; that insensitivity may partially explain the frequent ineffectiveness of such services and their underutilization by ethnic minority families.[1]

Since most counselors come from, or achieve, middle- or upper-middle-class status, and are infrequently of African-, Hispanic-, or Asian/Pacific-American background, lack of knowledge or understanding of each other's culture and social status may lead to a counseling process that is fraught with strife and dissatisfaction for both the counselor and the client (Acosta, Yamamoto, & Evans, 1982).

## COUNSELING AFRICAN-AMERICAN FAMILIES

While African Americans comprise approximately 12% of the population in the United States, and together share a common heritage, they are by no means a homogeneous group and, as Hines and Boyd-Franklin (1982) contend, there is no such entity as the African-American family. African Americans not only arrived here by different routes (although most were brought directly from Africa as slaves, many came later from the Caribbean and elsewhere and thus represent different subcultural groups), but also are characterized by different religious backgrounds, socioeconomic status, educational level, and levels of acculturation, to say nothing

---

[1] All three groups considered in this chapter tend to underutilize mental health services (Cheung & Snowden, 1990). Poor African Americans have historically been wary of seeking out these services, frequently fearing that they will be stigmatized as crazy or perhaps that they will require hospitalization (Poussaint, 1990). Poor Hispanic and Asian/Pacific Americans often find that geographic isolation, language barriers, and perceived class differences between themselves and white counselors discourage access to mental health services (Homma-True, Greene, Lopez, & Trimble, 1993).

of diverse sets of values and lifestyles. Despite these differences, however, color remains the predominant and distinguishing fact of life for all members of the African-American community and, as Hines and Boyd-Franklin (1982) emphasize, it is impossible for counselors to work with African-American families without taking into account the social, economic, and political realities of living with racism in this society. Understanding the realities they face, and the culture developed in response to those conditions, is essential if the counselor hopes to help such families cope with these realities.

Billingsley (1968) maintains that the African-American family must be understood as a social system in ongoing interaction with other systems, and that its family structure represents an adaptation to a unique set of historical and social/political conditions that are an everyday part of African-American life. He emphasizes the duality of the African-American experience, depicting the African-American community as an ethnic subsociety in which there is considerable intragroup commonality but also variation. He identifies three social dimensions on which the members of this subsociety vary: social class, rural or urban residence, and region of the country where that residence occurs. African Americans are represented among upper-, middle-, and lower-class families (predominantly the last), with urban and rural backgrounds (overwhelmingly in metropolitan areas), in various parts of the United States (after a huge migration during the 1940s from the South to the North, the Midwest, and the West Coast).

## POWERLESSNESS AND THE AFRICAN-AMERICAN EXPERIENCE

Despite the hardships and discrimination they have been exposed to, and the condition of powerlessness that greeted their ancestors upon arrival in the United States as slaves, African-American families have developed an amazing ability to survive. However, a sense of economic, social, and political powerlessness still characterizes much of their existence (Billingsley, 1968). Pinderhughes (1990) notes that this sense of powerlessness is magnified by the vicious circle in which many African-American people find themselves: denial of access to resources reduces the opportunity to develop self-esteem and function adequately in the family role; the consequent poverty and strain on family role cause problems in individual growth and development; problems in individual functioning further stress the community system, which is the expected source of support for individuals and families. The community that is under stress already has fewer resources (jobs, schools, housing), leading to increased disorganization and creating the conditions for crime and other forms of social pathology. The ironic point here, as Pinderhughes (1990) emphasizes, is that the political, economic, and social forces to which the community might expect to look for help are the same forces that cause the powerlessness.

Part of the social reality confronted by African-American families is that there exists a wide discrepancy between African-American and white median family income, and a significantly larger percentage of African-American households are headed by women (Ho, 1987). However, while the popular stereotype is that all

African Americans are members of low-income families, the facts are otherwise: there is an upwardly mobile middle-class group, aided in part by greater opportunity through higher education and affirmative action programs in the last several decades. However, as McAdoo (1988) observes, African-American families have historically been more vulnerable to external economic conditions and have been affected by economic downturns earlier than other groups ("last hired, first fired"). She believes improved circumstances for African Americans peaked and then deteriorated during the 1980s, leading to a decline in their college enrollment, especially among males, and a steady erosion in the proportion of African Americans employed by the traditional professions. McAdoo (1988) suggests that the upwardly mobile patterns that have occurred in African-American families would have been impossible in many cases without the help provided by their extended families. (We'll return to the significant role of the extended family and kinship network in African-American family life later in this chapter.)

Overall, while there is great diversity in economic level—African-American families may range from the inner-city single mother on public assistance to the suburban dual-career professional couple—salaries typically lag behind whites', even for the same work; their unemployment rates are the highest of any American group, and the proportion of African Americans in poverty continues to increase. As Boyd-Franklin (1989) concludes, the reality of being African American and poor is to live an underclass life: doing without; coping with endless cycles of unemployment, with substandard housing and inadequate community services, and with underfinanced inner-city schools from which the dropout rate is high; and living in fear of street crime and young family members' exposure to neighborhood "crack houses." Often, domestic violence and child abuse erupt as despairing families struggle to survive.

## RACISM, DISCRIMINATION, AND THE VICTIM SYSTEM

No discussion of African-American culture can overlook the effect of racism and discrimination on overall functioning and identity formation. As Boyd-Franklin (1989) points out, racism can be insidious, pervasive, and constant, impacting the lives of all African-American persons regardless of social class or attained position, sometimes experienced externally as discrimination and sometimes internally as a sense of shame. Poor urban parents who attempt to motivate their children to achieve, when the evidence of discrimination and hopelessness are all around them, are engaging in a struggle that often ends in defeat, as the children lose hope and succumb to drugs, truancy, or other forms of destructive, antisocial behavior. The more affluent, living in predominantly white suburbs, may experience subtle (social isolation) or overt (front-lawn cross burning) forms of racism. Regardless of where or how the discrimination occurs, the blow to self-esteem is real and powerful, and the counselor's task in such cases is to help clients develop a positive racial and cultural identification ("black pride") and to gain a sense of empowerment in order to achieve some reasonable control over their own destinies.

Pinderhughes (1982) refers to the circular feedback process described earlier, which threatens self-esteem and reinforces problematic responses in communities, families, and individuals, as a **victim system**. She contends that victimization has exerted a pervasive effect on African-American families throughout history, preventing the establishment of a unified culture and its integration with that of the American mainstream. In effect, she maintains, African-American ethnic identity is likely to be influenced by three cultural sources: residuals from Africa; identification with mainstream America; and adaptation and responses to the victim system that results from poverty, racism, and oppression. African residual values stress collectivity, sharing, affiliation, belief in spirituality, and obedience to authority. Mainstream American values emphasize individualism, autonomy, planning, efficiency, and achievement. Victim-system values represent responses to oppression and characteristically stress cooperation to combat powerlessness, strict obedience to powerful authority, a toughness of character, the suppression of feelings, and a belief in luck, magic, and spirituality. Values and beliefs from all three systems are found in African-American families.

According to Pinderhughes (1982), the victim system of racism and oppression is akin to a societal projection process, in which victims are blamed and poor African-American families are viewed as lazy and thus having brought about their own poverty and other misfortunes. Similarly, many who are achieving are also made to feel inferior: it is suggested that their middle-class professional status was attained as a result of affirmative-action concessions rather than ability or hard work. Boyd-Franklin (1989) argues that, whereas most ethnic groups experience some form of discrimination, particularly among first-generation immigrants, African-Americans have had to endure this experience for 400 years.

To break out of the victim system, to gain a sense of self-determination, to overcome despair—these can all be viewed as efforts to gain a sense of power and status. The counselor must look for ways to help African-American individuals or families identify what they need in order to cope with their realities, and then to clarify the kind of functioning required to achieve those goals (Pinderhughes, 1990). The danger here is that the counselor may become overwhelmed by the magnitude of the task, begin to despair about reaching the goals, and finally succumb to his or her own sense of powerlessness. As a consequence, he or she may also give up hope and withdraw.

## FAMILY LIFE AND KINSHIP NETWORKS

The family has always held a central place in the African-American community, despite efforts to obliterate African family heritage during slavery; such efforts, nevertheless, probably did serve to loosen family boundaries, as family members were separated by slave sales and new slaves were thrust into existing family structures. Extended families and the role of "significant others" in African-American families (Manns, 1988) have always been important, as individuals look to one another for help and support; this pattern has no doubt been intensified by the difficulty that African Americans experience in receiving validation from the larger society (McGoldrick, Garcia Preto, Hines, & Lee, 1991).

Extended families commonly are composed of relatives who have a variety of blood ties but are nevertheless absorbed into a coherent network of mutual support, economically, emotionally, socially, and interpersonally. In such a loose arrangement, roles and boundaries between members of the kinship network are not rigidly defined, allowing for considerable role flexibility (and occasional boundary confusion). This fluid interchanging of roles within the African-American nuclear-family structure, arising initially from the economic imperatives of an underclass life (Ho, 1987), often means that older children care for younger siblings, and that fathers and mothers exchange roles, jobs, and family functions (caring for economic, expressive, emotional, or nurturant needs) depending on availability.

Beyond actual relatives (uncles, aunts, siblings, grandparents, cousins, even in-laws), other nonblood "relatives" (or fictive kin) also may be intimately involved in family matters. These are likely to include neighbors, godparents, preachers, teachers, work colleagues, baby sitters, family friends, boarders, and sweethearts. Because of economic necessity, extended families, especially in low-income areas, may spill over into neighboring apartments: different family members may reside in different households, or two or more families (or parts of families) may live in one household for periods of time. Whatever the arrangement, according to Boyd-Franklin (1989), extended families, regardless of social class, provide reciprocity—helping one another and sharing support along with goods and services. (This diffuse boundary arrangement may, of course, also lead to a lack of privacy, role confusion, jealousies, competitiveness, and perhaps a struggle for limited resources, thus leading to subsequent family conflict.) In the process, extended-family members may provide role models, offer nurturing and supplemental parenting, encourage achievement in the children, and together participate in the rearing of the African-American child. Counselors thus must be willing to expand their definition of what constitutes a family and be flexible about whom to include in family counseling sessions.

Since three-generational households are commonplace (Hines & Boyd-Franklin, 1982), the culturally sensitive counselor would be wise too to assume the client may have participated in this experience, perhaps having been reared by a grandmother while one or both parents were away at work or school. The counselor should refrain from necessarily assuming that such an arrangement indicates a rejection of a child by a parent, or that the child perceives it as such, since the practice represents a cultural norm. Furthermore, the counselor needs to explore some of the possible benefits of such practices. Similarly, a child may be cared for temporarily by a relative while a parent seeks employment, perhaps in another city. Again, the counselor should evaluate the circumstances and not automatically assume that rejection or neglect are involved.

Since living arrangements are flexible and changeable, depending on circumstances (loss of a job, temporary breakup of a relationship, a teenage pregnancy, someone down on his or her luck) it behooves the counselor to think of African-American family life as typically involving permeable boundaries that are responsive to troubling situations and emergency circumstances. Elderly family members such as grandparents may be taken in, partly in recognition of the role grandparents often play in parenting African-American children. Family elders may be supported by the collective efforts of members both within and outside the nuclear family (Hines & Boyd-Franklin, 1982).

Informal adoption (Hill, 1977), practiced since slavery days, involves adult relatives or family friends caring for children whose parents, for a variety of circumstances, cannot do so themselves. This may take the form of long-term foster care, day care for working parents, services for children born out of wedlock, or simply helping out a friend or family member during a transitional period such as a new marriage. Essentially, the informal adoption process functions as an unofficial social-service network for African-American families. For example, following divorce, children may be divided up among extended-family members for a brief period of time until the custodial parent, most likely the mother, gets back on her feet and is able to resume custody herself. A similar scenario may occur when a young parent is seriously ill or requires hospitalization. If a parent dies, a kinsman may be asked to keep and raise one or more of the children for an indefinite period of time.

For the most part, there are few problems over informal adoptions. Occasionally, disputes may arise over the duration of adoption, if the adoptive familiy believes the child will be theirs permanently but the biological parent chooses, after a lengthy period of time, to reclaim the child; serious allegiance problems may need to be resolved at this point. It is important to note that the length of an informal-adoption arrangement may not be predetermined, so that in many cases it may end up as permanent if long-term emotional ties are established.

In the following case, an unmarried African-American teenager becomes depressed and no longer can care for her children, provoking a family crisis and decisions about informal adoption.

❊   ❊   ❊   ❊   ❊

Wynona, 16, was the only child in an intact low-income family in which the father, Andre, worked at an automobile assembly line and the mother, Bernice, helped out in a local cafe as a part-time cashier. Doing reasonably well in her studies, Wynona was nevertheless socially shy and tended to be with girlfriends rather than go out with boys. Although many of her girlfriends talked about having had sexual experiences with boys, Wynona was hesitant and scared, until she met George, with whom she fell in love. When he pressed her for sexual intercourse, she acquiesced and, having little knowledge of birth control measures, soon found herself pregnant.

Although her parents were upset, Wynona's mother agreed to care for the child, Jamal, so that her daughter could finish high school. Unfortunately, Andre, Wynona's father, was laid off from work, finances became tight, Bernice took a full-time job, and Wynona was forced to drop out of school and care for Jamal on her own. Living with her parents, she did manage his care, but soon felt lonely and isolated from her high school friends. Money too was a problem; what money she did receive from public-assistance programs she paid to her parents, to help out during their hard times. When she met Ellis, a 23-year-old, at the supermarket one day, she was attracted to him, and soon they began what Wynona hoped would be a long relationship. Once again inattentive to contraception—she had dropped out of school before taking the class offered for unwed mothers regarding the use of various birth control devices—she became pregnant for the second time. Ellis, unemployed, decided to join the Army before Althea, their daughter, was born. He offered no financial support beyond the vague promise that he would send her money when he could—a promise, it turned out, that he never kept.

Now with the full responsibility of caring for two children by herself, Wynona became depressed. Her father, home without work and himself depressed and drinking, and her mother, tired and angry at all the responsibilities that awaited her at home after a hard day's work, added to the overall gloom in the house. Feeling isolated and seeing her young life slip by with nothing to look forward to, Wynona began neglecting her two children. Despite the scolding from her mother, Wynona found herself less and less able to function, some days forgetting to eat or comb her hair.

Uncertain about what to do to help, Wynona's parents took her to a local community mental health clinic, where she was seen for counseling by an African-American female social worker. After several sessions, the counselor decided on a three-prong set of interventions—getting her evaluated for antidepressant medication, helping her develop a stronger sense of herself as an individual, and enlisting her family to provide whatever support they could muster.

As the counselor explored the possibility of help from the grandparents, Wynona mentioned that she had remained friendly with Harriette, George's mother and Jamal's grandmother. Although 60 years of age, Harriette agreed to care for Jamal and Althea both, while Wynona returned to finish high school. Under the arrangement, the children stayed with Harriette during weekdays, but were taken home on weekends by Wynona.

Harriette's child-care role was not without its problems. She was not in good health, it had been a long time since she cared for young children, and her childrearing attitudes were stricter than Wynona thought desirable. Here the counselor was able to arrange for Harriette and her second husband to get some parent training, which they enjoyed and looked forward to each week. They especially needed help with Jamal, who was showing signs of hyperactivity and an attention-deficit disorder; the grandparents initially took this to mean he was a bad child, but became aware through the classes that it reflected his psychological problems.

A multiproblem family, they needed extensive, coordinated social services, including weekly family therapy sessions attended by Wynona, her parents, Harriette and her husband, William, and occasionally the children. During family sessions, the counselor attempted to help them construct the best family arrangement possible, offering them a great deal of support as they struggled to work together as a unit. George, Jamal's father, had become a heavy drug user and, although he saw his son from time to time and was not disruptive, Wynona believed she could not depend on him for help, which he did not offer. She lost contact with Ellis, who remained in the Army but did not ever contact Wynona or his daughter, Althea. On her own, Wynona, with the counselor's help, was encouraged to develop a social group of which she could feel a part, and to return to school for training that would help her develop a stronger sense of competence. When last seen by the counselor, she had started in an office computer-training class, was working part-time, had started dating again, and was preparing to get her children back home with her.

❊    ❊    ❊    ❊    ❊

## SOCIALIZATION EXPERIENCES AND MALE/FEMALE RELATIONSHIPS

The social rift between African-American males and females begins early, according to Chapman (1988), as females are encouraged to seek scholastic achievement while their male counterparts are often discouraged from attaining such a goal. Young males, for a variety of reasons, frequently drop out of school before developing competitive job skills; this furthers their distance from females in the economic strata. Frustrated by lack of opportunity and without the skills needed to transcend their circumstances, many young men during adolescence drift into drugs, homicide, and, ultimately, incarceration. Chapman estimates that 40% of the African-American male population is functionally illiterate. As a consequence, African-American females have had greater access to economic opportunities in our society, and in times of high unemployment have worked outside the home, often as the sole wage earner (Ho, 1987). The shift in recent years from an industrial to a high-tech economy has pushed ever larger numbers of unskilled African-American males into unemployment.

Male/female relationships are thus often shaped by economic factors and, because of limited job options and the dismal odds of fulfilling the functions our society expects of adult men, the roles of African-American males as husbands and fathers is further undermined (McGoldrick, Garcia Preto, Hines, & Lee, 1991). Since jobs have been more available to women, particularly during times of high employment, an African-American family's economic survival very often depends primarily (if not solely) on her, thus accounting in part for the large number of female-headed households, married or unmarried. Some men, unable to provide for their families, may leave their homes in order to ensure that their family members will receive government assistance. However, the counselor should not assume that all contact between father and children or between marital partners has ceased, despite appearances.

African-American men, particularly in urban, inner-city settings, are socialized to play a "macho" role; in Boyd-Franklin's (1989) words, to "act bad even if you're scared." That is, they learn to survive by never showing weakness, often using the sexual area to show their prowess and strength. Women, on the other hand, grow up observing and emulating the women in the family, who are often strong, competent, and self-reliant, and learning to further their own education, get a job, and prepare to provide for themselves. Growing up in female-led families, with fathers frequently absent, African-American females have likely seen their mothers rearing children, working outside the home, attending church, and engaging in transitory, if any, relationships with men—all of which reinforces the myth that "Black men are no good" or that "They won't be there for you when you need them" (Boyd-Franklin, 1989). It is hardly any wonder that many African-American men and women grow up perpetuating powerful and controlling myths—that African-American men are shiftless, lazy, can't be counted on for support; that African-American women are domineering, hostile, and controlling (Chapman, 1988). As a result, male/female struggles are common, divorce rates are high, and the chasm between men and women is often great.

Adding to the imbalance, African-American men are often viewed by African-American women as powerless, economically and politically; this may lead to estrangement or may be acted out angrily in their intimate relations. The high mortality rate among men—many are incarcerated, are substance abusers, delay seeking health care, are in the military, or die as a result of homicide—means that fewer are available for marriage or stable long-term relationships. Chapman (1988) describes a mate-sharing arrangement in which two or more women share a man, with or without knowledge of one another. According to Staples (1985), African-American women from both poor and middle-class backgrounds are opting for children without benefit of marriage, more because of the shortage of marriageable males than because of any devaluation of the institution of marriage.

Clients, whether African American or white, grow up in different households: some in traditional two-parent families and others in divorced or widowed or never married ones; some in poor working-class families and others in middle-class surroundings; some with strong fathers who are good providers and good role models and others with no fathers or a series of father substitutes; some in abusive homes and others in more loving and egalitarian surroundings. It is imperative that the counselor explore the family histories of both partners to better understand their choices, expectations, and senses of entitlement from male/female relationships. In the case of African-American clients, Hines and Boyd-Franklin (1982) caution that the counselor proceed slowly, since many families are suspicious of white counselors, whom they view as prying, and are likely to be reluctant to discuss openly such family secrets as illegitimate births, the couple's unmarried status, or the true paternity of the children.

## SPECIAL ASPECTS OF AFRICAN-AMERICAN FAMILY LIFE

Many African Americans grow up regularly attending church, most probably Baptist or African Methodist, and the church plays a central role, sometimes nightly, in their family and community life. A wide variety of activities—trips, dinners, church socials, choir participation, Sunday-school classes—take place in connection with the church, which serves as an available support system for its congregants, especially during troubled times. Hines and Boyd-Franklin (1982) contend that the church is frequently the most important institution in this community, providing an outlet for leadership and creative talents, while simultaneously providing a forum for their expression. As examples, they cite a father who might be a porter during the week but takes on the responsible role of deacon or trustee in his church, or a mother or grandmother, overwhelmed by family responsibilities during the week, who finds her outlet in church choir singing on Sunday. Particularly for the nonreligious counselor, an understanding of the role that religion and spirituality play in the lives of disenfranchised African-American clients—providing respect for their abilities or mere escape from daily painful experiences—is essential.

Beyond providing a social network and an opportunity to be somebody significant, the church offers hope (frequently in short supply among these families) and a belief that adversity can be overcome. The numerous functions provided by the African-American church may offer a refuge in a hostile white world (Frazier, 1963). Indeed, it is often the epicenter of African-American life, socially, politically, culturally, educationally, and interpersonally. Much like the extended family, the church offers help, counsel, child care, food, role models, and schooling, to say nothing of the emotional outlet evoked by provocative preachers.

While many African Americans proclaim that "black is beautiful," they may nevertheless harbor many negative and self-deprecating feelings and attitudes about their racial identity (Acosta, Yamamoto, & Evans, 1982). Nowhere is this more evident than in mind-sets toward skin color, a remnant of slavery days when "mulatto" or light-skinned children of white masters and African female slaves were given greater privileges than their darker-skinned counterparts. Thus, class distinctions within the African-American community began in slavery, when lighter skin meant special treatment in the plantation system—living in the master's house (house slaves) and receiving some education, benefits not accorded field slaves. Grier and Cobbs (1968) suggest that the mark of slavery has never fully disappeared from the consciousness of African-American people, despite the end of slavery, and a class system based on skin color persists in many communities. In this sense, African Americans collude with the dominant white culture in rejecting dark-skinned people.

Bass (1982) contends that such differential treatment historically led to discrimination and intraracial conflict based on skin color alone, and that skin color, along with hair texture, became a preoccupation among many African-Americans, who tried to become as much like white people as possible. She argues that in the case of hairstyle, wearing a "natural" or African style, beginning with the black-pride movement of the late 1960s, represented an attempt at liberation from the notion that only straight hair was attractive. Skin color, on the other hand, has remained a factor leading to discrimination: it is usually easier for a light-skinned person to get a job or education than an equally qualified dark-skinned African American. Although the exact number is unclear, some light-skinned members in each generation have denied their blackness and passed for white.

---

**Box 8.1   A Problem-Appraisal Checklist for African-American Families**

African-American families may experience problems in the following areas:

- Effects of poverty (poor housing, health care, unemployment, etc.)
- Lack of kinship and community support
- Skin-color–related problems
- Religion and spirituality issues
- Suspicion of institutions
- Feelings of powerlessness
- Problems with self-esteem
- Feelings of hopelessness and rage

---

Boyd-Franklin (1989) observes that, because skin color is such a toxic issue in our society, the darkest or perhaps lightest child in a family may be singled out as different and thus scapegoated at an early age with constant reminders about the color of his or her skin. In her experience, in some families dark-skinned people are preferred, and light skin color is viewed negatively, as a constant reminder of abuse of African-American women by white men. In either case, being different from others in the family can lead to feelings of self-hatred, rejection, and ostracism.

## SOME COUNSELING GUIDELINES

Counseling as typically practiced by majority-culture (white) counselors has not usually been a source of help or comfort to African-American families in times of crisis, and so it is not surprising that they typically look elsewhere: first to family and kinship network members, then to ministers and other respected "church-family" members—elders, deacons, deaconesses, and on occasion close, trusted friends (Franklin & Boyd-Franklin, 1990). Grier and Cobbs (1968) describe a legacy of suspicion and mistrust of many of society's institutions among this population; this legacy, developed over generations, is more self-protective than pathological, and is manifested as a "healthy cultural paranoia" about efforts from white professionals (and African-American professionals in "white institutions") to engage them in counseling. As indicated earlier, the counselor must proceed carefully and sensitively, and trust must be built slowly, lest well-intentioned interventions be perceived as prying into family secrets (unwed pregnancies, true paternity, welfare entitlements) whose disclosure may be dangerous, as their previous experiences with social agencies have taught them.

An understanding of the broader social and political context in which many poor African-American families live is essential to working with this group. For example, Aponte (1987) describes poor,[2] underorganized families as learning to view as normal their own impotence and their dependence on the community's network of institutions. He insists that any therapeutic intervention not only address the problems facing all families, but also help African-American families develop a structure for effectively dealing with the institutional resources in their own community. Because their clients are likely to live with low self-esteem and little hope, counselors need to take an active, positive approach that builds on the clients' abilities, offering support and direction as they strive to achieve immediate, perceptible, concrete solutions to real-life problems. Grievous (1989) observes that family therapists working with low-income families are often called upon to assume a variety of roles—educator, director, advocate, problem solver, and role model.

Working with multiproblem families, the counselor inevitably will need to intervene on several levels—working with the individual, the family, and the extended family, as well as with such community agencies and institutions as schools, jobs, courts, hospitals, police, and welfare—in order to offer effective help (Franklin & Boyd-Franklin, 1990).

Such help is likely to be time-limited, highly focused, and aimed at solving specific problems. Because the experience may be viewed as suspect or perhaps dangerous, especially by poor clients, considerable time may have to be spent initially in overcoming distrust, and the counselor may be scrutinized for signs of prejudice, condescension, or disrespect. Solomon (1982) cautions that the counselor may well be asked many personal questions—whether married, how many children, and so on—as the clients deliberate whether to trust the counselor, not as a counselor per se but as a person.

African-American men may present a special problem to the counselor, often expressing resistance, distrust, suspicion, and frequently rage at efforts to involve them in couples or family counseling. The counselor may need to pursue them by telephone in order to engage them in the counseling process, and in some cases may opt to proceed with the woman alone until the man, if ever, can be brought into the process. Should the counselor need to proceed with the woman alone, Boyd-Franklin (1989) urges that he or she remain committed to working with a dyadic relationship, even in the absence of a key player. Should the man become available, he must learn to trust the counselor before being encouraged to express his feelings, something he has seen in the past as a sign of weakness and as unmasculine.

As with all families, African-American clients must learn strategies for strengthening relationships. This is particularly true with those families that have little history

---

[2]Although we have chosen to emphasize working with poor, underorganized, and dysfunctional families, often led by female single parents, we need to note that there also exist well-functioning poor families, as well as an increasing number of middle-income African-American families. In the latter case, high achievers may feel isolated from other African Americans in their jobs or as a result of living in predominantly white neighborhoods, may have run up against a "glass ceiling" limiting their advancement at work, or may sometimes experience guilt over the other African-American people they have left behind (Davis & Watson, 1982).

of positive male/female communication patterns or few appropriate role models. Thus, counseling includes an educational component, in which family members learn techniques for the direct communication of feelings, whether positive or negative. For many African Americans, directness, expressiveness, and open communication between equals represent a new experience, and they must be convinced that it pays off in greater intimacy and ultimate satisfaction. Resistance can be expected, especially from men who fear that, by urging the expression of feelings, the counselor is aligning with the woman.

The issue of empowerment is likely to become a central element in the counseling process with any minority family. Within the constraints of the social, political, and economic realities of their lives, families must learn to use power appropriately within the family system and when dealing with external systems within the community. Given the legacy of racism and discrimination, this is especially true when attempting to engage African-American families, who come with a multigenerational history of oppression and powerlessness and must learn, to the extent possible, to strengthen the family's ability to become effective problem solvers and take greater control of their own lives. In practice, according to McGoldrick, Garcia Preto, Hines, and Lee (1991), the goal of empowerment should be interwoven with every intervention made by the counselor.

Wilson (1971) offers the following guidelines, appropriate for all clients considered in this chapter:

> Counselors should relate to clients with cultural differences in ways that will enhance the cultural identities of their clients. Counselors should relate to clients in ways which will permit the cultural identities of their clients to become positive sources of pride and major motivators of behavior. To do less is to ask a client to give up his values in order to participate in the dominant culture. To do less is to contribute to the destruction of life; and our mission is not to destroy life but to enhance life. (p. 424)

## COUNSELING HISPANIC-AMERICAN FAMILIES

The term *Hispanic* is generic, referring to Spanish roots, and has gained prominence, if not complete acceptance, in recent years as an overall way of alluding to all Spanish-speaking or Spanish-surnamed people residing in the United States. While Hispanic Americans may have migrated originally from any number of places (Spain, Central or South America, the Caribbean), the three major groups, in order of population size, are Mexican Americans (63% of all Hispanics), Puerto Ricans living on the mainland (11%), and Cuban Americans (5%). Together, Hispanic Americans make up 8.4% of the American population (U.S. Bureau of the Census, 1991b).

Because each country of origin has its own history, complex culture, traditions, mores, value systems, and migration patterns, and because members of each group may be intensely nationalistic, it would be naive to assume a homogeneity among members of this overall group. Some Latin Americans do not consider themselves Hispanic, because *Spanish* for them connotes white European colonists with racist policies; they may refer to themselves as *Latinos* or people of Latin American origin, reflecting a biculturality without specifying racial or linguistic characteristics (Munoz, 1982). People of Mexican ancestry living in the United States may consider themselves *Chicanos*, a term that once was considered a slur but now has taken on a connotation of raised consciousness committed to a full share of rights as American citizens. *La Raza* (literally, the race) has an even more militant and political connotation: people so self-identified refer to themselves as a new ethnic group, a western-hemispheric mixture of European (largely Spanish) and Indian (indigenous American) descent, thus sharing a social and cultural legacy of Spanish colonists and Native American peoples.

With these caveats made clear, recognizing that no single term is acceptable to all groups, and having alerted the counselor to carefully determine how the client family identifies itself, we have chosen to call these clients Hispanic Americans, the term most frequently used in the growing literature on such families. Taken together as a single entity, they constitute the second largest minority group (after African Americans) in the United States and the fastest growing ethnic group in the country.

Among Hispanic-American groups are varying socioeconomic, regional, and demographic characteristics, making cultural generalizations risky. Within groups, the counselor needs to be alert to the client's generation level, acculturation level, languages spoken, educational background, socioeconomic status, rural or urban residence, adherence to cultural values, and religiosity/spirituality (Homma-True, Greene, Lopez, & Trimble, 1993). We mention such diversity to help the counselor avoid unwarranted generalizations, and to reiterate that before undertaking counseling it is imperative to learn as much as possible about the characteristics both of the specific Hispanic-American group and of the particular family seeking help.

## FAMILY STRUCTURE—THE ROLE OF THE EXTENDED FAMILY

No better introduction to the social and cultural environment of Hispanic Americans is available than gaining some insight into the role of family and extended family in their lives. Language, culture, and ethnicity are interrelated influences not only in forging individual self-concepts, but also in strengthening family bonds and carrying on family traditions. Family loyalty, unity, and honor, as well as family commitment, obligation, and responsibility, characterize most Hispanic-American families, so much so that sacrifices of family members' own needs or pleasures for the sake of the family group are often encouraged if not expected. Family members struggling to rise out of poverty may at the same time feel an obligation to provide a similar opportunity for other family members.

In Puerto Rican families, for example, family ties are strong and relationships intense; separations are cause for extreme grief and reunions bring extreme joy, so that one who leaves the family does so only at extreme risk (McGoldrick, Garcia Preto, Hines, & Lee, 1991). In this patriarchal pattern, husbands as heads of the family are expected to be dignified and hard working, to protect and provide for the family, and traditionally to feel free to make decisions without consulting their wives. This form of *machismo* or maleness, in the self-perception of the Puerto Rican man, is not seen as negative, but rather as representing a desirable combination of virtue, courage, romanticism, and fearlessness. Because respect plays such an important role—raising respectful children is a source of pride for Hispanic parents—family arrangements are such that, although a wife may assume power behind the scenes, she and the children nevertheless overtly support and acknowledge the father's authority and do not openly challenge his rules.

In Mexican-American families, too, especially among poor and working-class people (but also to a large extent with middle-class families), the family structure is typically hierarchical, with authority given the husband and father (Acosta & Evans, 1982). Machismo operates here too but, beyond the popular stereotype of a swaggering or autocratic man, it pertains to the way a self-respecting Mexican-American man sees himself and his sex role, not simply how he dominates women. (Young boys may be taught "Be macho. Respect and protect your mother and sisters. Don't be weak and feminine. Don't cry.")

This attitude, so much a part of traditional family life, may prove to be an obstacle in counseling, as the Hispanic man may deny feelings or pain, remain silent, or divert feelings should they surge to the surface. Crying in front of the counselor means a loss of self-respect or the respect of other family members, and telling the counselor too many personal details may be perceived as giving power to another and assuming a one-down position. The counselor needs to recognize that feelings are being experienced and not expect to evoke an Americanized form of their expression. In some cases, the culturally aware counselor may need to give explicit permission, early in the counseling process, for all participants to express feelings, or may simply observe aloud "I see that your father feels sad about this problem."

Cuban families, in the Hispanic tradition, also view the family—including extended-family members—as the most important social unit in their lives (Bernal, 1982). Once again, the man's self-esteem rests on his ability to care for and protect his family and, should he lose his job, for example, or be unable to find work, he fears the loss of face and possibly the respect of his wife and family. A large group of middle- and upper-class Cubans has arrived in the United States within the last 25 years in order to escape Castro's regime. Overall, they became easily acculturated despite their initial lack of economic security, and their viewpoints may be somewhat different from those of earlier immigrants. When working with Cuban Americans, the counselor should be aware that the specific phase of the family migration often provides important clues as to the family's original socioeconomic status, political orientation, and educational level.

Extended-family life among all Hispanic Americans tends to be tightly knit; family membership and belonging are a source of great pride, and the collective needs of the family supersede those of the individual member. Ho (1987) even suggests that an individual's self-confidence, worth, security, and identity are determined by his or her relationships with other family members. Grandparents, uncles, aunts, cousins, lifelong friends, and even godparents created through a Catholic baptism custom may share responsibilities for the family's welfare and form coparenting bonds with parents. During times of crisis, for example, children may be transferred from one nuclear family to another within the extended-family system; as in the African-American family, this should not necessarily be viewed by the counselor as rejection or neglect (although some children may, of course, be adversely affected).

Given the socioeconomic conditions under which most Hispanic families live, a major function of this close-fitting family life is often economic survival (Bernal, Bernal, Martinez, Olmedo, & Santisteban, 1983). Low income, unemployment, undereducation, poor housing, prejudice, and discrimination—to say nothing of cultural-linguistic barriers or perhaps a traumatizing experience after having sought political refuge in this country—make life a struggle for most Hispanic Americans, and extended-family life helps provide an essential resource to buffer the stresses that result from these conditions. In addition, documented or undocumented Mexican Americans or Cuban Americans (Puerto Ricans are American citizens and need no documentation) typically look to a surrogate extended-family network or to priests for direction regarding the process of acculturation.

This point should not be lost on the counselor, who needs to be aware that when a strong extended-family system is operating, as it does in Hispanic-American families, members are more likely to seek out the advice and support of other family members or close family acquaintances than to seek help from professional counselors (Carrillo, 1982). To do otherwise would be insulting to the family. Although this attitude may be changing as more Hispanics live in the United States longer and become more acculturated, it is essential that the counselor respect this tradiiton and recognize the efforts taken by clients to seek help outside the extended-family circle.

A great deal of personal strength may result from such close family ties, but these ties may also lead to problems. For example, young adults may experience considerable difficulty, and in some cases may be overwhelmed with anxiety and guilt when attempting to separate, geographically as well as psychologically, from the family. Younger women, especially more assimilated ones, may find traditional sex-assigned roles unacceptable, provoking family conflict. Finally, cultural differences between children born in this country and parents from the old country are frequently associated with intergenerational conflict. Because the issues are complex and often go to the heart of cultural tradition, Acosta and Evans (1982) contend that, whenever possible, the counselor encourage inclusion of as many family members as feasible in the treatment process.

## ACCULTURATION AND ETHNIC IDENTITY

The acculturation process of most immigrant groups is usually accompanied by considerable stress and value-system clashes. Especially for recent immigrants, integrating their own ethnic identity with the majority culture is often hazardous, slow, and conflict-laden, as participants strive to develop a sense of self and define a place for themselves in the new society. In the case of Hispanic Americans, the retention of Spanish surnames, the continued preference for, and use of, the Spanish language, and the predominantly brown skin color help set the group apart and leave them open to stereotyping and discrimination. Since most new arrivals are poor and without skills, their chances for adaptation and advancement in the new country often are minimal, and in many cases they can find affordable housing and a sense of community only in ghetto areas. Because they are then unable to make contact with members of the dominant culture, any assimilation is further retarded.

The Hispanic American often is caught in a dilemma between collectivism and individualism, according to Bernal, Bernal, Martinez, Olmedo, and Santisteban (1983): to assume American values that stress individualism, he or she must adopt behavior patterns that tend to disrupt the close-knit family ties from which that individual derives a sense of self, or risk becoming a socially marginal person. In the view of these authors, culture conflict arises because American cultural values are based on a pragmatic approach, effectiveness, and efficiency, while Hispanics are more attuned to a personal approach, idealism, and informality. To be respectful runs the risk of seeming obsequious; to passively avoid offending others may be viewed as weak and servile or insufficiently assertive by Anglo standards. Such value clashes often lead to conflict and loss of self-esteem. Thus, counselors must gauge the degree of acculturation of clients, in order to have a better framework for evaluating their possible conflict over abandoning characteristics of the culture of origin and accommodating to the host culture.

Retaining the Spanish language serves as a link to cultural roots, as well as a way of perpetuating group values. Unfortunately, its use often effectively cuts off potential clients from utilizing counseling services, especially for non–English-speaking clients. Even in well-staffed clinics that utilize the services of bilingual interpreters, the overall results frequently are unsatisfactory to counselor and client alike, and much nuance in communication may be missed. Even when English has been learned as a second language, there may be a language barrier affecting proper assessment or choice of intervention by the counselor. Ruiz (1982) reports studies indicating that, when psychiatric evaluations of Hispanic patients were carried out in English, even by experienced clinicians, the clients were judged to show greater psychopathology than when interviewed in their native language. Laval, Gomez, and Ruiz (1989) contend that language barriers have a significant effect in both the evaluation of psychopathology and in the counseling or therapeutic process. In the latter case, they argue that counselors may misinterpret client verbalizations and may not be able to utilize client's potential resources for therapeutic gain.

As we noted at the beginning of this chapter, clinicians and clients alike are affected by their own cultural background, and problems arise when they come from different ethnic heritages and/or hold differing social-class membership. In this regard, counselors must be especially vigilant not to impose culturally specific standards or middle-class values regarding such issues as childrearing, male/female relationships, and assigned sex roles on others, especially clients from poor working-class environments. Similarly, nonreligious counselors should take care not to dismiss the use of prayer as a therapeutic agent. Catholicism is a powerful force in most Spanish-speaking countries.

Care too must be taken not to denigrate attitudes of suffering and self-denial, or to underestimate the importance of an Hispanic person's idealism regarding service to God and fellow man, since these religious beliefs are a socially and culturally stabilizing factor and represent an affirmation of traditional Catholic values (Bach-y-Rita, 1982).

Families in cultural transition may develop multiple situational-stress problems, impairing their ability to cope with the demands of the existing society. In the case of Mexican Americans, Falicov (1982) cites such issues as problems over social isolation, lack of knowledge regarding social or community resources, or perhaps the experience of dissonance between the normative expectations of the home and of the school, peer group, or other institutions. In many cases, it may be difficult to distinguish the problems created by poverty from those caused by the family's migration. In the following case, what appears to be a problem of school truancy can be seen in broader social context as a sociocultural problem:

❖ ❖ ❖ ❖ ❖

The Ortiz family, consisting of Roberto, 47, the father, Margarita, 44, the mother, and two daughters, Magdelena, 12, and Rosina, 10, had never been to a counselor before, and arrived together at the school counseling office for their early evening appointment with little prior understanding of what the process entailed. Unaware that they could talk to a counselor at school about child-related problems at home, they were summoned by the school authorities as a result of poor and sporadic school attendance by the children during the previous six months. Magdalena, the older, had actually stopped attending, and her younger sister, Rosina, had recently begun to copy her sister's behavior, although she did go to some classes from time to time.

Arranging for the Ortiz family to come to counseling presented several problems. Although she had been in this country for two decades, having arrived from El Salvador by illegally crossing the border at Tijuana, Mexico, with an older brother when she was 25, Mrs. Ortiz spoke English poorly, and she felt self-conscious about her speech in front of the school authorities. Mr. Ortiz, himself an undocumented immigrant from rural Mexico, had been in this country longer, and had taken classes in English soon after he arrived. However, he too had to be persuaded that all the family members needed to be present. Both parents had recently been granted amnesty under federal immigration regulations, and had looked forward to their children having better lives in the United States than they had had an opportunity to have. Needless to say, both were very upset upon learning that their children were school truants.

The school counseling office arranged for Augusto Diaz, one of the counselors, to see the Ortiz family. Although of Mexican heritage, Mr. Diaz was a third-generation Hispanic American who himself learned Spanish in high school, never having heard it spoken at home growing up. However, he was sensitive to what each of the Ortiz family members was feeling and what was the proper protocol in reaching this family. He began respectfully by addressing the father as the head of the house, thanking him for allowing his family to attend, but indicating that the children could not be allowed to skip school, and that there were legal consequences if they continued to do so. Aware that Mrs. Ortiz seemed to be having trouble following his English, he enlisted Magdalena as translator. From time to time, he used Spanish words or idioms when appropriate, although he himself was quite self-conscious about his Americanized Spanish and he too turned to Magdalena when uncertain of whether he had said in Spanish exactly what he had intended.

The first session was essentially designed to familiarize the family with what they could expect from counseling, to build trust in the counselor, and to show them that he was interested in their situation and would try to help. He encouraged all family members to participate and remarked several times, especially for the father's benefit, that openly discussing personal problems was not a sign of weakness. They arranged another evening appointment for the following week, at a time that would not interfere with Mr. Ortiz' daytime gardening job or Mrs. Ortiz' daytime work as a domestic worker.

When Mr. Ortiz finally felt comfortable enough to share his thoughts, he said that girls did not need education, that they already knew how to read and write, and that had he had boys it would have been different. He was upset, however, that they were disobedient and disrespectful in not telling the parents that they were not attending school, but lying instead about how they spent their days. While Mrs. Ortiz seemed to agree, she also revealed that she herself was fearful of school as well as much of the outside world. She hinted that she knew about the truancy, adding that she was afraid for them in the mixed Hispanic/African-American neighborhood in which they lived, and was just as happy that they stayed home rather than mingle with their classmates. She saw their being home alone as an opportunity for them to learn to care for a house as preparation for their eventual marriages.

Both Magdalena and Rosina, quiet until asked direct questions in the first two sessions, began to open up in the middle of the third family meeting with the counselor. They admitted feeling isolated at school, especially because their parents would not allow them to bring classmates home or to visit others after dark. They confessed to being intimidated by gangs at the school, something they had been afraid to reveal to their parents, who, they felt, would not understand. Staying away from school had started as a result of Magdalena being attacked by an older girl on the school playground, after which she was warned to stay away or she would be seriously hurt. Rosina largely was following her older sister's lead, although she herself had not had the terrorizing experience Magdalena had had.

By the fifth session, the counselor had succeeded in opening up communication among the family members. Mrs. Ortiz expressed an interest in learning English better, and had begun to inquire about an English-as-a-second-language

(ESL) class at the high school at night. Mr. Ortiz was persuaded to allow her to go out in the evening to attend class with one of their neighbors, another woman from El Salvador. He was proud that she was trying to improve her English, as were her children. Learning English would also free up her daughter, Magdalena, from her pivotal role as translator and pseudo-adult in the family. As the counselor learned of their need for other special services, such as filling out various insurance forms and income tax returns, he directed them to the local Catholic church, where some volunteers were helping parishioners with these problems.

The children were given added support by their mother, who walked them to school every day before she left for work. The older girl still looked menacing, but as Magdalena and Rosina joined other children in the playground rather than being social isolates, they felt safer, and soon the terrorizing stopped. Magdalena joined the school drill team and Rosina expressed an interest in learning to play an instrument and join the school band.

The counselor, in an active, problem-solving fashion, was able to act successfully as a social intermediary between the family, the school, and the church, mobilizing the family to make better use of neighborhood and institutional resources and feel more a part of the overall community.

❊   ❊   ❊   ❊   ❊

## SEX-ROLE ISSUES IN HISPANIC CULTURES

We are aware that, in emphasizing traditional family structures in Hispanic-American families, we run the risk of reinforcing the stereotype that all such families adhere to such a pattern. Certainly this is not the case, and clearly with increased acculturation such strict gender-defined roles diminish. Generational differences, differences in socioeconomic status, the greater incidence of single-parent families, working wives, the Chicano movement, and the feminist movement all may contribute to making specific Hispanic families less like the traditional families we have been describing. As Carrillo (1982) observes, norms for Hispanic families indeed are changing, if slowly, leading to intrafamilial stresses and personal conflicts for family members. However, she adds that, despite these changes, the counselor still can expect a greater adherence to sex role behavior within the Hispanic culture than among non-Hispanic groups.

Virility and male supremacy are taught to young Hispanic males from childhood; acts of courage, aggressiveness, and honor are especially rewarded. To be a man is never to run from a fight and always to honor one's word. From adolescence on, virility is measured primarily by sexual conquest and secondarily by showing physical prowess in relation to other men (Carrillo, 1982). Traditionally, the man has been the undisputed authority at home and in all other functions in relation to women. Older boys are expected to protect their sisters, and it is still commonplace for girls to assist mothers in serving their father and brothers.

Both boys and girls learn sex-role–determined behaviors from an early age. Thus, in traditional homes, boys do not do tasks that are regarded as feminine, such as helping with the dishes or household chores. Instead, they can come and go as they please, something their female siblings do not have the freedom to do.

Both boys and girls are raised to respect their parents, who are esteemed and accorded high status, while the children have low status. If the father is authoritarian and feared as a disciplinarian, the mother is usually submissive, self-sacrificing, and dependent, but nevertheless is assured an honored place in the family. Fathers are unlikely to involve themselves in the caretaking of children, but they will protect the mother and insist the children obey her. If men need to prove their virility through sexual conquest, women are expected to remain pure—sexually naive and faithful to men (Canino, 1982). In addition, they are expected to be tender, affectionate, sentimental, and overprotective mothers— all characteristics that give women status within the Hispanic community.

Young girls growing up in traditional Hispanic families emulate their mother's role. They learn from observing their parents that the man is the final authority; he ultimately determines whether she will be permitted to realize her plans, and it is he who must be pleased. More likely than not, her father will expect her to live a chaste life, far more sheltered than her brothers.

Mate selection in traditional families requires the young man to speak to the young woman's parents about his intentions, and it is the father's permission that is particularly important. Once married, the hierarchical role of male dominance and female submissiveness tends to be followed. However, this power discrepancy may be more facade or social fiction than actuality. Canino (1982) suggests that many Hispanic women develop covert manipulative strategies, exerting power and influence in the family but in a socially acceptable manner. (This tactic frequently is practiced by oppressed or lower-status people in all cultures, and should not be considered necessarily Hispanic.) Especially as Hispanic Americans become upwardly mobile and assimilate Anglo lifestyles, traditional husband-wife sex-role delineations become less strict (Ho, 1987).

---

### Box 8.2   A Problem-Appraisal Checklist for Hispanic-American Families

The counselor must take the following circumstances into account in appraising the problems of Hispanic-American families:

- Country of origin
- Circumstances of immigration
- Degree of acculturation
- Generation in the United States
- English fluency
- Sex-role assignments
- Socioeconomic status
- Devotion to church
- Machismo
- Male/female relationships

## SOME COUNSELING GUIDELINES

Despite the myriad of problems that would seem to put them at risk—immigration, low income, unemployment, undereducation, and discrimination, as well as various cultural and language barriers and, in some cases, the traumatic aftermath of political persecution—it is nevertheless true that Hispanic Americans as a whole tend to underutilize counseling and other mental health services (Padilla, Ruiz, & Alvarez, 1989). In part, this is due to the shortage of trained bilingual and bicultural counselors; in part, perhaps, to a low level of cultural sensitivity among clinicians to this group's special needs; and, in part, to the geographic or financial inaccessibility of many programs to Hispanic populations (Bernal, Bernal, Martinez, Olmedo, & Santisteban, 1983). Resources in Hispanic communities typically are inadequate in number to meet needs, and when services are offered they are more likely to be carried out by paraprofessionals with limited training than by professionals (Carrillo, 1982). Padilla, Ruiz, and Alvarez (1989) contend that, even where services are available, Hispanic Americans will not refer themselves to agencies when they perceive them as alien institutions intruding into their community, and when such agencies are staffed by non–Spanish-speaking personnel.

Acosta and Evans (1982) suggest that Mexican Americans, whether faithful churchgoers or not, are likely to turn to the Catholic church in times of stress—using prayer or seeing a priest for the sacrament of confession and immediate absolution—rather than enter a more prolonged professional counseling arrangement. Similarly, Puerto Ricans are likely to wait until there is a crisis, and then expect the same help they are accustomed to in a hospital emergency room—brief, immediate, concrete, direct, problem-oriented, and offered by an authority (McGoldrick, Garcia Preto, Hines, & Lee, 1991). Bernal (1982) agrees that to involve Cubans in any ongoing counseling situation calls for Spanish-language skills as well as sensitivity to cultural issues. As noted earlier, how long the Cuban family has resided in the United States, why they moved and who initiated the move, and what family members remain behind in Cuba are all important questions that will help the counselor determine the family's migration phase, its level of acculturation, and any invisible obligations to those left behind—whom they never expect to see again—that may affect current family functioning.

Establishing a warm, personal, and respectful relationship, rather than a distant and professional one, is crucial if counseling with Hispanic-American families is to proceed and be successful. Trust must be built up slowly, attention paid to nuances in language, and community resources enlisted whenever feasible. A plan for treatment may need to be explained early on: what the counselor will be doing, what will be expected of the family members, and approximately how long all this will take, with some specific statement regarding ultimate goals.

Since Hispanics consider the family their primary source of support, the counselor must remain aware that the integrity of the family must be retained. To suggest that the father has failed to provide proper family leadership, that the mother is less than loving or sacrificing, or that the children no longer respect their parents is to cast a shattering blow; great sensitivity is demanded if the counselor must explore these areas.

Especially for newly arrived or unacculturated groups, counseling seems more familiar and more palatable if regarded as a form of medical treatment: a person going to a physician is simply ill and does not carry the stigma—particularly among uneducated and unsophisticated families—of being crazy. Before beginning to counsel family members, it is wise to secure the permission of the husband or father; this facilitates the process and helps guard against abrupt termination, even if he only participates sporadically.

Clinical interventions with Hispanics are greatly enhanced if extended-family members, such as grandparents, are included in the process. Because of their close-knit family ties and their sense of being responsible to one another, Hispanic Americans are apt to respond to a family counseling approach more readily than if individual counseling were attempted. Padilla and Salgado de Snyder (1985) suggest that Minuchin's (1974) structural approach is particularly applicable, specifically because it emphasizes the role of socioeconomic and cultural factors as individual subsystems in the formation of the problem as well as in its solution.

To function successfully, the Anglo-American counselor must be sensitized to the subtleties of Hispanic-American family structure and lifestyle patterns, able to refrain from imposing value judgments based on majority cultural standards, and respectful of the special strengths and expectations of culturally distinct Hispanic families.

# COUNSELING ASIAN/PACIFIC-AMERICAN FAMILIES

Although we group them together for classification purposes, we hasten to point out at the outset of our discussion that immigrants from Asia and the Pacific Islands and their descendants do not represent a homogeneous, monolithic group. Rather, these communities represent a heterogeneity of history, religion, language, culture, and appearance, to say nothing of differential patterns of immigration and acculturation. Counselors should be careful to avoid categorizing all clients from this area as the same or interchangeable, any more than it would make sense to aggregate the Irish, Poles, Swedes, and Italians into one group—European—ignoring their vast language and cultural differences (Morishima, 1978).

Instead, counselors might take heed of the observation made by Kuramoto, Morales, Munoz, and Murase (1983) that vast differences exist among Asian and Pacific families; as an example, they cite the obvious gulf between an affluent, fourth-generation Japanese American and the poverty, bewilderment, and despair felt by the family of an uneducated fisherman who fled Vietnam in a fishing boat. The constant influx of recent refugees from Southeast Asia has made for an even more diverse and heterogeneous Asian/Pacific-American population.

Asian and Pacific Americans come from such diverse places as East Asia (China, Japan, Korea), South Asia (India, Pakistan), Southeast Asia (the Philippines, Thailand, Vietnam, Cambodia, Laos, Indonesia), and the Pacific Islands (Hawaii, Samoa, and Guam). While a majority of Japanese Americans and many Chinese Americans have been in the United States for several generations, the vast majority of Chinese, Koreans, Filipinos, Vietnamese, Cambodians, Indians and Pakistanis living here are foreign born (Homma-True, Greene, Lopez, & Trimble, 1993).

The Asian/Pacific-American population is expected to increase sharply within the next few decades as new immigrant groups continue to arrive, especially from Hong Kong, Korea, the Philippines, and Southeast Asia. Each national group not only has a distinctive cultural heritage but also a different history and, equally important, a different reason for immigration (Takaki, 1990). Taken together, they represent the fastest growing group of immigrants in our society, now at about 3% of the total U.S. population. Currently, the Chinese, Filipino, and Japanese represent the three largest groups.

## CULTURAL TRANSITIONS

The immigration patterns of Asian and Pacific Americans reflect U.S. immigration policy. Earliest to arrive, in the mid-1800s, were the Chinese, induced to come here as laborers for the transcontinental railroads in the process of developing the West. They were initially welcomed as cheap labor but, when a diminishing labor market and fear of the "yellow peril" made their immigration no longer welcome, laws were enacted in the United States to deny them the rights of citizenship, ownership of land, and marriage (Sue, 1989). Prohibited by early exclusionary immigration legislation—the Federal Chinese Exclusion Act of 1882—from intermarrying or bringing brides to America, those Chinese already in this country remained living in essentially male Chinatown ghettos on the West Coast of the United States when the railroad work was completed. It was only with the end of World War II and the 1965 repeal of these exclusionary laws that the Chinese renewed their high immigration rates. As recently as 1980, according to one estimate (Lee, 1982), fully 60% of all Chinese Americans were first-generation immigrants, many of them women and children who had been separated from the other generations of their families but were now members of surrogate extended families in Chinatown.

The Japanese, immigrating primarily between 1890 and 1924, experienced similar resistance (for example, the Gentleman's Agreement of 1907 limiting the immigration of Japanese). Because they came from rural agricultural and fishing villages, this first generation, called *Issei,* moved into similar areas in this country to provide cheap agricultural labor. Later, they were joined by Japanese females ("picture brides"), whom they brought to the United States after an exchange of photographs (Kitano, 1982). Like many Asian Americans to follow, with modest expectations for themselves in terms of economic or social mobility, they placed their hopes and dreams on their U.S.-born children, the *Nisei* or second generation. Both foreign- and U.S.-born Japanese Americans living on the West Coast suffered innumerable hardships when they were relocated and incarcerated, as potential enemies, after the Japanese attack on Pearl Harbor in World War II.

Filipino immigrants also arrived in the 1920s and, like the Chinese, were not allowed citizenship privileges. Koreans, during the same period, were able to preserve family life by bringing wives and children. Pacific Islanders, such as

Samoans, were more recent arrivals; as their predecessors had done, they came in search of a better life but, lacking language and work skills, they often lived in poverty. The most recent Southeast Asian immigrants, from Vietnam, Cambodia, and Laos, came here to escape political persecution, only to face prejudice and discrimination in this country. In general, the newer immigrants from Southeast Asia, Samoa, Korea, and the Philippines are lower in socioeconomic status than those American-born descendants of earlier Chinese and Japanese immigrants.

Physical appearance and language are the most prominent features that immediately separate Asians from Westerners. Although it is difficult for Westerners to see beyond these primary physical and cultural distinctions, in actuality the countries of origin of Asian/Pacific peoples are themselves very different in historical, social, and economic development (Shon & Ja, 1982). In addition, each nation has its distinctive language, although some (Chinese, Japanese, Vietnamese) use common Chinese characters, which have been given different pronunciations as they became assimilated into separate native languages. Within groups, such as the Chinese, several dialects distinguish different parts of the country or, in some cases, different villages. Non–English-speaking Asians cannot communicate from one group to the other (Chien & Yamamoto, 1982).

Since cultural transitions play such significant roles in understanding Asian families, counselors must take care early on to identify problems in adapting to American society and assess the degree of acculturation exhibited by the family seeking help. They likely will find differences between family members—certainly between children and their parents but also between husband and wife—that may require attention. Helping families adapt more smoothly to the new majority culture may help alleviate some stress, but counselors must take care that, in the process, the family is not forced abruptly to give up all remnants of the life left behind (Lappin & Scott, 1982).

Ho (1987) distinguishes three types of Asian/Pacific American families:

1. Recently arrived immigrant families
2. Immigrant-American families
3. Immigrant-descendant families

The process of immigration inevitably causes a large number of life changes and adaptations over a short period of time. Immigrant families must simultaneously deal with: (1) the physical or material, economic, educational, and language transitions; and (2) the cognitive, affective, and psychological transitions for individuals and the family as a whole. Migration involves being uprooted from a familiar environment—neighbors, streets, sounds, customs, a supportive extended-family structure, cultural guidelines—and is inevitably stressful; it requires adaptation in stages as cultural boundaries are crossed (Sluzki, 1979). Some immigrants plan to stay a short time before returning to their native country, while others—in some cases political refugees—see the new land as a haven, an opportunity for a new life for themselves and their children.

As has been true of other immigrant groups, language is a major obstacle in the acculturation process of Asian/Pacific families. Because the parents are usually unable to communicate effectively with landlords, store clerks, school officials, potential employers, or neighbors, family hierarchy often is (temporarily) reversed, and children, having learned the new language and customs more quickly, may become interpreters for parents, throwing the customary patriarchy off balance (Lappin & Scott, 1982).

Economic necessities may force the adult family members to begin employment immediately upon arrival in the United States. Those who lack professional skills or proficiency in the English language may have no choice but to work long hours, six or seven days per week, at subminimum pay, with few if any employee benefits. Even with both parents working, the family is apt to live in substandard housing. New arrivals may grieve over the loss of support from family members left behind in the home country, which may or may not be partially replaced by relatives in the adopted country.

For newly arriving immigrants, according to Shon and Ja (1982), the initial phase of cognitive reactions almost certainly involves cultural shock and disbelief at the disparity between what was expected and what actually exists; this is often followed by anger and resentment and ultimately some accommodation and mobilization of family resources and energy. Because of cultural differences and language barriers, such families are not likely to seek psychological help from a counselor, although they may require referral for legal aid, information on educational opportunities to learn English, or overall advocacy.

Immigrant-American families (foreign-born parents, American-born children), if they seek help from a counselor, probably do so as a result of ongoing culture clash within the family. Younger members, usually better assimilated, are likely to value more Americanized characteristics—individuality, independence, assertiveness—while their elders frown upon their disrespectful behavior, perhaps express regret over coming to the United States, and may even threaten to return to the home country. (The case of the Singh family from India, in which intergenerational problems between parents and American-schooled adolescents threatened family unity, was presented in Chapter One.) Counselors need to provide negotiating tools so that such families can resolve parent-child conflicts and communication difficulties, and gain some role clarification (Ho, 1987).

Immigrant-descendant families, composed of second-, third-, or fourth-generation American-born families, are almost certainly highly acculturated to American values, speak English at home, may live outside traditional Asian/Pacific neighborhoods, and seek help when required in the same manner, and with the same degree of comfort or discomfort, as most other assimilated Americans.

## FAMILY STRUCTURE AND RESPONSIBILITIES

In most Asian and Pacific Island cultures, the family is the central unit and the individual is secondary. Chinese culture, for example, stresses kinship from birth to death, and it is expected that the family will serve as a major resource in providing stability, a sense of self-esteem, and satisfaction. Even if the person leaves for another country and is permanently separated from his or her family of origin, it is expected that devotion to family values and adherence to family standards will be maintained. So too in Japanese households, where, unlike the tendency in most American families to relate in an intimate fashion, self-expression is subordinate to acting in accordance with role expectations (Sue & Morishima, 1982).

Counselors can expect a restraint of feeling and self-disclosure, certainly in the early stages of the counseling process, and an apparent expectation that clients are there for advice and guidance from an authority and not to engage in two-way communication. Since an individual's actions during this lifetime traditionally are believed to reflect on his or her ancestors and future generations, emotional problems and the need for counseling may take on a powerful stigma in many Asian/Pacific families, who may then not avail themselves of psychiatric or psychological services (Wong, Lu, Shon, & Gaw, 1983).

Investment in children, as we have indicated, has very high priority among Asian/Pacific populations. Young children are indulged long beyond what is considered standard among traditional American families. Toilet training is often delayed, according to Berg and Jaya (1993), until the child insists on it, and older children, even up to the age of 10 or 11, frequently sleep with their parents. Adolescents are not encouraged to learn self-care skills (cleaning their rooms, doing their own laundry, cooking their own meals) and are permitted to maintain a dependent position as long as they wish. What they are expected to do, however, is to be well behaved and obedient and, above all, to bring honor to the family. School achievement is a particularly visible way to do so, but so is earning praise from others in the community for being respectful, knowing good manners, and eventually marrying into a good family.

Heavily influenced by Confucian philosophy and ethics, Asian/Pacific families' role definitions traditionally are hierarchical and patriarchal. Marriage represents a continuation of the male family line rather than the creation of a new family, and women are expected to show obedience toward their husbands (del Carmen, 1990). While this disparity has shifted to a more egalitarian marital relationship among contemporary Asian/Pacific Americans, it remains true that loyalty and respect are emphasized within the family. Though some culture conflict may occur as a result of increased exposure to American norms, values, and behavior patterns, adaptations evidently can readily be made: Asians have the lowest divorce rate among American households, as well as the lowest proportion of households headed by women. To what extent this represents successful marriages, and to what extent maintaining the appearance of success and avoiding the loss of face associated with bringing dishonor to the family is not clear.

In traditional Asian society, fathers are expected to be providers and to be responsible for educating and disciplining the children. Mothers in this arrangement are nurturing figures, protective of their offspring. Sons have traditionally been held in higher esteem than daughters; eldest sons are expected to be role models for the younger children and to take over family leadership after the death or incapacity of the father. By way of contrast, daughters are socialized as homemakers and expected to marry and be absorbed into their husbands' families (Shon & Ja, 1982). While this pattern is less rigidly adhered to among younger and more assimilated Asian/Pacific families, the basic role assignments and expectations continue today.

Berg and Jaya (1993) describe the Asian mother as failing to maintain boundaries with her son's family, and consequently appearing to meddle by maintaining a close relationship with him, from which his wife typically is excluded. These authors view this behavior as a way of solidifying her position when the first-born son becomes head of the household, and thus ensuring her security for her old age. They caution the counselor to take special note of this traditional arrangement as culturally appropriate and warn against any hasty attempt to restructure it—as too enmeshed by American standards—before its importance in Asian family patterns has been understood.

Intermarriage (or cross-cultural marriage) between partners of diverse ethnic backgrounds has become increasingly familiar as social tolerances increase,[3] but within such marriages the diverse outlooks and expectations of the spouses often produces strains and occasionally serious conflict (Falicov, 1986). Strains may also arise from family disapproval; one family may consider the new spouse a cultural outsider, at the same time that that person experiences culture shock or otherwise feels alienated from, or uncomfortable with, the attitudes and behavior patterns of the new in-law family. While we are in no way suggesting that marital happiness or unhappiness can be reduced simply to degrees of cultural commonality, it is nevertheless true that the lack of a shared cultural code—interpersonal expectations, childrearing values, anticipated boundary lines with extended family, styles of communicating—can lead to serious marital conflict, as in the following case:

❋    ❋    ❋    ❋    ❋

Darryl Chang and his wife, Rebecca Wilson Chang, were a middle-class couple in their early 30s, married for six years, when they sought help from a private-practice counselor. Darryl was a third-generation Chinese American, an oldest son with three younger sisters, brought up in Hawaii by well-to-do parents who were large landowners. Sent to the mainland to study as an undergraduate at a prestigious private Midwest university, he met Rebecca during his freshman year, and they were inseparable thereafter throughout their college careers. Rebecca was the only child of white middle-class parents, New Englanders, both professionals, who had to strain, financially, to send her to the university, but did so willingly because they wanted to encourage her to pursue a professional career. Darryl's goal, responding to family expectations, was to become a physician, while Rebecca had dreams of pursuing an academic career as an anthropologist.

[3]The degree to which marrying out occurs in any group affects the likelihood that a specific intermarriage will gain acceptance by the families or communities involved. For example, the *sansei* or third-generation Japanese Americans have a very high rate of outmarriage; more than half marry non-Asian partners (Kitano, 1982). The phenomenon reflects the degree of assimilation of Japanese Americans into U.S. society.

Married upon graduation, they returned to Hawaii, where Darryl received his medical training while Rebecca studied for her master's degree; her studies were interrupted when she gave birth to Robby. They resided in the Chang compound and ate their meals together every night with Darryl's parents, forming the close bond that Darryl insisted was the way respectful children should behave. Darryl's mother occasionally intimated to him that she and her husband were disappointed that he had married down, although she appeared cordial if somewhat distant with Rebecca. By way of contrast, Rebecca's parents accepted Darryl after some initial misgivings about the couple's differences in background, but did express some regrets that the young couple and their grandchild lived so far away that visiting was infrequent. While Rebecca was not happy about her mother-in-law's involvement in Robby's upbringing, she generally kept her feelings to herself, having learned that criticizing his parents only aroused Darryl's wrath.

An opportunity to gain intern and residency experience in dermatology brought Darryl, Rebecca, and Robby to California. Lack of sufficient income became a problem, and Rebecca especially resented her husband's parents' unwillingness to help them out when she knew they could well afford it. In addition, she became angry and depressed that Darryl not only was away for long periods of time but was fatigued and often irritable when they were together. He offered no help with Robby, and seemed puzzled that she should expect him to participate in childrearing activities.

Rebecca's insistence that they seek counseling was triggered when the Changs visited from Hawaii. Showing limited interest in Rebecca, Mrs. Chang spent a great deal of time with her son, lunching with him and shopping for clothes. Insisting that it was not proper for a doctor to dress poorly, she spent several thousand dollars on three suits and accessories for her son, but nothing comparable for her daughter-in-law or grandchild. Rebecca was furious, but Darryl argued that the behavior was appropriate, since his mother was apparently concerned that he would lose face if not properly attired. Rebecca was enraged at his lack of empathy with her feelings, and burst forth with a recitation of all of the slights and other grievances she had felt over the years when she felt treated as an outsider. She was sick of being deferential, sick of meeting a stone wall when she tried to talk to him about her unhappiness, and sick of being made to feel unwelcome by his family.

The couple saw the counselor for four sessions. In contrast to Rebecca's intensity, Darryl was taciturn, and had difficulty talking about family matters, which he finally acknowledged, but said belonged within the family and not in front of the counselor, an outsider. Careful not to give the appearance of taking sides, the counselor began by focusing on cultural differences and cultural expectations. She attempted as best she could to explain her perception of the cultural code each partner operated from, thus relabeling their differences as cultural (and thus fixable with increased understanding) rather than the result of irreconcilable personality differences. Her goal here was to help each partner start to understand underlying cultural issues, and in this way begin a dialogue with the goal of achieving better and more open communication.

The counselor next tried to get the couple to look at the structure of their relationship, stating that greater attention needed to be paid to Rebecca's sense that
she was a second-class person in Darryl's eyes, and Darryl's view that Rebecca
wanted too much, expecting him to do things—such as help with their child—
that he found completely alien and for which he had no role model. Careful to
keep them from blaming each other for their cultural blinders ("She's spoiled,
like all American women"; "He's a Chinese eldest son and thinks he's a crown
prince"), the counselor agreed that, while cultural factors were operating, that
did not make the situation unchangeable or exonerate either one from personal
responsibility to improving their relationship. Despite differences in background,
negotiations were nevertheless possible and some of their culturally unique
outlooks could be maintained but better integrated into new family traditions.

The couple made some progress, but Darryl in particular was minimally open
to change. By the start of the fourth session, he said he thought they were ready
to work out differences on their own, that they appreciated the help, and that
they would contact the counselor if needed in the future—all, it seemed to the
counselor, ways of exiting prematurely from counseling. Rebecca appeared reluctantly to go along with her husband's plans, and she too expressed relief that the
crisis in their marriage was over, although she seemed to be saying that it might
just erupt again some day.

❋    ❋    ❋    ❋    ❋

## VALUES, BELIEFS, OBLIGATIONS

In Asian/Pacific culture, form—how things are done—often takes precedence over
content—what is done. Proper protocol, procedures, and ways of addressing one
another, are all important, even before getting down to the business at hand. Berg
and Jaya (1993) advise counselors to be sure to pay proper respect to procedural
rules as the first step in achieving a positive alliance with the family. As examples,
they point out several possible errors: addressing parents by their first names,
allowing a wife to complain for too long about her husband, or confronting
parents directly about their mishandling of their children. In their experiences,
the first session might profitably be spent establishing a social relationship, paying proper deference to age (the counselor's or the client's, whichever is greater),
and establishing order, hierarchy, and social boundaries between the counselor
and the family. As part of this process, the counselor can expect to be asked many
personal questions.

Filial piety—loyalty, respect, and devotion of children to their parents—is of
prime importance in traditional Asian/Pacific families. Children are expected to
obey their parents in a deferential way and to respect and care for family elders
as they age (del Carmen, 1990). While some modification takes place with longer
residence in the United States, many traditions and values continue. Many such
traditions are dictated by adherence to Confucianism and Buddhism, which
specify more rules of behavior and conduct for family members than is usual
in most cultures (Shon & Ja, 1982). As we have indicated, an individual's adherence

to an established code of conduct becomes more than a reflection of that person's standards; it reflects the standards of the family and kinship network to which he or she belongs. Deeply rooted in the lives of most Asians, the philosophy of Confucianism, in particular, strongly emphasizes respect for elders, obedience, and close family ties.

Obligations, largely unspoken but understood by all, govern much of the lives of Asian family members. Regardless of what a parent does, Ho (1987) reports, the child is still obligated to show respect and obedience. Parents are considered to deserve the highest obligation because it was they who brought children into the world and cared for them when they were helpless. Obligation can be incurred in two ways: through the playing out of ascribed roles (parent/child; teacher/pupil) emphasizing status differences and the hierarchical or vertical nature of relationships; and through actions that incur obligation because of their kindness and helpfulness (Shon & Ja, 1982).

Closely related to obligation is the concept of shame and loss of face, which is frequently used to reinforce adherence to a prescribed set of obligations. In contrast to American ideals regarding self-sufficiency and self-reliance, Asian/Pacific people believe they are the product of their relationships, and consequently value the maintenance of harmony through proper conduct and attitudes. Shaming someone is a way of getting that person to adhere to societal expectations of proper behavior. To act in a shameful way not only leads to loss of face through exposure of errant action for all to see, but also leads to withdrawal of support and confidence in the person by family and community. In a society where interdependence is crucial, actual or threatened withdrawal of support is a powerful weapon to force conformity to family and societal expectations (Shon & Ja, 1982).

Counselors need to assess the role of obligation and fear of being shamed by revealing personal problems in their clients, if they are to fully understand and evaluate what information is being given and what withheld by client families. Direct confrontation, which some counselors question for any clients, is likely to be especially unsuccessful with Asian/Pacific clients because it runs the risk of forcing them to expose previously unacknowledged feelings and/or making them fearful of committing a social error and thus facing the dread of losing face. Nevertheless, Root (1989) reports that most Asian/Pacific families will come in together with a distressed family member, and at least give the outward appearance of support for the counseling process. However, the identified patient is likely to believe that his or her recovery rests on the exercise of willpower and, despite the need for support, may not want family members involved.

## SOME COUNSELING GUIDELINES

A useful starting point for counselors working with any ethnic family is to gain some awareness of the ethnic and cultural traditions of their own family. In most cases they are likely to discover that particular beliefs or behavior patterns previously attributed to idiosyncracies in their family may actually be more

---

**Box 8.3   A Problem-Appraisal Checklist for Asian/Pacific Families**

The counselor must take the following circumstances into account in appraising the problems of Asian/Pacific families:

- Country of origin
- Generation in the United States
- Social class (in country of origin and in the United States)
- Degree of identification with home country
- Language barriers
- Culture shock and degree of assimilation
- Prejudice and discrimination
- Role and status reversal
- Intergenerational family conflicts
- Lack of community support systems
- Expectations of temporary or permanent residence

---

accurately linked to their ethnic background. Further investigation may lead to the surprising discovery of the commonality of much of the behavior in their family with the larger ethnic community (Preli & Bernard, 1993). Multiculturalism is likely to become a more meaningful and relevant construct to a counselor as a result of becoming sensitized to his or her own ethnic and cultural roots. A dividend of such increased self-awareness might be raised consciousness regarding the experiences of ethnic minorities.

As we have indicated, the beginning phase of counseling, always important in establishing a relationship and helping clients learn what to expect, takes on special significance for Asian/Pacific-American clients, particularly those who are less acculturated. According to Ho (1987), the first interview, if not conducted sensitively, may also be the last. He suggests that the counselor from the start confidently assume the role of authority figure and actively direct the counseling process. When asked, even in a subtle or indirect manner, the counselor must be willing to disclose his or her educational background and work experience, and even to respond openly to more personal questions about marriage or children. Only after the family has developed a sense of trust in the counselor, and in the leadership they expect that person to provide, will they be able to begin to form a closer relationship with the counselor—a task that usually proceeds deliberately among Asian/Pacific peoples.

Especially when working with first-generation families, Sluzki (1979) attempts early in the counseling process to determine what phase of the migration process best characterizes their situation. He contends that the migration process follows a predictable pattern, occurring in phases, each with corresponding manifestations of family conflict. Contrary to expectations, he believes migratory stress is not greatest in the weeks and months following the move, but rather that families overcompensate as they attempt to deal with the adaptational tasks needed for survival. In Sluzki's experience, while family disorganization may occur under extreme circumstances or where there is a lack of effective coping skills, the majority of families show no symptoms during this phase of their acculturation, although conflicts may remain dormant. Several months later, however, a major crisis may develop; it is typically at this phase—which Sluzki labels *decompensation*—that counselors are likely to see such families, who are now struggling to come to terms with maximizing the family's continuity and its compatibility with the new environment. Later, especially if there is a long-term delay in the family's adaptive process, conflict will likely break out into the open, perhaps in the form of intergenerational conflicts between parents and children raised in the adopted country.

In many cases, families may fail to perceive any correlation between the move and their conflicts, seeing their migration in historical perspective but not as any longer impinging on their adaptive capabilities. Sluzki (1979) urges the counselor to convey his or her recognition to the family that the migratory process is stressful and that any presenting symptoms are understandable and a frequent by-product of the migration experience. This is an attempt to depathologize the presenting complaint and set it in its larger, overall context. He advises a future orientation and planning as part of any counseling process, especially for those families still stunned and confused by the migratory experience and not yet anchored to their new community.

Sufficiently detailed knowledge about the family's ethnic, cultural, and religious background is the key to effectively assessing the content of the material introduced by family members (Lau, 1986). In the same vein, it is helpful to be aware of the political and economic stresses—both present and historical—experienced by the particular ethnic group of which the client family is a member. Client language skills, years in the United States, age at time of arrival, and immigration and relocation history all need to be evaluated as the counselor attempts to assess family adaptation.

Mobilizing the family to work together on a specific problem, the counselor must take care not to usurp parental authority or, by his or her leadership, cause the parents to lose face in front of their children. Since shame is so much a part of Asian life, the non-Asian counselor must be especially sensitive about not embarrassing family members in front of each other and the counselor. To encourage the open expression of negative feelings by children toward their parents might be viewed as disrespectful, shaming the parents, and is likely in the long run to be countertherapeutic. One tactic recommended by Ho (1987), when there is an impasse between counselor and family or perhaps an impenetrable language barrier, is to enlist the aid of an extended-family member or trusted friend, normally an older male, who might attend family sessions and help negotiate conflict resolution, as between generations.

Counseling is likely to be brief, concrete, highly focused, and directed at achievable goals. Leong (1986) suggests that Asian/Pacific-American clients tend to prefer structured situations and practical, immediate solutions to problems. Because they tend to view counseling as a directive, paternalistic, and authoritarian process, they are likely to expect the counselor, as an experienced person, to provide advice and recommend a specific course of action. Accustomed to medical visits in which symptomatic relief is offered and treatment is short-term, Asian/Pacific families may focus on the improvement of symptoms or problems rather than seek long-term understanding or insight (Chien & Yamamoto, 1982).

Most authorities (Berg & Jaya, 1993; Homma-True, Greene, Lopez, & Trimble, 1993) suggest the counselor be active and offer pragmatic "how-to" suggestions designed more to solve problems than to emphasize feelings or provide insights. Reasonable, practical, result-oriented solutions are more effective than cause-and-effect explanations regarding the origins of the presenting problem. Helping the family achieve a consensus and discover what will help them achieve family harmony is more consistent with Asian/Pacific philosophy than any attempts to place the needs and desires of individuals above family considerations. It is essential that the counselor not attempt to disengage family members from one another, even if in his or her non-Asian view the family lacks clear boundaries. Since the expression of anger and hostility is often discouraged in these families, counselor confrontational techniques are not likely to be effective and will more probably alienate the family.

Asian/Pacific Americans as a group underutilize counseling services (Root, 1989) and, according to Shon and Ja (1982), generally seek psychological help only when all else has failed. Particularly among older or less assimilated people, in addition to the social stigma, there exists a lack of familiarity with Western mental health concepts. Problem solving is supposed to take place at home and within the family context; seeking help from a counselor is often seen as shameful public exposure that the parents have failed the family by not fulfilling what was expected of them. Kitano (1982) suggests that the inability to use community resources may be a symptom of a group that remains apart from the mainstream, and as a consequence is relatively disadvantaged and deprived of what the community has to offer.

# SUMMARY

The United States, increasingly, is a pluralistic society, which represents a gain in diversity and vitality, but also creates the conditions for intergroup misunderstanding and strife. Assimilation, if too rapid, runs the risk of separating people from their ethnic and cultural roots. Counselors need to cultivate sensitivities to various minority families—African Americans, Hispanic Americans, Asian/Pacific Americans serve as examples—in order to broaden their focus and develop an understanding of the sociocultural contexts that influence family behavior. Knowledge of a family's cultural background helps the counselor to differentiate cultural from idiosyncratic family attitudes and behavioral patterns.

African-American families are not a homogeneous group, although color remains the predominant and distinguishing fact of life for most members of the community. Counselors must take into account the realities of African-American life in our society in order to understand the culture developed in response to the prejudice and racial discrimination experienced on an ongoing basis. Economic, social, and political powerlessness characterize the existence of most African Americans; although a middle class has emerged in recent years, the proportion in poverty continues to increase. All classes reflect attitudes that combine residual values from Africa, American mainstream values, and a set of attitudes, values, and behavior that are the result of living as part of a victim system.

African-American family life relies heavily on a kinship network in which boundaries are loose and help and support is exchanged with a large extended family as well as nonblood "relatives." Informal adoptions of children by adult relatives or family friends provide an unofficial social-service network. Females are likely to have more economic opportunities than their male counterparts, whose roles as husbands and father are frequently undermined by a dismal future outlook. Female-led families are common, and divorce rates are high among African-Americans. Skin color further divides the community, with lighter skin often accorded greater status. The church often serves as the epicenter of African-American life. In stressful times, members of this community are more likely to reach out to kinsmen or the church than to counselors, of whom they are suspicious. Effective counseling with African Americans demands an active, positive approach, in which trust is built slowly and the counselor may need to intervene simultaneously on several levels—individual, family, and community—to strengthen the family's problem-solving abilities.

Hispanic Americans too are a heterogeneous population; immigrants from Mexico, Cuba, and Puerto Rico form the largest groups. Language, cultural ties, and ethnicity all play a part in strengthening family bonds and continuing family traditions in each group. Families tend to be patriarchal, with a hierarchical structure in which most overt authority resides with the father. Machismo is highly valued, and males, who typically have more privileges than females, are raised to be strong, courageous, and protective of their mothers and sisters. Respect for parents is considered essential, and open challenge to paternal authority is rare. Extended-family life is usually tightly knit, family membership is a source of pride, and the collective needs of the family are believed to supersede those of individual members. Economic survival often requires reliance on extended family; undocumented aliens largely turn to surrogate family members for direction in the acculturation process. While personal strength may be reinforced by family ties, separation from family may be difficult and family conflict may result from women's resistance to playing out traditional sex-assigned roles.

Many Hispanic-American families find the acculturation process extremely stressful as they attempt to assume American values that, with their emphasis on individualism, may disrupt the close family ties of their cultural heritage. Non-Hispanic counselors need to be especially careful not to impose culturally specific Anglo-American standards on those whose cultural background has led them to live by other standards, unless that adoption has led to problematic behavior. Hispanics tend to underutilize counseling services, often turning to the Catholic church rather than professional counselors, with whom there is likely to be a language barrier as well as fear of a lack of cultural sensitivity. However, traditional Hispanic Americans who do seek counseling are more likely to regard the experience as akin to a medical service and to go as a family rather than individually.

Asian/Pacific Americans encompass immigrants from East Asia (China, Japan), South Asia (India, Pakistan), Southeast Asia (Thailand, Vietnam), and the Pacific Islands (Hawaii, Samoa), and thus are not a homogeneous or monolithic group. Different groups arrived in the United States during different periods over the last century and were greeted with various forms of discrimination, including a series of exclusionary immigration laws. As such restrictions have lifted, and as a result of groups seeking political refuge, the influx has increased in recent years, and many current Asian/Pacific Americans are first-generation immigrants. Physical appearance and language immediately separate Asians from Westerners and may give the erroneous impression that their differences from one another are minimal. In reality, their histories, languages, and social and economic backgrounds are markedly different, and the counselor must take care to understand the specific country of origin and its distinctive features before commencing counseling with an Asian/Pacific-American family. The culturally sensitive counselor needs also to pay attention to whether they are recent arrivals, immigrant-American families (foreign-born parents, American-born children), or descendants of immigrants, since each group is likely to present a unique set of problems.

The family is of prime importance in Asian/Pacific-American families, and family members are required to behave with loyalty and devotion to its values. Role expectations are carefully followed, especially in less acculturated families; even in more assimilated populations, hierarchical and patriarchal patterns are likely to be continued in a somewhat abated fashion. Marriage represents a continuation of the male family line. Filial piety and obeying parents in a deferential manner follow from the dictates of Confucianism. Family obligation, and fear of being shamed and losing face are strong motivational forces. Counseling is more likely to succeed, particularly with less acculturated clients, if the counselor acts confidently and with authority and actively directs the process, mobilizing the family to work together on a problem but taking care not to arouse disrespect within the family or to cause someone to lose face.

# Counseling the Dual-Career Family

Dual-earner families per se are hardly a new phenomenon in the United States; throughout our country's history, many wives have joined their husbands as bread-winners, largely out of economic necessity. Moreover, wives in low-income, immigrant, African-American, and farm families, in particular, have always contributed money, working at home or away, either as supplement to a husband's income or in some cases as sole support for their families (Aldous, 1982).

The dual-earner family is the most common family style in the United States; in families with school-aged children, this has been the case for more than twenty years (Hoffman, 1989). In such a two-wage arrangement, both partners are employed for pay, the wife typically employed because the family needs her income for economic survival or because her paycheck enhances the family's standard of living. Not surprisingly, considering the nurturing role traditionally assigned to women in the family, the wife often finds herself torn between the demands of work and family responsibilities. Hochschild (1989) refers to the woman's day-time paid employment as her *first shift;* she then comes home in the evening to begin her *second shift,* sometimes with little backup from husband and children. Even if her family members do help, which is increasingly the case, she is likely to remain primarily responsible for household-related chores. As Hochschild (1989) suggests, as long as such a second shift is defined as a woman's problem, a covert struggle between husband and wife is inevitable, intimate relations between the two will be strained, and the family system is likely to be in disharmony.

Two-person careers (Papanek, 1974) represent another familiar American phenomenon. Here the wife, often well educated but without employment outside the home, channels her talents and energies into assisting her husband's high-achievement, high-commitment career rather than advancing her own occupational or professional development.[1] She offers primarily emotional and practical support rather than household labor; the breadwinner-male/supportive-homemaker-female role structure goes largely unchallenged by the participants, both of whom appear to benefit from the arrangement. By freeing himself of family-based roles and domestic responsibilities, the man can pursue a productive public career. In this traditional "egalitarian" marriage, benefits also accrue to the domestically based wife. Her measure of success, however, comes from how successful her husband becomes, with the understanding that her help and support in furthering his career, while simultaneously managing family responsibilities and providing for their social lives, plays a key role in his attainments. According to a popular notion, "behind every successful man there is a [perhaps exhausted] woman" or, possibly more accurately, "it takes two people to further one career."

A two-person career is one version of a traditional marriage, usually involving mid-level or upper-level executives, in which the wife is committed to management of the home and family, while at the same time giving both technical and social support to her husband (Bruce & Reed, 1991). Hochschild (1989) suggests that the man in such a situation has *backstage wealth,*[2] as in the case of a high-level executive "with a highly educated, unemployed wife who entertains his clients and runs his household; and a secretary who handles his appointments, makes his travel arrangements, and orders anniversary flowers for his wife" (p. 255).

The link between gender, work, and family did not gain the attention of social scientists until World War II, when married women left home in large numbers to seek employment in offices and factories. Although most women returned to the home at war's end, a sizeable number did not. When it became clear in the postwar period that married women's role in the workplace was not merely a wartime phenomenon, "working wives" became the target of studies investigating the impact of a wife's work on her children and her marriage. Underlying these early studies, as Walker and Wallston (1985) contend, was the assumption that

---

[1]Perhaps the most familiar example in recent years of a wife furthering her husband's high-visibility career while playing a traditional role herself involves former First Lady Barbara Bush. Addressing the 1990 graduating class at Wellesley, made up largely of career-oriented young women, she spoke of the value of putting husband and children first, thus basing her success on her husband's accomplishments.

[2]We are emphasizing a male executive's backstage wealth here, but sometimes, although less frequently, the roles can be reversed: a man might stay at home and help manage his wife's career (movie star, politician), providing support and backup as together they work at advancing her professional achievements.

the family's viability depended on sex-typed divisions of roles, and that therefore women pursuing careers were somehow entering into a deviant lifestyle that could threaten society's well-being.

Initially more the exception than the rule, families in which both parents work outside the home have grown in number enormously within a single generation, to the point where they are now the rule rather than the exception. As noted above, the majority of married women have now joined their husbands in the workforce. According to U.S. Department of Labor (1985) statistics, 64% of married couples with children under 18 both worked outside the home in 1985; half of the women with children under 3 were working mothers (up from one-third a decade earlier). Winfield (1988), a futurist, predicts that nine out of every ten married couples will be part of a dual-earner family by the end of this decade. As Silberstein (1992) observes, this rapidly developing phenomenon offers a window onto the changing landscape of gender roles and relations in contemporary society.

The preceding brief background is important in understanding one of the most dramatic changes in family structure and relationship patterns to have occurred over the last two decades: the emergence of substantial numbers of dual-career families, in which both spouses pursue careers characterized by strong commitment, personal growth, and increasing levels of responsibility (Bruce & Reed, 1991). This relatively new phenomenon, unlike dual-earner marriages or two-person careers, represents a variation of a nuclear family in which both partners simultaneously seek intellectual challenges from careers as well as emotional fulfillment from their family lives.

As Hunt and Hunt (1977) note, the concept of a two-person career emphasizes the necessity of a second person in an emotionally supportive role to make a single career work. The liability carried by dual-careerists, these authors argue, is precisely the lack of such a necessary auxiliary partner. In their view, the greatest challenge of two careers lies not in the required juggling of family and work responsibilities nor in the necessity for a new division of domestic labor between husband and wife, but in the lack of the nonworking wife at home that they *both* require, as a symbol of support and success.

## DUAL-CAREER MARRIAGES: BALANCING WORK AND FAMILY LIFE

At the core of every dual-career marriage, according to Silberstein (1992), there exists an attempt to redefine the relationship between work and family, the two primary spheres of modern life. In a traditional marriage, in which the husband was away at work and the wife cared for the children and took household responsibilities, sex-linked role assignments to single spheres were easily made. Work outside the home was viewed as masculine and the husband was assigned to caring for the family's instrumental needs; caring for the family and its expressive needs were viewed as the wife's responsibilities. Only when women entered the workforce in large numbers, and especially as many pursued careers, did this notion of men and women living in neat gender-determined divisions of work and family get challenged.

In the 1960s, a period of heady optimism concerning the possibility of significant changes in the structure of American life, many women, including those with young children, entered the professional work force. By 1974, according to Klein (1975), close to 5 million women were in career-level positions, a sudden jump of 68% over the previous decade. Close to half were married and residing with their husbands, who themselves were likely to be pursuing careers.

By the mid-1980s—a time of swollen university enrollments with women pursuing career-oriented goals, greater career opportunities for women, two-career couples living together outside of marriage, and greater public acceptance of the two-career phenomenon—there were probably 5 million dual-career families (Goldenberg & Goldenberg, 1984). Bruce and Reed (1991) suggest that this category now includes over 20% of all working couples.

Gilbert (1985, 1988) describes the changing attitudes and expectations of women in dual-career relationships over the past three decades. According to her studies, women of the 1960s, encouraged by the growing women's movement, could be characterized as willing to continue traditional household and child-care responsibilities while adding the opportunity to have a career. As Hunt and Hunt (1982) point out in describing this earlier period, the work world largely excluded women but had special rules for those allowed to enter. Those rules permitted men in dual-career marriages to continue to lead lives similar to those of other career men, while women in dual-career marriages were expected to engage in a balancing act that allowed a measure of career involvement as long as it did not inconvenience the family.

Women in the 1980s, according to Gilbert (1985), made a more conscious effort to share both home and work roles with their spouses. However, it is still true that, although both careerists may declare a willingness to share power and domestic responsibilities and to support their partner's career aspirations, in practice their efforts may frequently fall short of the mark. While progress has been made in reaching egalitarian goals, women in general still are likely to assume a larger proportion of child and household responsibilities than their husbands, to defer career aspirations in favor of their mate's career advancement, and to cut back career activities during critical periods of family development (Farber, 1988).

Some of the attraction of pursuing a career while simultaneously maintaining a family has been replaced, for many women in the 1990s, by a greater awareness of problems stemming from the changing family lifestyle. Counselors can expect to see many dual-career couples seeking help with work-overload problems, gender-role conflicts, struggles over power and dependency, conflicts over achievement and competition, patterns of role sharing, and relationship difficulties. Achieving a workable balance—a more or less smoothly functioning interpersonal system in which each partner maintains a sense of independence, uniqueness, and wholeness, all within the context and security of the spousal relationship—is never an easy task for any couple. As Goldenberg (1986) observes, the task is made all the more difficult for contemporary dual-career couples by the lack of prior role models from which to draw support. He argues that significant changes in the role structure between men and women are required to make a dual-career marriage work, and very few road maps for this journey presently exist.

## CONCEPTUALIZING THE DUAL-CAREER LIFESTYLE

In a dual-career family, according to Rapoport and Rapoport (1969), who are generally credited with coining the term and are themselves a two-career couple, both the husband and the wife pursue active professional careers as well as active, involved family lives. By the term *career* these authors mean rather precisely, "those types of job sequences that require a high degree of commitment and that have a continuous developmental character" (Rapoport & Rapoport, 1976, p. 9).

Obviously, many noncareer jobs may be performed with considerable commitment, although they may bring little personal development or advancement in status or salary. These authors argue that careers typically have an intrinsically demanding character. They are likely to require educational preparation and related professional work experience. Gilbert (1985) emphasizes continuous full-time commitment by both partners in her definition of a dual-career family as "a variation of the nuclear family in which both spouses pursue an uninterrupted lifelong career and also establish and develop a family life that often includes children" (p. 6). A less strict and probably more realistic definition is offered by a number of authors, including Shaevitz and Shaevitz (1980), who regard couples as dual-careerists when both spouses have made a "significant commitment full or part time to a role outside of the home" (p. 12).

Unlike partners in a two-person career, one of whom (in most cases, the wife) derives vicarious pleasure, achievement, and status from helping the other advance in a career, dual-careerists each pursue separate and distinct work roles, presumably offering support and encouragement to the career aspirations of the other. Ideally, the wife's career, no less than her husband's, is an integral part of her identity, representing a professional commitment that is more than a way to supplement the family income. Greater intellectual companionship, more adult contacts, increased financial freedom, added stimulation, more opportunity for self-expression, sharing of the provider role, an expanded sense of personal fulfillment, escape from household drudgery, and a possible closer relationship between father and children as a result of his greater participation in their upbringing are claimed as the potential benefits. The potential danger is in romantically overlooking the numerous sources of stress, and naively assuming that dual-career families have the best of it all: plenty of money, fulfilling family relationships, satisfying careers, an exciting and filled-to-the-brim lifestyle. To imagine typical dual-career marriages to be composed of the brilliant but sensitive nuclear-physicist husband who enjoys changing diapers and the hot-shot female lawyer balancing a briefcase on her knees while nursing a newborn child is to engage in fantasy that often bears little resemblance to real life.

In reality, making a two-career marriage work requires the ability to challenge traditional views about the rights and roles of men and women in our society. Tension often results as each spouse attempts to transcend earlier social conditioning in order to take on tasks ordinarily associated with the opposite sex. As Silberstein (1992) points out, the tension is caused not simply by performing out-of-role behavior, but also by not performing in-role behavior (for example, a mother not getting a chance to stay home for very long to nurture her infant). Successful adaptation to a dual-career lifestyle involves changing gender-role expectations, and inevitably changes the system context and subsequent lives of men as much as the more obvious change it brings to women.

## PROFESSIONAL WOMEN IN DUAL-CAREER MARRIAGES

Not all dual-career couples are the same. Each maintains a relationship that is constantly in flux, evolving over time as careers develop and diminish, children grow and leave home, and marital compatibilities wax and wane. Some start out together at college, preparing for careers that they then both pursue in an uninterrupted fashion. Some prepare together, but the woman stops to raise a family while her husband continues his career. In the past especially, some women did not think of careers until later in life, perhaps when their children were grown or they had gotten divorced or been widowed. One partner in a couple (most likely the woman) may work part-time at a career throughout the childrearing years. The point is that no "one-size-fits-all" pattern exists, especially for women. Nor are all professionals, men or women, equally committed to their careers or equally involved with their families.

In a longitudinal study carried out over an eight-year period, Poloma, Pendleton, and Garland (1981) examined the consequences for a group of married professional women of having a dual-career marriage. In particular, they were interested in the relationship between careers and stages in the family's life cycle. What effect does marriage and motherhood have on career development? How well are professional women able to coordinate their careers with those of their husbands? In the vast majority of cases, these researchers found that women who had children limited their career involvement, turning down promotions with increased responsibilities and opting for part-time employment instead of full-time work, and also foregoing geographic mobility.

For example, a female professor might turn down an opportunity for an administrative promotion (a demanding 11-month job) in favor of a more flexible teaching assignment geared to the normal academic year (hers and her children's). A woman physician choosing between work and family responsibilities might decide to work half-time. A woman attorney with a bright future in a prestigious law firm might find it necessary to relocate to another city in order to enhance her husband's career opportunities. In each case, career development is curtailed and possible marital and family tensions heightened. Most couples in Poloma, Pendleton, and Garland's (1981) sample chose to combine a career with childrearing; inevitably, this was associated with some reduction of career involvement, depending on age, stamina, and childrearing philosophy.

These researchers were able to differentiate four major career types among professional women. The first, pursuing what is termed a *regular career*, begins her career before marriage, right out of college or shortly thereafter, and may continue in her work with minimal interruption, possibly stopping for brief periods to bear children or to engage in part-time employment during early childrearing years. While this career pattern resembles men's in the same profession, being a mother as well as a professional has its costs, especially when the children are younger (for example, allowing less evening work, less travel).

A woman's *interrupted career* begins as a regular career but is halted, possibly for several years, so she can be with her children; eventually, she resumes professional work. In this case, professional growth or opportunities for promotion may be reduced. On the other hand, there may well be a gain for some women who look forward to taking such a sabbatical from their careers. A brief hiatus after early career demands may be most welcome, although there is a risk of resentment from a husband not customarily granted such an opportunity for an interrupted career.

The woman with a *second career* usually receives her professional training near the time her children are grown or after they leave. Thus, the heaviest demands of early childbearing years are behind her before she embarks on professional training and a future career. Although she gets off to a late start and is likely to be behind age cohorts in income and status for a long time, in most cases she ultimately pursues a career pattern much like regular female careerists.

A *modified second career* begins earlier: the woman obtains training and subsequent career development after the last child is deemed no longer in need of full-time mothering (perhaps when entering kindergarten). Family demands are still present, so this woman may begin her career slowly, increasing the momentum of her work involvement step by step as her child-care responsibilities lessen over the years. Like the regular careerist, but with her childbearing years behind her, she may seek full-time or part-time work, but may need to be available for family demands for a period of time.

These patterns indicate that, even with help from their husbands or live-in housekeepers, married career women with children have serious difficulty in following career paths like those of their male counterparts. Attempting to combine career and family is possible, of course, but it is a pressure-prone situation that frequently leads to conflicts over the multiple and sometimes conflicting demands.

A number of innovative family-friendly employment procedures for balancing work and family responsibilities have recently been introduced, largely in recognition of the considerable proportion of women of childbearing age in today's workforce (Hudson Institute, 1988). In addition to family-leave benefits offered to men as well as women, affordable on-site child day care at places of employment may relieve some dual careerists (as well as single parents and other dual-earner couples) of the never-ending search for reliable care for their children while they are at their job.

Beyond that, flexible working arrangements may often be adopted, making use of flexitime (adjusting the times at which the work day begins and ends, as well as the number of work days per week; for example, a working week may consist of four 10-hour days), flexiplace (working out of one's home and communicating with the office by telephone or computer), and job sharing (two part-time employees fulfilling the duties ordinarily performed by a single employee). These options are often seen by women careerists as preferable to part-time professional work, in which there usually are few opportunities for advancement. Bruce and Reed (1991) view flexible work arrangements, leave policies, and child day care as effective strategies for retaining qualified employees.

## CHANGING DOMESTIC ROLE PATTERNS

Flexibility in defining and learning new roles and in accommodating family-rule changes are essential elements in making a two-career relationship work. Establishing a new division of labor based on available time, interest, and skills is necessary if the couple is to avoid **role overload**, a frequent complaint of couples seriously trying to meet all work and family demands. Basic child care, meal preparation and cleanup, shopping, laundry, doctors' appointments, bill paying, monitoring children's homework and attending school conferences, directing baby-sitters and housekeepers, arranging for maintenance of cars and household appliances, indoor and outdoor cleaning, travel planning, pet care, maintaining social relationships, staying home with a sick child—these are just some of the tasks every couple must deal with that can become especially taxing when the couple is already overcommitted.

As we indicated earlier, most of these responsibilities ordinarily are handled by a wife at home, a key player lacking in a dual-career family. In the past, for the small number of women working away from home, relatively inexpensive and reliable female domestic help or cheap baby-sitting was available to help ease some of the burden but, as more women enter the workplace, fewer of them are willing to work at the low salaries these jobs command. Nor are female relatives (mothers, grandmothers, sisters) as likely to be at home or nearby as in the past. To pay for child care means the couple must work harder or more hours, increasing fatigue and reducing family time together.

What impact has the entry of women into employment had on their husbands' participation in household chores and child care? Hoffman (1989) suggests a modest increase, particularly if the mother is employed full time, there is more than one child, and there are no older children, especially daughters, at home. According to Walker and Wallston's (1985) survey, with some exceptions a non-egalitarian division of labor at home still tends to exist for families of professional women. However, husbands of employed wives take on more family responsibilities than do husbands whose wives are not employed. Rapoport and Rapoport (1982) suggest that, despite progress toward greater equity, the prevailing assumption remains that the major responsibility for domestic work resides with women, even though their husbands might be willing to help. Aldous (1981) contends that one reason for the imbalance in child care between mothers and fathers may be that some women are loath to part with such responsibilities, often feeling guilt over time away from their children.

How much change has occurred in dividing responsibilities for household tasks in recent years, as two-career families have become more commonplace? Using data from two national studies concerned with how husbands and wives allocate time to household responsibilities, Pleck (1985) has determined that the nature of employed wives' overload and husbands' response to their wives' employment are both changing. Although such overload for women still exists, it is declining as "men's time in the family is increasing while women's is decreasing" (p. 146). Moreover, according to this research, not only have husbands with employed wives increased their domestic involvements (child care, housework), but so have husbands whose wives do not work outside the home. Overall, Pleck concludes, a value shift in our society is occurring—no doubt stimulated in part by the surge of married women into the labor market—toward greater family involvement by husbands as well as a greater sharing of breadwinner responsibilities.

According to Gilbert's (1985) research, husbands who perceive their wives as highly committed to careers are especially likely to participate in domestic work. She found dual-career husbands more willing to take on child-care tasks than to do housework; indeed, her results indicate that one of the motivations of men who choose dual-career lifestyles is the desire to nurture their children. However, household tasks are likely to be divided in a sex-stereotypic manner. Gilbert (1988) suggests that, when a husband contributes to domestic work, it is often with the understanding that he is operating in female territory and he is apt to undertake the task jointly with another family member. Hochschild (1989) indicates that, while men may choose household tasks they like to do, women are far more apt to attend to tasks that need to be done.

Silberstein's (1992) more recent survey concludes that the arrival of children often propels dual-career couples into more egalitarian role sharing. Her data reveal that the contributions of both parents were approximately equal on certain school-related tasks and some household chores. Nevertheless, women still tend to shoulder more of the responsibility for meal-related tasks (planning meals, grocery shopping, cooking dinner) and child-care tasks (getting children ready for bed, taking children to appointments, staying home with a sick child), while men take primary responsibility for traditional male tasks such as arranging car repairs, lawn and garden maintenance, and doing home repairs. She found that resistance to household chores on the part of men stems partly from the fact that these are by and large undesirable duties. While women also may find them uninviting, they are more likely to have been socialized to believe such chores are an inevitable part of adult life and, whether they work outside the home or not, they anticipate responsibilities inside the home. According to Silberstein's respondents, men's early experiences, which are deeply socialized and often resistant to change, lead them to assume that these tasks will be done for them.

Despite these gender-role socialization experiences, Silberstein found that times are indeed changing: approximately one-third of the 20 dual-career couples in her study (ages 32–42) were engaged in a significant attempt to recalibrate their work and family assignments. Succeeding generations, growing up in families with two working parents, are likely to go beyond this group (just as this group has gone beyond its parents) and to achieve even greater equity in the division of labor.

# SOURCES OF STRESS IN DUAL-CAREER LIFESTYLES

Beyond changes in the division of labor, often calling for significant role restructuring within the family, all two-career couples must deal with a number of other issues that are potential sources of interpersonal conflict and family tension. Shaevitz and Shaevitz (1980) enumerate the following as a minimum list of such problems to be addressed:

How will household tasks be assigned?

Who will do what and according to whose standards?

Should they have children? How many? Who will be responsible for their care? Who will be available in emergencies? Are child-care facilities available?

Who controls the money? Separate or joint accounts? What are the rights of each in spending the money?

How do they deal with job relocations? Is one partner's commuting to and from another city a realistic solution?

What if one partner is significantly more successful in her or his career than the other?

How can they learn to recognize and deal with overload or burnout? What special things must they do, as a dual-career couple, to enhance their relationship?

Frequently, the counselor's first task is to help two-career couples distinguish which of their problems are caused by the makeup of their specific marital relationship and which are problems inherent in a dual-career lifestyle. The issue is complex and the two are clearly interrelated. Box 9.1 offers the counselor a list of strains that may result from the dual-career lifestyle. Role overload, as we have noted, is a common complaint of dual-careerists, who assume responsibilities for multiple roles while lamenting the fatigue, the limited leisure time, and the drained energies caused by their chosen lifestyle. This is particularly true of those super-achievers, men or women, who insist on having it all—successful careers, fulfilling marriages, prize-winning children, glorious vacations, and complex social lives.

Women, however, are more likely to experience role strain as they attempt to add career roles to their traditional gender-related roles. Who is more willing to stay home with a sick child, the mother or father? Which of the parents should defer the day's work plans to stay home if no trusted outside support (a housekeeper, a grandmother) is available? Most likely it is the woman—perhaps feeling guilty over failing to fulfill her traditional task with children, or perhaps unable

---

**Box 9.1   A Problem-Appraisal Checklist for Dual-Career Couples**

Dual-career couples may experience problems in the following areas:

- Role overload
- Career demands vs. personal and family demands
- Competition between spouses
- Achieving equity in their relationship
- Division of labor
- Job-related geographic mobility
- Child-care arrangements
- Time allocation
- Establishing social networks
- Maintaining a personal identity

---

to mobilize her husband, who has not been socialized to give child care his highest priority, and so feels less guilty. Her conflict, as a result of loyalties to work and family both, may lead to considerable strain and resentment toward her spouse and children. Or, in some cases, she may try to deny the feeling of resentment at being primarily responsible for certain family activities. In such instances, some more traditional women may berate themselves that a good mother should be able to do whatever her family requires without complaining. Even those women less invested in motherhood may withhold any complaints, fearing that their husbands may suggest that, if it is too difficult for them, then perhaps they should consider less involvement in their careers.

It has been common (far more in the past than among younger dual-careerists) for a woman to deal with the conflict between career demands and family needs by adjusting the former to accommodate the latter. As we noted in an earlier section, she was likely to interrupt a career to have children, work part-time while her children were young, or perhaps even delay starting a career until her children were self-sufficient or fully grown. She and her husband may have chosen not to have children or to have put off their arrival. If they opted for children, the couple might have arranged to work at different hours, so as to take turns with child-care responsibilities (although seeing each other only in passing was hardly conducive to a fulfilling relationship). While these options remain, priorities have shifted for many dual-careerists. In the past, the decision as to who must make the accommodation was simple: probably the man's career took precedence; he was almost certainly the major breadwinner, and accustomed to making fewer adjustments to family needs than his wife. Today, the solution is not always so cut and dried, and a number of factors beyond gender and economic gain (personal gratification, potential for the future, the other person's turn to develop a career) may prevail.

In the following case, both partners begin their relationship with high degrees of career involvement, but the situation changes:

❈  ❈  ❈  ❈  ❈

Tony and Abby had each been married before when they met at a business conference. Tony, 45, had divorced four years earlier, having been married for 20
years to Florence, a homemaker. Their marriage had been unhappy for many years
and, although both had agreed to stay together for the sake of the children, they
had found it increasingly difficult to stick to their plan, and they had divorced
as soon as their three children (Ben, 19; Howard, 18; Gillian, 16) were well into
adolescence. Tony, a successful executive, had agreed to a generous alimony and
child-support settlement. After the "miserable" marriage and "painful" divorce,
Tony had vowed not to remarry.

Abby, on the other hand, had been married three times, briefly each time, and
at age 36 believed she did not want children and thus would have no reason to
marry again. Because she was quite self-sufficient financially, as vice-president
in charge of labor negotiations for a large firm, she had not sought nor did she
receive any alimony from any of her failed marriages.

When they met, Tony was immediately smitten by Abby's intelligence and
vivaciousness. She was extremely attractive, he thought, and her independent
and nonclinging behavior was a welcomed relief from Florence's overdependency.
He respected her as an ambitious career woman, earning an impressive salary
and eager to advance in her company. She too appreciated his no-strings-attached
attitude, and together they enjoyed travel, going to the theater, and socializing
with friends. Except for the irritation of paying large amounts of money to his
ex-wife, Tony was content, and Abby had never been happier.

After living together for three years without being married, the two needed
to make a serious decision when Abby discovered she was pregnant. She now
had a change of heart and wanted to marry and have the baby. At 39, this was
probably her last possible pregnancy, and she felt for the first time that a child
of hers would have a father she respected. Tony was conflicted about the idea
of marrying and especially of becoming a father again. He remembered well the
demands of an infant and felt he was getting too old to deal with them comfort-
ably. He felt too that he deserved to have some free time with his wife, after the
heavy demands of their two careers, and the infant would interfere with that.
Wanting to please Abby, he acquiesced on the condition that Abby take major
responsibility for raising the child. He insisted that they hire a housekeeper to
look after their child, so that their lives would be interrupted only minimally and
they could enjoy their pleasurable life as before.

Tony and Abby married, and Abby continued to work while pregnant. However,
toward the end of her pregnancy, her firm decided to cut back on personnel in
her department, and she took that opportunity to resign but continue working
for them as an independent consultant from her home. In addition to enabling
her to work convenient hours, this seemed like a good opportunity to build a
labor consulting business of her own at home while raising their child. The
housekeeper she hired was helpful in freeing her from many domestic chores.

Unfortunately, soon after their son Donny was born, Abby's contract with the firm expired and she had trouble getting more accounts. With their combined income now seriously reduced, she fired the housekeeper and, while she enjoyed being with her child all day, the drop in income was troublesome to both Tony and Abby.

Abby now began to resent quite intensively the alimony and child-support money they were sending to Florence and her children each month. Tony too was becoming more and more annoyed at Abby's loss of income, and especially with her requests that he do more with their child in the evenings and on weekends. Their relationship began to deteriorate, with a great deal of acrimony and blaming.

Abby complained that he indulged his children from his previous marriage with money: he was helping with college tuition and extra spending money. She thought this financial arrangement was unfair to her and would have to stop; the children should get part-time jobs. He demanded she become more frugal, and began to control her expenditures. She claimed to have fired the housekeeper in an economy move, but kept secret from him her hiring of a cleaning woman on a once-per-week basis. When he asked her to get a baby-sitter and join him and his business associates for dinner at a gourmet restaurant one evening, she agreed but showed up with her year-old son. The event turned out to be miserable for all concerned, and Abby swore she would not go out with him under those circumstances again.

When they contacted a counselor, it was readily apparent that both were misusing money to fight with each other. Each spouse was bitter and felt betrayed. The counselor chose not to deal with specific issues at first, but instead to focus on the inappropriateness of maintaining their premarital agreement on the kind of life they were to live, and to reopen negotiations about a new arrangement. Abby, in particular, no longer believed in what she had agreed to before Donny was born, namely that she could handle matters at home, continue working, and not bother Tony with the day-to-day operations of the home. Tony remained angry at her because he believed she had reneged on her earlier promises in an unfair and uncaring way. Slowly they began to renegotiate a new contract based on a more realistic appraisal of their current situation and what each wanted from the relationship.

During counseling, Abby decided to return to full-time work, leaving their son, now 2, with an older neighborhood woman with whom she felt comfortable. The housekeeper had never been her idea, and the baby-sitter provided a more home-like atmosphere. Tony was persuaded to become more involved with Donny, who now was more responsive to his dad. The couple was encouraged by the counselor to return to many of the things they had enjoyed before, with recognition that the circumstances of having a child required some modification of earlier patterns. The parents began to take brief weekend vacations alone, leaving Donny with the baby-sitter, to whom he was now attached. Tony reported before counseling terminated that Abby had once again become more attractive to him, and that he was enjoying parenting for the first time in his life. Abby stated that being a successful working woman and a good mother did wonders for her self-esteem. She no longer felt she needed to placate her husband by being "supermom," able single-handedly to care for job, husband, and child without missing a step or experiencing exhaustion and occasional despondency. She remained an independent individual, which he admired, and he was the strong, consistent family man she had hoped for when she first learned she was pregnant.

❋    ❋    ❋    ❋    ❋

Redistributing household and child-care responsibilities and renegotiating an outdated contract were key elements in making this marital system functional once again. However, successful counseling came about not so much from helping the couple achieve complete equality—an equal division of roles and work opportunities—but rather from accomplishing greater equity through a fairer and more flexible distribution of roles. The goal here is for each partner to experience, over time and across situations, a sense of fairness, trusting that the opportunities and constraints of each partner's role will balance out. In our example, Abby felt better when she believed that her needs were being heard and that she had some choices in the roles she chose to play. Even if a major portion of the responsibility for caring for her son fell on her, for example, she came to feel her husband recognized her contribution, did what he could to help, and took greater responsibility in other areas, such as earning a living. Tony felt less exploited in his temporary role as sole breadwinner when he understood Abby's conflict between career and family demands. He also came to realize that she was committed to a career and not planning to become a dependent individual like his first wife. Having resolved her dilemma over satisfactory child care, which was central to her sense of being a good mother, Abby no longer viewed the work role as incompatible with her maternal role and was able to return to work. Together, they had achieved a greater sense of equity.

Money was an important issue with Abby and Tony, as it is with all dual-career couples. The ability to earn money represents power, and any change in the amount contributed to the family changes both the power balance and, inevitably, the family's well-being. Money going outside the family to ex-wives, children, or even old debts[3] creates stress, especially if it has not been discussed or agreed upon beforehand. A change in status (power) from a self-supporting woman to a lower-paid part-time worker often damages a woman's sense of confidence, since she is no longer contributing her share, and the change unbalances the family system. Similarly, a man experiencing economic problems at work also suffers a loss of self-esteem. The counselor must address these money issues with couples

[3]Dual-career couples frequently enter marriage after long periods of schooling, and one or both often bring college loans and other debts into the new marriage. Much of the early stress may revolve around paying off such debts and striving to catch up with their peer group (buying furniture, a house, a car) after having delayed gratification for many years.

rather specifically, even if such topics often are taboo in social situations. Female counselors, because of early socialization, may collude with the wife not to bring up money and embarrass the husband, and thus may miss dealing with an important manifestation of the central power issue in any relationship.

The decision to have children is a key one for working parents. The birth of a child puts a strain on any marriage, as the dyadic family system changes to a far more intricate triadic form. Husband-wife relationships inevitably change as new forces operate within the system. In the case of dual-careerists, the presence of children further complicates their lives, especially if both are heavily committed to career development and advancement. Time allocations must be restructured, less leisure time is available, professional and domestic responsibilities need to be renegotiated. Juggling work and child care is rarely easy, and feelings of guilt and/or resentment are often the result. Some parents worry that being a good parent and being in a career are incompatible, and that choosing the career may have a serious negative effect on the child's well-being. Other parents feel guilty over their resentment that the child has somehow infringed on their time, career, or marital relationship. In many cases, unable or unwilling to deal with the causes of the increased pressures, they search for scapegoats to blame: overcommitment to friends and work or too much time spent with relatives (including, in the case of remarrieds, time spent with children from the previous marriage).

Working parents inevitably worry about whether they are providing proper parenting. Quality day care for youngsters is essential if parental anxieties are to be kept in check. In the absence of high-quality organized workplace facilities—still relatively rare, although improving as employers recognize the need for a stable work force—grandparents, trusted and dependable baby-sitters, and part-time or at-home work by one parent may fill the need. Each of these makeshift solutions carries positive and negative consequences. Parents who take turns in shifts caring for their children at home manage to provide them with at least one parent at home at all times, a definite plus, but often do so at the expense of feeling exhausted and of minimizing adult time together for the sake of the children, a negative result. By doing so, too, they deny the children the opportunity to experience parental interaction and interaction of the family unit as a whole.

Bringing children to a day class provides the stimulation of other children, a plus for the child, but often involves complicated pickup and drop-off arrangements, to say nothing of having to keep a sick child at home, for which stress-inducing last-minute adult plans must be made. Day classes also rob the child of a needed chance to be alone for periods of time. Hiring a full-time housekeeper can be more convenient and less disruptive, but it adds another person to the family system, changing possible alliances and coalitions. Grandparents, especially grandmothers, may help out, but their input regarding child care may introduce conflict; adults who relinquish a parental role to their own parent may feel reduced to children themselves. Besides, many grandparents themselves are now part of the nonchild workplace.

Some child-care plans (for example, driving children to and from schools in a car pool with other parents) are usually easily worked out, although parents may run up against scheduling problems with other parents or, worse, people with whom it is difficult to be compatible. Nevertheless, barring unforeseen emergencies, which may require cutting into work responsibilities, such joint efforts are relatively anxiety-free for most working parents. Caring for a sick child, on the other hand, is a far more difficult matter to resolve. Men in general are more willing to pick up and deliver than to stay home and minister to the sick. On the other hand, serving only as a backup parent for emergencies or routine activities (for example, chauffeuring children) may not feel right for some men, who may wish to be more central to their child's daily emotional life. This is especially so if their wives get to do the satisfying, fun things (for example, going to the school play, attending "Mommy and Me" classes). Since many of these trade-offs are typically made covertly, the counselor may need to bring the issue of gender and responsibility into the open for joint discussion and resolution.

Dual-career couples must be helped to work out an emergency backup system, a secondary group of caregivers who can be turned to when extraordinary events (a sick child, a school holiday) require a change of plans. Without such a secondary support system, stress on one or both dual-careerists is inevitable, and a frequent result is conflict and competition over whose work plans are more important and thus less subject to interruption.

Finally, one barrier to intimacy and marital harmony comes from feelings of competition between two high-achieving and ambitious people who happen to be married to each other (Vannoy-Hiller & Philliber, 1989). This is especially the case if one or both feel insecure or anxious or frustrated in their careers. Even if they deny the feeling, insisting they are completely supportive of each other's career, some competition may lurk below the surface and intrude on the relationship. Especially if the two are in the same field or at the same career stage—or, worse yet, both—comparisons of success and recognition are inevitable. While the competition need not be fierce, the counselor will need to explore its presence with the couple, attending specifically to when and under what circumstances it occurs. Even when couples generally are supportive of each other's professional strivings, feelings of competition may be exacerbated by scarcity (for example, when both spouses, just out of graduate school, apply for the same job opening). Competition over who earns more (presumably a measure of who is more successful) is ever-present; men in general still feel their salary should exceed their spouse's (which in most cases it does). Dual-career couples need to accept that competitive feelings are a normal part of being high-achieving people and are not necessarily destructive. Counselors might encourage each partner to voice, and thus help exorcise, any lingering guilt that might surround normal feelings of competition.

Whatever the sources of stress, the goal of equity based on mutual trust represents the ideal, if not the most easily achieved, solution for dual-career partners. As Hall and Hall (1979) point out, "One of the factors that strengthens a relationship is the feeling of equity for both parties—the feeling that each partner is benefitting from the relationship as much as he or she is contributing to it" (p. 154). The couple must bear in mind that equity is not achieved through a perfect 50/50 split in responsibility—never a real possibility—but rather is attainable only through a sense that both partners are striving toward a common goal, not reachable at the expense of either one.

## COMMUTER MARRIAGES

For most people in North America, intact marriages are assumed to involve two spouses sharing a single residence. In the past, when the man was offered a job opportunity in another city, his wife and children followed him, thus maintaining the intact household. Many two-career couples also follow the man's relocation, frequently because his work usually commands a higher salary. Yet, with the growth in the number of dual-career families today, it should not be surprising that an attractive career opportunity in another locale may lead one person to move away from his or her spouse and children temporarily, without altering or upsetting the family's location. Known as **commuter marriages**, such arrangements entail the maintenance of separate residences by spouses who may live apart and independently for periods ranging from several days per week to months at a time (Gerstel & Gross, 1984).

Needless to say, such an arrangement contains many built-in sources of stress, as couples strive to adjust to feelings of loneliness or mistrust, and learn to maintain intimacy and emotional continuity on a long-distance basis. Couples who have a stronger and more established relationship, are older, and are free from childrearing responsibilities are usually in the best position to deal with the tensions of the commuter lifestyle. According to Gerstel and Gross (1984), the couple tends to fare better when at least one spouse's career is well established than when both partners at the same time must contend with the demands and uncertainties of new professional and marital identities. Older couples have a backlog of experiences together to better cushion the impact of separation; in some cases, where a husband's career has had priority in the past, both spouses accept the fact that it is now only fair and equitable that the wife have her turn.

Commuters—sometimes dubbed married singles—live apart precisely because each simultaneously wants to pursue a career, not because one or the other has an occupation that requires living separately for periods of time. (Examples of the latter include merchant marines, professional athletes, politicians, and entertainers.) Nor are they likely to commute for reasons of financial gain alone. While two active professional careers may yield high family income, that income often fails to compensate for the additional expense of maintaining two residences, travel, and telephone bills. Most often, commuter couples are people intensely committed to their careers, who at the same time value their marriage enough to be willing to put up with the hardship, cost, and effort involved in trying to make it all work.

While some couples manage to stay together precisely because they only see one another from time to time, most dual-career commuters are committed to their family and wish to keep their marriage strong. Both spouses are, at the same time, strongly committed to their professional identification. Most couples view the separation as a forced choice that benefits their sense of personal autonomy and work achievement, but at the same time generates new tensions in the marital relationship (Walker & Wallston, 1985).

Most married commuters struggle to balance the tangible rewards of professional advancement—money, recognition, status—against the more intangible rewards of a continuing personal connection with spouse and children. Rather than requiring one partner to make a career sacrifice for the other, young professionals in particular may opt for a more equitable solution in which both are willing to give up time together now for the excitement and challenge of advancing their long-range individual careers (Winfield, 1985). While a commuter arrangement could loosen the marital bond, it might also have benefits for the commuter. He or she may welcome the freedom from family pressures and daily constraints—from having to accommodate to another's mealtime or bedtime patterns or from being interrupted by child-care responsibilities. Kirschner and Wallum (1978) go so far as to suggest that the commuter may actually intensify his or her dedication to career, perhaps to justify having chosen such an unorthodox living arrangement.

The resolution of issues involving job mobility is essential for many of today's young married couples. An attractive career opportunity, a chance for advancement but in another town, or perhaps offers to both spouses from different locales are common dilemmas in which difficult choices must be made. In some cases, a transfer within an organization for one leads to a predicament for others in the family, as they attempt to determine the wisdom of the other spouse's giving up a satisfying job, the children's changing schools in mid-year, selling the house, and uprooting everyone. Whose job is more important? Is disrupting a partner's promising career too much to ask for the sake of living together seven days a week? What stresses are really involved in relocating the family? What about living apart? For how long? How often and under what circumstances will they reunite? Can the marriage sustain the strain? What about the effect on the children? How will the family's customary way of functioning change to adjust to the missing person?

In the following case, two young high-achievers, recently married and with a 2-year-old daughter, opt for living apart temporarily as the best solution in a tight job market:

❈    ❈    ❈    ❈    ❈

Stacy and John met and married while both were attending graduate school. Both ambitious for careers, they loved the academic life and were certain that as professors they could have it all—intellectual stimulation, a social network of interesting friends, time off for travel, prestigious jobs, periodic sabbatical leaves, and enough income to lead a comfortable life. Both also wanted what a family life would provide, and in her last year at the university Stacy got pregnant, as planned, gave birth to Robin, their daughter, during summer break, and without missing any school time received her Ph.D. in Greek literature on schedule. John, however, seemed to be less well organized and became bogged down in his dissertation in psychology during his fourth year in graduate school. As a result, he found himself needing to return to the university for at least an additional year when she was ready to look for a university teaching job.

Finding a job proved to be more of a hurdle than Stacy had imagined. Only a handful of universities offered courses she was prepared to teach and, at those schools, teacher turnover was slow and job openings rare. After sending her resume to 150 colleges and universities, she discovered only 2 had openings, and there were eight applicants for each. Fortunately, her outstanding school performance, plus strong letters of recommendation from her major advisor, helped her land a two-year contract at one of these schools, a small university 600 miles away.

The job offer stirred up much soul searching in both Stacy and John. Should she take the one offer she had received or wait until a better one opened up later, perhaps next year, when, presumably, John would also enter the job market? What would she do in the meantime? What were the chances they could ever teach at the same or nearby schools? If she took the job, how often would they see one another? What about Robin?

These and other questions and uncertainties led them to make an appointment with a counselor at the university's student-health center. Both appeared very upset by the pending decision, blaming themselves for not having been realistic about poor job opportunities for Stacy when they planned their academic lives together. John also blamed his dissertation chairman for throwing what John considered to be needless roadblocks in his way, delaying progress in completing his study and thus not allowing him to follow Stacy. He admitted to feeling competitive with Stacy for the first time, envying the apparent ease with which she had completed her graduate work in four years. Stacy too admitted impatience with John's progress, criticizing him for taking on an impossible dissertation topic, choosing the wrong chairman, and in general not moving fast enough. Stacy talked of becoming a housewife and forgetting any academic aspirations, although she soon realized that such an act would be motivated by utter frustration and would ultimately be self-destructive. There was also the issue of money to be considered.

With the counselor's help over several sessions, they decided that Stacy would take the teaching post and that she would take Robin with her. Perhaps with fewer distractions at home, John could devote full time to finishing his dissertation and joining her. They believed their marriage could stand the necessary strain; in any case, they had few choices and it would only be for a short period. They agreed to talk to each other at least five nights per week—after 11 P.M. to keep telephone costs at a minimum—and to plan reunions every two months.

Not surprisingly, the separation turned out to be more painful than either had thought. Both became lonely and depressed. In particular, they reported missing the small things that as a loving couple they had taken for granted—the daily exchange of small talk and gossip about school, the shared mealtimes when the three of them were alone together, even studying in silence next to one another in their bedroom. They missed their sexual intimacy, touching one another, being tender. John missed seeing Robin grow up.

Stacy did enjoy her students and colleagues and had begun to make friends. She found a female undergraduate student to help baby-sit when necessary in the evenings, and a good day-care center near the university where she could leave Robin during the day. John did less well, gaining a great deal of weight, neglecting his household chores, too distracted to devote his limited energies to completing his dissertation. When they spoke on the phone, they frequently bickered, each feeling cheated by the separation. Their calls became less frequent, as each began to spend more (nonsexual) time with friends. When they did meet, usually at some halfway point, for the weekend, there was initial tension, and they invariably had a fight. Perhaps they expected too much or wanted to crowd too much into their brief reunion, but the feeling of awkwardness and discomfort with one another never left them.

Six months after their separation, John contacted the counselor once again for individual help. He expressed a deep longing to be with his wife and child, indicating he could not go on this way much longer. Continuing his systems view, although working with one member only, the counselor focused on what John felt was happening to his family. Reviewing the family transactions within the last half year, John was asked to tally up the sacrifices and to see if any benefits might have accrued. He revealed that he was beginning to manage and to look at his manuscript again, but he was frustrated and lonely, and blamed Stacy for the decision that he realized they had made together.

John was asked to clarify for himself how much of the current conflict with Stacy resulted from their present temporary situation, and how much represented previously unspoken but never resolved marital issues from the past. He confessed to resenting her apparent ease in graduate school when he was stumbling through, and her time away from him devoted to school at first and then the baby. He acknowledged that the friends they had together had tried to help after Stacy left, but he had failed to respond and soon they had stopped calling.

John was offered a number of techniques for allocating his time better. In particular, the counselor urged him to focus on the primary goal—finishing his dissertation and getting back with his wife and child. While doing so, he needed to rebuild his social life, since friends were essential if he was to avoid feeling lonely and depressed. He needed to strengthen his sense of personal identity, and being by himself while Stacy and Robin were away was a good opportunity to work on that.

Stacy and John came to see the counselor together during her academic breaks and in the summer when she and Robin returned home. As the couple worked out some unfinished conflict from the past, their bond, weakened by the separation, seemed to grow stronger. John said he was proud of himself for learning to carry out domestic chores efficiently for the first time in his life. He still did not like to cook, relying too much on fast-food restaurants, but he was starting to watch his diet better. He said too that he was proud of Stacy's accomplishments and her independence, but he was afraid she no longer needed or wanted him.

She reassured him that his fears were unfounded, and that she had begun making inquiries at her school about possible openings in psychology for him next year. For one week she went back to another state to visit some friends, leaving Robin with her father, a situation John enjoyed immensely.

During their second year of separation, John and Stacy talked less on the phone, saving money in order to meet more frequently. Each tried to make that meeting more relaxed, not expecting a two-day weekend would compensate for a month apart. They became physically closer than they had been all of the previous year, and each looked forward to their next rendezvous when parting. John finished his dissertation early in the second year and moved to be with his family. Together, he and Stacy sent applications for common employment to a large number of universities, hoping they might be able to teach at the same place. When they last sent a postcard to the counselor, it was to notify him of their new address at a university town in the Midwest, where both were getting ready to start teaching in the fall.

❋　❋　❋　❋　❋

## ADAPTATIONAL STRATEGIES AND FAMILY SYSTEMS

It should be clear by now that there is more than one way to make a go of dual-career marriage. Hall and Hall (1979) offer a thumbnail sketch of several distinct patterns followed by effective two-career couples—couples satisfied in their homes, their family relationships, their lifestyles, and their careers. From these authors' description it is clear that no single role structure is satisfactory to all dual-career pairs; each one must forge an adaptational style that takes into account both work and family involvements and priorities. These authors distinguish four general types: accommodators, adversaries, allies, and acrobats.

Accommodators represent a marital relationship in which one partner is high in career involvement and low in home involvement while the second partner holds the opposite priorities. One assumes primary (but not total) responsibility for family-centered roles while the second takes major (but not sole) responsibility for career development. More than likely, this combination approximates gender-based roles in a traditional marriage. In most cases the main breadwinner is the professional man; it is the professional woman who involves herself more at home. If a move to another locale should become necessary, the family would likely follow him, since his career is paramount. Thus, a part-time or substitute teacher would accompany her computer-executive husband if he were transferred to another city.

Adversaries both are highly involved in their careers and only minimally involved in home, family, or parental roles. Each partner defines himself or herself primarily by career, while retaining some interest in maintaining a well-run home and smoothly functioning family life. Conflict in such an arrangement may arise over which of the two will perform non–career-related tasks at home (for example, staying home from the office to wait for the repairman). While each wants the support of the other, neither is willing to make major career sacrifices to facilitate the other's career or fulfill family roles. Competition is probably more severe here than in the other transactional patterns (who won the grant, who got the promotion, who will follow whose job relocation). Children, if present, are a problem, since each partner prefers the other to assume major child-rearing responsibilities.

Allies are both either highly engrossed in their careers or in their home roles, but not in both areas. Their priorities are clear. They may view their roles as parents or as a couple as paramount, gaining satisfaction from home and family rather than from career advancement. Conflict tends to be low in this arrangement, since each is willing to support the other at home, and neither accedes to potentially stressful career demands. On the other hand, if both view their careers as all-important, conflict is kept low by minimizing domestic roles and the need for a well-organized home. Those who value careers often choose to be childless. Neither resents purchases by the other—they treasure each other's independence—and together they may rely on a housekeeper or dinner out instead of bothering with fixing meals at home. Commuting marriages for the sake of career advancement are more easily tolerated here than in other configurations.

Acrobats hope to have it all, since they both actively engage in careers and in home roles. That is, they seek satisfaction and fulfillment from playing all roles; they juggle demanding career activities with performing family duties well. High achievement in their careers, a good marriage, happy children, a well-run home, exotic vacations, a reputation as top-notch host and hostess are all pursued, sometimes in a seemingly never-ending, frantic manner. Neither looks to the other to take over; both want to do it all themselves. No speaking engagement is turned down, no call for volunteers ignored, no office in a professional organization allowed to go unfilled, no child's birthday allowed to pass without a large, elaborate party, no soccer practice or musical recital by the children unattended. If conflict is experienced, it is apt to be internal (for example, work overload) rather than adversarial.

## SOME COUNSELING GUIDELINES

Various counseling approaches, ranging from the problem-solving to the developmental to the interpersonal, have been proposed in dealing therapeutically with dual-careerists. For example, Sekaran (1986), a management and organizational authority, suggests ways in which counselors can help such couples identify and resolve conflict by providing them with better decision-making, stress-management, and time-management strategies. In addition to encouraging client couples to clarify (and perhaps reassess) their concepts of success, she offers suggestions for helping organizations change policies (offering parental leave, flexible work schedules, child-care assistance) so as to more effectively address the needs of employees from dual-career households.

With a similar organizational outlook, Bruce and Reed (1991) argue that the dual-career couple is the prototype of the future employee, struggling to balance the demands of work and family. Addressing public-sector employers, they urge the restructuring of organizational policies, such as the adoption of family-oriented benefits (family leave, flexitime, flexiplace, part-time employment, job sharing), the hiring of husband-wife couples (doing away with policies restricting nepotism), and increased supervisory awareness and support for working spouses, in order to maximize the talents of career-oriented men and women with families. With this in mind, some counselors and organizational psychologists are being recruited to work within larger systems, helping resolve work-family conflicts.

Hall and Hall (1979) suggest that helping each partner confront and resolve his or her own unfinished developmental business is a useful way of beginning to untangle current relationship conflicts. Glickauf-Hughes, Hughes, and Wells (1986) support this effort, arguing that, while learning coping skills may help some dual-career couples, others may feel frustrated until more basic developmental issues (for example, trust, autonomy, and intimacy) get resolved for each partner. For example, these authors contend that power conflicts (over household divisions of labor, career moves, use of leisure time, sex) may reflect each partner's childhood experience that others cannot be counted on to meet his or her needs, and that therefore he or she must "look out for number one." Until both spouses sufficiently master the developmental tasks of trust or autonomy (following the schema of Erik Erikson [1963]), their current ability to resolve power dilemmas and thus achieve equity will be seriously compromised.

A more interpersonal systems-oriented view is offered by Goldenberg (1986). He maintains that, to be effective, counseling for dual-career couples must be highly focused and must involve both partners conjointly. In his experience, their sessions together may well be the first time that one partner has been forced to attend to the other partner's agenda. When this happens, each partner may begin to become sensitized to the fact that more is happening interpersonally between the spouses than his or her individual unhappiness alone. According to Goldenberg (1986), such recognition is an essential first step in reorganizing the faulty relationship system.

Certain conflict areas increase the probability that two-career families will seek counseling. Gilbert (1988) lists five such problem areas:

1. Managing stress (which may have reached the breaking point).
2. Matching career expectations (not only career expectations and career reality within one spouse but career accomplishment and satisfaction between spouses).
3. Struggles with role sharing (overcoming resistances rooted in traditional sex roles).
4. Deciding whether to have children or not (if so, at what point in the woman's career?).
5. Accommodating aged parents (as members of the "sandwich generation," middle-aged couples more and more may be caught between the demands of adolescent children and aging parents).

Maintaining their carefully achieved balance may make some dual-careerists especially resistant to change. By focusing on achievement and pursuing success, the busy couple may shield themselves from acknowledging marital or family strains until they are unavoidable, or an external event (such as an extramarital affair) forces the couple to face their disintegrating relationship. With both accustomed to success in their professional lives, neither is eager to examine their failing marriage. As Price-Bonham and Murphy (1980) observe, dual-career couples often delay entering counseling until their relationship has deteriorated to an almost irreversible point.

Once in the counseling situation, it is essential that the couple be treated even-handedly. The counselor's approach must not be tied to the values and sex-role assignments of the traditional marriage. Counselors thus not only must be aware of the dynamic struggles within their client couples, but also must look for similar struggles within themselves that may be counterproductive to the counseling (Goldenberg & Goldenberg, 1984). The dual-careerist spouse who senses a bias in the counselor's attitude toward role stereotypes and gender-related domestic assignments "is likely to withdraw, feel ganged up on and probably pessimistic, if not despairing, about being understood" (Goldenberg, 1986, p. 4).

In the following case, we see two highly successful married individuals, at somewhat different stages of their careers, try to resolve pressing differences between them that add considerable stress to their already overburdened lives. At the wife's insistence, they contact a woman counselor:

❊    ❊    ❊    ❊    ❊

Marilyn and Frank, both physicians, met when she began her residency training to become a surgeon and Frank headed the Department of Surgery training program in a large city hospital. Although a mere five years older, at 35, Frank was considerably more advanced in his career than Marilyn, who had just finished her internship and begun her training under Frank to become a surgeon. They were attracted to one another from their first meeting, and soon began to date one another exclusively. Within a year of their meeting, they made plans to marry.

While their backgrounds seemed worlds apart—Frank came from a large working-class Hispanic family, Marilyn from an upper-middle-class WASP upbringing—they felt confident that, as intelligent people who had common values and career interests, they could make a go of marriage. Marilyn had been married before, to a man from an Armenian background, and had experienced no strain with his family or friends, so she believed she could overcome any social or cultural differences with Frank. He had been alienated from his family for some time and, although they lived in the same city, he saw them only rarely.

When Marilyn first met Frank, she was dazzled by his intelligence and clinical ability in surgery. While she was immediately attracted to him, she was at the same time taken aback by his reputation as a "womanizer." Within the hospital there was considerable gossip about his sexual promiscuity; he was known as someone who sought out all attractive nurses, as well as female medical students, interns, and residents. She thus distrusted his obvious interest in her but, as she got to know him, this concern subsided somewhat, since he stopped pursuing anyone else. Besides, Marilyn was drawn to the combination of danger and romance he exuded. Frank, on the other hand, found her quick intelligence very appealing, and as he got to know Marilyn he realized and appreciated her steadying influence on him.

As they got to know one another better, they found they both came from hard-working, achieving families, each with a number of siblings and cousins with M.D.s and Ph.D.s. Moreover, they discovered that problems with alcoholism permeated both families, although neither Marilyn nor Frank had a particular drinking problem. Marilyn was the oldest child in her family, accustomed to caring for her younger siblings. Frank was the youngest in his family, the baby everyone adored and wanted to indulge.

Even before they married, the couple quarreled a great deal. Marilyn was jealous and suspicious when she didn't know Frank's whereabouts for long periods of time, suspecting he was with another woman. Frank protested his innocence, but was frequently irritated by her lack of trust. He felt, too, that she never let anything pass, insisting that the smallest issue between them had to be examined and worked out in detail. In his family, he had been allowed considerable latitude—"space"—and he expected the same in this relationship. She had always been the "rescuer" in her family, and her close scrutiny of the basis for any tension between her and Frank was often done in the pursuit of clarification to reduce the stress and make things between them right again.

When they decided to marry, Marilyn persuaded Frank that they should see a professional for premarital counseling. In particular, she wanted them to see a married woman, whom she felt would understand the feelings and potential conflicts of a young professional woman in a dual-career marriage. Together they saw the counselor for a total of six sessions. They seemed to benefit from the experience in that their communication patterns improved and they both felt more free to express to one another what they were experiencing in the relationship.

Frank and Marilyn married about a year after they met. After a brief honeymoon, both plunged back into extremely demanding work schedules, putting off children due to the large debts they had incurred and their desire that she finish her training. Marilyn was determined to be the best resident in the training program, a goal she seemed to reach. However, she was now aware that their unequal status bothered her; Frank seemed to her to be giving off a double message: "We are equal; I still am superior." She also became more sensitive to his behavior with the other residents, feeling that any decision he made that was not to someone's liking reflected poorly on her. He, on the other hand, felt her observing and evaluating him whenever he lectured or demonstrated a surgical procedure, and he became very uncomfortable and defensive whenever he felt she was criticizing him or trying to improve him. Frank now found it harder and harder to maintain his position with Marilyn as her teacher, retaining her admiration and his superior status in her eyes. She still tended to put him on a pedestal, only to become disappointed when he didn't behave as she thought a concerned teacher should, or when he was not as interested in the evening in her cases as she felt he should be, tired or not.

As both devoted themselves to work and career advancement, their social contacts shrank, and their dependence on one another for stimulation and fulfillment deepened. More and more they behaved as "workaholics," without many friends, their careers all-consuming. He no longer went to the gym after work, as he had done several nights each week before their marriage. She stopped seeing girlfriends for lunch or evenings out together.

After one year of this regime, both felt overburdened, put upon, and quarrelsome. Their pressure-cooker lives now became further complicated when Marilyn was offered a chance to move to another, more prestigious surgery training at a university hospital in the same city. Both felt ambivalent about making the change: she was tempted to go but wanted Frank to insist she stay; he would miss her but felt some relief that he would be less open to her daily assessment of his job performance. They decided to schedule a new series of appointments with their counselor to work out some solutions.

The counselor immediately made them focus on exactly what a pressure-filled existence their lives had become. In their drive for success, she helped them realize, they seemed to have neglected nourishing the intimate emotional bond that drew them together in the first place. The counselor suggested they now pause and make some decisions about what precisely they wanted out of their lives together. She stated her belief that they needed to reevaluate how they dealt with time demands, making certain that they left time and energy for fun, play, and relaxation together. They needed time too to dream and plan a little for their future. In addition, the counselor asked them to attend to their increasing social isolation, and the couple soon recognized that a network of friends with whom to share work and marital experiences might prove to be a good antidote to becoming insular. Beyond those immediate goals, the counselor indicated that they needed to reconsider the long-term effects of the lessening of differences in their professional status, since without doubt those differences would narrow in the future. By doing so, the counselor helped them focus and begin to work through the issue of competitiveness between them. Could they imagine their lives together 15 or 20 years from now? Would they be together? Would there be children? How many? How far did each expect to advance in his or her career? How did they see the balance of family and career in their future together?

The couple initially contracted for five sessions, and when the counseling series was completed they seemed to be in better contact with the unresolved issues between them. They agreed to work further on their own, and to see the counselor again in six months. When they did, it was clear that some progress had been made—in particular, they seemed to have achieved a better balance between career demands and time for one another—but significant problems remained between them. For example, there were the differences in cultural background. When Frank and Marilyn went together to the fiesta celebrating his mother's 65th birthday, there was open tension between them. She worried that he would behave in his old macho way in front of his cousins, appearing to ignore and thus dominate his Anglo wife. He worried that she would appear withdrawn, particularly if his family did not welcome her with open arms, a highly likely possibility.

Instead of denying dissimilarities in background, the counselor encouraged them to examine these past differences and to work through their impact on their present lives. The couple became aware that differences in social class and ethnic background led to basic differences in expectations regarding the role of women and the importance of family. The differences in their birth order—she the oldest child, he the youngest—also led to different expectations of roles and entitlements. These dissimilarities might or might not be significant, but they could not be buried or covered up.

The counselor also encouraged both spouses to separate their personal identities, in their case best accomplished by seeking separate work environments. In that way, competition between them would be minimized, although they needed to acknowledge it would not be eliminated completely. As they moved away from the teacher-student roles, each sought recognition in related, but not identical, fields in surgery. Frank remained primarily a teacher and trainer, Marilyn became a practitioner as a thoracic surgeon.

The couple planned to have children within two years. They realized that the divisions of labor at home would have to be renegotiated when a child arrived, and they began now to plan to add on a nursery room to their house. They also began to discuss how their lives would change with the arrival of a baby, and how emergencies at home would be handled, since Marilyn intended to return to her career as soon as feasible. In the process, they started to socialize with other young couples from their places of work, and talked with them at great length about family and career responsibilities.

Future sessions with the counselor were left open on an as-needed basis. While Marilyn had learned to become less intrusive and Frank less withdrawn, they both knew more work on their communication patterns was necessary, and occasional backslides were probably inevitable. In all likelihood, they assured the counselor upon completing the current round of counseling sessions, they would be calling her again.

❋ ❋ ❋ ❋ ❋

Many of the rewards and benefits of a dual-career marriage are seen in this case: an opportunity for self-fulfillment for both partners, greater intellectual stimulation, and the chance to lead a more economically enriched life together. At the same time, many of the common problems are also present: competition, restricted job mobility, difficulties with time allocations, and work overload.

The counselor needs to help any dual-career couple understand that they are undertaking a marriage that may well give them both a sense of accomplishment, perhaps even elation, but often at the price of exhaustion and guilt over goals not achieved. To romanticize the dual-career family as "having it all" is to invite inevitable disappointment. Rather, the counselor must aid the couple in exploring their values and priorities, pursuing what is important to both partners, relinquishing experiences to which they assign less urgency, and accepting the limitations of their demanding lives.

# SUMMARY

Working wives are a familiar phenomenon, but dual-career families have emerged in significant numbers only within the last 20 years. Such families contain husband and wife professionals both actively pursuing work that requires a high degree of career commitment, as well as involving themselves in their family lives.

Dual-career couples are not always equally committed to their careers or to their domestic roles. Women, depending on the stage of the family life cycle, may resolve the sometimes-conflicting demands of the two roles by interrupting their careers for childrearing, by seeking part-time or temporary employment, or by restricting their geographic mobility in order to fulfill parental responsibilities. Some may postpone careers; others may return to earlier careers only after their children no longer need them at home or after becoming divorced or widowed. Several new family-friendly employment procedures, such as flexitime, flexiplace, and job sharing, are often chosen by married women careerists as preferable to part-time employment.

To make a dual-career relationship work and to avoid role overload, especially for the woman, changes in who carries out domestic tasks, including child care, must be negotiated. Recent research data indicate that men are devoting more time to family responsibilities while women devote less. A greater sharing of both family involvement and breadwinner responsibilities by the two partners represents a value shift in today's society, although women still are expected to be primarily responsible for family and home-related chores.

Beyond role overload, a number of stresses are potential sources of interpersonal conflict between dual-careerists. Clashes between career and family demands, competition between the spouses, and difficulties in making time available for all their work and family commitments are common. The presence of children may add to their responsibility overload, especially if adequate child care is unavailable or too costly. Whatever the sources of stress, the counselor needs to help the dual-career couple try to achieve the goal of equity: for each partner to feel that, overall, fairness exists both in their role opportunities and in their constraints and responsibilities.

Commuter marriages—in which one adult lives apart from spouse and child for a period of time, usually for a job opportunity—place considerable strain on the marital bond, particularly among newly married couples with young children. Such married singles must often cope with feelings of loneliness and mistrust as they attempt to maintain intimacy and commitment to the marriage on a long-distance basis.

A number of alternative strategies are open to dual-careerists who attempt to find satisfaction at home and in their careers. Some may adapt to the situation by one partner's remaining high in career ambition but low in home involvement while the other partner adopts the reverse priorities. Others may become adversarial, both pursuing careers with only minimal attention to home, family, or parental responsibilities. In another configuration, the two may become allies in their careers or their home life, but not in both. A final group may resemble acrobats who strive to have it all, seeking satisfaction from playing career and domestic roles fully, while never missing an opportunity to add on another responsibility.

A variety of approaches may be used in counseling dual-career families: helping them manage decision-making and time allocation; having each partner separately resolve unfinished developmental issues from the past; or focusing conjointly on their interpersonal transactions. Managing stress, matching career expectations, struggling with role sharing, deciding whether to have children, and accommodating aged parents are typical conflicts requiring resolution. Whatever the counseling technique—and a combination is likely—the counselor must adopt an evenhanded approach to both careerists that is not bound by the values and sex-role assignments of the traditional marriage.

# GLOSSARY

**AIDS**  Acquired Immune Deficiency Syndrome, an infectious disease in which the body's immune system is damaged, often in progressive degrees, making the person vulnerable to fatal opportunistic infections and malignancies; gay men and drug abusers are at greatest risk

**anorexia**  Prolonged, severe diminution of appetite, particularly although not exclusively in adolescent females, to the point of becoming life-threatening

**behavioral**  The viewpoint that objective and experimentally verified procedures should be the basis for modifying maladaptive, undesired, or problematic behavior

**behaviorists**  Advocates of the behavioral view, in which tangible events and measurable data are sought rather than subjective reports or inferences

**binuclear family**  A postdivorce family structure in which the ex-spouses reside in separate but interrelated households; the maternal and paternal households thus form one family system

**bisexual**  An individual sexually attracted to both males and females

**boundaries**  Abstract delineations between parts of a system or between systems, typically defined by implicit or explicit rules regarding who may participate and in what manner

**centrifugal**  Tending to move outward or away from the center; within a family, forces that push the members apart, especially when the family organization lacks cohesiveness

**centripetal**  Tending to move toward the center; within a family, forces that bind or otherwise keep the members together so that they seek fulfillment from intrafamilial rather than outside relationships

**circular causality**  The view that causality is nonlinear, occurring instead within a relationship context and by means of a network of interacting loops; any cause is thus seen as an effect of a prior cause, as in the interactions within a family

**closed system**  A self-contained system with impermeable boundaries, operating without interactions outside the system, resistant to change, and thus prone to increasing disorder

**community divorce**  That stage in the divorce process in which each participant publicly redefines himself or herself, to family members, friends, and the community at large, as a divorced person

**commuter marriage**  An intact marriage in which the partners maintain separate households, usually in distant cities, typically to pursue dual careers simultaneously

**constructionist**  A view that emphasizes the subjective ways in which each individual creates a perception of reality

**coparental divorce**  That stage in the divorce process in which issues surrounding child custody, visitation, and coparenting are resolved and arrangements defined

**countertransference**  According to psychoanalytic theory, the analyst's unconscious emotional responses to a patient that may interfere with objectivity

**crisis intervention**  Brief, direct therapy focused on the present in response to an immediate psychological emergency situation

**custody**  The assignment of children to one or both parents in a postdivorce family system, as well as the determination of the children's living arrangements (see also **joint legal custody, joint physical custody, sole custody,** and **split custody**).

**cybernetics**  The study of methods of feedback control within a system, especially the flow of information through feedback loops

**delinquency**  Antisocial or illegal behavior by a minor

**disengagement**  A family process in which members become psychologically isolated from one another because of overly rigid boundaries among the participants

**divorce mediation**  A form of divorce arbitration in which the couple voluntarily learns to negotiate a mutually satisfying settlement through brief nonadversarial contact with a team knowledgeable in counseling and the law

**dual-career marriage**  A marriage in which husband and wife both pursue active professional careers as well as active, involved family lives

**economic divorce**  That stage in the divorce process in which matters of money, property, and the redistribution of family assets are settled

**emotional divorce**  That early stage in the divorce process in which both partners are forced to deal with their deteriorating marital relationship

**enmeshment**  A family process in which boundaries become blurred and members become overconcerned and overinvolved in each other's lives, limiting the autonomy of individual family members

**entropy**   The tendency of a system to go into disorder—that is, to reach a disorganized and undifferentiated state

**equifinality**   In contrast to simple cause-and-effect explanations, the principle that similar outcomes may result from different origins

**ethnicity**   The defining characteristics of a cultural subgroup, transmitted over generations and reinforced by the expectations of the subgroup in which the individual or family maintains membership

**family mapping**   A symbolic representation of a family's organizational structure, particularly its boundaries and coalitions, used by structural counselors to plan their inverventions

**feedback**   The reinsertion into a system of the results of its past performance, as a method of controlling the system

**feedback loops**   Those circular mechanisms by which information about a system's output is continuously reintroduced into the system, initiating a chain of subsequent events

**gay couples**   Partners of the same gender who develop and maintain a homosexual male or lesbian relationship

**genogram**   A schematic device of a family's relationship system in the form of a genetic tree, usually including at least three generations, often used by the counselor to trace recurring behavior patterns within the family

**homeostasis**   A dynamic state of balance or equilibrium in a system, or a tendency toward achieving and maintaining such a state in an effort to ensure a stable environment

**homophobic**   Excessively fearful of being homosexual oneself or of associating with homosexuals

**homosexual**   A person of either sex with a sexual preference for, and sexual activity with, a person of his or her same sex

**identified patient**   The family member with the presenting symptom or problem; thus, the person who initially seeks counseling or for whom counseling is sought

**joint legal custody**   A term used in the law to denote the rights of both parents to share in certain major decisions (for example, religious upbringing, choice of schools) regarding their children

**joint physical custody**   A shared legal arrangement between ex-spouses in which their children spend time on a regular basis with one and then the other parent

**legal divorce**   That stage in the divorce process in which the judicial system becomes involved officially in ending the marriage; the marriage may be dissolved through civil annulment, no-fault divorce, or a contested divorce hearing before a judge

**lesbian**  A female engaged with another female in a sexual relationship

**linear causality**  The view that a nonreciprocal relationship exists between events in a sequence, so that one event causes the next event, but not vice versa

**morphogenesis**  A process by which a system changes its basic structure, typically in response to positive feedback, in order to adapt to changing environmental demands or conditions

**morphostasis**  A process by which a system maintains constancy in its structure or organization, usually in response to negative feedback, in the face of environmental changes

**negative feedback**  The flow of corrective information from the output of a system back into the system in order to attenuate deviation and keep the system functioning within prescribed limits

**negentropy**  The tendency of a system to remain flexible and open to new input, necessary for change and survival of the system

**nonmarital cohabitation**  An arrangement in which two unmarried adults of the opposite sex live together in a sexual relationship

**nuclear family**  A family composed of a husband, wife, and their offspring, living together as a family unit

**open marriage**  A nonexclusive marital arrangement whereby extramarital sex by both partners is sanctioned

**open system**  A system with more or less permeable boundaries that permits interaction between component parts or subsystems, and is thus likely to function in an orderly manner

**parentified child**  A child forced by his or her parents into a caretaking or nurturing parental role within the family; in extreme cases, the parents may abdicate the position of authority and assign the adult role to the child

**physical custody**  An arrangement, usually following divorce, in which a child lives with one parent, although visitation with the other is possible

**positive feedback**  The flow of information from the output of a system back into the system in order to amplify deviation from the state of equilibrium, thus leading to instability and change

**prognosis**  A prediction or forecast about the outcome of a condition or disorder, including an indication of its probable duration and course

**psychic divorce**  The final stage in the divorce process, in which the ex-spouses must learn to accept the finality of their separation from one another and commence regaining a sense of individual identity and autonomy

**psychoanalytic**  A viewpoint reflecting the theory of personality formation as well as the therapeutic approach developed by Sigmund Freud

**psychoeducational**  A view emphasizing educating the family so that they might better understand and cope with a symptomatic family member

**psychopathology**  Severe problematic, maladaptive, or dysfunctional behavior

**reframing**  Relabeling behavior by putting it into a new, more positive perspective ("Mother is trying to help" in place of "She's intrusive"), thus altering the context in which it is perceived and inviting new responses to the same behavior

**role overload**  Stress that occurs in a family when members, most likely one or both parents, attempt to fulfill a greater variety of roles than their energies or time will permit

**single parent**  A divorced person of either sex with whom the children of the marriage reside

**sole custody**  The award by the court of total physical and legal responsibilities for the children to one of the parents in a divorcing couple

**split custody**  The award by the court of custody of one or more of the children to each of the parents in a divorcing couple

**stepfamily**  A linked family system created by the marriage of two persons, one or both of whom has been previously married, in which one or more children from the earlier marriages lives with the remarried couple

**strategic**  A therapeutic approach in which the counselor develops a plan or strategy and designs interventions aimed at solving a specific presenting problem

**structural**  A therapeutic approach directed at changing or realigning the family organization or structure in order to alter dysfunctional transactions and clarify subsystem boundaries

**subsystems**  Organized, coexisting components within an overall system, each having its own autonomous functions as well as a specific role in the operation of the larger system; within families, a member can belong to a number of such units

**suprasystem**  A higher-level system in which other systems represent component parts and play subsystem roles; within a remarried family, a network of people (the former couple and their current family members, grandparents, aunts and uncles, cousins, and so on) who influence the remarried system

**system**  A set of interacting units or component parts that together make up a whole arrangement or organization

**victim system**  A circular-feedback process, most noticeable among African Americans, whereby regularly experiencing poverty, racism, and discrimination lowers self-esteem and produces problematic antisocial behaviors; these in turn impede the integration of African-American culture with that of the American mainstream and lead to despair

# REFERENCES

ABC NEWS. (1986, August 1). *After the sexual revolution*. [Television documentary].

ABRAHAMSE, A. F., MORRISON, P. A., & WAITE, L. J. (1988). *Beyond stereotypes: Who becomes a single teenage mother?* Santa Monica, CA: Rand Corporation.

ACOSTA, F. X., & EVANS. L. A. (1982). The Hispanic-American patient. In F. X. Acosta, J. Yamamoto, & L. A. Evans (Eds.), *Effective psychotherapy for low-income and minority patients*. New York: Plenum Press.

ACOSTA, F. X., YAMAMOTO, J., & EVANS, L. A. (1982). *Effective psychotherapy for low-income and minority patients*. New York: Plenum Press.

AHRONS, C. R., & RODGERS, R. H. (1987). *Divorced families: A multidisciplinary view*. New York: W. W. Norton.

ALDOUS, J. (1981). From dual-earner to dual-career families and back again. *Journal of Family Issues, 2,* 115–125.

ALDOUS, J. (1982). *Two paychecks: Life in dual-career families*. Newbury Park, CA: Sage Publications.

ANDERSON, C. L. (1982). Males as sexual assault victims: Multiple levels of trauma. In J. C. Gonsiorek (Ed.), *Homosexuality and psychotherapy: A practitioner's guide to affirmative models*. New York: Haworth Press.

ANDERSON, C. M., REISS, D., & HOGARTHY, B. (1986). *Schizophrenia and the family*. New York: Guilford Press.

ANDOLFI, M. (1979). *Family therapy: an integrative approach*. New York: Plenum Press.

APONTE, H. (1987). The treatment of society's poor: An ecological perspective on the underorganized family. *Family Therapy Today, 2*(1), 1–7.

ATKINSON, D. R., MORTEN, G., & SUE, D. W. (Eds.). (1989). *Counseling American minorities: A cross-cultural perspective* (3rd ed.). Dubuque, IA: Wm. C. Brown.

AXINN, W. G., & THORNTON, A. (1992). The relationship between cohabitation and divorce: Selectivity or causal influence? *Demography, 29*(3), 357–374.

BACH-Y-RITA, G. (1982). The Mexican American religious and cultural influences. In R. M. Becerra, M. Karno, & J. I. Escobar (Eds.), *Mental health and Hispanic Americans: Clinical perspectives*. New York: Grune & Stratton.

BAGAROZZI, D. A. (1985). Dimensions of family evaluation. In L. L. L'Abate (Ed.), *The handbook of family psychology and therapy* (Vol. II). Pacific Grove, CA: Brooks/Cole.

BAGAROZZI, D. A. (1986). Premarital counseling. In F. P. Piercy, D. H. Sprenkle, and Associates (Eds.), *Family therapy sourcebook*. New York: Guilford Press.

BARTH, J. C. (1988). Family therapist's dilemma: Systems therapy with divorcing couples. *Journal of Family Psychology, 1,* 469–475.

BASS, B. A. (1982). The validity of sociocultural factors in the assessment and treatment of Afro-Americans. In B. A. Bass, G. E. Wyatt, & G. J. Powell (Eds.), *The Afro-American family: Assessment, treatment, and research issues.* New York: Grune & Stratton.

BATESON, G. (1979). *Mind and nature.* New York: Dutton.

BAYDAR, N. (1988). Effects of parental separation and reentry into union on the emotional well-being of children. *Journal of Marriage and the Family, 50,* 967–981.

BEAL, E. (1980). Separation, divorce, and single-parent families. In E. A. Carter & M. McGoldrick (Eds.), *The family life cycle: A framework for family therapy.* New York: Gardner Press.

BEAVERS, W. R. (1977). *Psychotherapy and growth.* New York: Brunner/Mazel.

BEAVERS, W. R. (1981). A systems model of family for family therapists. *Journal of Marriage and Family Therapy, 7,* 299–307.

BEAVERS, W. R. (1982). Healthy, midrange, and severely dysfunctional families. In F. Walsh (Ed.), *Normal family processes.* New York: Guilford Press.

BEAVERS, W. R. (1988). Attributes of a healthy couple. *Family Therapy Today, 3*(1), 1–4.

BEAVERS, W. R., HAMPSON, R. D., & HULGAS, Y.F. (1985). Commentary: The Beavers System approach to family assessment. *Family Process, 24,* 398–405.

BEAVERS, W. R., & VOELLER, M. N. (1983). Family models: Comparing and contrasting the Olson circumplex with the Beavers model. *Family Process, 22,* 85–98.

BELL, A. P. & WEINBERG, M. S. (1978). *Homosexualities: A study of diversity among men and women.* New York: Simon & Schuster.

BELLE, D. (Ed.). (1982). *Lives in stress: Women and depression.* Newbury Park, CA: Sage Publications.

BENNETT, N. G., BLANC, A.K., & BLOOM, D. E. (1988). Commitment and the modern union: Assessing the link between premarital cohabitation and subsequent marital stability. *American Sociological Review, 53*(1), 127–138.

BERG, I. K., & JAYA, K. P. (1993). Different and same: Family therapy with Asian-American families. *Journal of Marital and Family Therapy, 19*(1), 31–38.

BERMAN, E. M., & GOLDBERG, M. (1986). Therapy with unmarried couples. In N. S. Jacobson & A. S. Gurman (Eds.), *Clinical handbook of marital therapy.* New York: Guilford Press.

BERNAL, G. (1982). Cuban families. In M. McGoldrick, J. K. Pearce, & J. Giordano (Eds.), *Ethnicity and family therapy.* New York: Guilford Press.

BERNAL, G., BERNAL, M., MARTINEZ, A. C., OLMEDO, E. L., & SANTISTEBAN, D. (1983). Hispanic mental health curriculum for psychology. In J. C. Chunn, II, P. J. Dunston, & F. Ross-Sheriff (Eds.), *Mental health and people of color: Curriculum development and change.* Washington, DC: Howard University Press.

BERNARD, J. (1956). *Remarriage: A study of marriage.* New York: Dryden Press.

BERNSTEIN, A. C. (1990). *Yours, mine, and ours: How families change when remarried parents have a child together.* New York: W. W. Norton.

BERTALANFFY, L. von (1968). *General systems theory: Foundation, development, applications.* New York: Braziller.

BERZON, B. (1979). *Positively gay.* Los Angeles: Mediamix Press.

BILLINGSLEY, A. (1968). *Black families in white America.* Englewood Cliffs, NJ: Prentice-Hall.

BLASBAND, D., & PEPLAU, L. A. (1985). Sexual exclusivity versus openness in gay male couples. *Archives of Sexual Behavior, 14,* 395–412.

BLUMSTEIN, P., & SCHWARTZ, P. (1983). *American couples.* New York: William Morrow.

BOHANNAN, P. (1970). *Divorce and after.* Garden City, NY: Doubleday.

BOHANNAN, P. (1984). *All the happy families: Exploring the varieties of family life.* New York: McGraw-Hill.

BOOTH, A., & JOHNSON, D. (1988). Premarital cohabitation and marital success. *Journal of Family Issues, 9,* 255–272.

BORNSTEIN, P. H., & BORNSTEIN, M. T. (1986). *Marital therapy: A behavioral-communications approach.* New York: Pergamon Press.

BOULD, S. (1977). Female-headed families: Personal fate control and the provider role. *Journal of Marriage and the Family, 39,* 339–349.

BOWEN, M. (1978). *Family therapy in clinical practice.* New York: Jason Aronson.

BOYD-FRANKLIN, N. (1989). *Black families in therapy: A multisystems approach.* New York: Guilford Press.

BOZETT, F. W. (1982). Heterogeneous couples in heterosexual marriages: Gay men and straight women. *Journal of Marital and Family Therapy, 8,* 81–89.

BOZETT, F. W. (1985). Gay men as fathers. In S. M. H. Hanson & F. W. Bozett (Eds.), *Dimensions of fatherhood.* Newbury Park, CA: Sage Publications.

BRADT, J. O., & BRADT, C. M. (1986). Resources in remarried families. In M. Karpel (Ed.), *Family resources: The hidden partner in family therapy.* New York: Guilford Press.

BRANDWEIN, R., BROWN, C., & FOX, E. (1974). Women and children last: The social situation of divorced mothers and their families. *Journal of Marriage and the Family, 36,* 498–514.

BRAVER, S. L., WOLCHIK, S. A., SANDLER, I. N., SHEETS, V. L., FOGAS, B., & BAY, R. C. (1993). A longitudinal study of noncustodial parents: Parents without children. *Journal of Family Psychology, 7*(1), 9–23.

BRAY, J. H. (1988). *What's in the best interest of the child? Custodial arrangements and visitation issues.* Unpublished manuscript.

BRAY, J. H. (1992). Family relationships and children's adjustment in clinical and nonclinical stepfather families. *Journal of Family Psychology, 6,* 60–68.

BRAY, J. H. & ANDERSON, H. (1984). Strategic interventions with single-parent families. *Psychotherapy, 21,* 101–109.

BROSS, A. (1982). *Family therapy: Principles of strategic practice.* New York: Guilford Press.

BROWN, L. S., & ZIMMER, D. (1986). An introduction to therapy issues of lesbians and gay male couples. In N. S. Jacobson & A. S. Gurman (Eds.), *Clinical handbook of marital therapy.* New York: Guilford.

BRUCE, W. M., & REED, C. M. (1991). *Dual-career couples in the public sector: A management guide for human resource professionals.* New York: Quorum Books.

BUMPASS, L. L., & SWEET, J. A. (1989). National estimates of cohabitation. *Demography, 26*(4), 615–625.

BUMPASS, L. L., SWEET, J. A., & MARTIN, T. C. (1990). Changing patterns of remarriage. *Journal of Marriage and the Family, 52,* 747–756.

BURDEN, D., & KLERMAN, L. (1984). Teenage parenthood: Factors that lessen economic dependence. *Social Work, 29*(1), 11–16.

BUUNK, B. M., & van DRIEL, B. (1989). *Variant lifestyles and relationships.* Newbury Park, CA: Sage Publications.

CAILLE, P. (1982). The evaluation phase of systemic family therapy. *Journal of Marital and Family Therapy, 8,* 29–39.

CANINO, G. (1982). The Hispanic woman: Sociocultural influences on diagnoses and treatment. In R. M. Becerra, M. Karno, & J. I. Escobar (Eds.), *Mental health and Hispanic Americans: Clinical perspectives.* New York: Grune & Stratton.

CARRILLO, C. (1982). Changing norms of Hispanic families: Implications for treatment. In E. E. Jónes & S. J. Korchin (Eds.), *Minority mental health.* New York: Praeger.

CARTER, E. A., & McGOLDRICK, M. (Eds.). (1980). *The family life cycle.* New York: Gardner Press.

CARTER, E. A., & McGOLDRICK, M. (1988). Overview: The changing family life cycle: A framework for family therapy. In E. A. Carter & M. McGoldrick (Eds.), *The changing family life cycle: A framework for family therapy* (2nd. ed.). New York: Gardner Press.

CASHON, B. (1982). Female-headed families: Effects on children and clinical implications. *Journal of Marital and Family Therapy, 8,* 77–85.

CAZENAVE, N. A. (1980). Alternative intimacy, marriage, and family lifestyle among low-income Black-Americans. *Alternative Lifestyles, 4*(4), 425–444.

CHAPMAN, A. B. (1988). Male-female relations: How the past affects the present. In H.P. McAdoo (Ed.), *Black families* (2nd ed.). Newbury Park, CA: Sage Publications.

CHERLIN, A. J., & McCARTHY, J. (1985). Remarried couples households: Data from the June 1980 current population survey. *Journal of Marriage and the Family, 47,* 23–30.

CHEUNG, F. K., & SNOWDEN, L. R. (1990). Community mental health and ethnic minority populations. *Community Mental Health Journal, 26,* 277–291.

CHIEN, C., & YAMAMOTO, J. (1982). Asian-American and Pacific-Islander patients. In F. X. Acosta, J. Yamamoto, & L. A. Evans (Eds.), *Effective psychotherapy with low income and minority patients.* New York: Plenum Press.

CHILDREN'S DEFENSE FUND. (1993, June). Birth to teens. *CDF Reports, 14*(7), 7–10.

CHILMAN, C. S. (1988). Never-married, single, adolescent parents. In C. S. Chilman, E. W. Nunnally, & F. M. Cox (Eds.), *Variant family forms.* Newbury Park, CA: Sage Publications.

CLINGEMPEEL, A. J., BRAND, E., & IEVOLI, R. (1984). Stepparent-stepchild relationships in stepmother and stepfather families: A multimethod study. *Family Relations, 33,* 465–473.

CLINGEMPEEL, A. J., & REPPUCCI, N. D. (1982). Joint custody after divorce: Major issues and goals for research. *Psychological Bulletin, 91,* 102–127.

COLE, C. L. (1988). Family and couples therapy with nonmarital cohabiting couples: Treatment issues and case studies. In C. S. Chilman, E. W. Nunnally, & F. M. Cox (Eds.), *Variant family forms.* Newbury Park, CA: Sage Publications.

COLEMAN, E. (1982). Developmental stages of the coming out process. In J. C. Gonsiorek (Ed.), *Homosexuality and psychotherapy.* New York: Haworth Press.

CONGER, J. J. (1981). Freedom and commitment: Families, youth, and social change. *American Psychologist, 36,* 1475–1484.

CONSTANTINE, L. L. (1986). *Family paradigms: The practice of theory in family therapy.* New York: Guilford Press.

COOGLER, O. J. (1978). *Structured mediation in divorce settlement.* Lexington, MA: Lexington Books.

COWAN, P., & HETHERINGTON, M. (Eds.). (1990). *Family transitions.* Hillsdale, NJ: Erlbaum.

CRAWFORD, S. (1987). Lesbian families: Psychosocial stress and the family-building process. In Boston Lesbian Psychologies Collective (Eds.), *Lesbian psychologies: Explorations and challenges.* Urbana: University of Illinois Press.

CROHN, H., SAGER, C. J., BROWN, H., RODSTEIN, E., & WALKER, L. (1982). A basis for understanding and treating the remarried family. In J. C. Hansen & L. Messinger (Eds.), *Therapy with remarried families.* Rockville, MD: Aspens Systems.

DAVIS, G., & WATSON, G. (1982). *Black life in corporate America.* New York: Doubleday.

DAVIS, K. (Ed.). (1985). *Contemporary marriage.* New York: Russell Sage Foundation.

DEL CARMEN, R. (1990). Assessment of Asian-Americans for family therapy. In F. C. Serafica, A. I. Schwebel, R. K. Russell, P. D. Isaac, & L. B. Myers (Eds.), *Mental health of ethnic minorities.* New York: Praeger.

DELL, P. (1982). Beyond homeostasis: Toward a concept of coherence. *Family Process, 21,* 21–41.

DERDEYN, A. P. (1976). Child custody contests in historical perspective. *American Journal of Psychiatry, 133,* 1369–1376.

DeSHAZER, S. (1983). Diagnosing + researching + doing therapy. In B. Keeney (Ed.), *Diagnosis and assessment in family therapy.* Rockville, MD: Aspen Systems.

DOHERTY, W. J., & BAIRD, M. A. (1983). *Family therapy and family medicine: Toward the primary care of families.* New York: Guilford Press.

DUBERMAN, L. (1975). *The reconstituted family: A study of remarried couples and their children.* Chicago: Nelson-Hall.

DUCK, S. (1982). A topography of relationship disengagement and dissolution. In S. Duck (Ed.), *Personal relationships.* London: Academic Press.

EIDELSON, R. J. (1983). Affiliation and independence issues in marriage. *Journal of Marriage and the Family, 45,* 683–688.

EINSTEIN, E. (1982). *The stepfamily: Living, loving and learning.* Boston: Shambhala.

EMERY, R. E. (1988). *Marriage, divorce, and children's adjustment.* Newbury Park, CA: Sage Publications.

EPSTEIN, N. B., BALDWIN, L. M., & BISHOP, D. S. (1983). The McMaster family assessment device. *Journal of Marital and Family Therapy, 9,* 171–180.

EPSTEIN, N. B., BISHOP, D. S., & BALDWIN, L. M. (1982). McMaster model of family functioning: A view of the normal family. In F. Walsh (Ed.), *Normal family processes.* New York: Guilford Press.

ERIKSON, E. H. (1963). *Childhood and society.* New York: W. W. Norton.

EVERETT, C. A. (1987). *The divorce process: A handbook for clinicians.* New York: Haworth Press.

FALICOV, C. J. (1982). Mexican families. In M. McGoldrick, J. Pearce, & J. Giordano. (Eds.), *Ethnicity and family therapy.* New York: Guilford Press.

FALICOV, C. J. (1986). Cross-cultural marriages. In N. S. Jacobson & A. S. Gurman (Eds.), *Clinical handbook of marital therapy.* New York: Guilford Press.

FALICOV, C. J. (1988). Learning to think culturally. In H. A. Liddle, D. C. Breunlin, & R. C. Schwartz (Eds.), *Handbook of family therapy training and supervision.* New York: Guilford Press.

FARBER, R. S. (1988). Integrated treatment of the dual-career couple. *Journal of Family Therapy, 16,* 46–57.

FELDMAN, L. (1992). *Integrating individual and family therapy.* New York: Brunner/Mazel.

FISHMAN, H. C. (1985). Diagnosis and context: An Alexandrian Quartet. In R. L. Ziffer (Ed.), *Adjunctive techniques in family therapy.* New York: Grune & Stratton.

FOLBERG, J., & MILNE, A. (Eds.). (1988). *Divorce mediation: Theory and practice.* New York: Guilford Press.

FOWERS, B. J., & OLSON, D. H. (1986). Predicting marital success with PREPARE: A predictive validity study. *Journal of Marital and Family Therapy, 12,* 403–413.

FOWERS, B. J., & OLSON, D. H. (1992). Four types of premarital couples: An empirical typology based on PREPARE. *Journal of Family Psychology, 6*(1), 10–21.

FRADKIN, H. R. (1987). Counseling men in the AIDS crisis. In M. Scher, M. Stevens, G. Good, & G. A. Eichenfield (Eds.), *Handbook of counseling and psychotherapy with men.* Newbury Park, CA: Sage Publications.

FRANCES, A., CLARKIN, J. F., & PERRY, S. (1984). *Differential therapeutics in psychiatry: The art and science of treatment selection.* New York: Brunner/Mazel.

FRANKLIN, A. J., & BOYD-FRANKLIN, N. (1990). Psychotherapy with African-American clients. *Register Reports, 16*(3), 20–22.

FRAZIER, E. F. (1963). *The Negro church in America.* New York: Schocken Books.

FRIESEN, J. D. (1985). *Structural-strategic marriage and family therapy.* New York: Gardner Press.

FULMER, R. H. (1983). A structural approach to unresolved mourning in single-parent family systems. *Journal of Marital and Family Therapy, 9,* 259–269.

FURSTENBERG, F. F., JR. (1980). Reflections on marriage. *Journal of Family Issues, 1,* 443–453.

FURSTENBERG, F. F., JR. (1987). The new extended family: The experience of parents and children after remarriage. In K. Pasley & M. Ihinger-Tallman (Eds.), *Remarriage and stepparenting: Current research and theory.* New York: Guilford Press.

FURSTENBERG, F. F., JR., BROOKS-GUNN, J., & CHASE-LANSDALE, L. (1989). Teenage pregnancy and childbearing. *American Psychologist, 44,* 313–320.

FURSTENBERG, F. F., JR., & CHERLIN, A. J. (1991). *Divided families: What happens to children when parents part.* Cambridge, MA: Harvard University Press.

GANONG, L. H., & COLEMAN, M. (1987). Effects of parent remarriage on children: An updated comparison of theories, methods, and findings from clinical and empirical research. In K. Pasley & M. Ihinger-Tallman (Eds.), *Remarriage and stepfamilies: Current research and theory.* New York: Guilford Press.

GARTRELL, N. (1983). Gay patients in the medical setting. In C. C. Nadelson & D. B. Marcotte (Eds.), *Treatment interventions in human sexuality.* New York: Plenum Press.

GERSTEL, N., & GROSS, H. (1984). *Commuter marriage.* New York: Guilford Press.

GETTY, C. (1981). Considerations for working with single-parent families. In C. Getty & D. B. Marcotte (Eds.), *Understanding the family: Stress and change in American family life.* New York: Appleton-Century-Crofts.

GILBERT, L. A. (1985). *Men in dual-career families: Current realities and future prospects.* Hillsdale, NJ: Erlbaum.

GILBERT, L. A. (1988). *Sharing it all: The rewards and struggles of two-career families.* New York: Plenum Press.

GLICK, P. C. (1980). Remarriage: Some recent changes and variations. *Journal of Family Issues, 1,* 455–478.

GLICK, P. C. (1984a). American household structure in transition. *Family Planning Perspectives, 16,* 205–211.

GLICK, P. C. (1984b). How American families are changing. *American Demographics, 5,* 21–25.

GLICK, P. C. (1984c). Marriage, divorce, and living arrangements: Prospective changes. *Journal of Family Issues, 5,* 7–26.

GLICK, P. C., & SPANIER, G. B. (1980). Married and unmarried cohabitation in the United States. *Journal of Marriage and the Family, 42,* 19–30.

GLICKAUF-HUGHES, C. L., HUGHES, G. B., & WELLS, M. C. (1986). A developmental approach to treating dual-career couples. *American Journal of Family Therapy, 14,* 254–263.

GOLDENBERG, H. (1977). *Abnormal psychology: A social/community approach.* Pacific Grove, CA: Brooks/Cole.

GOLDENBERG, H. (1986). Treating contemporary couples in dual-career relationships. *Family Therapy Today, 1*(1), 1–7.

GOLDENBERG, I., & GOLDENBERG, H. (1984). Treating the dual-career couple. *American Journal of Family Therapy, 12,* 29–37.

GOLDENBERG, I., & GOLDENBERG, H. (1991). *Family therapy: An overview* (3rd ed.). Pacific Grove, CA: Brooks/Cole.

GOLDSTEIN, J., FREUD, A., & SOLNIT, A. (1979). *Beyond the best interests of the child.* New York: Free Press.

GOODE, W. J. (1956). *After divorce.* New York: Free Press.

GRANVOLD, D. K. (1983). Structured separation for marital treatment and decision-making. *Journal of Marital and Family Therapy, 9,* 403–412.

GREEN, J. (1989). Post-test counselling. In J. Green & A. McCreaner (Eds.), *Counselling in HIV infection and AIDS.* Oxford: Blackwell Scientific Publications.

GREEN, R. G., KOLEVZON, M. S., & VOSLER, N. R. (1985). The Beavers-Timberlawn model of family competence and the Circumplex model of family adaptability and coherence: Separate, but equal? *Family Process, 24,* 385–398.

GREIF, J. B. (1979). Fathers, children, and joint custody. *American Journal of Orthopsychiatry, 49,* 311–319.

GREIF, J. B. (1985). *Single fathers.* Lexington, MA: Lexington Books.

GRIER, W. H., & COBBS, P. M. (1968). *Black rage.* New York: Basic Books.

GRIEVOUS, C. (1989). The role of the family therapist with low-income Black families. In D. R. Atkinson, G. Morten, & D. W. Sue (Eds.), *Counseling American minorities: A cross-cultural perspective.* Dubuque, IA: Wm. C. Brown.

GROTEVANT, H. D., & CARLSON, C. I. (1989). *Family assessment: A guide to methods and measurements.* New York: Guilford Press.

GUERIN, P., FAY, L., BURDEN, S., & KAUTTO, J. (1987). *The evaluation and treatment of marital conflict.* New York: Basic Books.

GULLOTTA, T. P., ADAMS, G. R., & ALEXANDER, S. J. (1986). *Today's marriages and families: A wellness approach.* Pacific Grove, CA: Brooks/Cole.

GUTIERREZ, M. J. (1987). Teenage pregnancy and the Puerto Rican family. In M. Lindblad-Goldberg (Ed.), *Clinical issues in single-parent households.* Rockville, MD: Aspen Publishers.

GWARTNEY-GIBBS, P. A. (1986). The institutionalization of premarital cohabitation: Estimates from marriage license applications, 1970 to 1980. *Journal of Marriage and the Family, 48,* 423–434.

HALEY, J. (1976). *Problem solving therapy.* San Francisco: Jossey-Bass.

HALL, F. S., & HALL, D. T. (1979). *The two-career couple.* Reading, MA: Addison-Wesley.

HANSEN, J. C. (Ed.). (1983). *Clinical implications of the family life cycle.* Rockville, MD: Aspen Systems.

HAREVEN, T. K. (1982). American families in transition: Historical perspective on change. In F. Walsh (Ed.), *Normal family processes.* New York: Guilford Press.

HARRISON, J. (1987). Counseling gay men. In M. Scher, M. Stevens, G. Good, & G. A. Eichenfield (Eds.), *Handbook of counseling and psychotherapy with men.* Newbury Park, CA: Sage Publications.

HARRY, J. (1983). Gay male and lesbian relationships. In E. D. Macklin & R. H. Rubin (Eds.), *Contemporary families and alternative lifestyles.* Newbury Park, CA: Sage Publications.

HARRY, J. (1988). Some problems of gay/lesbian families. In C. S. Chilman, E. W. Nunnally, F. M. Fox (Eds.), *Variant family forms.* Newbury Park, CA: Sage Publications.

HENGGELER, S. W., & BORDUIN, C. M. (1990). *Family therapy and beyond: A multi-systemic approach to treating the behavior problems of children and adolescents.* Pacific Grove, CA: Brooks/Cole.

HERNANDEZ, D. J. (1988). Demographic trends and the living arrangements of children. In E. M. Hetherington & J. D. Arasteh (Eds.), *Impact of divorce, single parenting, and stepparenting on children.* Hillsdale, NJ: Erlbaum.

HETHERINGTON, E. M. (1987). Family relations six years after divorce. In K. Pasley & M. Ihinger-Tallman (Eds.), *Remarriage and stepparenting: Current research and theory.* New York: Guilford Press.

HETHERINGTON, E. M. (1993). An overview of the Virginia Longitudinal Study of Divorce and Remarriage with a focus on early adolescence. *Journal of Family Psychology, 7*(1), 39–56.

HETHERINGTON, E. M., COX, M., & COX, R. (1976). Divorced fathers. *Family Coordinator, 25,* 417–428.

HETHERINGTON, E. M., COX, M., & COX, R. (1982). Effects of divorce on parents and children. In M. E. Lamb (Ed.), *Nontraditional families: Parenting and child development.* Hillsdale, NJ: Erlbaum.

HETHERINGTON, E. M., STANLEY-HAGAN, M., & ANDERSON, E. R. (1989). Marital transitions: A child's perspective. *American Psychologist, 44,* 303–312.

HILL, R. (1977). *Informal adoption among black families.* Washington, DC: Urban League Research Department.

HILL, R. (1986). Life cycle stages for types of single-parent families: Of family development theory. *Family Relations, 35,* 19–29.

HINES, P. M., & BOYD-FRANKLIN, N. (1982). Black families. In M. McGoldrick, J. K. Pearce, & J. Giordano (Eds.), *Ethnicity and family therapy.* New York: Guilford Press.

HO, M. K. (1987). *Family therapy with ethnic minorities.* Newbury Park, CA: Sage Publications.

HOCHSCHILD, A. (1989). *The second shift: Working parents and the revolution at home.* New York: Viking.

HODGES, W. F. (1991). *Intervention for children of divorce: Custody, access, and psychotherapy* (2nd ed.). New York: Wiley.

HOFFMAN, L. (1981). *Foundations of family therapy.* New York: Basic Books.

HOFFMAN, L. W. (1989). Effects of maternal employment in the two-parent family. *American Psychologist, 44,* 283-292.

HOMMA-TRUE, R., GREENE, B., LOPEZ, S. R., & TRIMBLE, J. E. (1993). Ethnocultural diversity in clinical psychology. *The Clinical Psychologist, 46,* 50–63.

HOOKER, E. (1957). The adjustment of the male homosexual. *Journal of Projective Techniques, 21,* 18–31.

HOOKER, E. (1967). The homosexual community. In J. H. Gagnon & W. Simon (Eds.), *Sexual deviance.* New York: Harper & Row.

HOWELL, R. J., & TOEPKE, K. E. (1984). Summary of the child custody laws for the fifty states. *American Journal of Family Therapy, 12,* 56–60.

HUBER, C. H., & BARUTH, L. G. (1987). *Ethical, legal, and professional issues in the practice of marriage and family therapy.* Columbus, OH: Merrill.

HUDSON INSTITUTE. (1988). *Opportunities 2000: Creative affirmative action strategies for a changing workforce.* Washington, DC: U.S. Department of Labor.

HUMPHREYS, L., & MILLER, B. (1980). Identities and the emerging gay culture. In J. Marmor (Ed.), *Homosexual behavior: A modern reappraisal.* New York: Basic Books.

HUNT, J. G., & HUNT, L. L. (1977). Dilemmas and contradictions of status: The case of the dual-career family. *Social Problems, 24,* 407–416.

HUNT, J. G., & HUNT, L. L. (1982). Dual-career families: Vanguards of the future or residue of the past? In J. Aldous (Ed.), *Two paychecks: Life in dual-earner families.* Newbury Park, CA: Sage Publications.

HUSTON, T. L. & ROBINS, E. (1982). Conceptual and methodological issues in studying close relationships. In L. H. Brown & J. S. Kidwell (Eds.), Methodology: The other side of caring. *Journal of Marriage and the Family, 44*(4), 901–925.

IHINGER-TALLMAN, M. (1987). Sibling and stepsibling bonding in stepfamilies. In K. Pasley and M. Ihinger-Tallman (Eds.), *Remarriage and stepparenting: Current research and theory.* New York: Guilford Press.

IHINGER-TALLMAN, M., & PASLEY, K. (1987). Divorce and remarriage in the American family: A historical review. In K. Pasley & M. Ihinger-Tallman (Eds.), *Remarriage and stepparenting: Current research and theory.* New York: Guilford Press.

IMBER-BLACK, E. (1990). Multiple embedded systems. In M.P. Mirkin (Ed.), *The social and political contexts of family therapy.* Boston: Allyn & Bacon.

IRVING, H. H., BENJAMIN, M., & TROCME, N. (1984). Shared parenting: An empirical analysis using a large data base. *Family Process, 23,* 561–569.

ISAACS, M. B. (1982). Facilitating family restructuring and relinkage. In J. C. Hansen & L. Messinger (Eds.), *Therapy with remarried families.* Rockville, MD: Aspen Systems.

ISAACS, M. B., MONTALVO, B., & ABELSOHN, D. (1986). *The difficult divorce: Therapy for children and families.* New York: Basic Books.

JACKSON, J. (1973). Family organization and ideology. In D. Miller (Ed.), *Comparative studies of blacks and whites in the United States.* New York: Seminar Press.

JACOBS, J. W. (1982). The effect of divorce on fathers: An overview of the literature. *American Journal of Psychiatry, 139,* 1235–1241.

JACOBSON, D. S. (1987). Family type, visiting patterns, and children's behavior in the stepfamily: A linked family system. In K. Pasley & M. Ihinger-Tallman (Eds.), *Remarriage and stepparenting: Current research and theory.* New York: Guilford Press.

JEMAIL, J. A., & NATHANSON, M. (1987). Adolescent single-parent families. In M. Lindblad-Goldberg (Ed.), *Clinical issues in single-parent households.* Rockville, MD: Aspen Publishers.

KANTOR, D., & LEHR, W. (1975). *Inside the family: Toward a theory of family process.* San Francisco: Jossey-Bass.

KARPEL, M. A. (Ed.) (1986). *Family resources: The hidden partner in family therapy.* New York: Guilford Press.

KARPEL, M. A., & STRAUSS, E. S. (1983). Family evaluation. New York: Gardner Press.

KASLOW, F. W. (1985). To marry or not: Treating a living-together couple in midlife. In A. S. Gurman (Ed.), *Casebook of marital therapy.* New York: Guilford Press.

KASLOW, F. W. (1988). The psychological dimensions of divorce mediation. In J. Folberg & A. Milne (Eds.), *Divorce mediation: Theory and practice.* New York: Guilford Press.

KASLOW, F. W., & SCHWARTZ, L. L. (1987). *The dynamics of divorce: A life cycle perspective.* New York: Brunner/Mazel.

KESHET, J. K. (1980). From separation to stepfamily. *Journal of Family Issues, 1,* 517–531.

KESHET, J. K., & MIRKIN, M. P. (1985). Troubled adolescents in divorced and remarried families. In M. P. Mirkin & S. L. Koman (Eds.), *Handbook of adolescents and family therapy.* New York: Gardner Press.

KESSLER, S. (1975). *The American way of divorce: Prescriptions for change.* Chicago: Nelson-Hall.

KIRSCHNER, B., & WALLUM, L. (1978, November). Two-location families: Married singles. *Alternative Lifestyles, 1,* 513–525.

KITANO, H. H. (1982). Mental health in the Japanese-American community. In E. E. Jones & S. J. Korchin (Eds.), *Minority mental health.* New York: Praeger.

KITSON, G. C., & SUSSMAN, M. B. (1982). Marital complaints, demographic characteristics, and symptoms of mental distress in divorce. *Journal of Marriage and the Family, 44,* 87–101.

KLEIN, D. P. (1975, November). Women in the work force: The middle years. *Monthly Labor Review,* 10–16.

KNISKERN, D. P., & GURMAN, A. S. (1983). Future directions for family therapy research. In D. A. Bagarozzi, A. P. Jarich, & R. M. Jackson (Eds.), *New perspectives in marital and family therapy: Issues in theory, research and practice.* New York: Human Sciences Press.

KOMAN, S. L., & STECHLER, G. (1985). Making the jump to systems. In M. P. Mirkin & S. L. Koman (Eds.), *Handbook of adolescents and family therapy.* New York: Gardner Press.

KRAJESKI, J. P. (1986). Psychotherapy with gay men and lesbians: A history of controversy. In T. S. Stein & C. J. Cohen (Eds.), *Contemporary perspectives on psychotherapy with lesbians and gay men.* New York: Plenum.

KRESSEL, K. (1985). *The process of divorce: How professionals and couples negotiate settlements.* New York: Basic Books.

KRESTAN, J., & BEPKO, C. (1980). The problem of fusion in the lesbian relationship. *Family Process, 19*(3), 277–290.

KURAMOTO, F. H., MORALES, R. F., MUNOZ, F. U., & MURASE, K. (1983). Education for social work practice in Asian and Pacific American communities. In J. C. Chunn, II, P. J. Dunston, & F. Ross-Sheriff (Eds.), *Mental health and people of color: Curriculum development and change.* Washington, DC: Howard University Press.

KURDEK, L. A. (1981). An integrative perspective on children's divorce adjustment. *American Psychologist, 36,* 856–866.

LAPPIN, J., & SCOTT, S. (1982). Intervention in a Vietnamese refugee family. In M. McGoldrick, J. K. Pearce, & J. Giordano (Eds.), *Ethnicity and family therapy,* New York: Guilford Press.

LAU, A. (1986). Family therapy across cultures. In J. L. Cox (Ed.), *Transcultural psychiatry.* London: Croom Helm.

LAVAL, R. A., GOMEZ, E. A., & RUIZ, P. (1989). A language minority: Hispanic Americans and mental health care. In D. R. Atkinson, G. Morten, & D. W. Sue (Eds.),

*Counseling American minorities: A cross-cultural perspective.* Dubuque, IA: Wm. C. Brown.

LEE, E. (1982). A social systems approach to assessment and treatment for Chinese American families. In M. McGoldrick, J. K. Pearce, & J. Giordano (Eds.), *Ethnicity and family therapy.* New York: Guilford Press.

LEONG, F. T. L. (1986). Counseling and psychotherapy with Asian-Americans: Review of the literature. *Journal of Counseling Psychology, 33,* 196–206.

LEVANT, R. F. (1988). Facilitating fathering skills through psychoeducational programs. *Family Therapy Today, 3*(12), 1–5.

LEVINGER, G. (1979). A social psychological perspective on marriage dissolution. In G. Levinger & O. C. Moles (Eds.), *Divorce and separation: Context, causes, and consequences.* New York: Basic Books.

LEVINGER, G., & HUSTON, T. L. (1990). The social psychology of marriage. In F. D. Fincham & T. N. Bradbury (Ed.), *The psychology of marriage: Basic issues and applications.* New York: Guilford Press.

LEWIS, J. M., BEAVERS, W. R., GOSSETT, J. T., & PHILLIPS, V. A. (1976). *No single thread: Psychological health in family systems.* New York: Brunner/Mazel.

LEWIS, R. A., & SPANIER, G. B. (1979). Theorizing about the quality and stability of marriage. In W. R. Burr, R. Hill, F. I. Nye, & I. L. Reiss (Eds.), *Contemporary theories and alternative lifestyles.* Newbury Park, CA: Sage Publications.

LINDBLAD-GOLDBERG, M. (1989). Successful minority single-parent families. In L. Combrinck-Graham (Ed.), *Children in family context: Perspectives on treatment.* New York: Guilford Press.

MACKLIN, E. D. (1978). Non-marital heterosexual cohabitation: A review of research. *Marriage and Family Review, 1,* 1–12.

MACKLIN, E. D. (1983). Nonmarital heterosexual cohabitation: An overview. In E. D. Macklin & R. H. Rubin (Eds.), *Contemporary families and alternative lifestyles.* Newbury Park, CA: Sage Publications.

MACKLIN, E. D. (1988). Heterosexual couples who cohabit nonmaritally: Some common problems and issues. In C. S. Chilman, E. W. Nunnally, & F. M. Cox (Eds.), *Variant family forms.* Newbury Park, CA: Sage Publications.

MADDOX, B. (1982). Homosexual parents. *Psychology Today, 16*(2), 62–69.

MAKOSKY, V. P. (1982). Sources of stress: Events or conditions? In D. Belle (Ed.), *Women and depression.* Newbury Park: Sage Publications.

MALYON, A. K. (1982). Psychotherapeutic implications of internalized homophobia in gay men. In J. C. Gonsiorek (Ed.), *Homosexuality and psychotherapy: A practitioner's handbook of affirmative models.* New York: Haworth Press.

MANNS, W. (1988). Supportive roles of significant others in Black families. In H. P. McAdoo (Ed.), *Black families* (2nd ed.). Newbury Park, CA: Sage Publications.

MARKS, R., & GOLDBLUM, P. B. (1989). The decision to test: A personal choice. In J. W. Dilley, C. Pies, & M. Helquist (Eds.), *Face to face: A guide to AIDS counseling.* Berkeley, CA: Celestial Arts.

MARMOR, J. (1980). Overview: The multiple roots of homosexual behavior. In J. Marmor (Ed.), *Homosexual behavior: A modern reappraisal.* New York: Basic Books.

MARUYAMA, M. (1968). The second cybernetics: Deviation-amplifying mutual causal process. In W. Buckley (Ed.), *Modern systems research for the behavioral scientist.* Chicago: Aldine.

McADOO, H. P. (1977). Family therapy in the black community. *Journal of the American Orthopsychiatric Association, 47,* 74–79.

McADOO, H. P. (1988). Transgenerational patterns of upward mobility in African-American families. In H. P. McAdoo (Ed.), *Black families* (2nd ed.). Newbury Park, CA: Sage Publications.

McCREANER, A. (1989). Pre-test counselling. In J. Green & A. McCreaner (Eds.), *Counselling in HIV Infection and AIDS.* Oxford: Blackwell Scientific Publications.

McGOLDRICK, M. (1982). Ethnicity and family therapy: An overview. In M. McGoldrick, J. K. Pearce, & J. Giordano (Eds.), *Ethnicity and family therapy.* New York: Guilford Press.

McGOLDRICK, M., & CARTER, E. A. (1988). Forming a remarried family. In E. A. Carter & M. McGoldrick (Eds.), *The changing family life cycle: A framework for family therapy.* (2nd ed.). New York: Gardner Press.

McGOLDRICK, M., GARCIA PRETO, N., HINES, P. M., & LEE, E. (1991). Ethnicity and family therapy. In A. S. Gurman & D. P. Kniskern (Eds.), *Handbook of family therapy* (Vol. II). New York: Brunner/Mazel.

McGOLDRICK, M., & GERSON, R. (1985). *Genograms in family assessment.* New York: W. W. Norton.

McNAUGHT, B. (1979). Gay and Catholic. In B. Berzon (Ed.), *Positively gay.* Los Angeles: Mediamix Press.

McWHIRTER, D. P., & MATTISON, A. M. (1982). Psychotherapy for gay couples. In J. C. Gonsiorek (Ed.), *Homosexuality and psychotherapy.* New York: Haworth Press.

MEDNICK, M. T. (1987). Single mothers: A review and critique of current research. In S. Oskamp (Ed.), *Family processes and problems: Social psychological aspects.* Newbury Park, CA: Sage Publications.

MEYER, D. R., & GARASKY, S. (1991). *Custodial fathers: Myths, realities, and child support policy.* Washington, DC: U.S. Department of Health and Human Services.

MILLER, J. G. (1978). *Living systems.* New York: McGraw-Hill.

MILNE, A. (1988). The nature of divorce disputes. In J. Folberg & A. Milne (Eds.), *Divorce mediation: Theory and practice.* New York: Guilford Press.

MINUCHIN, S. (1974). *Families and family therapy.* Cambridge, MA: Harvard University Press.

MORAWETZ, A., & WALKER, G. (1984). *Brief therapy with single-parent families.* New York: Brunner/Mazel.

MORISHIMA, J. K. (1978). The Asian American experience: 1850–1975. *Journal of the Society of Ethnic and Special Studies, 2,* 8–10.

MORRISON, P. A. (1986). *Changing family structure: Who cares for America's dependents?* Santa Monica, CA: Rand Corporation.

MORRISON, P. A. (1991). *Congress and the year 2000: A demographic perspective on future issues.* Santa Monica, CA: Rand Corporation.

MOSES, A., & HAWKINS, R., JR. (1982). *Counseling lesbian women and gay men: A life-issues approach.* St. Louis: Mosby.

MUNOZ, R. F. (1982). The Spanish-speaking consumer and the community mental health center. In E. E. Jones & S. J. Korchin (Eds.), *Minority mental health.* New York: Praeger.

NATIONAL CENTER FOR HEALTH STATISTICS. (1985). Annual summary of births, marriages, divorces, and deaths, United States, 1984. *Monthly Vital Statistics Report, 33*(13). Available as DHHS Publication No. PHS85-1120. Hyattsville, MD: Public Health Service.

NELSON, J. B. (1982). Religious and moral issues in working with homosexual clients. In J. C. Gonsiorek (Ed.), *Homosexuality and psychotherapy.* New York: Haworth Press.

NEVILLE, W. G. (1990). Mediation. In M. R. Textor (Ed.), *The divorce and divorce therapy handbook.* Northvale, NJ: Jason Aronson.

NEWCOMB, M. D. (1983). Relationship qualities of those who live together. *Alternative Lifestyles, 6,* 78–102.

NEWCOMB, M. D. (1987). Cohabitation and marriage: A quest for independence and relatedness. In S. Oskamp (Ed.), *Family processes and problems: Social psychological aspects.* Newbury Park, CA: Sage Publications.

NICHOLS, M. P. (1987). *The self in the system: Expanding the limits of family therapy.* New York: Brunner/Mazel.

NICHOLS, S. E. (1986). Psychotherapy and AIDS. In T. S. Stein & C. J. Cohen (Eds.), *Contemporary perspectives on psychotherapy with lesbians and gay men.* New York: Plenum.

NICHOLS, W. C., & EVERETT, C. A. (1986). *Systemic family therapy: An integrative approach.* New York: Guilford Press.

NORTON, A. J., & GLICK, P. C. (1986). One-parent families: A social and economic profile. *Family Relations, 35,* 9–17.

*Not all parents are straight.* (Television documentary). (1987, July). Los Angeles, CA: KCET Television Production.

NUNGESSER, L. G. (1980). Theoretical bases for research on the acquisition of social sex-roles by children and lesbian mothers. *Journal of Homosexuality, 5*(3), 177–187.

OLSON, D. H. (1986). Circumplex model VII: Validation studies and FACES III. *Family Process, 26,* 337–351.

OLSON, D. H. (1990). Marriage in perspective. In F. D. Fincham & T. N. Bradbury (Eds.), *The psychology of marriage: Basic issues and applications.* New York: Guilford Press.

OLSON, D. H., FOURNIER, D. G., & DRUCKMAN, J. M. (1986). *Prepare/Enrich counselor's manual.* Minneapolis: Prepare/Enrich, Inc.

OLSON, D. H., RUSSELL, C. S., & SPRENKLE, D. H. (1983). Circumplex model of marital and family systems: VI. Theoretical update. *Family Process, 22,* 69–83.

OLSON, D. H., RUSSELL, C. S., & SPRENKLE, D. H. (1989). *Circumplex model: systemic assessment and treatment of families.* New York: Haworth Press.

PADILLA, A. M., RUIZ, R. A., & ALVAREZ, R. (1989). Community mental health services for the Spanish-speaking/surname populations. In D. R. Atkinson, G. Morten, & D. W. Sue (Eds.), *Counseling American minorities: A cross-cultural perspective.* Dubuque, IA: Wm. C. Brown.

PADILLA, A. M., & SALGADO DE SNYDER, V. N. (1985). Counseling Hispanics: Strategies for effective intervention. In P. Pedersen (Ed.), *Handbook of cross-cultural counseling and therapy.* Westport, CT: Greenwood Press.

PAPANEK, H. (1974). Men, women, and work: Reflections on the two-person career. *American Journal of Sociology, 78,* 852–872.

PAPP, P. (1983). *The process of change.* New York: Guilford Press.

PARNELL, M., & VANDERKLOOT, J. (1989). Ghetto children: Children growing up in poverty. In L. Combrinck-Graham (Ed.), *Children in family contexts: Perspectives on treatment.* New York: Guilford Press.

PASLEY, K. (1985). Stepfathers. In S. M. H. Hanson & F. W. Bozett (Eds.), *Dimensions of fatherhood.* Newbury Park, CA: Sage Publications.

PASLEY, K., & IHINGER-TALLMAN, M. (1987). The evolution of a field of investigation: Issues and concerns. In K. Pasley & M. Ihinger-Tallman (Eds.), *Remarriage and stepparenting: Current research and theory*. New York: Guilford Press.

PASLEY, K., & IHINGER-TALLMAN, M. (1988). Remarriage and stepfamilies. In C. S. Chilman, E. W. Nunnally, & F. M. Cox (Eds.), *Variant family forms*. Newbury Park, CA: Sage Publications.

PATTERSON, C. J. (1992). Children of lesbian and gay parents. *Child Development, 63,* 1025–1042.

PAUL, G. L. (1967). Strategy of outcome research in psychotherapy. *Journal of Consulting Psychology, 31,* 109–118.

PEARCE, D. (1978). The feminization of poverty: Women, work, and welfare. *Urban and Social Change, 2,* 24–36.

PEPLAU, L. A., & AMARO, H. (1982). Understanding lesbian relationships. In J. Weinreich & W. Paul (Eds.), *Homosexuality: Social, psychological, and biological issues*. Newbury Park, CA: Sage Publications.

PETERMAN, D., RIDLEY, C., & ANDERSON, S. (1974). A comparison of cohabiting and noncohabiting college students. *Journal of Marriage and the Family, 36,* 344–354.

PIES, C. (1985). *Considering parenthood: A workbook for lesbians*. San Francisco: Spinsters/Aunt Lute.

PINDERHUGHES, E. (1982). Afro-American families and the victim system. In M. McGoldrick, J. K. Pearce, & J. Giordano (Eds.), *Ethnicity and family therapy*. New York: Guilford Press.

PINDERHUGHES, E. (1990). Legacy of slavery: The experience of Black families in America. In M. P. Mirkin (Ed.), *The social and political contexts of family therapy*. Boston: Allyn & Bacon.

PLECK, J. H. (1985). *Working wives, working husbands*. Newbury Park, CA: Sage Publications.

POLLACK, S., & VAUGHN, J. (Eds.). (1987). *Politics of the heart: A lesbian parenting anthology*. Ithaca, NY: Firebrand Books.

POLOMA, M. M., PENDLETON, B. F., & GARLAND, T. N. (1981). Reconsidering the dual-career marriage: A longitudinal approach. *Journal of Family Issues, 2,* 205–224.

PONSE, B. (1980). Lesbians and their world. In J. Marmor (Ed.), *Homosexual behavior: A modern appraisal*. New York: Basic Books.

POUSSAINT, A. (1990). The mental health status of Black Americans. In D. S. Ruiz (Ed.), *Handbook of mental health and mental disorder among Black Americans*. New York: Greenwood Press.

PRELI, R., & BERNARD, J. M. (1993). Making multiculturalism relevant for majority culture graduate students. *Journal of Marital and Family Therapy, 19,* 5–15.

PRICE, S. J., & McKERNRY, P. C. (1988). *Divorce*. Newbury Park, CA: Sage Publications.

PRICE-BONHAM, S., & MURPHY, D. C. (1980). Dual-career marriages: Implications for the clinican. *Journal of Marital and Family Therapy, 6,* 181–188.

RAMIREZ, M., III. (1991). *Psychotherapy and counseling with minorities: A cognitive approach to individual and cultural differences*. Boston: Allyn & Bacon.

RAPOPORT, R., & RAPOPORT, R. (1969). The dual-career family. *Human Relations, 22,* 3–30.

RAPOPORT, R., & RAPOPORT, R. (1976). *Dual-career families reexamined: New integration of work and family*. New York: Harper.

RAPOPORT, R., & RAPOPORT, R. (1982). The next generation in dual-career research. In J. Aldous (Ed.), *Two paychecks: Life in dual-career families.* Newbury Park, CA: Sage Publications.

REISS, D. (1980). Pathways to assessing the family: Some choice points and a sample route. In C. K. Hofling & J. M. Lewis (Eds.), *The family: Evaluation and treatment.* New York: Brunner/Mazel.

RICE, D. G. (1989). Marital therapy and the divorcing family. In M. R. Textor (Ed.), *The divorce and divorce therapy book.* Northvale, NJ: Jason Aronson.

RICE, D. G., & RICE, J. K. (1986a). Separation and divorce therapy. In N. S. Jacobson & A. S. Gurman (Eds.), *Clinical handbook of marital therapy.* New York: Guilford Press.

RICE, J. K., & RICE, D. G. (1986b). *Living through divorce: A developmental approach to divorce therapy.* New York: Guilford Press.

RICE, S., & KELLY, J. (1988). Choosing a gay/lesbian lifestyle: Related issues of treatment services. In C. S. Chilman, E. W. Nunnally, & F. M. Cox (Eds.), *Variant family forms.* Newbury Park, CA: Sage Publications.

RICHARDS, C. A., & GOLDENBERG, I. (1985). Joint custody: Current issues and implications for treatment. *American Journal of Family Therapy, 4,* 33–40.

RIDLEY, C. A., PETERMAN, D. J., & AVERY, A. W. (1978). Cohabitation: Does it make for a better marriage? *The Family Coordinator, 27,* 129–137.

ROCHLIN, M. (1979). Becoming a gay professional. In B. Berzon (Ed.), *Positively gay.* Los Angeles: Mediamix Press.

ROOSA, M. W., FITZGERALD, H. E., & CRAWFORD, M. (1985). Teenage parenting, delayed parenting, and childlessness. In L. L'Abate (Ed.), *The handbook of family psychology and therapy* (Vol. I). Pacific Grove, CA: Brooks/Cole.

ROOT, M. P. P. (1989). Guidelines for facilitating therapy with Asian American clients. In D. R. Atkinson, G. Morten, & D. W. Sue (Eds.), *Counseling American minorities: A cross-cultural perspective.* Dubuque, IA: Wm. C. Brown.

ROTH, S. (1989). Psychotherapy with lesbian couples: Individual issues, female socialization, and the social context. In M. McGoldrick, C. M. Anderson, & F. Walsh (Eds.), *Women in families: A framework for family therapy.* New York: W. W. Norton.

RUIZ, P. (1982). The Hispanic patient: Sociocultural perspectives. In R. M. Becerra, M. Karno, & J. I. Escobar (Eds.), *Mental health and Hispanic Americans: Clinical perspectives.* New York: Grune & Stratton.

SACHS, N. (1986). The pregnant lesbian therapist. In T. S. Stein & C. J. Cohen (Eds.), *Contemporary perspectives on psychotherapy with lesbians and gay men.* New York: Plenum.

SAGER, C. J., BROWN, H. S., CROHN, H., ENGEL, T., RODSTEIN, E., & WALKER, L. (1983). *Treating the remarried family.* New York: Brunner/Mazel.

SAGER, C. J., WALKER, L., BROWN, H. S., CROHN, H. M., & RODSTEIN, E. (1981). Improving functioning of the remarried family system. *Journal of Marital and Family Therapy, 7,* 3–13.

SAGHIR, M. T., & ROBINS, E. (1980). Clinical aspects of female homosexuality. In J. Marmor (Ed.), *Homosexual behavior: A modern reappraisal.* New York: Basic Books.

SALTS, C. J. (1985). Divorce stage theory and therapy: Therapeutic implications through the divorcing process. In D. H. Sprenkle (Ed.), *Divorce therapy.* New York: Haworth Press.

SAUBER, S. R. (1983). *The human services delivery system.* New York: Columbia University Press.

SCHWARTZ, L. L. (1987). Joint custody. *Journal of Family Psychology, 1,* 120–134.

SEGAL, L. (1987). What is a problem? A brief therapist's view. *Family Therapy Today, 2*(7), 1–7.

SEGAL, L., & BAVELAS, J. B. (1983). Human systems and communication theory. In B. B. Wolman & G. Stricker (Eds.), *Handbook of family and marital therapy*. New York: Plenum Press.

SEKARAN, U. (1986). *Dual-career families: Contemporary organizational and counseling issues*. San Francisco: Jossey-Bass.

SERAFINA, F. C., SCHWEBEL, A. I., RUSSELL, R. K., ISAAC, P. D., & MYERS, L. B. (Eds.). (1990). *Mental health of ethnic minorities*. New York: Praeger.

SEWARD, R. (1978). *The American family: A demographic history*. Newbury Park, CA: Sage Publications.

SHAEVITZ, M. H., & SHAEVITZ, H. J. (1980). *Making it together as a two career couple*. Boston: Houghton-Mifflin.

SHON, S. P., & JA, D. Y. (1982). Asian families. In M. McGoldrick, J. K. Pearce, & J. Giordano (Eds.), *Ethnicity and family therapy*. New York: Guilford Press.

SHUSTER, R. (1987). Sexuality as a continuum: The bisexual identity. In Boston Lesbian Psychologies Collective (Eds.), *Lesbian psychologies: Explorations and challenges*. Urbana: University of Illinois Press.

SILBERSTEIN, L. R. (1992). *Dual-career marriage: A system in transition*. Hillsdale, NJ: Erlbaum.

SILVERSTEIN, C. (1981). *Man to man: Gay couples in America*. New York: Morrow.

SILVERSTEIN, C. (Ed.) (1991). *Gays, lesbians, and their therapists: Studies in psychotherapy*. New York: W. W. Norton.

SKOLNICK, A. (1991). *Embattled paradise: The American family in an age of uncertainty*. New York: Basic Books.

SKYNNER, R. (1982). Frameworks for viewing the family as a system, In A. Bentovim, G. G. Barnes, & A. Cooklin (Eds.), *Family therapy: Complementary frameworks of theory and practice*. (Vol.I). London: Grune & Stratton.

SLUZKI, C. (1979). Migration and family conflict. *Family Process, 18*(4), 379–390.

SOBOL, M. P. & DALY, K. J. (1992). The adoption alternative for pregnant adolescents: Decision making, consequences, and policy implications. *Journal of Social Issues, 48*(3), 143–161.

SOLOMON, B. B. (1982). The delivery of mental health services to Afro-Americans and their families: Translating theory into practice. In B. A. Bass, G. E. Wyatt, & G. J. Powell (Eds.), *The Afro-American family: Assessment, treatment, and research issues*. New York: Grune & Stratton.

SPERRY, L. (1992). Tailoring treatment with couples and families: Resistances, prospects, and perspectives. *Topics in Family Psychology and Counseling, 1*(3), 1–6.

SPRENKLE, D. H. (Ed.). (1985). *Divorce therapy*. New York: Haworth Press.

SPRENKLE, D. H. (1990). The clinical practice of divorce therapy. In M. R. Textor (Ed.), *The divorce and divorce therapy book*. Northvale, NJ: Jason Aronson.

STAHMANN, R. F., & HIEBERT, W. J. (1987). *Premarital counseling: The professional's handbook*. Lexington, MA: Lexington Books.

STAPLES, R. (1985). Changes in Black family structures: The conflict between family ideology and structural conditions. *Journal of Marriage and the Family, 47,* 1005–1013.

STIER, S. (1986). Divorce mediation. *Family Therapy Today, 1*(3), 1–7.

STORMS, M. (1986). *The development of sexual orientation*. Washington, DC: American Psychological Association.

STUART, R. B. (1980). *Helping couples change: A social learning approach to marital therapy.* Champaign, IL: Research Press.

SUE, D. W. (1989). Ethnic identity: The impact of two cultures on the psychological development of Asians in America. In D. R. Atkinson, G. Morten, & D. W. Sue (Eds.), *Counseling American minorities: A cross-cultural perspective.* Dubuque, IA: Wm. C. Brown.

SUE, S. (1988). Psychotherapeutic services for ethnic minorities: Two decades of research findings. *American Psychologist, 43,* 301–308.

SUE, S., & MORISHIMA, J. K. (1982). *The mental health of Asian-Americans.* San Francisco: Jossey-Bass.

TAKAKI, R. (1990). *Strangers from a different shore: A history of Asian Americans.* Boston, MA: Little, Brown.

TAYLOR, A. (1988). A general theory of divorce mediation. In J. Folberg & A. Milne (Eds.), *Divorce Mediation: Theory and Practice.* New York: Guilford Press.

TEXTOR, M. R. (Ed.). (1989). *The divorce and divorce therapy book.* Northvale, NJ: Jason Aronson.

THOMAS, A., & SILLEN, S. (1974). *Racism and psychiatry.* Secaucas, NJ: Citadel.

THOMPSON, E. H., JR., & GONGLA, P. A. (1983). Single parent families: In the mainstream of American society. In E. D. Macklin & R. H. Rubin (Eds.), *Contemporary families and alternative lifestyles.* Newbury Park, CA: Sage Publications.

THORNTON, A. (1988). Cohabitation and marriage in the 1980s. *Demography, 25*(4), 497–508.

TODER, N. (1979). Lesbian couples: Special issues. In B. Berzon (Ed.), *Positively gay.* Los Angeles: Mediamix Press.

TURNER, N. W. (1985). Divorce: Dynamics of decision therapy. In D. H. Sprenkle (Ed.), *Divorce therapy.* New York: Haworth Press.

UMBARGER, C. C. (1983). *Structural family therapy.* New York: Grune & Stratton.

U.S. BUREAU OF THE CENSUS. (1980). *Marital status and living arrangements: March 1979* (Current population reports, series P-20, No. 349). Washington, DC: U.S. Government Printing Office.

U.S. BUREAU OF THE CENSUS (1986). *Households, families, marital status, living arrangements: March 1986* (Current population reports, Series P-20, No. 412). Washington, DC: U.S. Government Printing Office.

U.S. BUREAU OF THE CENSUS. (1991a). *Poverty in the United States: 1990* (Current population reports, Series P-60, No. 175). Washington, DC: U.S. Government Printing Office.

U.S. BUREAU OF THE CENSUS. (1991b). *The Hispanic population in the United States: March 1991* (Current population reports, Series P-20, No. 455). Washington, DC: U.S. Government Printing Office.

U.S. DEPARTMENT OF LABOR. (1985). *Labor force activity of mothers with young children continues at record pace.* (Publication No. USDL 85-381). Washington, DC: Bureau of Labor Statistics.

VANNOY-HILLER, D., & PHILLIBER, W. W. (1989). *Equal partners: Successful women in marriage.* Newbury Park, CA: Sage Publications.

VISHER, E. B., & VISHER, J. S. (1979). *Stepfamilies: A guide to working with stepparents and stepchildren.* New York: Brunner/Mazel.

VISHER, E. B., & VISHER, J. S. (1982). Stepfamilies in the 1980s. In J. C. Hansen & L. Messinger (Eds.), *Therapy with remarried families.* Rockville, MD: Aspen Systems.

VISHER, E. B., & VISHER, J. S. (1986). *Stepfamily workbook manual.* Baltimore, MD: Stepfamily Association of America.

VISHER, E. B., & VISHER, J. S. (1988a). *Old loyalties, new ties: Therapeutic strategies with stepfamilies.* New York: Brunner/Mazel.

VISHER, E. B., & VISHER, J. S. (1988b). Treating families with problems associated with remarriage and step relationships. In C. S. Chilman, E. W. Nunnally, & F. M. Cox (Eds.), *Variant family forms.* Newbury Park, CA: Sage Publications.

WACHTEL, E. F., & WACHTEL, P. L. (1986). *Family dynamics in individual psychotherapy: A guide to clinical strategies.* New York: Guilford Press.

WALKER, G. (1987, April and June). AIDS and family therapy. *Family Therapy Today, 2,* (4), 1–7; *2*(6), 1–7.

WALKER, L. S., & WALLSTON, B. S. (1985). Social adaptation: A review of dual-earner family literature. In L. L'Abate (Ed.), *The handbook of family psychology and therapy.* Pacific Grove, CA: Brooks/Cole.

WALLERSTEIN, J. S. (1986). Women after divorce: Preliminary report from a ten-year follow-up. *American Journal of Orthopsychiatry, 56,* 65–77.

WALLERSTEIN, J. S. (1988). Children of divorce: The dilemma of a decade. In E. W. Nunnally, C. S. Chilman, & F. M. Cox (Eds.), *Troubled relationships.* Newbury Park, CA: Sage Publications.

WALLERSTEIN, J. S., CORBIN, S. B., & LEWIS, J. M. (1988). Children of divorce: Report of a ten-year follow-up of early latency-age children. In E. M. Hetherington & J. D. Arasteh (Eds.), *Impact of divorce, single parenting, and stepparenting on children.* Hillsdale, NJ: Erlbaum.

WALLERSTEIN, J. S., & KELLY, J. B. (1974). The effects of parental divorce: The adolescent experience. In E. J. Anthony & C. Koupernik (Eds.), *The child in his family: Children at psychiatric risk.* New York: Wiley.

WALLERSTEIN, J. S., & KELLY, J. B. (1975). The effects of parental divorce: Experiences of the preschool child. *Journal of the American Academy of Child Psychiatry, 14,* 600–616.

WALLERSTEIN, J. S., & KELLY, J. B. (1976). The effects of parental divorce: Experiences of the child in later latency. *American Journal of Orthopsychiatry, 46,* 256–269.

WALLERSTEIN, J. S., & KELLY, J. B. (1980a). Effects of divorce on the visiting father-child relationship. *American Journal of Psychiatry, 137,* 1534–1539.

WALLERSTEIN, J. S., & KELLY, J. B. (1980b). *Surviving the breakup: How parents and children cope with divorce.* New York: Basic Books.

WALSH, F. (1983). The timing of symptoms and critical events in the family life cycle. In J. C. Hansen (Ed.), *Clinical implications of the family life cycle.* Rockville, MD: Aspen Systems.

WALSH, F. (1991). Promoting healthy functioning in divorced and remarried families. In A. S. Gurman & D. P. Kniskern (Eds.), *Handbook of family therapy* (Vol. II). New York: Brunner/Mazel.

WARREN, C. (1980). Homosexuality and stigma. In J. Marmor (Ed.), *Homosexual behavior: A modern reappraisal.* New York: Basic Books.

WEATHERLEY, R. A., & CARTOOF, V. G. (1988). Helping single adolescent parents. In C. S. Chilman, E. W. Nunnally, & F. M. Cox (Eds.), *Variant family forms.* Newbury Park, CA: Sage Publications.

WEBER, T., McKEEVER, J. E., & McDANIEL, S. H. (1985). A beginner's guide to the problem-oriented first family interview. *Family Process, 24,* 356–364.

WEED, J. A. (1980). *National estimates of marriage dissolution and survivorship: United States.* (Vital and Health Statistics, Series 3, Analytic Statistics, No. 19. DHHS Publication No. PHS81-1403). Hyattsville, MD: National Center for Health Statistics.

WEINBERG, G. (1972). *Society and the healthy homosexual.* New York: St. Martin's Press.

WEISS, R. S. (1975). *Marital separation.* New York: Basic Books.

WEISS, R. S. (1979). *Going it alone: The family life and social situation of the single parent.* New York: Basic Books.

WEITZMAN, L. (1985). *The divorce revolution: The unexpected social and economic consequences for women and children in America.* New York: Free Press.

WELTNER, J. S. (1982). A structural approach to the single-parent family. *Family Process, 21,* 203–210.

WELTNER, J. S. (1992). Matchmaking: Therapist, client, and therapy. *Topics in Family Psychology and Counseling, 1*(3), 37–52.

WESTLEY, W. A., & EPSTEIN, N. B. (1969). *The silent majority.* San Francisco: Jossey-Bass.

WESTOFF, L. (1977). *The second time around: Remarriage in America.* New York: Viking Press.

WHITAKER, C. A. (1977). Process techniques of family therapy. *Interaction, 1,* 4–19.

WHITAKER, C. A., & BUMBERRY, W. M. (1988). *Dancing with the family: A symbolic-experiential approach.* New York: Brunner/Mazel.

WHITE, M. (1989). *Selected Papers.* Adelaide: Dulwich Centre Publications.

WHITE, S. L. (1978). Family therapy according to the Cambridge Model. *Journal of Marriage and Family Counseling, 4,* 91–100.

WHITESIDE, M. F. (1982). Remarriage: A family developmental process. *Journal of Marital and Family Therapy, 8*(2), 59–68.

WHITESIDE, M. F. (1983). Families of remarriage: The weaving of many life cycles. In J. C. Hansen & H. A. Liddle (Eds.), *Clinical implications of the family life cycle.* Rockville, MD: Aspen Systems.

WHITESIDE, M. F. (1989). Remarried systems. In L. Combrinck-Graham (Eds.), *Children in family contexts: Perspectives on treatment.* New York: Guilford Press.

WIENER, N. (1967). *The human use of human beings: Cybernetics and society (2nd ed.).* New York: Avon.

WILSON, M. E. (1971). The significance of communication in counseling the culturally disadvantaged. In R. Wilcox (Ed.), *The psychological consequences of being a Black American.* New York: Wiley.

WINFIELD, F. E. (1985). *Commuter marriage: Living apart together.* New York: Columbia University Press.

WINFIELD, F. E. (1988). *The work and family sourcebook.* Greenville, NY: Panel.

WONG, N., LU, F. G., SHON, S. P., & GAW, A. C. (1983). Asian and Pacific American issues in psychiatric residency training programs. In J. C. Chunn, II, P. J. Dunston, & F. Ross-Sheriff (Eds.), *Mental health and people of color: Curriculum development and change.* Washington, DC: Howard University Press.

WOODMAN, N. J., & LENNA, H. R. (1980). *Counseling with gay men and women.* San Francisco: Jossey-Bass.

WOODY, J. D. (1983). Sexuality in divorce and remarriage. In J. C. Hansen, J. D. Woody, & R. H. Woody (Eds.), *Sexual issues in family therapy.* Rockville, MD: Aspen Systems.

WORTHINGTON, E. (1989). Matching family treatment to family stressors. In C. Figley (Ed.), *Treating stress in families.* New York, Brunner/Mazel.

WORTHINGTON, E. (1992). Strategic matching and tailoring of treatment to couples and families. *Topics in Family Psychology and Counseling, 1*(3), 21–32.

NAME INDEX

# SUBJECT INDEX

Abortion, 92
Adoption, 4, 92, 93, 234–236
African Americans, 3, 4, 8, 18, 89, 91, 92, 93, 213, 225, 227, 229–241
AIDS, 21, 168, 194–196, 205–208, 215–221
Alimony, 177
Anorexia, 54
Asian/Pacific Americans, 3, 227, 251–262
Assessment (*See* Family assessment)

Beavers systems model, 78–82
Behavioral view, 62, 75
Binuclear family, 15, 102, 111, 128, 135
Boundaries, 12, 51–52, 68, 71, 102, 112, 113, 128, 133, 135–138, 146–147, 158, 214, 233, 256
Brief Therapy Center, 59, 65

California Children of Divorce Project, 105–107, 110
Cases:
  African-American teenager, 234–236
  AIDS denial, 218–219
  anorexia, 54
  Asian couple, 256–258
  circumplex model, 78
  cohabitation, 20–21, 171–178
  commuter marriage, 282–285
  divorce counseling, 31–33
  dual-career families, 31–33, 276–278, 288–291
  elderly unmarried couple, 177–178
  father-daughter coalition, 48–50
  gay "coming out," 198–199
  gay couples, 21, 214–216
  gay father, 209–211

Cases (*continued*)
  "ghosts" of earlier marriage, 112–113
  Hispanic family, 246–248
  immigrants, 24, 153–154
  intergenerational problems, 24, 47–48, 48–50, 48–50
  joint custody, 158–161
  lesbian couple, 202–203
  parentified child, 113
  premarital counseling, 187–191
  single-parent-led families, 22, 115–118
  stepfamilies, 19, 130–133, 153–154, 155–158, 158–161
  teenage parent, 234–236
  unmarried parent, 121–123, 176–177
  widowhood, 96, 113
  young divorcee, 96–98
Centrifugal families, 81
Centripetal families, 81
Child-care arrangements, 100, 114
Child custody, 4, 14, 18, 98–102, 107–111, 125, 139, 182
Child support payments, 14, 88, 93, 97, 100, 102, 110, 139–140, 177
Church, 206, 237–239, 250, 237, 258
Circular causality, 39–41, 53, 119
Circumplex model, 76–79, 185, 187, 190
Closed systems, 43–46
Cohabitation, 4, 9, 10, 165–192
"Coming out," 197–200, 205
Commuter marriage, 281–285
Constructionist view, 60
Crisis intervention, 61–62, 69, 104
Custodial parent, 90, 98–102, 107–108, 112, 114, 120, 128, 135, 182
Cybernetics, 40

# C R E D I T S

This page constitutes an extension of the copyright page. We have made every effort to trace the ownership of all copyrighted material and to secure permission from copyright holders. In the event of any question arising as to the use of any material, we will be pleased to make the necessary corrections in future printings. Thanks are due to the following authors, publishers, and agents for permission to use the material indicated.

Page 8. Figure 1.2. From *Congress and the Year 2000: A Demographic Perspective on Future Issues,* by P. A. Morrison. Copyright © 1991 by Rand Corporation.

Page 16. Table 1.1. From "The psychological dimensions of divorce mediation," by F. W. Kaslow. In *Divorce Mediation: Theory and Practice* by J. Folbert & A. Milne (Eds.), pp. 88–89. Copyright © 1988 by Guilford Press. Reprinted by permission.

Page 26. Figure 1.4. Reprinted from J. S. Weltner, "Matchmaking: Therapist, Client, and Therapy," in *Topics in Family Psychology and Counseling,* Vol. 1, No. 3, pp. 39, with permission of Aspen Publishers, Inc., © 1992.

Page 27. Figure 1.5. Reprinted from J. S. Weltner, "Matchmaking: Therapist, Client, and Therapy," in *Topics in Family Psychology and Counseling,* Vol. 1, No. 3, pp. 40, with permission of Aspen Publishers, Inc., © 1992.

Page 42. Figure 2.1. From *Living Systems,* by J. G. Miller, p. 36. Copyright © 1978 by McGraw-Hill. Reprinted by permission.

Page 55. Figure 2.2. From *Structural-Strategic Marriage and Family Therapy,* by J. D. Friesen, p. 46. Copyright © 1985 by Garner Press. Reprinted by permission.

Page 72. Figures 3.3 and 3.4. Reprinted by permission of the publishers from *Families and Family Therapy,* by Salvador Minuchin, p. 53. Cambridge, Mass.: Harvard University Press, Copyright © 1974 by the President and Fellows of Harvard College.

Page 77. Figure 3.5. From "Circumplex model VII: Validation studies and FACES III," by D. H. Olson in *The Psychology of Marriage: Basic Issues and Applications,* p. 339. Copyright © 1986 by Guilford Press. Reprinted by permission.

Page 80. Figure 3.6. From "Family models: Comparing and contrasting the Olson circumplex with the Beavers model," by W. R. Beavers & M. N. Voeller in Family Process, p. 90, 1983.

Page 129. Table 5.1. From *Treating the Remarried Family,* by C. J. Sager, H. S. Brown, H. Crohn, E. Rodstein, & L. Walker, p. 65. Copyright © 1983 by Brunner/Mazel. Reprinted by permission.

To the owner of this book:

We hope that you have enjoyed *Counseling Today's Famlies*, 2nd edition, as much as we have enjoyed writing it. We'd like to know as much about your experiences with the book as you care to offer. Only through your comments and the comments of others can we learn how to make *Counseling Today's Families* a better book for future readers.

School: _____

Your instructor's name: _____

1. For what course was this book assigned? _____

2. What did you like most about *Counseling Today's Families*, 2nd edition? _____

_____

_____

3. What did you like least about the book? _____

_____

_____

4. Were all of the chapters of the book assigned for you to read? _____

   If not, which ones weren't? _____

_____

5. If you used the Glossary, how helpful was it as an aid in understanding psychological concepts and terms? _____

_____

6. In the space below, or in a separate letter, please let us know what other comments about the book you'd like to make. (For example, were any chapters or concepts particularly difficult?) We'd be delighted to hear from you!

_____

_____

_____

_____

_____

Optional:

Your name: _____ Date: _____

May Brooks/Cole quote you either in promotion for *Counseling Today's Families*, 2nd edition, or in future publishing ventures?

     Yes: _____ No: _____

     Sincerely,

     *Herbert Goldenberg*
     *Irene Goldenberg*

---

FOLD HERE

BUSINESS REPLY MAIL

FIRST CLASS     PERMIT NO. 358     PACIFIC GROVE, CA

POSTAGE WILL BE PAID BY ADDRESSEE

ATT:    *Herbert Goldenberg & Irene Goldenberg*

**Brooks/Cole Publishing Company**
**511 Forest Lodge Road**
**Pacific Grove, California  93950-9968**

NO POSTAGE
NECESSARY
IF MAILED
IN THE
UNITED STATES

---

FOLD HERE

Brooks/Cole is dedicated to publishing quality publications for education in the human services fields. If you are interested in learning more about our publications, please fill in your name and address and request our latest catalogue, using this prepaid mailer.

Name: _____

Street Address: _____

City, State, and Zip: _____

FOLD HERE

FOLD HERE